T0178801

Mathematics for Engineers

Mathematics for Engineers

Georges Fiche
Gérard Hébuterne

Series Editor
Pierre-Noël Favennec

First published in France in 2007 by Hermes Science/Lavoisier entitled: "Mathématiques pour les télécoms"
First published in Great Britain and the United States in 2008 by ISTE Ltd and John Wiley & Sons, Inc.

ISTE Ltd
27-37 St George's Road
London SW19 4EU
UK

www.iste.co.uk

John Wiley & Sons, Inc.
111 River Street
Hoboken, NJ 07030
USA

www.wiley.com

© ISTE Ltd, 2008
© GET et LAVOISIER, 2007

Library of Congress Cataloging-in-Publication Data

Fiche, Georges.
  [Mathématiques pour les télécoms. English]
  Mathematics for engineers / Georges Fiche, Gérard Hébuterne.
    p. cm.
  Includes bibliographical references and index.
  ISBN 978-1-84821-055-4 (talk. paper)
  1. Engineering mathematics. I. Hébuterne, Gérard. II. Title.
  TA330.F5313 2008
  621.38201'51--dc22

2008030348

British Library Cataloguing-in-Publication Data
A CIP record for this book is available from the British Library
ISBN: 978-1-84821-055-4

Cover image created by Atelier Isatis.
Printed and bound in Great Britain by CPI/Antony Rowe Ltd, Chippenham, Wiltshire.

FSC
Mixed Sources
Product group from well-managed forests and other controlled sources

Cert no. SGS-COC-2953
www.fsc.org
© 1996 Forest Stewardship Council

Contents

Preface

Communication techniques and services are changing rapidly, and so are the techniques for the design and analysis of communicating systems and networks transporting and processing information: both in terms of data or images generated in a professional environment and – increasingly – in a personal environment (personal terminals: computers and mobiles). We have felt the need to reconsider basic mathematic tools, usually known by engineers but seldom presented as a whole, in the context of communication technologies. So, this book presents the major mathematical techniques in use in the field of telecommunications and more generally in the domain of information and communication technologies. Engineers, as well as students, will be led to tackle problems related to various subjects, such as signal and information processing, traffic or performance analysis, reliability, etc. Possibly they will become specialists, or responsible for one or several of these domains. We attempt here to provide the mathematical basis necessary to open constructive exchanges with experts, and also to efficiently begin the study of specialized publications.

The present publication has naturally been constructed around the notion of probability. Indeed, we should not be surprised that random variables play a major role in the mathematics deployed to solve problems related to the processing and transport of "information", in essence an unknown quantity. This has naturally guided the structure of this book, providing something of a framework for a unified theoretical approach of communications, with the following chapters.

Probability theory is naturally the subject of Chapter 1, as it constitutes the basis of numerous developments in all the fields addressed by this book, from simple combinatorics to queueing theory, signal processing, statistics or reliability. The chapter presents the main theorems and introduces the notion of random variables and their handling. Transform properties, and their use, are also detailed. Indeed, transforms happen to offer an essential tool for the solution of numerous problems arising when dealing with linear systems, birth and death systems or stochastic relationships. They will find many applications in each of the following chapters.

Chapter 2 complements Chapter 1 and presents the major *probability distributions* we should encounter when describing or modeling the events observed in systems and networks. This refers to, for instance, the analysis of a signal, the volume of data to process, or the reliability of a piece of equipment. All these distributions will be of constant use in the later chapters.

Statistics constitute the object of Chapter 3. Engineers face uncertainty at every step – in observation, measurement, modeling – and have to rely on statistical techniques in order to support their decisions. Estimation will be a constant necessity, e.g. when observing traffic flows, measuring equipment reliability or recognizing a signal.

Chapter 4 presents *signal theory* and its *digital processing*. Every communication relies on signals, and more and more sophisticated methods guarantee the quality of its transport and reconstruction. Sampling makes it possible to represent the actual analog signal in the form of a digital signal. The latter can then be easily stored or transported. Finally, digital processing techniques allow signal filtering in order to restore it as accurately as possible, or even to synthesize new signals. The complex variable, the Fourier and z-transforms, as well as correlation analysis are the major tools for these operations.

Chapter 5, devoted to *information and coding theory*, is the natural successor of Chapter 4. Considering the random nature of information and its perturbations, digitalization and coding bring considerable improvements, both for its transmission (error correction) and for resource optimization (thanks to compression techniques). The chapter first presents a probabilistic model of the information (measure of information and notion of entropy, source and channel modeling, Shannon's theorems), then the major theoretical and practical aspects of coding algorithms are introduced (detecting codes and correcting codes, data compression, for text, image and sounds). For this, probabilities, transforms and modulo 2 algebra will be used.

Chapter 6 presents *traffic and queueing theory*. In networks, traffic represents the information transported globally, its volume, time characteristics (arrival epochs, duration of resource seizing). Here we encounter the well-known *Erlang* concept and the associated dimensioning procedures. Traffic and queueing theory are the essential tools for performance analysis of networks and computers, in order to guarantee the fulfilment of quality of service constraints, through systems and protocols modeling. This is above all the area of Markov processes, of stochastic relations as well as Laplace transforms, generating and characteristic functions.

Chapter 7 presents *reliability theory*. Facing all defects present in any equipment and software involved in a given communication task, and given the catalectic (random) nature of failures, studying their reliability makes it possible to evaluate the probability that the mission will be successful. Observation and statistical processing of the observed events allows us to collect all the data needed to forecast the reliability of systems under design. Using statistical laws will then allow a judicious dimensioning of spare parts, for an acceptable probability of stock outage.

Finally, Chapter 8 presents the theoretical bases of *simulation*, which offers an essential complement to analytical methods. Whatever the approach, Monte Carlo or discrete-event, it aims at reproducing the random aspects of events of interest, and at estimating probabilities of interest, by observing a large number of their occurrences.

To complete these topics, the reader will find a mathematical refresher in the Appendix, recalling a few "elementary" results relevant to the proofs.

As complete as it strives to be, this book cannot pretend to present all the details and ramifications of these theories. However, besides the tools to solve most of the problems he/she could encounter, the reader should find here the essential background information allowing them to tackle specific topics, and for which purpose a bibliography is provided.

Obviously all the subjects presented in this book have a wider application field than pure communications (i.e. carrying information through a media), even if most examples belong to this field. For instance, signal processing plays a major role in medicine, climatology and astronomy, as well as entertainment. Equally, birth and death processes are at the basis of financial mathematics. The same comment holds for statistics, simulation or reliability. All these mathematical techniques cover a wider range of applications, and it is our belief that this book meets the needs of numerous students as well as practitioners in many fields involved with probabilities – communications, and much besides.

Writing this book has given us the opportunity for fruitful exchanges with specialists in various domains. In particular, it is our pleasure to address our thanks to A. Gilloire and M. Joindot, France Télécom R&D, and also to N. Moreau, Telecom-ParisTech (formerly GET/ENST), for their suggestions and for having re-read Chapters 4 and 5.

Chapter 1

Probability Theory

In this chapter we introduce the fundamental concepts of probability theory. Indeed, telecommunication systems are mainly concerned with basically unpredictable phenomena. In order to analyze a signal, as well as to process information or to characterize the performance and reliability of equipment, the engineer is permanently faced with random phenomena. This explains the need to handle them using the tools and methods of probability theory.

We present the notions and properties of random variables, and the major theorems underpinning the theory. We also develop the properties of the *transforms* of distribution functions, which appear as essential tools in solving complex probabilistic problems.

1.1. Definition and properties of events

1.1.1. *The concept of an event*

Probability theory is mainly built on the concept of *random events*. The particular outcome of an experiment cannot be predicted, although the set of all possible outcomes is known: any particular outcome will be called a "random event".

The concept of a random event is quite natural. Consider the traditional example consisting of tossing a die: the outcome is that one of the six faces will come up, numbered $1, 2, \ldots, 6$. "I toss the die and 3 comes up" is an event. Each such occurrence is an *elementary event*. Six different outcomes are possible corresponding to any one of the six faces of the die coming up. Nothing is known about the next outcome, except that it belongs to a certain set, one which is usually able to be described. The set of all the possible outcomes (here, the six possible faces coming up) is the *event space*, or the *sample space*, and is usually denoted as Ω.

The formalism of set theory method is useful when describing events and their properties. Indeed, the properties of events may be stated in terms of the traditional operations of the set theory. This last provides methods to analyze combinations of events in order to predict properties of more complex events. The terminology and correspondence are summarized below in Table 1.1.

Event	Any subset of the sample space
Sure event	Ω: the sure event is the occurrence of anyone of the elements of Ω
Impossible event	$\emptyset$: the impossible event is the occurrence of an event which is not an element of Ω, thus belonging to the empty set $\emptyset$. $\emptyset$ does not contain any elementary event
Elementary event	$\omega \in \Omega$: ω belongs to Ω
Compound event	A is a subset of Ω. It is denoted that the elementary event ω belongs to set A by $\omega \in A$
Complementary event	$\overline{A}$ is the complement of A (the event A does not occur)
A or B	$A \cup B$, union of A and B. The union of sets A and B contains all the elements which belong to *at least* one of the two sets
A and B	$A \cap B$, intersection of A and B. The intersection of sets A and B contains all the elements which belong *both* to A and B
A and B mutually exclusive	$A \cap B = \emptyset$. There is not any event common to A and B
A equivalent to B	$A = B$, which can be read as A equals B

Table 1.1. *Events and sets*

All these definitions are in fact quite natural. Consider again the experiment of tossing a die: "3 comes up" is an elementary event, while "I draw an even number" is a compound event. Similarly, "I draw an odd number" is the complementary event to the previous one, and "7 comes up" is an impossible event, etc. The experiment could be extended, for instance when tossing two dice: the outcome "the sum of the two faces coming up is 6" is a compound event, etc.

From these basic definitions, we are now in a position to introduce the following definitions and properties, which are themselves quite intuitive.

1.1.2. *Complementary events*

Let A stand for an event (i.e. a subset of the sample space Ω). $\overline{A}$ denotes the complementary event (it contains all the elementary events which are not in A).

1.1.2.1. *Basic properties*

The following relations hold and have an immediate and intuitive understanding:

○ $A \cup \overline{A} = \Omega$.

○ $\overline{A} = \Omega - A$ (the symbol "$-$" denotes the difference, sometimes called the reduction of Ω by A).

○ $A \cup \Omega = \Omega$; $A \cap \Omega = A$.

○ $A \cap \emptyset = \emptyset$: A being a subset of Ω, there is no element of A in the empty set.

○ $A \cap \overline{A} = \emptyset$: A and its complement have no common element.

○ $A \cup A = A$; $A \cap A = A$.

and also:

○ $\overline{\Omega} = \emptyset$, $\overline{\emptyset} = \Omega$.

○ $\overline{\overline{A}} = A$, the complement of the complement of A is A itself.

1.1.3. *Properties of operations on events*

1.1.3.1. *Commutativity*

Union and intersection are commutative. The proof is straightforward, starting from the definitions:

$$A \cup B = B \cup A, \quad A \cap B = B \cap A.$$

1.1.3.2. *Associativity*

Union and intersection are associative. Let A, B and C be subsets of Ω:

$$A \cup (B \cup C) = (A \cup B) \cup C, \quad A \cap (B \cap C) = (A \cap B) \cap C.$$

1.1.3.3. *Distributivity*

Union is distributive over intersection, and intersection is distributive over union. The proof is straightforward, starting from commutativity and associativity properties.

$$A \cup (B \cap C) = (A \cup B) \cap (A \cup C), \quad A \cap (B \cup C) = (A \cap B) \cup (A \cap C).$$

1.1.3.4. *Difference*

The difference between A and B is composed of all the elements in A that do not belong to B:

$$A - B = A \cap \overline{B}. \tag{1.1}$$

If B is included in A, then $A - B$ is said to be the complement of B with respect to A. The complement of B with respect to Ω is merely called the complement of B.

1.1.3.5. *De Morgan's rules*

$$\overline{A \cap B} = \overline{A} \cup \overline{B}. \tag{1.2}$$

$$\overline{A \cup B} = \overline{A} \cap \overline{B}. \tag{1.3}$$

Consider the first rule; the proof is straightforward using the distributivity and commutativity properties:

$$
\begin{aligned}
(A \cap B) \cup (\overline{A} \cup \overline{B}) &= (A \cup \overline{A} \cup \overline{B}) \cap (B \cup \overline{A} \cup \overline{B}) \\
&= \big((A \cup \overline{A}) \cup \overline{B}\big) \cap \big((B \cup \overline{B}) \cup \overline{A}\big) \\
&= (\Omega \cup \overline{B}) \cap (\overline{A} \cup \Omega) = \Omega,
\end{aligned}
$$

so that $(\overline{A} \cup \overline{B}) = \overline{(A \cap B)}$, as $(A \cap B) \cap (\overline{A} \cap \overline{B}) = \emptyset$.

The second rule is directly derived from the first rule:

$$\overline{(\overline{A} \cap \overline{B})} = \overline{(\overline{A})} \cup \overline{(\overline{B})} = A \cup B, \quad \text{thus } \overline{A} \cap \overline{B} = \overline{A \cup B}.$$

NOTE. These formulae are easily verified by building the corresponding Venn diagram. We will use this type of diagram below to illustrate some probability properties (see Figure 1.1).

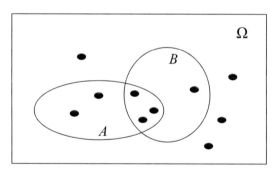

Figure 1.1. *Venn diagram illustrating the notion of conditional probability*

These rules offer a systematic way to deal with complex logical relations. They constitute the basic design techniques for logic circuits such as those encountered in automatisms and computer systems. More generally, event algebra will be a preferred tool for the analysis of linked structures (switching systems, reliability, etc.). This is naturally the foundation of probability theory, as explained hereafter.

1.2. Probability

1.2.1. *Definition*

We are given a phenomenon that is observed through the occurrence of events denoted A, B, etc. The concept of probability will be defined on the set Ω of all the possible events. The probability of an event A, denoted by $P(A)$, is a positive number verifying the following conditions:

1) $0 \le P(A) \le 1$;

2) $P(\Omega) = 1$, the probability of the "sure event" is 1;

3) $P(\emptyset) = 0$, probability of the "impossible event" is zero;

4) if A and B are two exclusive events (i.e., $A \cap B = \emptyset$), then $P(A \cup B) = P(A) + P(B)$.

The mathematical concept of event probability corresponds to the relative frequency of the event during a sequence of experimental trials. We consider that this relative frequency goes to a limit, which is the event probability, as the number of trials increases to infinity.

If n is the number of times the event A occurs during an experiment of N trials, then:

$$P(A) = \lim_{N \to \infty} \frac{n}{N}. \tag{1.4}$$

1.2.2. *Basic theorems and results*

1.2.2.1. *Addition theorem*

Given two events A and B from set Ω,

$$P(A \cup B) = P(A) + P(B) - P(A \cap B). \tag{1.5}$$

The above theorem results directly from properties of operations on the event, as we have just seen. Indeed:

$$A \cup B = A \cup \big(B - (A \cap B)\big).$$

The sets A and $(B - (A \cap B))$ are mutually exclusive, thus:

$$P(A \cup B) = P(A) + P\big((B - (A \cap B))\big) = P(A) + P(B) - P(A \cap B).$$

This result can be understood intuitively if we think about the way to count events in the different subsets: in summing the number of elements in A and in B, the common elements, i.e. those in $A \cap B$, are counted twice.

In applied probability the following symbolism is generally adopted:

$$P(A \cup B) = P(A + B), \qquad P(A \cap B) = P(AB),$$

so that the basic expression is often written as:

$$P(A + B) = P(A) + P(B) - P(AB). \tag{1.6}$$

It is easy to extend the result to the general case of n events:

$$P(A_1 + \cdots + A_n) = P(A_1) + P(A_2) + \cdots + P(A_n)$$
$$- P(A_1 A_2) - \cdots - P(A_{n-1} A_n) \tag{1.7}$$
$$+ P(A_1 A_2 A_3) + \cdots + (-1)^{n-1} P(A_1 A_2 \cdots A_n).$$

This is the so-called Poincaré's theorem. Moreover, if the events are mutually exclusive:

$$P(A_1 + A_2 + \cdots + A_n) = P(A_1) + \cdots + P(A_n). \tag{1.8}$$

1.2.2.2. *Conditional probability*

The notion of conditional probability is of central importance. It formalizes the idea according to which knowledge of an event is modified by any information we can acquire about the system. To give an elementary example: consider throwing two dice. "I bet the faces coming up sum to 12." What is the probability I am right? If I know nothing about the trial, the event is given probability 1/36 (36 possible outcomes, only one favorable if both dice come up with 6). Now, assume I am told the first trial gives 3. I am bound to lose. If on the other hand the first throw gives 6, the probability of a win is 1/6 (I only need the second throw to come up with 6 in order to win).

This illustrates the notion. It is commonly denoted as $P(B \mid A)$, which reads as "probability of B given (or knowing) A". Its expression is defined as:

$$P(B \mid A) = \frac{P(AB)}{P(A)}. \tag{1.9}$$

The Venn diagram above serves to verify this property, in an example where the knowledge about the realization of the event B depends on the realization of A. In this example, A contains $n_A = 5$ elementary events, B contains $n_B = 4$ elementary events, of which 3 are common with A ($n_{AB} = 3$). The total number of outcomes is $N = 10$: $P(AB) = 3/10$, $P(A) = 5/10$, $P(B/A) = 3/5 = 6/10$, $P(B) = 4/10$, and $P(A)P(B) = (5/10)(4/10) = 2/10$.

Such a situation corresponds, for example, to the probability of finding, among 10 people taken at random, boys (event A, probability around 0.5) taller than a value (event B of probability 0.4 in the example). This should illustrate the property according to which boys are likely to be taller than girls.

1.2.2.3. *Multiplication theorem*

Given two events A and B from the sample space Ω:

$$P(AB) = P(A)P(B|A). \tag{1.10}$$

This is merely the preceding result under its product form. Similarly we have:

$$P(AB) = P(B)P(A|B). \tag{1.11}$$

Generalization to n events.

$$P(ABC) = P(A)P(B \mid A)P(C|AB).$$

Indeed:

$$P(ABC) = P(AB)P(C \mid AB) = P(A)P(B \mid A)P(C \mid AB),$$

and thus, also: $P(C \mid AB) = \frac{P(ABC)}{P(AB)}$, and so on for n events.

Independent events. Two events are said to be independent if:

$$P(A \mid B) = P(A).$$

Knowing that B occurred brings no special knowledge about A: the occurrence of B (resp. A) does not affect the probability of the occurrence of A (resp. B). Then:

$$P(AB) = P(A)P(B). \tag{1.12}$$

Coming back to our previous example, assume that we are interested in the color of the eyes. We can admit that this color is independent of gender. Assume a 40% proportion of blue eyes among girls as well as boys. When a total of $N = 10$ people are taken at random, we should observe $n_A = 5$ (5 boys), $n_B = 4$ (4 blue eyed people), and $n_{AB} = 2$.

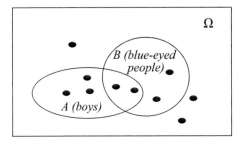

Figure 1.2. *Independent events*

Then $P(A) = 5/10$, $P(B/A) = 2/5$, $P(AB) = 2/10$, equal to $P(A)P(B) = (5/10)(4/10) = 2/10$ (compare with the previous case in Figure 1.1).

More generally, events (A_i) are said to be mutually independent if, for any combination A_i, A_j:

$$P(A_1 A_2 \cdots A_j \cdots A_n) = P(A_1)P(A_2) \cdots P(A_i) \cdots P(A_n).$$

1.2.2.4. *The posterior probability theorem*

Let an event A be associated with one of the events B_i, the B_is being mutually exclusive. B_i is said to be a cause for A. Assume we know the set of conditional probabilities, $P(A \mid B_i)$. The conditional probability of B_i knowing A expresses the probability that B_i is the cause of A. This probability is called the *posterior probability*, or *a posteriori probability* of the event B_i.

First, the relation:

$$P(A) = \sum_{i=1}^{n} P(B_i A)$$

known as the *total probability theorem*, simply states that if the event occurs, it is necessarily associated with a cause which is one of the B_is (which are mutually exclusive). Moreover, introducing conditional probabilities:

$$P(B_i A) = P(B_i)P(A \mid B_i),$$

the total probability theorem may also be written in the form:

$$P(A) = \sum_{i=1}^{n} P(B_i)P(A \mid B_i). \tag{1.13}$$

Once again using conditional probabilities, $P(B_i \mid A) = P(B_i A)/P(A)$, we may state the following result, known as Bayes' formula (or *posterior probability theorem*):

$$P(B_i \mid A) = \frac{P(B_i)P(A \mid B_i)}{\sum_{j=1}^{n} P(B_j)P(A \mid B_j)}. \tag{1.14}$$

U_1 U_2 U_3

The following example will illustrate this result. Three urns U_1, U_2, U_3 contain red and black balls. There are 2 black balls and 1 red in U_1, 5 black and 1 red in U_2, 1 black and 5 red in U_3.

A black ball has just been drawn; what is the probability it comes from U_3? If B stands for the event "a black ball is selected", then:

$$P(U_3 \mid B) = \frac{P(U_3)P(B \mid U_3)}{\sum_{j=1}^n P(U_j)P(B \mid U_j)}.$$

We assume all urns are equally likely to be chosen:

- $P(U_1) = P(U_2) = P(U_3) = 1/3$.
- Also, $P(B \mid U_1) = 2/3$, $P(B \mid U_2) = 5/6$, $P(B \mid U_3) = 1/6$.
- Thus: $P(U_3 \mid B) = (1/3)(1/6)/((1/3)(2/3 + 5/6 + 1/6)) = 0.1$.

1.3. Random variable

1.3.1. *Definition*

A random variable is a function that associates a real number x with the realization of a random event. More formally, a random variable X is an application X of Ω into $\mathcal{R}$, the set of the real number. For instance, the height of the first person to enter in my office is a random variable, and so is the duration of the next telephone call that I will receive.

1.3.2. *Probability functions of a random variable*

1.3.2.1. *Notations*

As before, let us denote by ω an event from Ω. We write $X = x$ for the event $\{\omega : \omega \in \Omega$ and $X(\omega) = x\}$.

Similarly, we write $X \leq x$ for the event $\{\omega : \omega \in \Omega$ and $X(\omega) \leq x\}$.

1.3.2.2. *Cumulative distribution function*

The cumulative distribution function (or probability distribution function, or simply distribution function) of the random variable X is the function:

$$F(x) = P[X \leq x]. \tag{1.15}$$

This function is non-decreasing, that is, if $x < y$ then $F(x) \leq F(y)$. It is such that $F(\infty) = 1$. Also:

$$P[x < X \leq y] = F(y) - F(x). \tag{1.16}$$

1.3.2.3. *Probability density function*

Given a random variable X, with distribution function F, we may wonder about the probability that X takes some value. This leads us to make the following distinction between *discrete* random variable and *continuous* random variable. A random variable X is said to be discrete if:

$$\sum_{x \in T} p(x) = 1,$$

where $p(x) = p(X = x)$ is the *probability mass function*, with T the set of all the possible values x for X. T is either finite or denumerable (countably infinite), i.e. T consists of a finite or countable set of real numbers x_1, x_2, etc.

Now, for a continuous random variable, the probability of observing a given value is zero, as the variable X can take all the possible values x between two given values a and b. The set T of possible values x for X is then called non-denumerable. So, the only reasonable statement is "the value is between x and y". This leads us to introduce the notion of density. The probability density function of a random variable X is the function $f(x)$, such that:

$$\int_{-\infty}^{x} f(x) \mathrm{d}x = F(x). \tag{1.17}$$

Specifically we find:

$$\int_{-\infty}^{\infty} f(x) \mathrm{d}x = 1. \tag{1.18}$$

and if $a < b$:

$$P[a < X \leq b] = F(b) - F(a) = \int_{a}^{b} f(x) \mathrm{d}x.$$

Notice that for a strictly continuous variable $P[X = x] = 0$. In general, we can encounter distribution functions with continuous segments and jumps corresponding to *mass* (i.e. $P[X = x] \neq 0$). This explains the distinction between "$\leq$" and $<$ in equation (1.16), and in the following formula:

$$P[x < X \leq x + \mathrm{d}x] = F(x + \mathrm{d}x) - F(x)$$

thus

$$f(x) = \frac{\mathrm{d}F(x)}{\mathrm{d}x}. \tag{1.19}$$

1.3.3. *Moments of a random variable*

The moments of a random variable give a simple and synthetic characterization of its behavior. As a consequence they also make it easier to study combinations of several independent variables, as will be illustrated below.

1.3.3.1. *Moments about the origin*

The nth order moment of a random variable about the origin is, for a discrete variable:

$$m_n = \sum_k p_k x_k^n, \tag{1.20}$$

and for a continuous variable:

$$m_n = \int_x x^n f(x)\mathrm{d}x. \tag{1.21}$$

1.3.3.2. *Central moments*

The nth central moment of a random variable is, for a discrete variable:

$$m_n = \sum_k p_k \left(x_k - m_i\right)^n, \tag{1.22}$$

with m_i the ith moment about the origin. For a continuous variable:

$$m_n = \int_x \left(x - m_i\right)^n f(x)\mathrm{d}x. \tag{1.23}$$

In practice, central moments will generally be calculated about the mean (i.e. m_1), as defined below.

1.3.3.3. *Mean and variance*

In the application of probability theory, the two first moments of a random variable – namely its mean and variance – are of particular importance.

Mean (expectation) of a random variable. The *mean* (or *expected* value) of a random variable is the first order moment about the origin, and is conventionally denoted m, or $E[X]$. For a discrete variable:

$$m = E[X] = \sum_k p_k x_k. \tag{1.24}$$

For a continuous variable:

$$m = E[X] = \int_x x f(x)\mathrm{d}x. \tag{1.25}$$

The mean is also often denoted[1] as $E[X] = \overline{X}$.

---

1. The notation $\overline{X}$ is in current use, although it ought to be reserved to sample means, as explained in Chapter 3.

Intuitively, we can easily understand the physical meaning of expectation: it is the weighted value of the set of all possible outcomes. In a way this value summarizes the result of a great number of experiments. Note also that from these definitions we derive $E[X/N] = E[X]/N$.

Variance of a random variable. The *variance* of a random variable is the second order moment about the mean, and is conventionally denoted V or σ^2. For a discrete variable:

$$V = \sigma^2 = \sum_k p_k (x_k - m)^2, \tag{1.26}$$

and for a continuous variable:

$$V = \sigma^2 = \int_x (x - m)^2 f(x)\mathrm{d}x. \tag{1.27}$$

σ is called the *standard deviation*. This quantity is also of evident interest, as it takes account of the variations of the realizations around the mean, i.e. the *dispersion*. As its value increases, larger deviations from the mean are likely to occur.

The dispersion is often characterized by the *coefficient of variation*, $c = \sigma/m$.

Variance properties. Applying the variance definition, we obtain:

$$\sigma^2 = \overline{(X - \overline{X})^2} = \overline{X^2 - 2X\overline{X} + \overline{X}^2}$$

(the second expression, by developing the squared term). Now, as the expectation of a sum is the sum of expectations – because of the linear form of equations (1.24), (1.25) – it allows:

$$\sigma^2 = \overline{X^2} - 2\overline{X\overline{X}} + \overline{\overline{X}^2}$$
$$= \overline{X^2} - 2\overline{X} \cdot \overline{X} + \overline{X}^2$$

and finally

$$\sigma^2 = \overline{(X - \overline{X})^2} = \overline{X^2} - \overline{X}^2, \tag{1.28}$$

that is, we have the central relationship: the variance is equal to the mean of the squares minus the square of the mean. This result will be very useful throughout this book. Note that, from equations (1.28), we derive $\sigma^2(X/N) = \sigma^2(X)/N^2$.

1.3.3.4. *Example applications*

First, let us calculate the mean of a variable obeying a Poisson distribution, which will be further detailed in the rest of the book. Let X be a random variable whose possible values are $0, 1, 2, \ldots, k$, etc., with probability p_k:

$$X = \{0, 1, 2, \ldots, k, \ldots\}, \quad \text{and} \quad p_k = P[X = k] = \frac{\lambda^k}{k!} e^{-\lambda}.$$

This is the Poisson distribution. For the mean, we have:

$$E[X] = \sum k p_k = 0 \cdot e^{-\lambda} + \lambda e^{-\lambda} + 2 \frac{\lambda^2}{2} e^{-\lambda} + \cdots + k \frac{\lambda^k}{k!} e^{-\lambda}$$

$$= \lambda e^{-\lambda} \left(1 + \lambda + \frac{\lambda^2}{2!} + \cdots + \frac{\lambda^{k-1}}{(k-1)!} \right) = \lambda e^{-\lambda}(e^\lambda),$$

that is:

$$E[X] = \overline{X} = \lambda \tag{1.29}$$

for the variance:

$$\sigma^2 = \overline{X^2} - \overline{X}^2.$$

The mean square is given by

$$\overline{X^2} = \sum k^2 p_k = \lambda e^{-\lambda} + 2^2 \frac{\lambda^2}{2} e^{-\lambda} + \cdots k^2 \frac{\lambda^k}{k!} e^{-\lambda} + \cdots .$$

Now, we can write:

$$\frac{k^2}{k!} = \frac{k(k-1) + k}{k!} = \frac{k(k-1)}{k!} + \frac{k}{k!} = \frac{1}{(k-2)!} + \frac{1}{(k-1)!}.$$

Using this relation, the second moment is written as:

$$\overline{X^2} = \lambda^2 e^{-\lambda} \left(1 + \lambda + \frac{\lambda^2}{2} \cdots + \frac{\lambda^{k-2}}{(k-2)!} \right)$$

$$+ \lambda e^{-\lambda} \left(1 + \lambda + \frac{\lambda^2}{2} \cdots + \frac{\lambda^{k-1}}{(k-1)!} \right),$$

or

$$\overline{X^2} = \lambda^2 + \lambda.$$

Thus, finally:

$$\sigma^2 = \overline{X^2} - \overline{X}^2 = (\lambda^2 + \lambda) - \lambda^2 = \lambda. \tag{1.30}$$

This result is worth remembering: in the case of a random variable obeying a Poisson distribution with parameter λ, its mean and its variance are equal, and equal to λ.

1.3.4. *Couples of random variables*

We now consider the case of two random variables such as those defined before. In practice, we introduce the properties of several random variable functions – important applications will be found in signal and information theory, and in queueing theory. The results obtained for two variables will be easily more generally extended to many variables. Of particular importance for the following are the results for the sum of random variables.

1.3.4.1. *Definition*

A couple of random variables is the set of two random variables, each having its own variation domain and probability distribution (the generalization to n-tuples is straightforward).

As an example, consider tossing two coins (numbered 1 and 2). The result is a couple of variables, each having values "Heads" or "Tails". Denoting as H_1, T_1 and H_2, T_2 the possible realizations of the individual trials, the experiment results in four different outcomes $H_1 H_2$, $H_1 T_2$, $T_1 H_2$, $T_1 T_2$, each one being equally likely so that the probability of each outcome is $1/4$.

1.3.4.2. *Joint probability*

Joint distribution. Let X and Y be two random variables defined on Ω. The joint distribution function of the 2-tuple X, Y is the function:

$$F(x; y) = P[X \leq x;\ Y \leq y], \tag{1.31}$$

also denoted as F_{xy}. As in the case of the single random variable we can develop:

$$P\big[x_1 < X \leq x_2;\ y_1 < Y \leq y_2\big].$$

We have:

$$P\big[X \leq x_2;\ Y \leq y\big] = P\big[X \leq x_1;\ y_1 < Y \leq y\big] + P\big[x_1 < X \leq x_2;\ y_1 < Y \leq y\big]$$

so that (a):

$$P\big[x_1 < X \leq x_2;\ Y \leq y\big] = P\big[X \leq x_2;\ y_1 < Y \leq y\big] - P\big[X \leq x_1;\ y_1 < Y \leq y\big].$$

Then in the same way for the second variable:

$$P\big[x_1 < X \leq x_2;\ Y \leq y_2\big] = P\big[x_1 < X \leq x_2;\ Y \leq y1\big]$$
$$+ P\big[x_1 < X \leq x_2;\ y_1 < Y \leq y_2\big],$$

so that (b):

$$P\big[x_1 < X \le x_2;\; y_1 < Y \le y_2\big] = P\big[x_1 < X \le x_2;\; Y \le y_2\big]$$
$$- P\big[x_1 < X \le x_2;\; Y \le y_1\big].$$

Mixing expressions (a) and (b), we finally obtain

$$P\big[x_1 < X \le x_2;\; y_1 < Y \le y_2\big]$$
$$= F(x_2; y_2) - F(x_1; y_2) - F(x_2; y_1) + F(x_1; y_1). \tag{1.32}$$

In the field of signal theory, this expression is actually written as:

$$P\big[x_1 < X \le x_2;\; y_1 < Y \le y_2\big] = F_{x_2, y_2} - F_{x_1, y_2} - F_{x_2, y_1} + F_{x_1, y_1}.$$

Joint density function. The joint density function of two variables X and Y is the function:

$$f(x; y) = \frac{\partial^2 F(x; y)}{\partial x \partial y}. \tag{1.33}$$

Fundamental property of joint density:

$$P[x < X \le x + \mathrm{d}x;\; y < Y \le y + \mathrm{d}y] = \mathrm{d}^2 F(x; y) = f(x; y)\mathrm{d}x\mathrm{d}y. \tag{1.34}$$

Indeed, from the above result for joint distribution:

$$P[x < X \le x + \mathrm{d}x;\; y < Y \le y + \mathrm{d}y]$$
$$= F(x + \mathrm{d}x;\; y + \mathrm{d}y) - F(x + \mathrm{d}x; y) - F(x;\; y + \mathrm{d}y) + F(x; y),$$
$$P[x < X \le x + \mathrm{d}x;\; y < Y \le y + \mathrm{d}y]$$
$$= \mathrm{d}F(x + \mathrm{d}x; y) - \mathrm{d}F(x; y) = \mathrm{d}^2 F(x; y).$$

Consequently:

$$P\big[x_1 < X \le x_2;\; y_1 < Y \le y_2\big] = \int_{x_1}^{x_2} \int_{y_1}^{y_2} f(x; y)\mathrm{d}x\mathrm{d}y.$$

1.3.4.3. *Marginal probability of couples of random variables*

Marginal distribution function. The distribution of each variable in a pair of variables is called its marginal distribution.

The marginal distributions of X and Y are respectively the functions:

$$F_x = P[X \le x;\; -\infty < Y < \infty] \tag{1.35}$$

$$= \int_{y=-\infty}^{\infty} \int_{u=-\infty}^{x} f(u; y)\mathrm{d}u\mathrm{d}y, \tag{1.36}$$

and:

$$F_y = P[-\infty < X < \infty; \; Y \leq y] \tag{1.37}$$

$$= \int_{v=-\infty}^{y} \int_{x=-\infty}^{\infty} f(x; v) \mathrm{d}x \mathrm{d}v. \tag{1.38}$$

Marginal density function. From the above, it follows for X and Y respectively:

$$f_X(x) = \int_{-\infty}^{\infty} f(x; y) \mathrm{d}y \tag{1.39}$$

$$f_Y(y) = \int_{-\infty}^{\infty} f(x; y) \mathrm{d}x. \tag{1.40}$$

1.3.4.4. *Conditional probability of a couple of random variables*

Conditional distribution function. The conditional distribution function of X with respect to Y is the function:

$$F(x \mid y) = P[X \leq x \mid Y \leq y], \tag{1.41}$$

and according to the conditional probability theorem:

$$F(x \mid y) = \frac{F(x, y)}{F(y)}. \tag{1.42}$$

Thus:

$$F(x, y) = F(y)F(x \mid y) = F(x)F(y \mid x).$$

Conditional density function. From the above, it follows directly for X and Y respectively:

$$f_X(x \mid y) = \frac{f_{XY}(x, y)}{f_Y(y)}, \tag{1.43}$$

$$f_Y(y \mid x) = \frac{f_{XY}(x, y)}{f_X(x)}. \tag{1.44}$$

1.3.4.5. *Functions of a couple of random variables*

We consider here not only the relation between two random variables but a *function* of these variables. This is a common situation when dealing with random phenomena.

DEFINITION 1.1. Let X and Y be two random variables, and let U and V be two functions of these variables:

$$U = g(X, Y), \quad V = h(X, Y).$$

Let us denote by G and H the inverse functions:

$$X = G(U, V), \quad Y = H(U, V).$$

We obtain:

$$P[x < X \le x + dx; \; y < Y \le y + dy] = P[u < U \le u + du; \; v < V \le v + dv]$$

or, in other words:

$$f_{XY}(x, y) dx dy = f_{UV}(u, v) du dv.$$

Thus:

$$f_{UV}(u, v) = \frac{f_{XY}(x, y)}{\left| J_{\frac{uv}{xy}} \right|} \tag{1.45}$$

with J, the Jacobian of U and V:

$$J = \begin{vmatrix} \dfrac{dU}{dx} & \dfrac{dU}{dy} \\[2mm] \dfrac{dV}{dx} & \dfrac{dV}{dy} \end{vmatrix} \tag{1.46}$$

i.e. the determinant of the partial derivatives of U and V with respect to x and y.

Example application. In order to make this concept more concrete, consider the simple configuration of two pieces of equipment "in series", such as components in series in a material, or a chain of routers inside a network. Their characteristics (failure rate, processing time, etc.) are two random variables X and Y. We are interested in the probability density function of the sum variable (the total processing time for instance) $U = X + Y$. Taking here simply $V = X$, we obtain:

$$J = \begin{vmatrix} \dfrac{dU}{dx} & \dfrac{dU}{dy} \\[2mm] \dfrac{dV}{dx} & \dfrac{dV}{dy} \end{vmatrix} = \begin{vmatrix} 1 & 1 \\ 1 & 0 \end{vmatrix} = -1.$$

Hence:

$$f_{UV}(u, v) = f_{XY}(x, y),$$

a result which is obviously intuitive in such a simple case. Now consider U; its density is the marginal density of the pair (u, v):

$$f_U(u) = \int f_{UV}(u, v) dv,$$

and then:

$$f_U(u) = \int f_{UV}(u,v)dv = \int f_{XY}(x,y)dx = \int f_X(x)f_Y(y)dx.$$

Noting that $y = u - x$, we obtain:

$$f(u) = \int f(x)f(u-x)dx.$$

The density of the sum is the *convolution product* of the densities of x and y, and is usually symbolized as

$$f(u) = f(x) \otimes f(y).$$

In the following, we will see that many problems involving several random variables make use of convolution products. In many cases it will be possible to derive the solution directly from the definition. This is further developed in the next section. Then, we will present other resolution methods, based upon powerful tools such as Laplace transforms, generating functions or characteristic functions.

Of prime importance is the case of the sum of independent random variables.

1.3.4.6. *Sum of independent random variables*

Imagine a complex system, for which a global performance parameter is studied (e.g., some processing delay). The analysis often proceeds by decomposing the system into subsystems which are sequentially invoked during the processing. Thus, if the process is a sequence of n elementary tasks in the various subsystems, the total delay is the sum of the n elementary delays. This exemplifies the importance of studying the properties of the sum of random variables. We now establish the main results concerning these sums.

Probability density of the sum of independent random variables. Let X and Y be two independent random variables, and $Z = X + Y$ their sum. We have:

$$F(z) = P[Z \le z] = P[(X+Y) \le Z], \tag{1.47}$$

and thus:

$$F(z) = \int_{-\infty}^{\infty} dy \int_{-\infty}^{z-y} f(x;y)dx.$$

Since X and Y are independent variables, we can write:

$$F(z) = \int_{-\infty}^{\infty} \left[\int_{-\infty}^{z-y} f_X(x)dx \right] f_Y(y)dy$$

$$= \int_{-\infty}^{\infty} F_X(z-y)f_Y(y)dy, \tag{1.48}$$

and so:

$$f(z) = \int_{-\infty}^{\infty} f_X(z - y) f_Y(y) dy. \tag{1.49}$$

Once again, the convolution product appears, as in the previous example. In the case of discrete variables, we immediately find:

$$P[Z = k] = \sum_{i=0}^{k} p_X(i) p_Y(k - i). \tag{1.50}$$

Example application. Let X and Y be two variables, each one obeying a Poisson distribution with parameters λ_1 and λ_2 respectively. Recall the expression for the Poisson law given above:

$$p(k) = \frac{\lambda^k}{k!} \cdot e^{-\lambda}.$$

Then the density of their sum $Z = X + Y$ is given by:

$$P[Z = k] = \sum_{i=0}^{k} p_X(i) p_Y(k - i) = \sum_{i=0}^{k} \frac{\lambda_1^i}{i!} e^{-\lambda_1} \frac{\lambda_2^{k-i}}{(k - i)!} e^{-\lambda_2}$$

$$= \frac{e^{-(\lambda_1+\lambda_2)}}{k!} \sum_{i=0}^{k} \frac{k!}{i!(k - i)!} \lambda_1^i \lambda_2^{k-i} = \frac{e^{-(\lambda_1+\lambda_2)}}{k!} \sum_{i=0}^{k} \binom{k}{i} \lambda_1^i \lambda_2^{k-i}.$$

Now, we recognize in the last term the binomial expansion: $(a+b)^k = \sum_i \binom{k}{i} a^i b^{k-i}$, and thus:

$$P[Z = k] = \frac{e^{-(\lambda_1+\lambda_2)}}{k!} (\lambda_1 + \lambda_2)^k. \tag{1.51}$$

This is a remarkable result: the sum of two Poisson independent random variables is itself a Poisson variable. This is a basic property for all traffic and performance studies: for instance we conclude that a system which is offered several independent Poisson flows (calls, messages) will be globally offered a Poisson flow.

1.3.4.7. *Moments of the sum of independent random variables*

Mean. The mean of the sum of several variables $X, Y, \ldots$ is equal to the sum of their means:

$$E[X + Y + \cdots] = E[X] + E[Y] + \cdots. \tag{1.52}$$

Let us give the proof for two variables:

$$E[X + Y] = \int_{-\infty}^{\infty} \int_{-\infty}^{\infty} (x + y) f_{XY}(x, y) \mathrm{d}x\mathrm{d}y$$

$$= \int_{-\infty}^{\infty} \int_{-\infty}^{\infty} x f_{XY}(x, y) \mathrm{d}x\mathrm{d}y + \int_{-\infty}^{\infty} \int_{-\infty}^{\infty} y f_{XY}(x, y) \mathrm{d}x\mathrm{d}y$$

$$= \int_{-\infty}^{\infty} x f_X(x, y) \mathrm{d}x + \int_{-\infty}^{\infty} y f_Y(y) \mathrm{d}y = E[X] + E[Y].$$

The extension of this result to the sum of any number of variables is obvious. Furthermore, note that it follows from the proof that the result holds whether the variables are independent or not.

Variance. The variance of the sum of two independent random variables is equal to the sum of their variances:

$$V[X + Y] = \sigma^2(X + Y) = \sigma^2(X) + \sigma^2(Y). \tag{1.53}$$

Let us give the proof for two variables. By the definition of variance, we have:

$$V[X] = \sigma^2 = E\big[X - E[X]\big]^2.$$

Thus, for the sum of two variables – independent or not:

$$V[X + Y] = \sigma^2 = E\big[(X + Y) - E[X + Y]\big]^2,$$

and, as just proven above:

$$E[X + Y] = E[X] + E[Y].$$

So (noting the expectations as $\overline{X}, \overline{Y}$, for clarity):

$$V[X + Y] = E\big[(X - \overline{X}) + (Y - \overline{Y})\big]^2$$

$$= E\big[(X - \overline{X})^2 + (Y - \overline{Y})^2 + 2(X - \overline{X})(Y - \overline{Y})\big].$$

As the expectation of the sum is the sum of expectations,

$$V = E\big[X - \overline{X}\big]^2 + E\big[Y - \overline{Y}\big]^2 + 2E\big[(X - \overline{X})(Y - \overline{Y})\big],$$

the last term of this equation is called the covariance of X and Y, and is usually denoted as $\text{Cov}[X, Y]$:

$$\text{Cov}[X, Y] = E\big[(X - E[X])(Y - E[Y])\big].$$

Finally we find the important following result:

$$V[X+Y] = V[X] + V[Y] + 2\,\mathrm{Cov}[X,Y]. \tag{1.54}$$

Note that by observing:

$$E[X\overline{Y}] = E[Y\overline{X}] = \overline{X} \cdot \overline{Y},$$

the covariance can be written as:

$$\mathrm{Cov}[X,Y] = E[XY] - E[X]E[Y].$$

Notice the generality of the result, as up to now we did not make use of any independent assumptions. Now consider the case of independent variables. In the expression for the covariance, the term $E[XY]$ is:

$$E[XY] = \int_{-\infty}^{\infty}\int_{-\infty}^{\infty} xy f_{XY}(x,y)\mathrm{d}x\mathrm{d}y.$$

Now, if the variables are independent

$$E[XY] = \int_{-\infty}^{\infty}\int_{-\infty}^{\infty} xy\, f_X f_Y(x,y)\mathrm{d}x\mathrm{d}y = E[X]E[Y]. \tag{1.55}$$

The mean of the product of two independent random variables is equal to the product of their means. As for the sum, the extension of the result to any number of variables is obvious.

Thus, for independent variables:

$$\mathrm{Cov}[X,Y] = E[XY] - E[X]E[Y] = 0,$$

which yields the variance:

$$V[X+Y] = E[X-\overline{X}]^2 + E\big[(Y-\overline{Y})\big]^2 = V[X] + V[Y].$$

The variance of the sum of two independent random variables is equal to the sum of their variances. Once again, the extension of the result to any number of variables is straightforward.

1.3.4.8. *Practical interest*

The previous results have obvious and important applications, both in signal theory and for performance studies. When trying to derive the probability distribution of a phenomenon corresponding to the sum of individual variables, they enable us to derive exact characteristics of the resulting distributions, by summing up individual moments. This practical value will also be apparent in statistics, and especially in sampling theory.

1.4. Convolution

We now tackle the properties of this fundamental operation, introduced in the previous section, in greater detail.

1.4.1. *Definition*

Let $f(t)$ and $g(t)$, be two functions: their convolution product (convolution for brevity) is the function:

$$h(\tau) = \int_{-\infty}^{\infty} f(t)g(\tau - t)\mathrm{d}t = \int_{-\infty}^{\infty} f(\tau - t)g(t)\mathrm{d}t \tag{1.56}$$

when the integral exists.

Note that for the important case where the functions are defined on $[0, \infty[$, the convolution reduces to

$$h(\tau) = \int_{0}^{\tau} f(t)g(\tau - t)\mathrm{d}t = \int_{0}^{\tau} f(\tau - t)g(t)\mathrm{d}t. \tag{1.57}$$

The interpretation is obvious. Imagine that $f(t)$ and $g(t)$ represent the probability density functions for the processing delay of two elements in sequence, that the probability of a total delay equal to τ is the probability product, and that the first delay is t and the second is $\tau - t$, whatever the value for t (total probability theorem).

The convolution expresses the probability density of the sum of random variables.

Other important applications of this concept apply to the filtering process of signal theory. For instance, a noisy signal will travel through the filter transfer function, so as to subtract (which is logically equivalent to a sum) the parasitic signal.

Evidently, the concept of convolution product can be used for discrete variables. The convolution product is, in this case:

$$p(N) = \sum_{n=0}^{N} p_1(n)p_2(N - n)$$

with $p_1(n)$, $p_2(N - n)$ being the respective probabilities that the first variable has the value n and the second has the value $N - n$.

More generally, the convolution product of several functions is denoted using the following symbol:

$$f(t) \otimes g(t) \otimes h(t) \cdots$$

1.4.2. *Properties of the convolution operation*

1.4.2.1. *The convolution is commutative*

$$f(t) \otimes g(t) = g(t) \otimes f(t).$$

Indeed, changing the variables: $\theta = \tau - t$ i.e. $t = \tau - \theta$, $dt = -d\theta$:

$$\int_{-\infty}^{\infty} f(t)g(\tau - t)dt = -\int_{-\infty}^{\infty} f(\tau - \theta)g(\theta)d\theta = \int_{-\infty}^{\infty} f(\tau - \theta)g(\theta)d\theta.$$

Let us now calculate the convolution of two constant use functions:

1.4.2.2. *Convolution of exponential distributions*

We take the example of the exponential distribution of processing times. As the variables are positive, we make use of the convolution form (1.57). Given:

$$f(t) = Ae^{-at}, \quad g(t) = Be^{-bt},$$

with $a \neq b$. We obtain:

$$h(\tau) = \int_0^\tau Ae^{-a(\tau - t)} Be^{-bt}dt = ABe^{-a\tau} \int_0^\tau e^{(a-b)t}dt$$

$$= \frac{ABe^{-a\tau}}{a - b}\left(e^{(a-b)\tau} - 1\right) = \frac{AB}{a - b}\left(e^{-b\tau} - e^{-a\tau}\right).$$

See section 1.5.2.4 for an example where $a = b$.

1.4.2.3. *Convolution of normal (Gaussian) distributions*

We will define this important function precisely in the next chapter. For now we take only its simplest expression, called the *standard normal distribution*:

$$f(x) = \frac{1}{\sqrt{2\pi}} e^{-\frac{x^2}{2}}.$$

Then the convolution of two normal distributions is:

$$h(\tau) = \frac{1}{2\pi} \int_{-\infty}^{\infty} e^{-\frac{1}{2}[x^2 + (\tau - x)^2]}dx.$$

Note that the expression $u = x^2 + (\tau - x)^2$ can be rewritten as:

$$u = x^2 + (\tau - x)^2 = 2x^2 + \tau^2 - 2x\tau = \frac{\tau^2}{2} + \left(x\sqrt{2} - \frac{\tau}{\sqrt{2}}\right)^2,$$

so that, by taking $v = \frac{1}{\sqrt{2}}\left(x\sqrt{2} - \frac{\tau}{\sqrt{2}}\right) = x - \frac{\tau}{2}$, the expression reduces to:

$$h(\tau) = \frac{1}{2\pi}e^{-\frac{\tau^2}{4}}\int_{-\infty}^{\infty}e^{-v^2}\,\mathrm{d}x.$$

However:

$$\int_{-\infty}^{\infty}e^{-v^2}\,\mathrm{d}x = \sqrt{\pi}.$$

We thus have the remarkable result:

$$h(\tau) = \frac{1}{2\sqrt{\pi}}e^{-\frac{(\tau/\sqrt{2})^2}{2}}. \tag{1.58}$$

The convolution of two normal distributions is itself normal. This is a basis for many approximations, since the normal approximation is often a reasonable assumption, provided the variables are not too far from their mean, and in this case the sum is simply the normal distribution. This will be developed in the following sections.

Moreover, the *central limit theorem* is another fundamental property when summing a large number of random variables, and states that the limit goes to a normal distribution, independently of the individual distributions. This result is presented in Chapter 3.

We now introduce the notion of *transforms*, which allow an efficient manipulation of random variables. They provide essential tools in various problems, such as the resolution of systems of differential equations (Laplace transforms) or the use of stochastic relations for the resolution of complex queueing systems (characteristic functions). They also enable easy calculation of the successive moments of a distribution or the derivation of the distributions of sums on random variables.

1.5. Laplace transform

The appeal of the Laplace transform, as well as the other transforms we will introduce, is mainly that it decomposes the original function into a sum of exponential terms that are easy to manipulate. It will be applied when solving state equations, in queueing theory and reliability (see Chapters 6 and 7), and also calculating moments of sums of random variables. As we see now, Laplace transforms are a powerful means of deriving, in a simpler way, results already obtained. Note that the Laplace transform, as well as the other transforms, also appears in signal theory with a different usage but still based on the properties developed hereafter.

Note also that each of these transforms conserves all the information of the original function. This means that there is a one-to-one correspondence between a function and its transform.

1.5.1. *Definition*

The Laplace transform of a function $f(t)$ such that $f(t) = 0$ if $t < 0$ is the function

$$F^*(s) = \int_{0-}^{\infty} f(t)e^{-st}dt. \tag{1.59}$$

The bound "$0-$" is a short notation for:

$$\lim_{\epsilon > 0, \epsilon \to 0} \int_{-\epsilon}^{\infty} .$$

1.5.2. *Properties*

1.5.2.1. *Fundamental property*

The major property of the Laplace transform concerns the convolution, just as introduced above. Its formulation is: the Laplace transform of the convolution of functions is just the product of each transform. So for two functions $f(t)$ and $g(t)$ we have:

$$F^*\big[f(t) \otimes g(t)\big] = F^*(s)G^*(s). \tag{1.60}$$

Indeed, denoting the convolution as h, we find:

$$F^*\big[h(\tau)\big] = \int_{\tau=0}^{\infty} \int_{t=0}^{\tau} f(\tau - t)g(t)e^{-st}dtd\tau$$

$$= \int_{t=0}^{\infty} \int_{\tau=t}^{\infty} f(\tau - t)e^{-s(\tau-t)}g(t)e^{-st}dtd\tau$$

$$= \int_{t=0}^{\infty} g(t)e^{-st}dt \int_{\tau-t=0}^{\infty} f(\tau - t)e^{-s(\tau-t)}d\tau$$

and thus:

$$F^*\big[h(t)\big] = F^*\big[f(t) \otimes g(t)\big] = F^*(s)G^*(s). \tag{1.61}$$

The generalization of this result is straightforward. Furthermore, using the results of the previous section, it can be reformulated by stating that *the Laplace transform of the distribution of a sum of variables is the product of the individual transforms.* This is a basic property that the Laplace transform shares with other transforms (characteristic and generating functions), as will be seen below.

1.5.2.2. *Differentiation property*

From the definition of transform, we immediately obtain:

$$\frac{df(t)}{dt} \Longleftrightarrow sF^*(s),$$

and:

$$\frac{d^n f(t)}{dt^n} \Longleftrightarrow s^n F^*(s).$$ (1.62)

1.5.2.3. *Integration property*

$$\int_0^\infty f(t)dt \Longleftrightarrow \frac{F^*(s)}{s},$$

and for the nth order integration:

$$\int_0^\infty \cdots \int_0^\infty f(t)dt^n \Longleftrightarrow \frac{F^*(s)}{s^n}.$$ (1.63)

1.5.2.4. *Some common transforms*

Here we offer a few examples of results concerning the transforms of distributions most commonly found in telecommunication applications. More generally, tables of function couples (original/transform) can be established, so that deriving the original from the transform can normally be accomplished by inspecting the table.

Unit step function. By definition:

$$\mu(t) = \begin{cases} 1 & t \geq 0 \\ 0 & t < 0 \end{cases}$$

this function expresses the fact that a probability distribution exists only for positive epochs. For instance, the function denoted as $e^{-at}\mu(t)$ is an exponential function taking values only for $t \geq 0$. Using the definition, we obtain:

$$\mu(t) \Longleftrightarrow \frac{1}{s}.$$ (1.64)

Note that this result can also be obtained from the exponential transform function (see below) by making $a \to 0$.

Dirac delta function (unit impulse). By definition:

$$\int_{-\infty}^\infty \delta(t)dt = 1, \quad \text{with } \delta(t) \text{ being defined on } [-\epsilon, \epsilon], \text{ with } \epsilon \longrightarrow 0$$

(i.e. $\delta(t) = 0$ if $t \neq 0$). This function provides a way to deal with distribution discontinuities. For instance, it allows us to represent a discrete variable as a continuous function. An important application is presented in signal theory for the sampling function. Another important application is in the representation of discontinuities at the origin. For instance, some equipment, the reliability of which is governed by the exponential distribution during its operational life, might have a probability of being up (or down) at the instant of being put into service. This possibility is represented by the Dirac delta function.

Applying the transform definition, we have:

$$\int_{-\infty}^{\infty} \delta(t) e^{-st} dt = 1,$$

that is:

$$\delta(t) \Longleftrightarrow 1, \tag{1.65}$$

and in the same way:

$$\delta(t - \theta) \Longleftrightarrow e^{-s\theta}. \tag{1.66}$$

From the above, we deduce the important property:

$$f(t) \otimes \delta(t - \theta) \Longleftrightarrow F^*(s) e^{-s\theta},$$

and thus:

$$f(t) \otimes \delta(t - \theta) = f(t - \theta).$$

The convolution of a function with a Dirac delta function shifted on the time axis also shifts the function. The Dirac function is also denoted:

$$u_0(t) = \delta(t),$$

and:

$$u_{-1}(t) = \int_{-\infty}^{t} u_0(t) dt.$$

Thus, we have:

$$u_{-1}(t) = \mu(t).$$

The unit step function is the integral of the Dirac delta function. More generally, for the nth integrals and derivatives of these two functions, we find the following relationships:

$$u_{-n}(t) = \frac{t^{n-1}}{(n-1)!} \Longleftrightarrow \frac{1}{s^n}, \tag{1.67}$$

$$u_n(t) = \frac{d}{dt} u_{n-1}(t) \Longleftrightarrow s^n. \tag{1.68}$$

Exponential function:

$$Ae^{-at}\mu(t) \Longleftrightarrow \frac{A}{s+A}. \tag{1.69}$$

Notice that when taking the limiting case $a = 0$ we again find the result obtained for the unit step function, as we have already signaled.

Application. Let us apply this result to one of our preceding examples, the convolution of two exponential functions:

$$f(t) = Ae^{-at}$$

$$g(t) = Be^{-bt},$$

with $a \neq b$. From the previous results we immediately obtain:

$$F^*(s) = \frac{A}{s+a}, \qquad G^*(s) = \frac{B}{s+b},$$

$$F^*(s)G^*(s) = \frac{AB}{(s+a)(s+b)} = \frac{AB}{a-b}\left(\frac{1}{s+b} - \frac{1}{s+a}\right).$$

Now, by inspection (using the results above (see exponential transform)), we return to the original (untransformed) function, and we obtain:

$$f(\tau) = \frac{AB}{a-b}\left(e^{-b\tau} - e^{-a\tau}\right).$$

The result is of course the same as in the previous section.

Let us now consider the notable case of the sum of n identically distributed exponential variables (here we no longer impose $a \neq b$). The transform of the sum is

$$F^*(s) = \left(\frac{A}{s+a}\right)^n,$$

whose original is:

$$f(t) = \frac{A^n t^{n-1}}{(n-1)!} e^{-at}. \tag{1.70}$$

Clearly, for $n = 1$ the solution is $f(t) = Ae^{-at}$.

Let us verify that for $n = 2$ the solution is:

$$f(t) = A^2 t e^{-at}.$$

We have:

$$F^*(s) = \int_0^\infty A^2 t e^{-at} e^{-st} dy = A^2 \int_0^\infty t e^{-(s+a)t} dt.$$

After a simple integration by parts ($\int u dv$, with $u = t$ and $dv = e^{-(s+a)t} dt$), we obtain:

$$F^*(s) = \frac{A^2}{(s+a)^2}.$$

Proceeding stepwise in an identical way, we can verify that the general solution is

$$f(t) = \frac{A^n t^{n-1}}{(n-1)!} e^{-at}.$$

We will see in the following chapters that this is a very useful function, called the Erlang-n distribution.

1.6. Characteristic function, generating function, z-transform

These functions play a fundamental role in probability and statistics, mainly due to their relation with the moments of distributions, and for the simplicity they offer when dealing with sums of random variables. Among all these functions, the characteristic function has a major position. It provides another expression for Laplace transforms, and happens to be one of the basic tools in queueing theory. Some properties of these transforms will also be of constant use in signal theory, as we have already mentioned.

1.6.1. *Characteristic function*

The *characteristic function* provides another expression for the Laplace transform, and will be an essential tool in relation to the Pollaczek method, as will be seen in Chapter 6.

1.6.1.1. *Definition*

The characteristic function of a random variable X, whose distribution function is $F(x)$, is defined as:

$$\phi(u) = \int_{-\infty}^{\infty} e^{iux} dF(x). \tag{1.71}$$

This function has been introduced by Laplace for absolutely continuous functions. Its use in probability theory has mainly been developed through the work of Paul Lévy [LÉV 25].

The characteristic function ϕ always exists, is continuous, defined on the imaginary axis, and is such that $\phi(0) = 1$, $|\phi(u)| \leq 1$.

For commodity reasons, the purely imaginary variable iu is replaced by the complex number z. We thus write:

$$\phi(z) = \int_{-\infty}^{\infty} e^{zx} dF(x), \quad z \in \mathbb{C}. \tag{1.72}$$

In the case of a discrete variable we have:

$$\phi(z) = \sum_k p_k e^{zx_k}, \tag{1.73}$$

which is also written, for brevity (the symbol E stands for the expectation):

$$\phi(z) = E\left[e^{zX}\right].$$ (1.74)

The distribution function $F(x)$ can be obtained from the characteristic function $\phi(z)$ using the inversion formula (see below).

As we have mentioned, the integral always exists on the imaginary axis. This is not always true in the complex plane. However, introducing z, as in equation (1.72), offers a convenient way to retrieve the distribution $F(x)$ from $\phi(z)$, the derivation of the integral then starting from the study of singularities of ϕ. Thanks to the work of Lévy, it is possible to assert that if $F(x)$ exists for all x real, $\alpha < x < \beta$, the integral is convergent in the vertical strip $\alpha < Re(z) < \beta$, and $\phi(z)$ is holomorphic inside this strip. Moreover, the singularity closest to the origin is necessarily real – this property making the derivation of asymptotic limits easier.

Once again, we should note that the transform defines the original probability distribution completely. We present below its main properties and several significant results related to the use of residue theorem, leading to simple applications.

1.6.1.2. Inversion formula

At points where the function $F(x)$ is continuous we find:

$$F(x) = \frac{1}{2\pi i} \int_{-i\infty+\delta}^{i\infty+\delta} e^{zx} \phi(-z) \frac{dz}{z},$$ (1.75)

provided that this integral converges. We can recognize a Cauchy integral in the complex plane, where the contour of integration is a vertical line parallel to the imaginary axis at distance $x = \delta$ ($\delta > 0$), and traversed from below to above.

1.6.1.3. The concept of event indicator and the Heaviside function

Let us first introduce the Heaviside function. It is defined by: $H(x) = 1$, for $x > 0$; $H(x) = \frac{1}{2}$, for $x = 0$, $H(x) = 0$, for $x < 0$, and for $x \neq 0$ it is represented by the Dirichlet integral:

$$H(x) = \frac{1}{2\pi i} \int_{-i\infty+\delta}^{i\infty+\delta} e^{zx} \frac{dz}{z},$$ (1.76)

which is, as before, a Cauchy integral, taken in the complex plane, and where the integration contour (closed to ∞) is a vertical line parallel to the imaginary axis, at distance $x = \delta$, and traversed from $-\infty$ to $+\infty$. In the following, for convenience, we will denote this integral $\int_{C_s}$, its contour being located just on the right and close to the imaginary axis.

This function allows us to define of the probability of an event.

Indeed, given the event $x > 0$, the event *indicator* is defined as a function equal to 1 for $x > 0$, and equal to 0 otherwise, i.e. the function $H(x)$. Then we have the following fundamental relationship: *the probability of the event is the expectation of its indicator*, $F(x) = E[H(x)]$, as we now explain.

Event indicator and distribution function. Let X be a random variable, and $F(x)$ its probability distribution function. According to the definition its characteristic function is:

$$\phi(z) = \int_{-\infty}^{\infty} e^{zx} dF(x) = E\left[e^{zX}\right].$$

Consider the variable $x - X$. The indicator of the event $\{x - X > 0\}$, i.e. $X < x$, is $H(x - X)$, and thus:

$$F(x) = E\left[H(x - X)\right]. \tag{1.77}$$

Indeed,

$$E\left[\frac{1}{2i\pi} \int_{C_z} e^{z(x-X)} \frac{dz}{z}\right] = \frac{1}{2i\pi} \int_{C_z} e^{zx} E\left(e^{-zX}\right) \frac{dz}{z} = \frac{1}{2i\pi} \int_{C_z} e^{zx} \phi(-z) \frac{dz}{z}$$

(the permutation of operators $\int$ and $\sum$ being possible if the integral is uniformly convergent, i.e. if the line $x = \delta$ is in the analytic strip). This is simply the inversion of the formula presented above:

$$\frac{1}{2i\pi} \int_{C_z} e^{zx} \phi(-z) \frac{dz}{z} = F(x).$$

Finally, $E[H(x - X)] = F(x)$, provided $F(x)$ is continuous at point x.

1.6.1.4. *Calculating the inverse function and residues*

Now we present the means to calculate the integral in the inversion formula. First remember that if $f(z)$ is a holomorphic function of the complex variable z (see the Appendix) in the domain $\mathcal{D}$ bounded by a closed contour $\mathcal{C}$, and if $f(z)$ is continuous in $\mathcal{D} \cup \mathcal{C}$, then for any point z_0 of $\mathcal{D}$ we find:

$$\frac{1}{2\pi i} \int_{C+} \frac{f(z)}{z - z_0} dz = f(z_0),$$

the path being traversed in the positive direction (counter-clockwise).

Then we may verify that $f(z)$ can be expanded according to the powers of $(z - z_0)$ inside the circle centered on z_0, and that the series converges as long as z remains inside $\mathcal{C}$.

Consequently, we can apply the residue theorem to obtain the solution, which is: $\frac{1}{2\pi i} \int_{C+} \frac{f(z)}{z-z_0} \, dz = \sum R_i$, where R_i is the residue at the singularity z_i (see below).

The usefulness of the characteristic function is clear, as in most cases it is simpler to express functions of random variables through their characteristic functions (e.g., in the case of sums of variables), and then return to the distribution. However, integrating the inversion formula may happen to be difficult, or even impossible, and we sometimes have to rely on approximations. Most often, the original distribution function is directly obtained by a simple inspection, as was illustrated for the Laplace transform.

Nevertheless, the inversion formula is of great help in several cases, especially to derive asymptotic results (as illustrated below), and also to derive fundamental results by applying the Pollaczek approach (see section 6.6).

The use of the residue theorem is essential in these calculations, and its main aspects are presented here.

1.6.1.5. *The residue theorem*

Let us recall the residue theorem: let z_1 be a pole or an isolated singular point for the function $f(z)$, ($f(z)$ is holomorphic in a circle whose center is z_1, except in z_1), the residue of $f(z)$ at this point is the coefficient R_1 of $1/(z - z_1)$ in the Laurent expansion around z_1. Let C be a simple curve, closed, and traversed in the positive direction. If within C, $f(z)$ does not have any singularity other than z_1, then:

$$\frac{1}{2\pi i} \int_{C+} f(z) dz = R_1.$$

Indeed, we may replace C by any other similar curve, for instance a circle of center z_1, and we will then verify that this expression is the coefficient of $1/(z - z_1)$ in the Laurent expansion of $f(z)$ (see the Appendix). In a more general way (for several singularities), the residue theorem is:

$$\frac{1}{2\pi i} \int_{C+} f(z) dz = \sum R_i. \tag{1.78}$$

Calculating residues. Generally, in order to obtain the residue of $f(z)$ at the pole z_i, we expand $f(z)$ in its Laurent series around z_i, and the residue is the coefficient of the term $1/(z - z_i)$. The Taylor series may also be used (see the Appendix): z_i being an n order pole, the residue in that point is the coefficient of $(z - z_i)^{n-1}$ in the Taylor development of $\Psi(z) = [(z - z_i)^n f(z)]$, i.e.:

$$R_n = \frac{1}{(n-1)!} \cdot \frac{d^{n-1}}{dz^{n-1}} \left[(z - z_i)^n f(z) \right].$$

Especially for a simple pole (first order pole), if $f(z) = P(z)/Q(z)$ with $P(z_1) \neq 0$ and $Q(z_1) = 0$,

$$R_1 = \lim_{z \to z_1} \frac{(z - z_1)P(z)}{Q(z)} = \lim_{z \to z_1} \frac{P(z)}{(Q(z) - Q(z_1))/(z - z_1)},$$

i.e.

$$R_1 = \frac{P(z_1)}{Q'(z_1)}.$$

EXAMPLE. Consider the function $f(z) = \frac{1}{(z+1)(z-1)^2}$. It has two poles: a simple pole, $z_1 = -1$, and a multiple pole of order 2, $z_2 = 1$. In order to expand around z_2, we take $z = 1 + h$, (h infinitely small). Then the Laurent expansion is:

$$f(z) = \frac{1}{h^2(h+2)} = \frac{1}{2h^2} \times \left(1 - \frac{h}{2} + \frac{h^2}{4} - \frac{h^3}{8} \cdots \right) = \frac{1}{2h^2} - \frac{1}{4h} + \frac{1}{8} - \frac{h}{6} \cdots$$

The residue, coefficient of $1/h$ (i.e. of $1/(z-1)$), is thus $R_2 = -\frac{1}{4}$. Similarly, at the simple pole we take $z = -1 + h$ and obtain $R_1 = 1/4$ (the exercise is left to the reader). We may also apply the general formula directly. For instance:

$$R_1 = \left[(z+1)f(z)\right]_{z=z_1=-1} = \left[\frac{1}{(z-1)^2}\right]_{z=z_1=-1} = \frac{1}{4},$$

or also:

$$R_1 = \left[\frac{1/(z-1)^2}{(z+1)'}\right]_{z=z_1=-1} = \frac{1}{4}.$$

Similarly:

$$R_2 = \frac{d}{dz}\left[(z-1)^2 f(z)\right]_{z=z_2=1} = -\frac{1}{4}.$$

Evidently, we obtain the same results.

1.6.1.6. *Asymptotic formula*

Now we are in a position to establish an asymptotic expression of the distribution $F(x)$ for large values of x. This kind of expression is useful as it provides approximate results for many queueing problems.

Let us assume that the first singular point of our integral is a simple pole z_1 (necessarily real, as mentioned previously – see Lévy's theorem in the Appendix). Applying the residue theorem to the inversion formula at the poles $z = 0$ and z_1 yields:

$$F(x) = 1 + \frac{R_1}{z_1}e^{z_1 x} + \frac{1}{2\pi i}\int_{-i\infty+\delta_1}^{i\infty+\delta_1} e^{zx}\phi(-z)\frac{dz}{z},$$

with $\delta_1 < z_1$, and R_1 residue of $\phi(-z)$ at z_1. The last integral decays to zero when x grows to infinity, and then for very large values of x we obtain:

$$F(x) \approx 1 - \frac{-R_1}{z_1}e^{z_1 x}, \quad \text{and so } P(> x) \approx \frac{-R_1}{z_1}e^{z_1 x}, \tag{1.79}$$

which, taking $\phi(z)$ this time and its residue R'_1 at pole z_1, may also be written:

$$P(> x) \approx \frac{R'_1}{(-z_1)}e^{-z_1 x}. \tag{1.80}$$

We will develop several simple applications of this fundamental result in what follows. The solution is clearly exact when the singular point is a unique pole.

1.6.1.7. Moments

Returning to the definition and expanding in power series e^{zx}, we find:

$$e^{zx} = 1 + x\frac{z}{1!} + x^2\frac{z^2}{2!} + \cdots + x^n\frac{z^n}{n!} + \cdots,$$

and:

$$\phi(z) = 1 + m_1\frac{z}{1!} + m_2\frac{z^2}{2!} + \cdots + m_n\frac{z^n}{n!} + \cdots.$$

Thus, taking the nth order derivative:

$$\phi^{(n)}(0) = m_n, \tag{1.81}$$

m_n is the nth order moment about the origin, as defined previously. So, the moments are easily derived from the characteristic function.

Example application. Let X be a random variable having density $f(x) = \lambda e^{-\lambda x}$, with $f(x) = 0$ if $x < 0$. Its characteristic function is:

$$\phi(z) = \int_0^\infty e^{zx}\lambda e^{-\lambda x}dx = \lambda\int_0^\infty e^{(z-\lambda)x}dx = \frac{\lambda}{\lambda - z},$$

and:

$$\phi'(z) = \frac{\lambda}{(\lambda - z)^2}, \quad \phi''(z) = \frac{2\lambda}{(\lambda - z)^3}.$$

Thus:

$$E[X] = m_1 = \phi'(0) = \frac{1}{\lambda},$$

$$E[X^2] = m_2 = \phi''(0) = \frac{2}{\lambda^2},$$

and:

$$\sigma^2 = E[X^2] - (E[X])^2 = \frac{1}{\lambda^2}.$$

Sum and difference of independent random variables. Consider the variable $Y = X_1 + X_2$, with X_1 and X_2 two independent random variables. We denote their respective characteristic functions as $\phi(z)$, $\phi_1(z)$, $\phi_2(z)$. According to the definition:

$$\phi(z) = E\left[e^{z(X_1+X_2)}\right],$$

thus:

$$\phi(z) = E\left[e^{zX_1}e^{zX_2}\right] = E\left[e^{zX_1}\right]E\left[e^{zX_2}\right],$$

the last transformation being justified by the properties of the means of independent variables. We again find the basic relationship, used previously for Laplace transforms:

$$\phi(z) = \phi_1(z)\phi_2(z). \tag{1.82}$$

Similarly, for the difference $Y = X_1 - X_2$, we obtain:

$$\phi(z) = \phi_1(z)\phi_2(-z). \tag{1.83}$$

These results may be readily generalized to any number of independent variables.

1.6.1.8. *Some common transforms*

Just as for Laplace transforms, several basic transforms are of constant help in applications. Note that the correspondence with Laplace transforms is immediate, as $\phi(is) = F^*(s)$. Chapter 2 contains a more comprehensive set of the characteristic functions of common distributions (Poisson, binomial, etc.).

Sure (or almost sure) function. A constant service time provides a typical example:

$$F(x) = \begin{cases} 1 & x < a \\ 0 & x \geq a \end{cases}$$

for which:

$$\phi(z) = e^{az}. \tag{1.84}$$

Exponential function. This function is of constant use in queueing problems to describe inter-arrival delays or service durations:

$$f(x) = Ae^{-ax} \quad \text{for } x \geq 0$$

$$F(x) = \begin{cases} 0 & x < 0 \\ 1 - Ae^{-ax} & x \geq 0 \end{cases} \tag{1.85}$$

$$\phi(z) = \frac{A}{a - z}.$$

Geometric distribution:

$$p_n = pq^n \quad (n = 0, 1, 2 \dots) \text{ with } q = 1 - p$$

$$F(n) = 1 - q^{n+1} \tag{1.86}$$

$$\phi(z) = \frac{p}{1 - qe^z}.$$

1.6.2. *Generating functions, z-transforms*

1.6.2.1. *Definition*

For discrete random variables, the characteristic function is written as:

$$\phi(z) = \sum_k p_k e^{zx_k}.$$

Now assume that X takes only positive integer values. It may then be convenient to introduce the generating function of the p_k:

$$F(z) = \sum_k p_k z^k, \tag{1.87}$$

where z is a complex variable. It is also referred to as the z-transform, which we will particularly use in Chapter 4 on signal theory (it is then expressed as a function of z^{-k}). It is defined for $|z| < 1$, since $F(1) = 1$. We also find:

$$\phi(z) = F(e^z). \tag{1.88}$$

The characteristic function derives from the generating function through a simple change of variable.

1.6.2.2. *Moments*

We may derive the important relationships concerning moments directly from their definition. Indeed, we have:

$$F'(z) = \sum_k k p_k z^{k-1},$$

and so:

$$F'(1) = \sum_k k p_k.$$

Thus:

$$E[X] = \overline{X} = F'(1). \tag{1.89}$$

Similarly:

$$F''(z) = \sum_k k(k-1)p_k z^{k-2},$$

then:

$$F''(1) = \sum_k k(k-1)p_k = \overline{X^2} - \overline{X},$$

and finally:

$$\sigma^2 = \overline{X^2} - \overline{X}^2 = F''(1) + F'(1) - \left(F'(1)\right)^2. \tag{1.90}$$

1.6.2.3. *Some common transforms*

Here are the simplest and most common pairs of discrete distributions and their generating functions.

(Discrete) unit step function:

$$\mu_k = 1, \quad \text{for } k = 0, 1, 2, \dots$$

so that

$$F(z) = \sum_k 1 \cdot z^k = \frac{1}{1-z},$$

which is traditionally written as

$$\mu_k \Longleftrightarrow \frac{1}{1-z}. \tag{1.91}$$

Geometric function:

$$f_k = Aa^k, \quad \text{for } k = 0, 1, 2, \dots$$

$$F(z) = \sum_k Aa^k z^k = \frac{1}{1-az}. \tag{1.92}$$

$$f_k \Longleftrightarrow \frac{A}{1-az}.$$

The reader will easily link this result with formula (1.86).

1.6.3. *Convolution*

At last, just as for the other transforms, it can be shown that:

$$f_k \otimes g_k \iff F(z)G(z). \tag{1.93}$$

The transform of the convolution of functions is equal to the product of their transforms.

We will illustrate the use of these properties throughout the following chapters of this book, especially in Chapter 6 when mixing different bitrates.

Chapter 2

Probability Laws

Random phenomena are clearly of various kinds, and their probabilistic description makes use of numerous probability laws. In this chapter, we present the most important and most commonly used of these laws, giving their main characteristics (distribution function, transforms, moments) and commenting on the circumstances in which they are likely to appear.

The engineer is led to apply these laws in various situations. For instance, the experimental distribution of a character has been obtained in a measurement campaign, and the goal is to build a theoretical model capable of representing the result. This amounts to tailoring a mathematical law to the measurements. Another case is the *a priori* choice of a process model in an ongoing project (typically for a simulation experiment). Here, the choice is made by invoking intuitive or mathematical arguments sustaining a specific law (for instance the normal law for a random signal, or an exponential law – or a discrete law – for a service duration, etc.). Needless to say, such a choice relies mainly on the specialist's experience. Lastly, there is the need to analyze the behavior of a phenomenon of given probability distribution (e.g. obtained through one of the previous steps). The analysis is based upon properties of the law (moments, transforms) and makes it possible to draw various figures of interest (e.g. loss probabilities, average delays, etc.).

Depending on circumstances, observations are represented using discrete laws (number of events arriving in an observation window, number of failures, etc.) or continuous laws (e.g. service duration). Denoting the random variable as X, the law is thus either discrete, defined by a distribution function:

$$p_i = P[X = i] \tag{2.1}$$

or continuous, defined by the *probability distribution function* (PDF) or the *probability density function* (pdf):

$$F(x) = P[X \leq x], \quad f(x) = \frac{\mathrm{d}}{\mathrm{d}x} F(x). \tag{2.2}$$

2.1. Uniform (discrete) distribution

The uniform law is the simplest imaginable. Let X be a discrete random variable (the outcomes are represented as 0, 1, 2, etc., without loss of generality), such that each outcome has the same occurrence probability (this is a frequent modeling assumption). Tossing an unloaded die is the most obvious illustration, each face having the same frequency in the long term: the probabilistic model simply assigns a $1/6$ probability to each outcome.

A discrete random variable, taking values between a and b, has $b - a + 1$ possible values. It obeys the uniform distribution, denoted as $U(a, b)$, if its probability law is:

$$p_k = P(X = k) = \frac{1}{b - a + 1}, \quad a \leq k \leq b. \tag{2.3}$$

Its mean value is easily derived:

$$\text{Mean: } m = \sum_{k=a}^{k=b} k p_k = \sum_{k=a}^{b} \frac{k}{b - a + 1} = \frac{a + b}{2}. \tag{2.4}$$

Variance is obtained through a calculation of the same kind, making use of the sum of squares formula:

$$\sum_{k=1}^{n} k^2 = \frac{n(n + 1)(2n + 1)}{6},$$

yielding:

$$\text{Variance: } \mathrm{Var} = \frac{(b - a)(b - a + 2)}{12}. \tag{2.5}$$

The continuous version of this law will be addressed later on.

2.2. The binomial law

The binomial law is encountered in numerous applications of probability theory. Let us consider the quality control operation of a production line. Assume that each item has a probability p of being defective. The circumstances making the item faulty or not are such that the status of an item does not depend on the status of the previously produced items. Any element extracted at random is faulty with probability p. Now, assume that a batch of N items is controlled. How many of them are faulty? More precisely, as the experiment is of a random nature, what is the probability of observing $0, 1, 2, \ldots$ faulty items among the N items?

This is one of the problems traditionally addressed by combinatorial analysis. Each trial corresponding to the event "k faulty elements" consists of extracting, in any order, k faulty items and $N - k$ good ones. Several drawings lead to this result. For instance, denoting faulty elements as "0" and good ones as "1", the sequences 110011, 111100, 001111, etc. yields the same event; "2 faulty among 6". Each of these sequences has probability $p^k(1 - p)^{N-k}$ (k and only k defaults have been observed). Moreover, as the order in which faulty elements are observed is irrelevant, the probability of the event is simply the sum of individual sequence probabilities (which are clearly exclusive). Classical counting consists of putting k "balls" inside N "urns", so that each urn contains at most one ball. There are N ways to choose the first urn where a ball is put, $N - 1$ ways to choose the second one, and so on up to the $N - k + 1$th, so that there are $N!/(N - k)!$ possible outcomes. In this operation, however, the same sequence has been counted $k!$ times (as the k balls are not distinguishable, this is the number of permutations of k objects).

Finally, there were $\frac{N!}{k!(N-k)!} = \binom{N}{k}$ ways of observing the event, and the probability of the event is:

$$p_k = P(k \text{ faulty among } N) = \binom{N}{k} p^k (1 - p)^{N-k}. \tag{2.6}$$

This is the so-called binomial distribution, since p_k is the rank k term in the development of $[p + (1 - p)]^N$. Transforms are the easiest way to obtain its moments, and we derive them using its characteristic function (see Chapter 1).

The characteristic function is obtained by the following argument: for a single drawing, the characteristic function is $\phi(z) = E[e^{zX}] = q + pe^z$, with $q = 1 - p$, since the result is $x = 1$ with probability p, and 0 otherwise. Thus, for N independent drawings, since the characteristic function of the sum of independent variables is the product of the individual functions:

$$\phi(z) = \left(q + pe^z\right)^N, \tag{2.7}$$

from which the final result is:

$$m = \sum k p_k = \phi'(z)_{z=0} = N(q + pe^z)^{N-1} pe^z|_{z=0} = Np, \tag{2.8}$$

$$\text{Var} = \sum k^2 p_k - m^2 = \phi''(0) - \left(\phi'(0)\right)^2 = Np(1 - p). \tag{2.9}$$

Figure 2.1 displays the typical shape for the probability density function of the binomial distribution.

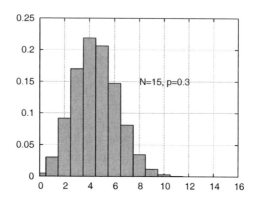

Figure 2.1. *Probability density function of the binomial distribution*

The binomial distribution is of repeated use each time a trial involves superposing independent elementary trials. In the traffic field, the Engset problem introduces it as a limiting distribution (see Chapter 6) of the number of busy lines in subscriber concentrators.

The binomial distribution enjoys the following property, concerning the sum of several variables:

THEOREM 2.1. *If two discrete random variables X and Y have binomial distributions with parameters respectively (N, p) and (M, p), the variable $X + Y$ has a binomial distribution with parameters $(N + M, p)$.*

The proof is straightforward, noting that the characteristic function of the sum is the product of the individual functions.

2.3. Multinomial distribution

This is the generalization of the binomial law. Assume that m types can be distinguished in the population (m kinds of defects, to take the previous example), so that the population has a proportion p_k of type k elements (with naturally $\sum p_k = 1$). The question is: what is the probability of observing, when extracting N items, n_1 of the type 1, etc., n_m of type m, with $n_1 + n_2 + \cdots + n_m = N$. The result is:

$$P(n_1, n_2, \ldots, n_m) = \frac{N!}{n_1! n_2! \cdots n_m!} p_1^{n_1} p_2^{n_2} \cdots p_m^{n_m}. \qquad (2.10)$$

This result has numerous applications. Imagine for instance observing a network element (e.g. a concentrator) to which various sources are connected. What is the traffic distribution the sources generate? Individual traffic intensity, expressed in Erlangs, is distributed between 0 and 1. We can usually define categories, according to the type of subscriber (professional, residential, in urban area, etc.), corresponding to traffic intensities. With two categories, the binomial distribution gives the answer. For several categories (typically: less than 0.03, between 0.03 and 0.05, etc., higher than 0.12), the distribution of customers among the categories is given by the multinomial law. Finally, knowing the distribution of the different customers among the categories allows the dimensioning of the subscriber concentrator, using the multinomial distribution. More generally, this result holds whenever a population, composed of different sub-populations, is observed.

2.4. Geometric distribution

A discrete variable obeys a geometric distribution if its distribution is given by:

$$p_k = (1-p)p^k, \quad 0 < p < 1, \ k = 0, 1, 2, \ldots \tag{2.11}$$

Consider for instance a data layer protocol which detects and corrects transmission errors (such as TCP, in its traditional Go-back-N version). Assume that each packet has a probability p of being erroneously received. Thus, a retransmission is needed with probability p. An error is corrected if the following retransmission is successful: probability $1 - p$. In general, the packet may be erroneous during the k first attempts, the $k + 1$th being correct. This event has probability:

$$p_k = P(k \text{ retransmissions}) = (1-p)p^k. \tag{2.12}$$

The moments of the distribution can be estimated directly:

$$m = \sum k p_k = \sum k(1-p)p^k = p(1-p)\sum k p^{k-1}$$

$$= p(1-p)\frac{\mathrm{d}}{\mathrm{d}p}\left(\sum p^k\right) = p(1-p)\frac{\mathrm{d}}{\mathrm{d}p}\frac{1}{1-p} = \frac{p}{1-p}.$$

The same kind of analysis gives the variance. Actually, this offers another opportunity to stress the efficiency of the transforms approach. We illustrate here the use of generating functions.

For the geometric law, the generating function is given by:

$$B(z) = \sum z^k p_k = \sum (zp)^k (1-p) = \frac{1-p}{1-zp} \tag{2.13}$$

from which the results are immediately derived:

$$\text{Mean value} = \sum k p_k = B'(z)_{z=1} = \frac{p}{1-p}, \tag{2.14}$$

$$\text{Variance} = \sum (k-m)^2 p_k = \frac{p}{(1-p)^2}. \tag{2.15}$$

As a comparison, here is the same calculation using the characteristic function:

$$\phi(z) = \sum e^{zk} p_k = \frac{1 - p}{1 - pe^z} \tag{2.16}$$

from which the derivatives, here taken at $z = 0$ (see Chapter 1), give:

$$m = \phi'(0), \quad \text{Var} = \phi''(0) - \left[\phi'(0)\right]^2$$

(The reader is encouraged to proceed through the calculation.)

The law is sometimes presented in a slightly different form. In the above example, we could have been concerned with the distribution of the total number of transmissions. This time:

$$P(k \text{ transmissions}) = (1 - p)p^{k-1}.$$

2.5. Hypergeometric distribution

Consider once again the configuration leading to the binomial distribution: random extraction from a population having a given proportion of a certain character. This time, assume the population is of finite size H, of which a proportion p is distinguished (defective elements, in the previous example): there are $M = Hp$ such elements. The experiment consists here of drawing N items without replacement (i.e. the items already drawn are not replaced in the population; this is also called an "exhaustive" drawing). At each trial, the size of the remaining population decreases and the proportion of faulty items evolves. The binomial distribution would hold only if the proportion remains constant. The hypergeometric distribution is to be used in this case.

The probability of drawing k type T elements while extracting N of them in a population size H containing M type T elements (proportion $p = M/H$) is:

$$p_k = \frac{\binom{M}{k}\binom{H-M}{N-k}}{\binom{H}{N}}, \tag{2.17}$$

for $\max(0, N + M - H) \leq k \leq \min(M, N)$.

This is the ratio of the number of ways to realize the event (choosing k among M, and $N - k$ others of the other type) to the total number of possible drawings. The moments are:

$$\text{Mean value: } m = M\frac{N}{H} = Np, \tag{2.18}$$

$$\text{Variance: } \text{Var} = N\frac{M(H-M)(H-N)}{H^2(H-1)}$$

$$= Np(1-p)\frac{H-N}{H-1}. \qquad (2.19)$$

The comparison with binomial distribution, of the same parameter p, shows that the average values are identical, while for variances:

$$\frac{\text{Var(HyperG)}}{\text{Var(Binom)}} = \frac{H-N}{H-1}. \qquad (2.20)$$

As the population size keeps growing ($H \to \infty$), the ratio goes to 1: for a large population, extracting N elements brings no significant change to the composition of the remaining elements. In other words, the hypergeometric distribution tends to the binomial law as the population size increases indefinitely.

2.6. The Poisson law

A discrete random variable taking unbounded positive values obeys a Poisson law with parameter A if its distribution is given by:

$$p_k = \frac{A^k}{k!}e^{-A}. \qquad (2.21)$$

The dimensionless parameter A characterizes the law. This distribution is encountered in various circumstances. Especially, if a flow arrives according to a Poisson process of intensity λ (see Chapter 6), then the number of arrivals observed in a window of width T is distributed according to the Poisson law with parameter $A = \lambda T$. This gives to this law a fundamental role in teletraffic studies, especially when describing call arrivals, sessions, etc., in communications systems. The conditions explaining the occurrence of such a law are detailed in Chapter 6.

The characteristic function, from which the moments are derived, is written:

$$\phi(z) = \sum e^{kz}\frac{A^k}{k!}e^{-A} = e^{A(e^z-1)} \qquad (2.22)$$

$$\text{Mean value: } m = \sum kp_k = \phi'(0) = Ae^z e^{A(e^z-1)} = A, \qquad (2.23)$$

$$\text{Variance: } \text{Var} = \sum(k-m)^2 p_k = A. \qquad (2.24)$$

The higher order central moments are:

$$\mu_3 = A, \quad \mu_4 = A + 3A^2. \qquad (2.25)$$

Figures 2.2 and 2.3 illustrate the general shape of the law. As this is a discrete distribution, the histogram resembles Figure 2.2. Figure 2.3 shows the effect of changing parameter A.

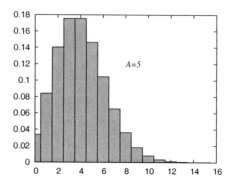

Figure 2.2. *Histogram of the Poisson distribution ($A = 5$)*

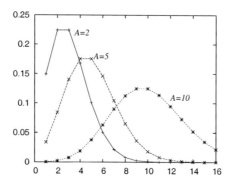

Figure 2.3. *Shape of a Poisson distribution for different values of parameter A*

Variables obeying a Poisson distribution enjoy the following property (theorem 2.2), so they combine easily.

THEOREM 2.2. *Let X and Y be two Poisson variables with parameters λ and μ respectively. Then, $X + Y$ obeys a Poisson distribution with parameter $\lambda + \mu$.*

The proof is immediate, using the transform approach explained in Chapter 1, the transform of the sum being the product of transforms (Laplace, characteristic function, etc.). This property is of great importance, as we are then often led to deal with a mix of Poisson streams.

Relationship with the binomial law. When the size of the population grows indefinitely, the Poisson law provides a useful approximation. Consider a binomial law, with average A and with growing population size N (so that $p = A/N$ goes to 0).

$$p_k = P(X = k) = \binom{N}{k}\left(\frac{A}{N}\right)^k\left(1 - \frac{A}{N}\right)^{N-k}.$$

Developing the binomial coefficient and rearranging the terms, we obtain:

$$P(X = k) = \frac{A^k}{k!}\left(1 - \frac{A}{N}\right)^N \left(1 - \frac{A}{N}\right)^{-k} \times \frac{N}{N} \times \frac{N-1}{N} \times \cdots \times \frac{N-k+1}{N}.$$

We make N extend to infinity, keeping A constant (thus p going to 0). Then:

$$\frac{A}{N} \longrightarrow 0; \quad \left(1 - \frac{A}{N}\right)^N \longrightarrow e^{-A}; \quad \left(1 - \frac{A}{N}\right)^{-k} \longrightarrow 0;$$

$$\frac{N}{N} \times \frac{N-1}{N} \times \cdots \times \frac{N-k+1}{N} \longrightarrow 1$$

and so:

$$P(X = k) \longrightarrow \frac{A^k}{k!} e^{-A}.$$

As the sample size increases, the average remaining constant, the limiting distribution conforms to the Poisson law. This is an appealing result, as the Poisson approximation is much easier to tabulate. Practically, the approximation holds as soon as $N > 40$ and $p < 0.1$.

Actually, a Poisson distribution may serve as the limit for several other laws, such as the Erlang distribution, as will be seen later on. This explains its use in many fields, such as statistics, reliability (e.g. for estimating spare parts), and, of course, traffic studies. Chapter 6 will offer an interesting interpretation of a system with N customers and R servers, which allows us to explain the natural relationship between Poisson, binomial and Engset laws.

2.7. Continuous uniform distribution

This is the simplest kind of continuous distribution, which corresponds to the limiting case of the discrete distribution. A random variable is uniformly distributed between a and b if the probability of finding it in any interval of length l is $l/(b-a)$. As the law is absolutely continuous, the probability density exists and is:

$$f(x)\mathrm{d}x = P[x < X \leq X + \mathrm{d}x] = \frac{\mathrm{d}x}{b-a}, \tag{2.26}$$

and the distribution is:

$$F(x) = \begin{cases} 0 & x < a, \\ \dfrac{x}{b-a} & a \leq x \leq b, \\ 1 & x > b. \end{cases} \tag{2.27}$$

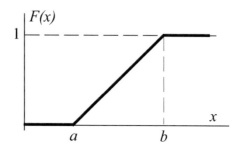

Figure 2.4. *Uniform distribution*

Such a distribution has a great variety of uses. This may be a service duration, for instance if the service epoch occurs periodically, with a constant interval T, the customers arriving randomly (packeting of speech samples). This is also the law which will serve as a basis for generating random variables with arbitrary distributions in simulation (see Chapter 8), and more generally in all Monte Carlo methods.

The characteristic function of the uniform distribution is:

$$\phi(z) = \frac{e^{bz} - e^{az}}{(b-a)z} \tag{2.28}$$

from which the moments are obtained (e.g. by developing the exponential functions):

$$\text{Mean value: } m = \phi'(0) = \frac{a+b}{2}, \tag{2.29}$$

$$\text{Variance: Var} = \phi''(0) - \left(\phi'(0)\right)^2 = \frac{(b-a)^2}{12}. \tag{2.30}$$

2.8. Normal (Gaussian) distribution

Normal (or Gaussian) distribution is probably among the most celebrated laws that engineers and scientists manipulate. Its popularity rests to a large extent on work which has been devoted to the theory of error measurements. Its justification relies on the central limit theorem, presented in Chapter 3, which states that normal distribution is the limiting distribution of the sum of a large number of independent and identically distributed variables. For instance, the causes of measurement errors are numerous and independent, and they combine so that the measured value is normally distributed around the "true" value.

In the telecommunications field, the applications of normal distributions are numerous for signal analysis, reliability, traffic and queueing, as well as simulation

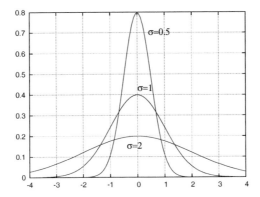

Figure 2.5. *Probability density function of the normal law*

where it allows us to estimate the measurement precision. Actually, the analysis of most physical phenomena involves the addition of a large number of independent variables – number of waiting customers, number of machines down, etc. – making it possible to invoke the central limit theorem.

A random variable is said to be normally distributed with mean m and standard-deviation σ, and usually denoted as $N(m, \sigma)$ if its probability distribution is given by:

$$F(x) = P(X \leq x) = \frac{1}{\sigma\sqrt{2\pi}} \int_{-\infty}^{x} e^{-(u-m)^2/2\sigma^2} du, \quad -\infty < x < \infty. \quad (2.31)$$

The coefficient before the integral guarantees normalization, so that $P(X < \infty) = 1$ as requested. The term σ, the standard-deviation, is responsible for the density flattening around the mean (see Figure 2.5). The expression $\sigma_r = \sigma/m$ is referred to as the relative dispersion, or coefficient of variation (also denoted as c).

The sum of normal random variables. With reference to the properties of the sum of independent variables, stated in Chapter 1, the following result allows easy manipulation of the sum of normal variables.

THEOREM 2.3. *Let $X = N(m_1, \sigma_1)$ and $Y = N(m_2, \sigma_2)$ be two independent random variables. The sum $X + Y$ is distributed according to $= N(m_1 + m_2, \sqrt{\sigma_1^2 + \sigma_2^2})$.*

This clearly generalizes to the sum of an arbitrary number of variables. Of special interest is the case of n variables identically distributed: the coefficient of variation of the sum is $\sigma_s = \frac{\sigma}{m\sqrt{n}}$. As n grows, the relative dispersion vanishes so that the sum goes to an almost constant variable.

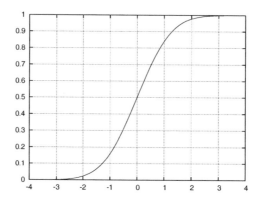

Figure 2.6. *Distribution of the normal law (standard deviation = 1)*

The curves in Figure 2.5 show how the dispersion varies as the standard deviation increases. Figure 2.6 illustrates the symmetric shape of the distribution function.

In fact, the normal distribution is rarely used this way. If X is normally distributed according to $N(m, \sigma)$, then clearly $X - m$ has a mean $= 0$, and the same variance as X. Moreover, $(X - m)/\sigma$ is a variable with variance equal to 1. This is the standard or reduced normal distribution (Laplace law). This form is "universal", in that it does not depend on any parameter, which justifies its tabulation. It is usually written as:

$$\Phi(x) = \frac{1}{\sqrt{2\pi}} \int_{-\infty}^{x} e^{-u^2/2}\,du, \quad \phi(x) = \frac{1}{\sqrt{2\pi}} e^{-x^2/2}, \tag{2.32}$$

and its characteristic function is:

$$\phi(z) = e^{\frac{z^2}{2}}. \tag{2.33}$$

A direct numerical evaluation of $\Phi(x)$ is difficult, except when using specific mathematical tools (tables or programs), and its estimation is most often based upon numerical tables. The following approximation is quite efficient, for $0 \le x \le 4$:

$$\Phi(x) = 1 - \phi(x)\left[a \cdot u^3 + b \cdot u^2 + c \cdot u\right], \quad u = \frac{1}{1 + 0.33267x}$$

$$\text{with} \begin{cases} a = 0.9372980 \\ b = -0.1201676 \\ c = 0.4361836 \end{cases} \tag{2.34}$$

This expression deviates from the exact value by a relative error of about 10^{-5}.

Statistical tables. All reference textbooks in statistics provide comprehensive tables for standardized normal distribution. An example of such a table is given below in Table 2.1. The first part gives the probability for a reduced normal variable to be less than x. For instance, in a sample, 84% of the values should be less than 1.

x	0	0.2	0.5	1	1.5	2
$P(\leq x)$	0.5	0.579	0.691	0.841	0.933	0.977

$P(> x)$	10^{-2}	10^{-3}	10^{-4}	10^{-5}	10^{-6}	10^{-7}	10^{-8}	10^{-9}
x	2.326	3.290	3.890	4.417	4.892	5.327	5.731	6.110

Table 2.1. *Table of the normal (reduced) distribution*

If needed, symmetric properties can help in calculating probabilities of finding the variable in an interval. For instance, 5% of the values are outside the interval $[-2 : 2]$. Indeed, according to the table:

$$P(X < -2.) = P(X > 2.) = 0.023.$$

Both parts of Table 2.1 are for reduced distribution. The second part gives the quantiles for small probability values. The correspondence with an arbitrary distribution is easy to establish. As an example, consider a normal variable X with mean $m = 10$ and standard-deviation $\sigma = 15$. We seek the probability that the value of X is greater than 40. This is written as:

$$P(X > 40) = P\left(\frac{X - 10}{15} > \frac{40 - 10}{15} = 2\right).$$

The value we are looking for, i.e. the probability of a variable greater than 40, is the probability that the reduced variable is greater than 2. Table 2.1 tells us that the probability is around $1 - 0.977 \simeq 0.023$.

The normal law as limiting distribution. The normal law is the limiting distribution of numerous distributions, either continuous or discrete, when one of their parameters increases. For discrete distributions already encountered:

– binomial law: $Z = B(n,p)$, then $(Z - np)/\sqrt{np(1-p)}$ goes to $N(0,1)$ as $n \to \infty$; in practice, we admit that generally the approximation holds as soon as $p > 0.5$ and $np > 5$, or $p < 0.5$ and $n(1-p) > 5$;

– Poisson law: $Z = P(\lambda)$, then $(Z - \lambda)/\sqrt{\lambda}$ converges towards $N(0,1)$ as $\lambda \to \infty$. The condition $\lambda > 10$ ensures the validity of the approximation.

Other continuous distributions, introduced in the next section, also have the normal law as limiting distribution.

2.9. Chi-2 distribution

We are given a set $X_1, X_2, \ldots, X_n$ of independent and identically distributed variables obeying the reduced normal distribution.

The variable $\chi^2 = X_1^2 + X_2^2 + \cdots + X_n^2$ is distributed as a Chi-2 with n degrees of freedom (written χ_n^2). This distribution enjoys the following property: the sum of two Chi-2 variables with respectively n and m degrees of freedom is a Chi-2 with $n + m$ degrees of freedom. This variable is used frequently in statistics, especially for hypothesis testing or estimating confidence intervals (see Chapter 3). It is particularly useful for the estimation of operational component failure rates, when monitoring reliability of equipment in operation. Figure 2.7 displays the density shape for several values of n.

$$f_n(\chi^2) = \frac{e^{-\frac{\chi^2}{2}}(\chi^2)^{\frac{n}{2}-1}}{2^{\frac{n}{2}}\Gamma(\frac{n}{2})}, \quad \text{for } \chi^2 > 0, \tag{2.35}$$

where $\Gamma(x)$ is the Gamma function:

$$\Gamma(\alpha) = \int_0^\infty x^{\alpha-1}e^{-x}dx;$$

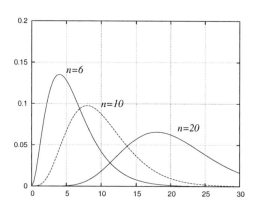

Figure 2.7. *Probability density function of Chi-2 distribution*

which is such that $\Gamma(\alpha + 1) = \alpha\Gamma(\alpha)$, which for integer values of α reduces to $\Gamma(n + 1) = n!$ (also, $\Gamma(1/2) = \sqrt{\pi}$):

$$\text{Mean value: } m = n, \tag{2.36}$$

$$\text{Variance: Var} = 2n. \tag{2.37}$$

Limiting behavior. Since a Chi-2 variable is the sum of independent variables, it clearly should go to a normal distribution as the number of degrees of freedom increases. A more precise result can be stated:

THEOREM 2.4. *Let X be a variable distributed according to a Chi-2 with n degrees of freedom. As n increases:*

$$\frac{X - n}{\sqrt{2n}} \longrightarrow N(0,1) \quad \text{as } n \longrightarrow \infty. \tag{2.38}$$

2.10. Student distribution

We are given a set of $n+1$ independent random variables, X and $(X_1, X_2, \ldots, X_n)$, each normally distributed with mean $m = 0$ and identical variance. Let:

$$Y = \sqrt{\frac{1}{n} \sum X_i^2}, \quad t = \frac{X}{Y}. \tag{2.39}$$

The variable t is distributed according to the Student law with n degrees of freedom. This distribution appears in estimation theory, especially with samples of limited size.

The density function is given by:

$$f_n(t) = \frac{1}{\sqrt{n\pi}} \cdot \frac{\Gamma\left(\frac{n+1}{2}\right)}{\Gamma\left(\frac{n}{2}\right)} \cdot \left(1 + \frac{t^2}{n}\right)^{-\frac{n+1}{2}}. \tag{2.40}$$

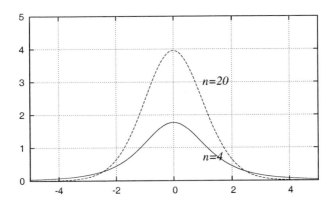

Figure 2.8. *Probability density function of the Student distribution*

For $n > 2$, moments exist and are given by:

$$\text{Mean value: } m = 0, \tag{2.41}$$

$$\text{Variance: } \text{Var} = \frac{n}{n - 2}. \tag{2.42}$$

The variance does not depend on the common variance of X_i. As the degrees of freedom increase in number, the Student distribution approaches the reduced normal distribution (intuitively, Y goes to a constant equal to 1).

2.11. Lognormal distribution

A variable is lognormally distributed if its logarithm has a normal distribution. If Y is $N(m, \sigma)$-distributed, then $X = e^Y$ is lognormally distributed with density function:

$$f(x) = \frac{1}{\sigma x \sqrt{2\pi}} e^{-(\log x - m)^2 / 2\sigma^2}, \quad \text{for } 0 \leq x < \infty. \tag{2.43}$$

The moments of the two distributions X and Y are related:

$$\text{Mean value: } E[X] = e^{m + \sigma^2 / 2}, \tag{2.44}$$

$$\text{Variance: } \text{Var}(X) = \left(e^{\sigma^2} - 1\right) e^{2m + \sigma^2}. \tag{2.45}$$

However, we usually proceed from the other direction: the parameters of X are known and we look for the (m, σ) needed, e.g. to generate a sample in a simulation experiment. The correspondence is simply:

$$\sigma^2 = \log\left(1 + \frac{\text{Var}(X)}{E[X]^2}\right), \tag{2.46}$$

$$m = \log E[X] - \frac{\sigma^2}{2}. \tag{2.47}$$

The reason for the lognormal distribution being encountered is described as the principle of *multiplicative accumulation*. The normal distribution appears naturally when a phenomenon results in the sum of independent perturbations. Assume now that the amplitude of the phenomenon is caused by the *product* of independent causes. Taking the logarithm transforms the products into sums, on which the arguments of the central limit theorem apply. The lognormal distribution is thus invoked in the analysis of a large number of economic phenomena related to income or consumption, or in life sciences.

2.12. Exponential and related distributions

2.12.1. *Exponential distribution*

Exponential distribution has a quite distinct position in traffic, queueing and reliability domains. The corresponding chapters will explain the reason for its endless use. The distribution depends on a single parameter, traditionally denoted as μ in the teletraffic field, and the density function is given by:

$$f(x) = \mu e^{-\mu x}, \quad \text{for } x \geq 0. \tag{2.48}$$

The distribution function is:

$$F(x) = 1 - e^{-\mu x}. \tag{2.49}$$

Remember its characteristic function (see Chapter 1):

$$\phi(z) = \frac{\mu}{\mu - z} \tag{2.50}$$

for which the moments are easily obtained:

$$\text{Mean value: } m = \frac{1}{\mu}, \tag{2.51}$$

$$\text{Variance: } \text{Var} = \frac{1}{\mu^2}. \tag{2.52}$$

The curve $k = 1$ in Figure 2.9 shows the shape of its density function (as this is a special case of Erlang-k distribution, see below).

2.12.2. *Erlang-k distribution*

A variable which is the sum of k independent variables having the same exponential distribution is said to have an Erlang-k distribution. It can serve for approximating an unknown distribution with a coefficient of variation lower than 1. This helps in building a model of service durations that have dispersion between the constant and exponential distributions.

For the simplest case, let $k = 2$. Let X denote the variable sum of the two variables X_1, X_2, having probability distributions F_1 and F_2. The distribution F of X is the *convolution* of F_1 and F_2 (see Chapter 1):

$$P(X \leq x) = P(X_1 + X_2 \leq x) = \int_{u=0}^{x} F_1(x - u) \mathrm{d}F_2(u).$$

As X_1, X_2 are exponentially distributed, it follows that:

$$P(X \leq x) = 1 - e^{-\mu x} - \mu x e^{-\mu x}.$$

More generally, we saw in Chapter 1 that cascading k exponential variables with the same parameter leads to the distribution:

$$F(x) = P(X_1 + X_2 + \cdots + X_k \leq x) = 1 - e^{-\mu x} \sum_{j=0}^{k-1} \frac{(\mu x)^j}{j!}. \tag{2.53}$$

This distribution is known as the Erlang-k distribution. As this is the sum of independent variables, the mean and variance are simply the sums of the mean and variance of each component:

$$\text{Mean value: } m = \frac{k}{\mu}, \tag{2.54}$$

$$\text{Variance: } \text{Var} = \frac{k}{\mu^2}, \tag{2.55}$$

$$\text{Coefficient of variation: } c = \frac{1}{\sqrt{k}}. \tag{2.56}$$

The Laplace transform facilitates the retrieval of these results. As the distribution is the convolution of k independent exponentially distributed variables, its transform is directly obtained:

$$B^*(s) = \left(\frac{\mu}{\mu + s}\right)^k. \tag{2.57}$$

From the distribution, moments are obtained by taking derivatives for $s = 1$. Moreover, returning to the original function provides the probability density:

$$f(x) = \mu e^{-\mu x} \cdot \frac{(\mu x)^{k-1}}{(k-1)!}. \tag{2.58}$$

Figure 2.9 displays the shape of this distribution, for different values of k.

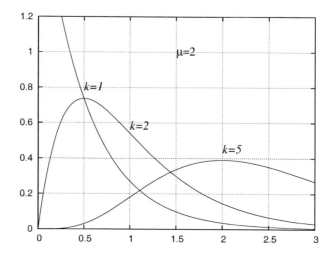

Figure 2.9. *Probability density function of the Erlang-k distribution for various k*

Note that the coefficient of variation $c = 1/\sqrt{k}$ is always less than 1, except for $k = 1$, which corresponds to the exponential function. This explains the use of this distribution as a means of representing a phenomenon with a low dispersion. It can even be used with a large value of k, keeping k/μ constant, thus providing an approximate representation of constant duration under the form of a Markovian system, thus keeping the memoryless property, the appeal of which will be made obvious in Chapter 6, section 6.3, which is devoted to Markov processes. It can be verified that the limit of equation (2.58) as k grows is indeed the constant distribution.

Laplace transforms provide an elegant way to prove this limit. Let $a = k/\mu$ be kept constant as k increases:

$$B^*(s) = \left(\frac{k/a}{s + k/a} \right)^k = \left(1 + \frac{as}{k} \right)^{-k},$$

so that

$$\lim_{k \to \infty} B^*(s) = \left(1 + \frac{as}{k} \right)^{-k} = e^{-as}$$

which is actually the transform of the constant duration with parameter a.

For practical purposes, we can introduce the new parameter $X = \mu x/k$, such that the new variable has a mean value equal to 1. We thus obtain the reduced law, just as was done for normal distribution:

$$f(X) = ke^{-kX} \frac{(kX)^{k-1}}{(k-1)!}, \tag{2.59}$$

having the characteristic function:

$$\phi(z) = \left(1 - \frac{z}{k} \right)^{-k} \tag{2.60}$$

and moments:

$$E[X] = 1, \quad \text{Var}[X] = 1/k. \tag{2.61}$$

Taking for k a real number instead of a positive integer generalizes to the Gamma distribution. This is presented hereafter. Note also, for statisticians, that Erlang-k distributions are analogous with a χ^2 distributions with k degrees of freedom.

2.12.3. Hyperexponential distribution

When it comes to representing service distributions with a coefficient of variation larger than 1, the hyperexponential distribution is introduced (as discussed in Chapter 6). The basic configuration depends on 3 parameters, usually denoted as α, μ_1, μ_2.

The distribution is:

$$P(X \leq x) = \alpha\left(1 - e^{-\mu_1 x}\right) + (1 - \alpha)\left(1 - e^{-\mu_2 x}\right). \tag{2.62}$$

The Laplace transform is readily obtained, as the sum of the transforms of the 2 exponential functions:

$$B^*(s) = \frac{\alpha \mu_1}{s + \mu_1} + \frac{(1 - \alpha)\mu_2}{s + \mu_2}. \tag{2.63}$$

The mean and variance are derived from the transform:

$$\text{Mean value: } m = \frac{\alpha}{\mu_1} + \frac{1 - \alpha}{\mu_2}, \tag{2.64}$$

$$\text{Variance: } \text{Var} = 2\left[\frac{\alpha}{\mu_1^2} + \frac{1 - \alpha}{\mu_2^2}\right] - \left[\frac{\alpha}{\mu_1} + \frac{1 - \alpha}{\mu_2}\right]^2, \tag{2.65}$$

$$\text{Squared coefficient of variation: } c^2 = \frac{2\left[\frac{\alpha}{\mu_1^2} + \frac{1-\alpha}{\mu_2^2}\right]}{\left[\frac{\alpha}{\mu_1} + \frac{1-\alpha}{\mu_2}\right]^2} - 1. \tag{2.66}$$

In the general case, the distribution is a combination of n exponential functions:

$$P(X \leq x) = \sum_k \alpha_k\left(1 - e^{-\mu_k x}\right), \quad \text{with} \quad \sum_k \alpha_k = 1. \tag{2.67}$$

The moments of the distribution are:

$$\text{Mean value: } m = \sum_k \frac{\alpha_k}{\mu_k}, \tag{2.68}$$

$$\text{Variance: } \text{Var} = 2\sum \frac{\alpha}{\mu_k^2} - \left(\sum_k \frac{\alpha_k}{\mu_k}\right)^2, \tag{2.69}$$

$$\text{Squared coefficient of variation: } c^2 = 2\frac{\sum \frac{\alpha_k}{\mu_k^2}}{\left[\sum \frac{\alpha_k}{\mu_k}\right]^2} - 1. \tag{2.70}$$

The *Cauchy-Schwarz inequality* states that $(\sum a_i b_i)^2 \leq \sum a_i^2 \sum b_i^2$. Applying it to the above expression, taking $a_i = \sqrt{\alpha_i}$ and $b_i = \sqrt{\alpha_i}/\mu_i$ shows that the coefficient of variation is always larger than 1. Thus, this law is representative of distributions more dispersed than exponential distributions.

2.12.4. *Generalizing: Coxian distribution*

The n-phase Coxian distribution is obtained by a combination of n exponential stages, in a way which generalizes the previous hyperexponential scheme, and is represented in Figure 2.10. Upon arrival in front of server k of service rate μ_k, the client chooses to enter the server (probability α_k) or leave the system (probability $1 - \alpha_k$).

The Laplace transform of the resulting distribution is

$$B(s) = 1 - \alpha_1 + \sum_{i \leq n} \prod_{j=1}^{n} \frac{\alpha_j \mu_j}{s + \mu_j} \left(1 - \alpha_{i+1}\right). \qquad (2.71)$$

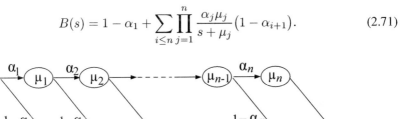

Figure 2.10. *Coxian distribution*

We can show that any distribution function may be approximated, as precisely as needed, by such a compound server.

2.12.5. *Gamma distribution*

A variable with a Gamma distribution $\gamma(\alpha, \beta)$ has a probability density given by:

$$f(x) = e^{-x/\beta} \frac{x^{\alpha-1}}{\beta^\alpha \Gamma(\alpha)}, \qquad \alpha, \beta > 0, \ x \geq 0 \qquad (2.72)$$

in which Γ is the Gamma function (introduced for the Chi-2 distribution). The reduced form with $\beta = 1$ can be used, being obtained by scaling the distribution: if X is distributed according to $\gamma(\alpha, \beta)$, then $Y = X/\beta$ is distributed according to $\gamma(\alpha, 1)$ – usually denoted simply as $\gamma(\alpha)$:

$$\text{Mean value: } m = \alpha\beta, \qquad (2.73)$$

$$\text{Variance: Var} = \alpha\beta^2. \qquad (2.74)$$

Reciprocally, given the moments, the parameters are obtained as $\beta = \text{Var}/m$, $\alpha = m^2/\text{Var}$.

For $\alpha = 1$ it reduces to the exponential distribution. More generally, $\gamma(k, \beta)$ with integer k is the Erlang-k distribution. For integer k and $\beta = 2$, this is a Chi-2 with $2k$ degrees of freedom.

If two variables X and Y, are Gamma distributed with the same parameter β – respectively $\gamma(\alpha, \beta)$ and $\gamma(\alpha', \beta)$ – then $Z = X + Y$ is Gamma distributed as $\gamma(\alpha + \alpha', \beta)$.

The Gamma distribution offers a means of representing various distributions, for which the analytical expression is either unknown or too complex to be numerically manipulated. It provides an extension of the Erlang family to configurations with non-integer parameters, giving arbitrary variances (larger or smaller than the mean).

The reduced form provides a means of effectively calculating the distribution, by observing that equation (2.72) can be re-written into:

$$f(x) = e^{-x/\beta} \frac{(x/\beta)^\alpha}{\beta \Gamma(\alpha)}. \tag{2.75}$$

From this we can build a table of the function (we should also consult statistical function handbooks):

$$F(u, \alpha) = e^{-u} \frac{u^\alpha}{\Gamma(\alpha)}. \tag{2.76}$$

For given values of α and β, we simply take

$$u = \frac{x}{\beta}, \quad f(x) = \frac{F(u, \alpha)}{\beta}. \tag{2.77}$$

Thus, the transform is given by:

$$\phi(z) = (1 - z\beta)^{-\alpha}.$$

2.12.6. Weibull distribution

A variable obeys the Weibull distribution if its probability density function is given by:

$$f(x) = \frac{\beta}{\delta} \left(\frac{x}{\delta} \right)^{\beta - 1} e^{-(\frac{x}{\delta})^\beta}, \quad F(x) = 1 - e^{-(\frac{x}{\delta})^\beta}. \tag{2.78}$$

It is used, in particular, in reliability studies, where the reliability function $R(t)$ is defined: this is the probability that the system is working correctly at time t. $R(t)$ is the complement of the distribution (see Chapter 7):

$$R(t) = 1 - F(t) = e^{-(\frac{t-\gamma}{\eta})^\beta}. \tag{2.79}$$

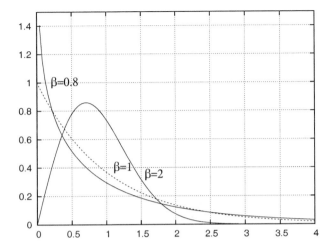

Figure 2.11. *Probability density of the Weibull distribution*

It represents distributions with reliability parameters as a function of time. For example: reliability increases with the beginning of the life, $\beta < 1$ (failure rate decreasing as the time increases), constant failure rate during the operational period, taking $\beta = 1$, $\gamma = 0$ (the exponential distribution), and the failure rate increasing at the end of the lifetime, with $\beta > 1$ (see Chapter 7).

The Weibull distribution can also be of help in traffic studies, where it is used for describing complex arrival processes, such as the inter-arrival duration between successive IP flows. The moments of the Weibull distribution are:

$$\text{Mean value: } m = \delta\Gamma\left(1 + \frac{1}{\beta}\right), \tag{2.80}$$

$$\text{Variance: } \text{Var} = \delta^2\left[\Gamma\left(1 + \frac{2}{\beta}\right) - \Gamma^2\left(1 + \frac{1}{\beta}\right)\right]. \tag{2.81}$$

2.13. Logistic distribution

Logistic distribution appears when modeling the evolution of a population characteristic, and more specifically in telecommunications when deploying new services. Indeed, this is the traditional model for the introduction of any consumer goods. To give a specific example, let us consider a communication service (e.g. cellular phone). Let x be the equipment ratio, i.e. the equipment density at time t (ratio of the number of equipped customers to the total population). Let s stand for the saturation density (it can be 100%, or even more if households are the reference population: e.g. 200% for two telephones in a single family).

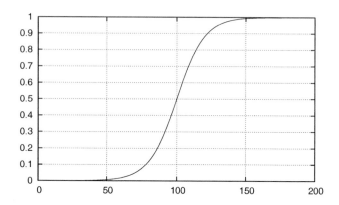

Figure 2.12. *Logistic curve*

The derivative dx/dt accounts for the growth rate. Assume the demand can be immediately satisfied: the equipment ratio is equal to the demand. Assume now that the demand is proportional to the number of customers already equipped. Assume also that it is proportional to the size of the unequipped population. The first assumption is related to the service usefulness, as more and more customers can be reached; the second assumption amounts to defining an individual need of the service, the demand thus being proportional to the size. The same kind of assumptions are made in epidemiological studies (x being here the density of contaminated subjects).

Under these assumptions, and with k being a coefficient that is assumed constant, the phenomenon is governed by the following equation:

$$\frac{dx}{dt} = kx(s - x),$$

the solution of which is readily obtained:

$$x = \frac{s}{1 + Ae^{-kst}}, \quad \text{or} \quad x = \frac{s}{1 + e^{-k(t-t_0)}}. \tag{2.82}$$

In this equation, A stands for the integration constant. The second form, equivalent to the first, introduces t_0, the median equipment time (the epoch where $x = s/2$).

A change in coordinates is most commonly used, taking $\log \frac{x}{s-x}$ instead of x. This is the *logit transformation*, which reduces the typical logistic curve in Figure 2.12 to a straight line. This provides a descriptive framework, rather than an explanatory model. In practice, several observations allow us to estimate the best values for the parameters. The validity of this model actually depends on the (questionable) validity of all the assumptions (for instance, k is taken as constant, which is probably erroneous for social phenomena). Figure 2.12 displays the shape of the curve, for $s = 1$, $k = 0.05$, $t_0 = 100$.

2.14. Pareto distribution

The Pareto distribution is given by the following law:

$$F(x) = 1 - \left(\frac{b}{x}\right)^a, \quad \text{with } a, b > 0, \ x \geq b. \tag{2.83}$$

Taking the derivative gives the density function:

$$f(x) = \frac{dF}{dx} = \frac{ab^a}{x^{a+1}}. \tag{2.84}$$

If the complementary distribution is drawn on a logarithmic scale, the parameters are readily identified:

$$\log\left[1 - F(x)\right] = a \log b - a \log x$$

so the curve appears as a straight line with slope $-a$:

$$\text{Mean value: } m = \frac{ab}{a-1} \quad a > 1, \tag{2.85}$$

$$\text{Variance: } \mathrm{Var} = \frac{ab^2}{2-a} - \left(\frac{ab}{a-1}\right)^2 \quad a > 2. \tag{2.86}$$

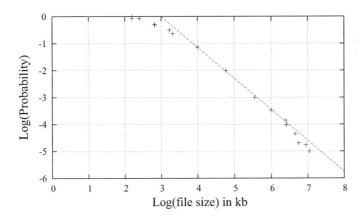

Figure 2.13. *Pareto distribution*

The Pareto distribution was first used in statistics. Recent studies concerning Internet traffic have seen it applied to traffic description. It has been shown that some of the characteristics of these flows are fairly well modeled using this law. This is particularly the case for the length of the files exchanged on the network, and the *self-similarity* we observe in Internet traffic could originate here. Self-similarity accounts for the observation that statistical observation properties are conserved through changes of scale. The term *fractal traffic* is also in use.

Figure 2.13 displays the shape of the complementary distribution function, plotted on a logarithmic scale (the unit length on the abscissa is proportional to $\log x$). The curve "$b = 3.\,\text{kB}, a = 1.15$" corresponds to the adjustment with a series of file size exchanges observed on the Internet (reported in [CRO 97]).

2.15. A summary of the main results

Mean values are denoted as m and variances as Var. μ_3 and μ_4 are the third and fourth order central moments. The generating function $B(z)$ and the characteristic function $\phi(z)$ are given. Most of these laws are tabulated: the reader is referred to specialized books, such as [FIC 04].

2.15.1. *Discrete distributions*

– *Uniform (discrete) distribution $U(a,b)$:*

$$p_k = P(X = k) = \frac{1}{b - a + 1}, \quad a \le k \le b.$$

$$B(z) = \frac{z^a - z^{b+1}}{(b - a + 1)(1 - z)}, \quad \phi(z) = \frac{e^{az} - e^{(b+1)z}}{(b - a + 1)(1 - e^z)}$$

$$m = \frac{a + b}{2}, \quad \text{Var} = \frac{(b - a)(b - a + 2)}{12},$$

$$\mu_3 = 0, \quad \mu_4 = \frac{(b - a)^4}{80} + \frac{(b - a)^3}{20} + \frac{(b - a)(b - a + 1)}{30}$$

– *Binomial distribution $B(p, N)$:*

$$p_k = P(k \text{ among } N) = \binom{N}{k} p^k (1 - p)^{N-k}, \quad k = 0, \ldots, N$$

$$B(z) = (1 - p + pz)^N, \quad \phi(z) = \frac{1 - p}{1 - pe^z}$$

$$m = Np, \quad \text{Var} = Np(1 - p), \quad \mu_3 = Np(1 - p)(1 - 2p)$$

$$\mu_4 = Np(1 - p)\left[1 + (3N - 6)p - (3N - 6)p^2\right]$$

– *Geometric distribution*:

$$p_k = (1-p)p^k, \quad 0 < p < 1, \quad k = 0, 1, \ldots$$

$$B(z) = \frac{1-p}{1-pz}, \quad \phi(z) = \frac{1-p}{1-pe^z}$$

$$m = \frac{p}{1-p}, \quad \text{Var} = \frac{p}{(1-p)^2}$$

– *Hypergeometric distribution*:

$$p_k = \frac{\binom{M}{k}\binom{H-M}{N-k}}{\binom{H}{N}} \quad \text{for } \max(0, N+M-H) \leq k \leq \min(M, N)$$

$$m = M\frac{N}{H} = Np, \quad \text{Var} = Np(1-p)\frac{H-N}{H-1} \text{ with } p = M/H$$

– *Poisson distribution*:

$$P(k) = \frac{\lambda^k}{k!}e^{-\lambda}$$

$$B(z) = e^{\lambda(z-1)}, \quad \phi(z) = e^{\lambda(e^z - 1)}$$

$$m = \lambda, \quad \text{Var} = \lambda, \quad \mu_3 = \lambda, \quad \mu_4 = \lambda + 3\lambda^2$$

2.15.2. *Continuous distributions*

The density and distribution are given when the expressions are simple enough to be of some help.

– *Uniform distribution* $U[a, b]$:

$$f(x)dx = P[x < X \leq X + dx] = \frac{dx}{b-a}, \quad F(x) = \begin{cases} 0 & x < a \\ \dfrac{x}{b-a} & a \leq x \leq b \\ 1 & x > b \end{cases}$$

$$\phi(z) = \frac{e^{bz} - e^{az}}{(b-a)z}$$

$$m = \frac{a+b}{2}, \quad \text{Var} = \frac{(b-a)^2}{12}, \quad \mu_3 = 0, \quad \mu_4 = \frac{(b-a)^4}{80}$$

– *Normal (Gauss) distribution* $N(m, \sigma)$:

$$P(X \leq x) = \frac{1}{\sigma\sqrt{2\pi}} \int_{-\infty}^{x} e^{-(x-m)^2/2\sigma^2} dx, \quad -\infty < x < \infty$$

$$\phi(z) = e^{zm+(z\sigma)^2/2}$$

(mean and variance are the parameters of the law); $\mu_3 = 0$, $\mu_4 = 3\sigma^4$.

– *Chi-2 distribution with n degrees of freedom*:

$$f_n(\chi^2) = \frac{e^{-\frac{\chi^2}{2}}(\chi^2)^{\frac{n}{2}-1}}{2^{\frac{n}{2}}\Gamma(\frac{n}{2})}, \quad \text{for } \chi^2 \geq 0$$

$$\phi(z) = (1 - 2z)^{-n/2}$$

$$m = n, \quad \text{Var} = 2n$$

– *Student distribution*:

$$f_n(t) = \frac{1}{\sqrt{n\pi}} \cdot \frac{\Gamma\left(\frac{n+1}{2}\right)}{\Gamma\left(\frac{n}{2}\right)} \cdot \left(1 + \frac{t^2}{n}\right)^{-\frac{n+1}{2}}$$

$$m = 0, \quad \text{Var} = \frac{n}{n-2}, \quad \mu_3 = 0$$

– *Log normal distribution*:

$$f(x) = \frac{1}{\sigma x\sqrt{2\pi}} e^{-(\log x-m)^2/2\sigma^2}, \quad \text{for } 0 \leq x < \infty.$$

$$m = e^{m+\sigma^2/2}, \quad \text{Var} = (e^{\sigma^2} - 1)e^{2m+\sigma^2}$$

– *Exponential distribution*:

$$f(x) = \mu e^{-\mu x}, \quad F(x) = 1 - e^{-\mu x}$$

$$\phi(z) = \frac{\mu}{\mu - z}$$

$$m = \frac{1}{\mu}, \quad \text{Var} = \frac{1}{\mu^2}, \quad \mu_3 = \frac{2}{\mu^3}, \quad \mu_4 = \frac{9}{\mu^4}$$

– Erlang-k distribution:

$$F(x) = P(X_1 + \cdots + X_k \leq x) = 1 - e^{-\mu x} \sum_{j=0}^{k-1} \frac{(\mu x)^j}{j!}$$

$$f(x) = \mu e^{-\mu x} \frac{(\mu x)^{k-1}}{(k-1)!}$$

$$\phi(z) = \left(\frac{\mu}{\mu - z} \right)^k$$

$$m = \frac{k}{\mu}, \quad \text{Var} = \frac{k}{\mu^2}$$

– Hyperexponential distribution:

$$F(x) = P(X \leq x) = \sum_k \alpha_k \left(1 - e^{-\mu_k x} \right),$$

$$\phi(z) = \sum_k \frac{\alpha_k \mu_k}{\mu_k - z}, \quad \text{with } \sum_k \alpha_k = 1$$

$$m = \sum_k \frac{\alpha_k}{\mu_k}, \quad \text{Var} = 2 \sum_k \frac{\alpha_k}{\mu_k^2} - \left(\sum_k \frac{\alpha_k}{\mu_k} \right)^2,$$

$$c^2 = 2 \frac{\sum \frac{\alpha_k}{\mu_k^2}}{\left[\sum \frac{\alpha_k}{\mu_k} \right]^2} - 1$$

– Gamma distribution:

$$f(x) = e^{-x/\beta} \frac{x^{\alpha-1}}{\beta^\alpha \Gamma(\alpha)}, \quad \alpha, \beta > 0, \ x \geq 0$$

$$m = \alpha\beta, \quad \text{Var} = \alpha\beta^2$$

– Weibull distribution:

$$f(x) = \frac{\beta}{\delta} \left(\frac{x}{\delta} \right)^{\beta-1} e^{-(\frac{x}{\delta})^\beta}, \quad F(x) = 1 - e^{-(\frac{x}{\delta})^\beta}$$

$$m = \delta \Gamma \left(1 + \frac{1}{\beta} \right) \quad \text{Var} = \delta^2 \left[\Gamma \left(1 + \frac{2}{\beta} \right) - \Gamma^2 \left(1 + \frac{1}{\beta} \right) \right]$$

– *Pareto distribution*:

$$f(x) = \frac{ab^a}{x^{a+1}},$$

$$F(x) = 1 - \left(\frac{b}{x}\right)^a, \quad \text{with } a, b > 0,\ x \geq b$$

$$m = \frac{ab}{a-1}, \quad \text{Var} = \frac{ab^2}{2-a} - \left(\frac{ab}{a-1}\right)^2 \quad \text{(for } a > 2\text{)}$$

Chapter 3

Statistics

In order to formulate any statement about a system, engineers need to acquire as precise a knowledge as possible about it and the environment in which it is to work. Such knowledge cannot result from pure reasoning alone, and has to rely on *observation* and *measurement*. In the telecommunications field, for instance, these measurements will allow us detect a signal, or to estimate flow volume or the *quality of service*. For example, the spectral analysis of an unknown signal amounts to measuring some of its statistical characteristics such as average value or covariance, etc., in order to recognize it. Similarly, during field trials, as well as during the normal life of a telecommunications network, we have to estimate traffic levels, response times and loss ratio. Again, for reliability studies, equipment lifetime, system availability, etc. are measured. Similar measurements can be made in the preliminary design step, during simulation studies.

As a consequence, a certain amount of data is collected on the system, and the question is now how to *interpret* them and to *summarize* them.

Descriptive statistics help us to choose the parameters of interest and present the results in a synthetic way – that is, in visualizable form.

Now, exhaustive measurements are clearly impossible to obtain. *Mathematical statistics* aim at providing tools to analyze data in order to extract all the possible information from it. For instance, *estimation theory* intends to evaluate the confidence level to be associated with the prediction of a parameter of interest. *Hypothesis testing* provides help when making decisions about the population under study, such as comparing two different samples or deciding the conformity of the measurements with a given theoretical distribution function.

Statistics are concerned with a set of elements, called the *population*. On each of the elements a *character* is observed, which varies from one element to another. Typical examples in telecommunications are the spectral density of a signal, duration of a communication, length of a message, number of busy elements in a pool of resources, the time between two failures of the equipment, etc. The implicit idea sustaining the statistical approach is that a kind of regularity exists behind the apparent randomness of our observations, and that the population is characterized by a (unknown) well-defined parameter value, with observations being distributed around this value according to some probability law.

3.1. Descriptive statistics

Interpreting the huge amount of raw data collected during a measurement campaign is always difficult, and the first step towards understanding such data is in visualizing it properly: that is, developing means to summarize the information and stress the relations involved, etc.

The tools of descriptive statistics are of invaluable help in this task, the importance of which must not be underestimated. The detail of the analysis the specialist may conduct is only convincing for his/her peers. For others, synthetic and convincing illustrations (charts, tables or other) must be the preferred communication media: a picture paints a thousand words.

3.1.1. *Data representation*

Numerous data have been gathered, and the point is to display them, so as to give a synthetic view, allowing us to visualize the results "at a glance", at least in a qualitative way. Numerous techniques have been conceived, which are readily available through contemporary specific software tools.

The most popular tool is the histogram. To begin with, assume that a discrete character is observed (to aid in the presentation, we take integer values 0, 1, 2, etc.). Let n_k be the frequency of value k, i.e. the number of times the value k has been observed. Figure 3.1 shows the histogram which summarizes the measurements. The outcome has been "0" for 1 element, while 5 elements exhibit the value "6", and an average around "8" can be guessed. Abnormal measurements may be discovered in this way (here, perhaps "16", but the sample size is far too small for such a firm statement).

The case of continuous variables calls for a more careful analysis. The previous approach is no longer valid, as the outcomes are real numbers, scattered throughout the axis, with no two identical values. The method is to group the observations into classes and to draw *cumulative frequencies*. I intervals are defined: $]x_i, x_{i+1}], i = 1, 2, \ldots, I$.

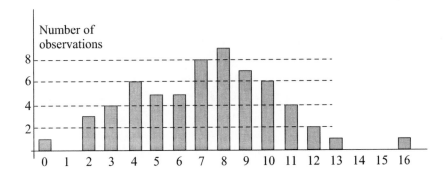

Figure 3.1. *Histogram, showing observation results for a discrete variable*

They are usually referred to as bins. Class i bin gathers all observations within interval i and contains observations:

$$n_i = \#\text{Elements}\left(x, \text{ s.t. } x_i < x \leq x_{i+1}\right).$$

With N for the whole population size, the relative frequency for class i is the ratio $f_i = n_i/N$. The cumulative frequency curve gives another view of the set of measurements:

$$F(x) = \sum_{i=1}^{j} f_j \quad x_i < x \leq x_{i+1}, \quad F\left(x_{i+1}\right) = \sum_{j=1}^{i+1} f_j. \qquad (3.1)$$

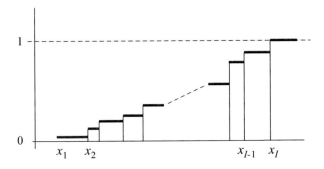

Figure 3.2. *The empirical distribution of a continuous variable*

The curve is made up of a series of horizontal segments (Figure 3.2). The histogram is also another representation, just as for discrete value observations, provided that the "equal area rule" is observed. This guarantees the validity of the interpretation given to the graph.

Class i is represented on the histogram by a rectangle with area (instead of height) proportional to n_i. For bins of equal width, the distinction makes no sense. In the general case, the rule is motivated by the following arguments:

– It allows the interpretation of the ordinate as an "empirical density".

– It allows an unbiased comparison between the different class frequencies to be made.

– It makes the histogram insensitive to class modifications (in particular, the shape remains the same if several bins are grouped).

Other representations. Numerous other descriptive tools have been imagined, the goal of which is to provide synthetic and intuitive access to the data. Various software packages make them easy to use. The reader is referred to the bibliography ([MOO 86, ALB 03]).

3.1.2. *Statistical parameters*

Direct data visualization is a first and important step. At that point, the need arises for a quantitative characterization for the parameter of interest. Here again, the assumption is that statistical laws (probability laws), which are often difficult to identify, govern the phenomena under study. To begin with, we make use of global parameters that introduce no specific assumption about the underlying probabilistic models.

3.1.2.1. *Fractiles*

Fractiles are read directly on the cumulative frequency curve. Let F be the cumulative frequency of variable X: $F(x)$ is the ratio of measured values equal to or less than x. The α-fractile (also referred to as *quantile* or *percentile*) is the number u such that $F(u) \leq \alpha$, $F(u + \epsilon) > \alpha$. It can be read directly on the curve (see Figure 3.3).

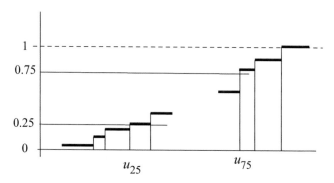

Figure 3.3. *Distribution function fractile*

This notion may help eliminate extreme values, which are most often abnormal. In the common situation where the measured character has no upper bound, the interest range should be chosen as, for instance, the interval between the 0.001-fractile and 0.999-fractile.

In economics use is made of quartiles (values for $\alpha = 25, 50$ or 75%). The 0.5 fractile is called the median. It splits the whole population into two subsets of the same size.

3.1.2.2. *Sample mean*

Among the global numeric indicators that are derived from the raw data, the mean value (or average) is certainly the most frequently used. The sample mean is the average measured on the data. The term *empirical mean* is sometimes used to emphasize the fact that this quantity is estimated, as opposed to the theoretical mean value of a probabilistic distribution. The sample mean of variable X, most commonly denoted as $\overline{X}$, is:

$$\overline{X} = \frac{\sum_{i=1}^{N} x_i}{N}, \tag{3.2}$$

N being the sample size.

3.1.2.3. *Sample variance*

In order to represent the dispersion (intuitively the distance from the average behavior given by the sample mean), sample variance V is introduced:

$$V = \frac{\sum_{i=1}^{N} \left(x_i - \overline{X} \right)^2}{N}. \tag{3.3}$$

Standard deviation σ is the square root of the variance: $\sigma^2 = V$.

3.1.2.4. *Moments*

The kth-moment of the distribution (k order moment) is usually denoted as μ_k. Most often, moments are taken about the mean:

$$\mu_k = \frac{\sum_{i=1}^{N} \left(x_i - \overline{X} \right)^k}{N}. \tag{3.4}$$

3.1.2.5. *Mode*

The mode is the most easily observed value. It is given by the peak of the histogram. Distributions with a single mode are referred to as being *unimodal*.

Mode, median and mean values should be carefully distinguished. The mode is visible on the histogram; the median separates the population into two subsets of equal size, and the mean into two subsets of equal weight. Unimodal distributions fit in one of the two categories:

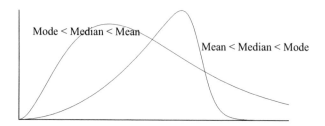

Figure 3.4. *Mean, mode, median of a density function*

– mode < median < mean (the distribution is spread to the right);

– mean < median < mode (the distribution is spread to the left).

3.1.2.6. *Other characterizations*

Mean and variance do not capture all the features of the distribution. Other indicators have been proposed, which take account of certain classes of shapes of the distribution functions. These indicators are derived from moments. Here too these indicators are to be seen as "empirical" (i.e. defined from the sample).

$$\gamma_1 = \frac{\mu_3}{\sigma^3}, \quad \text{or} \quad \beta_1 = \gamma_1^2. \tag{3.5}$$

These coefficients (respectively, Fisher and Pearson coefficients) reflect the *skewness* of the distribution. They take account of any symmetry the function may exhibit; they vanish when the curve is symmetric.

$$\beta_2 = \frac{\mu_4}{\mu_2^2}, \quad \gamma_2 = \beta_2 - 3. \tag{3.6}$$

These coefficients allow the comparison of distribution peaks (the *kurtosis*) with the normal distribution, which is such that $\mu_3 = 0$, $\mu_4 = 3\sigma^4$ (see Chapter 2), and so $\gamma_1 = \gamma_2 = 0$.

3.2. Correlation and regression

When a phenomenon implies more than one random variable, the possible relationships involved are an important issue.

This correlation effect will be of prime importance in signal theory, for instance to analyze and filter a random signal, as we will see in Chapter 4. We will also find many applications in other fields, such as traffic and reliability analysis, and of course more generally in sociology and economics.

For instance, when observing a sample of people, we can expect a kind of fuzzy relation between their size and weight. In a similar way, the socioeconomic category of a family, as given by its annual income, is related to its telephone or Internet usage (more precisely with the usage level, i.e. the traffic).

The same observation is made in reliability studies: typically, when characterizing a production process, we are interested in the possible relation between the rejection ratio and a production condition (e.g. date, or production line identity). A first approach is to illustrate the possible relation by displaying all the pairs (x, y) of observed data.

The *Jipp curve* (see Figure 3.5), although it was first observed in the 1960s, is still a good example of such a correlation. It shows the relation between the revenue per inhabitant and the equipment level for fixed telephony. There is no strict mathematical link, but only a quite typical trend. Interpreting this trend is beyond the scope of the statistical tools. There may be a direct causal relationship (phenomenon X provokes Y) or a more complex scheme (X and Y being two consequences of a third, hidden, cause).

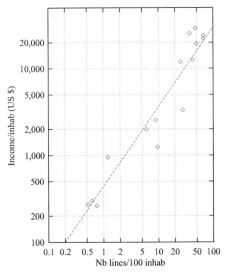

Figure 3.5. *Relation between income and equipment level for the telephone service, for various countries*

3.2.1. *Correlation coefficient*

The relationship between two random variables is numerically represented by the coefficient of correlation. This is a real number, between -1 and 1, defined as:

$$\widehat{\rho} = \frac{\sum (x_i - \overline{X})(y_i - \overline{Y})}{\sqrt{\sum (x_i - \overline{X})^2}\sqrt{\sum (y_i - \overline{Y})^2}}. \tag{3.7}$$

The reader may compare this with the covariance (see Chapter 1): the above quantity is nothing more than its empirical version (normalized).

3.2.2. *The regression curve*

When two variables X and Y are correlated, their mutual influence may be visualized through a causal relation $Y = f(X)$, although that correlation does not imply any direct causal relation. This operation is called a regression.

3.2.2.1. *The least squares method*

Let us imagine a linear model: that means that we are looking for a linear relation between x_i and y_i: $Y = aX + b$. Note that we can always limit ourselves to a linear model by the appropriate transformation of variables. It is also possible to define more elaborate models (e.g. quadratic relations).

The coefficients, denoted as $\widehat{a}$ and $\widehat{b}$, have to be estimated from the set of measurements providing N couples (x_i, y_i). The notation $\widehat{a}$ is intended to recall that the quantity is an *estimate* of the true coefficient. As the linear model does not capture the whole phenomenon, since other factors are neglected, an additional error term e, is introduced.

$$y_i = \widehat{a}x_i + \widehat{b} + e_i. \tag{3.8}$$

The *least squares method* proceeds by allocating values to parameters so as to minimize the residual error, i.e. the distance between the model and the values actually observed. This distance is written:

$$\Delta = \sum \left(y_i - \widehat{a}x_i - \widehat{b} \right)^2.$$

The optimal coefficients are such that they cancel the partial derivatives of Δ:

$$\frac{\partial \Delta}{\partial \widehat{a}} = 0, \quad \text{i.e.} \quad \sum x_i \left(y_i - \widehat{a}x_i - \widehat{b} \right) = 0, \quad \text{and} \quad \sum x_i y_i - N\widehat{a}\overline{x^2} - N\widehat{b}\overline{x} = 0$$

$$\frac{\partial \Delta}{\partial \widehat{b}} = 0, \quad \text{i.e.} \quad \sum \left(y_i - \widehat{a}x_i - \widehat{b} \right) = 0, \quad \text{and} \quad N\overline{y} - N\widehat{a}\overline{x} - N\widehat{b} = 0.$$

This yields the solution we are looking for:

$$\widehat{a} = \frac{\frac{\sum x_i y_i}{N} - \overline{x} \cdot \overline{y}}{\overline{x^2} - \overline{x}^2} = \widehat{\rho}\frac{S_y}{S_x},$$

$$\widehat{b} = \overline{y} - \widehat{a}\overline{x}. \tag{3.9}$$

(in these expressions, S_x and S_y stand for the empirical standard deviations of variables). The *regression line* goes through the center of gravity of the scatter diagram, and its slope is directly related with the correlation between variables. The residual error is often expressed by the variance of the e_i (residual error). After some calculations it results in:

$$S_e^2 = \frac{1}{N-2}\left(\overline{y^2} - (\overline{y})^2 - \hat{a}^2\left(\overline{x^2} - (\overline{x})^2\right)\right).$$

Coefficient $N - 2$ ensures that the estimator is unbiased (this concept will be clarified later on).

NOTE (*Using specific scales*). As we have seen in Figure 3.5, the Jipp curve is drawn with a logarithmic scale for the ordinate axis. Generally, for a non-linear relation between two quantities, the graphical representation of the cloud scatter diagram can be made using a specific scale, thanks to which a linear trend reappears.

This is especially the case with the celebrated "Gausso-arithmetic" plot, where the scale is such that any normal distribution appears as a straight line. For an empirical distribution, this gives a simple visual method to estimate the accuracy of a normal approximation and to give a rough idea of the moments: the mean is the abscissa corresponding to 50%, the standard deviation is half the distance between 16% and 84%, or the reverse of the slope. The graph (see Figure 3.6) is referred to as the *normal plot*.

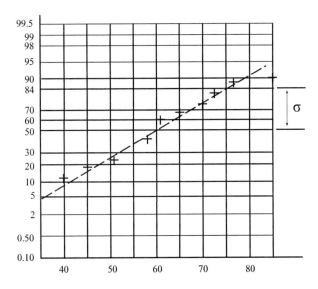

Figure 3.6. *Normal plot showing that the empirical measures are roughly normally distributed*

3.3. Sampling and estimation techniques

Visualizing data provides a synthetic characterization through global parameters; however, it by no means covers the needs of the analyst. In particular, the main issue is to predict general properties of the whole population from data coming from samples of limited size, for economic or technical reasons (and most often because the population is of infinite size). The question is thus: how to estimate the value of the (true) population parameters from the incomplete series of measurements, i.e. the sample. A basic assumption is needed here, which justifies using probability theory and its tools: all elements belong to the same population, and each element being tested has been drawn independently of the previous ones (this is called a random drawing). Most often the assumption is impossible to assert. This is particularly a crucial issue for people involved in sociological enquiries and polling activities. Note here that drawing random variables is also an important activity for the telecommunication engineer, for instance in reliability studies, traffic measurements or simulation. We address this point in more detail in Chapter 8.

Two basic results of mathematical statistics help in understanding the techniques traditionally related to sampling:

a) Sample mean and variance. Consider a sample of size N, drawn from an infinite sized population, or from a finite size population with replacements (then the draw is said to be *non-exhaustive*) where the character of interest has average m and variance σ^2. The sample mean $\overline{m}$ given by equation (3.2) is a random variable, with mean m, and with variance $\sigma^2(\overline{m})$ equal to σ^2/N:

$$E(\overline{m}) = m$$

$$\mathrm{Var}(m) = \sigma^2(\overline{m}) = \left(\frac{\sigma}{\sqrt{N}}\right)^2. \tag{3.10}$$

This last result is easy to verify: let the sample contain N elements. The classical results concerning the sum of independent random variables presented in Chapter 1, and the mean and variance properties of the variable X/N (see equations (1.24) and (1.28) in Chapter 1) make it possible to write:

$$\overline{m} = \frac{1}{N}(x_1 + x_2 + \cdots + x_N),$$

and thus:

$$E(\overline{m}) = \frac{1}{N}(E(x_1) + E(x_2) + \cdots + E(x_N)) = \frac{1}{N}Nm = m.$$

In the same way:

$$\sigma^2(\overline{m}) = \mathrm{Var}\left[\frac{x_1 + x_2 + \cdots + x_N}{N}\right] = N\,\mathrm{Var}\left[\frac{x_1}{N}\right] = N\frac{\mathrm{Var}(X)}{N^2} = \frac{\sigma^2}{N}.$$

b) Central limit theorem. The previous result concerns the first two moments but not the probability distribution of the sample mean. The next result concerns this distribution. The central limit theorem is of major importance when using statistical methods, as it introduces and motivates the endless references to *normal distribution*. Furthermore, it justifies most of the approximations presented hereafter. Its proof is beyond the scope of this book.

THEOREM 3.1. *Consider a set of N variables $X_1, X_2, \ldots, X_N$, independent and distributed according to a given, arbitrary distribution with average m and finite variance σ^2. Then, the variable:*

$$\overline{X} = \frac{1}{N} \sum_{i=1}^{N} X_i$$

goes, as N increases, to a limiting distribution which is normal, with average m and with variance σ^2/N.

This is a major improvement, as compared with the previous result: drawing a sample of size N, from a population with a character distributed according to an arbitrary distribution with mean m and standard-deviation σ, the sample mean goes to a normal law with mean m and standard-deviation $\sigma/\sqrt{N}$, as the sample size increases. Practically, the approximation is good when N is greater than 30 in most configurations. However, the independence assumption is mandatory.

These results presented above are the basis on which the remainder of this section is built. Two major techniques allow us to extract information from the sample: *estimation* and *hypothesis testing*. Estimating the value of a parameter, based upon the assumption of an underlying probabilistic model, may not be enough to support a decision such as "accept/reject". We may also need to justify the initial assumptions. The tools of hypothesis testing provide answers to these issues.

Finally, observations or tests (e.g. during simulations) are of limited duration, the question thus arises of taking into account the last time interval or the last test. This leads us to distinguish between truncated tests, for which the duration is chosen independently of the number of events observed, and curtailed tests, in which the total number of events is fixed in advance, the duration then having no limitation.

3.4. Estimation

The problem can be stated as follows: given a population, with a given character distributed according to a probability distribution function depending on a parameter p, estimate the numerical value of the parameter from the observations made on a limited sample size.

In *point estimation* the goal is to give the "best possible" estimate of the parameter, starting from the value obtained on the sample (it could be, for instance, the sample mean).

However, accepting the value obtained on the sample often leads to answers differing notably from the "true" value – especially if the sample is of moderate size. *Interval estimation* provides tools to prevent against such erroneous estimations. This introduces the notion of confidence into the result, which will thus be stated in the form of a *confidence interval* inside of which is the true value, with a given probability: the confidence level, expected as large as possible. So, the answer to the estimation problem is re-stated:

With a confidence level $1 - \alpha$ (i.e. a risk of error α), the parameter p lies in the interval $[p_{min}, p_{max}]$.

Clearly, the narrower the confidence interval, the higher the risk of error. This is the fundamental dilemma of every sampling and estimation activity.

3.4.1. *Point estimation*

We assume that the character is distributed according to a probability distribution function, the form of which is known, except for a certain parameter p, which we intend to estimate from the data.

Let the sample of size n be denoted $(x_1, x_2, \ldots, x_n)$. As previously mentioned, the estimator is usually denoted as $\widehat{p}$ to stress the fact that it is actually a random variable, and to distinguish it from the true value. The desirable properties for an estimator are as follows:

– As sample size increases, the estimated value ought to get closer to the true value: $\lim_{n \to \infty} \widehat{p_n} = p$ (where $\widehat{p_n}$ stands for the estimate built on a sample of size n): the estimator is said to be *convergent* (or consistent).

– The estimator ought to be *unbiased*, that is, for all n, $E(\widehat{p_n}) = p$, where $E(\widehat{p})$ is the expectation of $\widehat{p}$ (strictly speaking, we should put the same requirement on higher moments).

An estimator which is convergent and unbiased is said to be *absolutely correct*.

The natural approach is to identify the parameter under study from the measurement results. For instance, estimating the mean and variance of a distribution from the sample mean and sample variance. However, the question arises: how can we derive a "good" estimator?

Several methods have been proposed to derive a point estimator. In the following we concentrate on the *maximum likelihood* method. Other approaches have been developed (see e.g. [MOO 86]).

Let $f(x_1, x_2, \ldots, x_n,)$ – or $f(x_i)$ for short – denote the sample statistics probability density (i.e. the probability to draw $x_1, x_2, \ldots, x_n$, in any order). The maximum likelihood estimator is that which gives the higher value for $f(x_1, x_2, \ldots, x_n,)$, i.e. such that

$$\frac{d \log f(x_1, x_2, \ldots, x_n)}{dp} = 0 \quad \text{(the likelihood equation)}. \tag{3.11}$$

It can be shown that such an estimator is convergent. However, the method does not guarantee that it is unbiased. The estimation will be said to be *correct* but not absolutely correct. In order to make it absolutely correct the estimator will be adjusted, as is shown hereafter. The two following results are of central importance for estimation.

3.4.1.1. *Average*

The sample mean is an absolutely correct estimator of the actual mean:

$$\widehat{m} = \frac{1}{n} \sum_{i=1}^{n} x_i. \tag{3.12}$$

It is easy to verify that, whatever the value for n, $E[\widehat{m}] = m$, and so the estimator is unbiased.

3.4.1.2. *Variance*

The quantity s^2 is an absolutely correct estimator for variance:

$$s^2 = \frac{1}{n-1} \sum_{i=1}^{n} (x_i - \widehat{m})^2. \tag{3.13}$$

The quantity s^2 is known as the "sample variance". The careful reader has noticed the term $n - 1$, instead of n, on the denominator. Actually, the sample variance is:

$$\widehat{\sigma}^2 = \frac{\sum (x_i - \widehat{m})^2}{n}, \quad \text{and (as we show below)} \quad E[\widehat{\sigma}^2] = \frac{n-1}{n} \sigma^2.$$

It is thus a biased estimator. In order to correct the bias, statisticians introduce the substitution:

$$s^2 = \frac{n}{n-1} \widehat{\sigma}^2.$$

Let us verify this result:

$$(n-1)s^2 = \sum (x_i - \widehat{m})^2 = \sum [(x_i - m) - (\widehat{m} - m)]^2.$$

Developing and taking the mean of the right hand side expression and using results (3.10) about the mean and sample variance:

(1):

$$E\left[\sum (x_i - m)^2\right] = \sum E[x_i - m]^2 = n\sigma^2,$$

(2):

$$2E\left[\sum (x_i - m)(\widehat{m} - m)\right] = 2E\left[(\widehat{m} - m)\sum (x_i - m)\right]$$
$$= 2E[(\widehat{m} - m)(n\widehat{m} - nm)]$$
$$= \frac{2}{n}E[(n\widehat{m} - nm)^2] = 2\sigma^2,$$

(3):

$$E\left[\sum (\widehat{m} - m)^2\right] = E[n(\widehat{m} - m)] = nE[(\widehat{m} - m)^2] = \sigma^2,$$

(these last relations are just equation (3.10)); and finally

$$E[(n-1)s^2] = n\sigma^2 - 2\sigma^2 + \sigma^2 = (n-1)\sigma^2, \quad \text{thus } E[s^2] = \sigma^2.$$

Note that these results do not depend on any assumption about the distribution probability of the parameter under study.

Now, we can show that, for the case of normal variables, these estimators are actually the best possible.

3.4.1.3. *Estimating the mean and variance of a normal distribution*

a) The problem is to estimate the mean value m of a normal distribution with parameters (m, σ), where σ is known. The maximum likelihood method is used to derive the best estimator:

$$f(x_i) = \frac{1}{(\sigma\sqrt{2\pi})^n}e^{-\sum_{i=1}^{n}(x_i - m)^2/2\sigma^2}.$$

From this expression, we derive:

$$\frac{d\log(f)}{dm} = \frac{1}{\sigma^2}\sum_{i=1}^{n}(x_i - m),$$

and for the maximum likelihood:

$$\left(\frac{d\log f}{dm}\right)_{m=\widehat{m}} = 0.$$

Thus, $\widehat{m} = \frac{1}{n}\sum_{i=1}^{n} x_i = \overline{x}$.

We can verify that $E[\widehat{m}] = m$ whatever n. The estimator is unbiased and convergent, and is thus absolutely correct.

b) Similarly, when m is known, the best variance estimator is:

$$\widehat{\sigma^2} = \frac{1}{n}\sum_{i=1}^{n}(x_i - m)^2.$$

c) In general, however, both m and σ are unknown.

The mean is estimated as above, but the variance estimator $\widehat{\sigma^2} = (\sum_{i=1}^{n}(x_i - \widehat{m})^2)/n$ is biased, although convergent. Instead, we make use of the parameter already introduced $s^2 = \frac{n}{n-1}\widehat{\sigma^2}$.

The same results hold for the exponential distribution, as considered in the following example.

3.4.1.4. Example: estimating the average lifetime of equipment

As an example application, we show how to apply these results to estimate the average lifetime of equipment, the mortality having an exponential distribution (see Chapter 7). The same reasoning holds for other observations.

Consider a trial on a sample of n elements. The average lifetime θ is estimated by:

$$\widehat{\theta} = \frac{1}{n}\sum_{i=1}^{n}t_i = \frac{T}{n}, \tag{3.14}$$

where t_i is the lifetime of item i, and T is the total duration of the test. For practical purposes, the trial has limited duration, and the number of failures is limited. This refers to the notions of truncated tests and curtailed tests. For truncated tests, the test duration is limited to t_{max}. If, upon the n elements under test, $n - k$ are still operating at time t_{max}, then:

$$\widehat{\theta} = \frac{1}{k}(t_1 + \cdots + t_k + (n - k)t_{max}) = \frac{T}{k}, \tag{3.15}$$

where T is the cumulated duration of the test. If no failure at all has been detected it is mandatory to estimate a confidence interval. The number of elements to test is estimated using the simple formula:

$$k = n\left[1 - \exp\left(\frac{-t_{max}}{\theta}\right)\right].$$

As an example, estimating a failure rate around $\lambda = 1/\theta = 10^{-6}$/h, by observing 30 failures during 8,760 hours (one year) requires 3,450 elements to be tested. This clearly stresses the difficulty of characterizing elements with high reliability – or, otherwise stated, in considering the case of rare events. For curtailed tests, the test is stopped upon failure number k. Then:

$$\widehat{\theta} = \frac{1}{k}\left(t_1 + \cdots + t_k + (n - k)t_k\right) = \frac{T}{k}, \tag{3.16}$$

where T is the cumulative test duration at failure k.

3.4.2. *Estimating confidence intervals*

The maximum likelihood method provides a "good" way to estimate an unknown parameter, when the underlying probability distribution is known. However, if the same trial is repeated, or lengthened, it will give a different result. As already mentioned, the estimator is a random variable, as opposed to the parameter to be estimated, which is assumed to have a constant value. This leads us to question the accuracy of the prediction. Not only should a value be given for the parameter p, but also a range within which its "true" value is likely to be found (with a given probability). As above, the estimator of p is denoted as $\widehat{p}$. This is a random variable, with its own distribution function depending on the distribution of the character in the original population, itself function of the unknown p. For instance, we hereafter show that the mean value estimator of a normal law is itself normally distributed.

Let H be the probability distribution of the estimator. Let us choose two real numbers α_1 and α_2 ($\alpha = \alpha_1 + \alpha_2$). These numbers stand for the prediction risk. More precisely, they provide upper and lower bounds for the estimation, i.e. a *confidence interval I* such that:

$$P(\widehat{p} \in I) = 1 - \left(\alpha_1 + \alpha_2\right) = 1 - \alpha.$$

The approach consists, from the distribution H (or the associated density h), of finding two quantities u_1, u_2, such that $P(\widehat{p} < u_1) = \alpha_1$ and $P(\widehat{p} > u_2) = \alpha_2$ (see Figure 3.7). Any choice for the risk is possible (for instance $\alpha_1 = \alpha_2 = \alpha/2$, or $\alpha_1 = 0$, etc.). The exact shape of the curve depends on the unknown value p, as do u_1, u_2. Assume that we can give an explicit form to this relation, expressed by two curves $u_1 = H_1(p)$, $u_2 = H_2(p)$. Figure 3.8 illustrates the relation.

The curves H_1, H_2 delimit an area in the plane denoted as $D(\alpha)$ (it depends clearly on the risk, written simply α for short). Let us choose an arbitrary point p_0^* on the ordinate axis. The ordinate cuts the curves at the abscissas p_1 and p_2, given by the inverse functions $p_1 = H_1^{-1}(p_0^*)$ and $p_2 = H_2^{-1}(p_0^*)$. These functions are most often

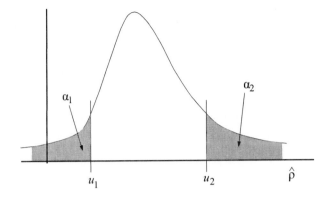

Figure 3.7. *Risks associated with the bounds of the confidence interval*

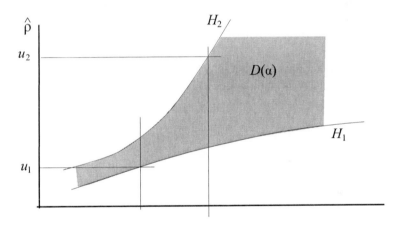

Figure 3.8. *Limits of the confidence interval*

impossible to derive explicitly, but can be obtained numerically. Now, let us consider the three following relations:

$$(p, \widehat{p}) \subset D(\alpha)$$

$$u_1 < \widehat{p} < u_2$$

$$p_1(\widehat{p}, \alpha) < p < p_2(\widehat{p}, \alpha).$$

All these relations describe the same set D. The elements thus have the same probability:

$$P(p_1 < \widehat{p} < p_2) = 1 - (\alpha_1 + \alpha_2) = 1 - \alpha$$

The series of measurements $x_1, x_2, \ldots, x_n$ is used to estimate $\widehat{p}$, and also the bounds (p_1, p_2), through the set of curves obtained above. The experimentation has given the result, within an interval, with a risk of error which can be limited. The examples below will help in understanding the method's principle and will illustrate it in typical cases.

3.4.2.1. Example 1: estimating the mean of a normal distribution

A random variable is distributed according to a normal distribution, with a known variance. The point estimator for the mean is, as explained in the previous section,

$$\widehat{m} = \frac{1}{n} \sum_{i=1}^{n} x_i.$$

Moreover, the estimator is normally distributed, with mean m and variance σ^2/n (remember that the sum of normal variables has a normal distribution). So, the parameter u, such that

$$u = \frac{\widehat{m} - m}{\sigma/\sqrt{n}}$$

is distributed according to the normalized normal distribution. Thus, given the risks α_1 and $\alpha_2 \, (= \alpha/2)$:

$$P\left(u_1 < u = \frac{\widehat{m} - m}{\sigma/\sqrt{n}} < u_2\right) = 1 - \alpha, \tag{3.17}$$

and finally:

$$P\left(\widehat{m} + u_1 \frac{\sigma}{\sqrt{n}} < m < \widehat{m} + u_2 \frac{\sigma}{\sqrt{n}}\right) = 1 - \alpha. \tag{3.18}$$

For example, with a risk symmetrically distributed: $\alpha_1 = \alpha_2 = 0.025$, we obtain $u_2 = 1.96$, $u_1 = -u_2$, i.e. an interval around the mean roughly equal to $\pm 2\sigma/\sqrt{n}$ (see the table in Chapter 2, and see also [FIC 04]).

Note that in the case where the variable is not normally distributed, the method can still be used, as the central limit theorem ensures that the estimator behaves approximately as a normal variable, with mean m and variance σ^2/n, σ being the population's standard deviation. In general, however, this parameter is unknown, and has to be estimated too.

3.4.2.2. Example 2: Chi-2 distribution in reliability

We revisit the problem of estimating the lifetime of items with an exponentially distributed lifetime. We assume that the number of failures within an interval obeys the Poisson distribution. This corresponds to a truncated test, in which a failed item is immediately replaced.

Let θ be the average lifetime, let n be the number of items tested, and $t_{\max}$ the test duration. With the Poisson distribution, the probability of having more than r failures during the interval θ is:

$$P(\leq r; \theta) = \sum_{i=0}^{r} \frac{(k)^i}{i!} e^{-k},$$

with $k = T/\theta$, and $T = nt_{\max}$, the cumulative test duration (the notation r is motivated by the Chi-2 distribution usage, which we are to obtain). Now, the following relation holds:

$$P(\leq r; \theta) = \sum_{i=0}^{r} \frac{(k)^i}{i!} e^{-k} = e^{-k}\left(1 + k + \cdots + \frac{k^r}{r!}\right) = \int_{t=k}^{\infty} \frac{t^r}{r!} e^{-t} dt,$$

and thus, with $t = u/2$:

$$P(\leq r; \theta) = \int_{u=2k}^{\infty} \frac{u^r}{r!2^{r+1}} e^{-u/2} du.$$

Referring to Chapter 2, we recognize the Chi-2 distribution. Indeed, by taking $u = \chi^2$ and $v = 2r + 2$, we obtain:

$$P(\leq r; \theta) = \int_{2k}^{\infty} \frac{1}{2^{v/2}\Gamma(v/2)} (\chi^2)^{\frac{v}{2}-1} e^{-\chi^2/2} d\chi^2. \tag{3.19}$$

This is the probability that a χ^2 with $2(r + 1)$ degrees of freedom is larger than $2k$. Finally,

$$P(\leq r; \theta) = P(\chi^2_{2r+2} > 2k). \tag{3.20}$$

This yields the upper and lower bounds at the levels α_1 and α_2:

$$\frac{2T}{\chi^2_{2r+2;\alpha_1}} < \theta < \frac{2T}{\chi^2_{2r;1-\alpha_2}}. \tag{3.21}$$

Especially, for a symmetric risk $\alpha_1 = \alpha_2 = \alpha/2$:

$$\frac{2T}{\chi^2_{2r+2;\alpha/2}} < \theta < \frac{2T}{\chi^2_{2r;1-\alpha/2}}. \tag{3.22}$$

Table 3.1 summarizes the main results for this important kind of test (including the case of curtailed tests).

Example applications in realistic situations will be developed in Chapter 7. Tables of the Chi-2 distribution are given in specialized handbooks (see also [FIC 04]).

	Truncated test at t, N parts, r failures		Curtailed test at t_r, r failures, N parts	
	With replacement	Without replacement	With replacement	Without replacement
Cumulated time T	$T = Nt$	$T = t_1+t_2+\cdots$ $+(N-r)t$	$T = Nt_r$	$T = t_1+t_2+\cdots$ $+(N-r)t_r$
Point estimator	$\theta = T/r$, (if $r=0$, take $\theta = 3T$)		$\theta = T/r$, (if $r=0$, take $\theta = 3T$)	
Lower limit at confidence level $1-\alpha$	$\theta_i = \dfrac{2T}{\chi^2_{2r+2;1-\alpha}}$		$\theta_i = \dfrac{2T}{\chi^2_{2r;1-\alpha}}$	
Confidence interval at confidence level $1-\alpha$	$\dfrac{2T}{\chi^2_{2r+2;\alpha/2}} < \theta < \dfrac{2T}{\chi^2_{2r;1-\alpha/2}}$		$\dfrac{2T}{\chi^2_{2r;\alpha/2}} < \theta < \dfrac{2T}{\chi^2_{2r;1-\alpha/2}}$	

Table 3.1. *Truncated and curtailed test: confidence intervals with Chi-2 distribution*

3.4.2.3. *Estimating proportion*

Suppose we intend to estimate the proportion p of faulty elements in a given infinite size population. The experiment proceeds by choosing a sample size N, the successive drawings being independent of each other, and by counting the number k of faulty items. In accordance with our intuition, the calculation confirms that the maximum likelihood estimator for p is the ratio $\widehat{p} = k/N$.

Under the independence assumption, the number of faulty items is distributed according to a Bernoulli distribution (for a finite size population, the distribution would be hypergeometric). The probability distribution is written:

$$P(k \text{ faulty among } N) = \binom{N}{k} p^k (1-p)^{N-k}. \tag{3.23}$$

The two curves delimiting the domain $D(\alpha)$ may be drawn numerically. The probability of observing less than k faulty elements is:

$$P(k; N) = \sum_{j=0}^{k} \binom{N}{j} p^j (1-p)^{N-j}.$$

Once the risk α_1 is chosen, the curve H_1 is obtained by "inverting" the relation (which is possible through exact numerical calculation, or using an approximate method, as we explain now).

In most cases, the experiment is such that the normal approximation holds (see Chapter 2): this is the case if $p > 0.5$, and $Np > 5$, or $p < 0.5$, and $N(1 - p) > 5$. The binomial distribution is then replaced by the normal law with mean $m = Np$ and variance $Np(1 - p)$, for which the mean is to be estimated. If the risk is taken symmetrically, it amounts to calculating $u(\alpha)$, and the confidence interval is:

$$\widehat{p} - u_\alpha \sqrt{\frac{\widehat{p}(1 - \widehat{p})}{N}} \leq p \leq \widehat{p} + u_\alpha \sqrt{\frac{\widehat{p}(1 - \widehat{p})}{N}}. \tag{3.24}$$

If the conditions for using the normal approximation are not fulfilled, the Poisson distribution is used instead: it has been shown that the binomial distribution goes to the Poisson distribution with parameter Np, as soon as $N \geq 40$ and $p < 0.1$ (see Chapter 2).

Building the curves H_1 and H_2. The solution can only be derived numerically. In the case where the normal approximation holds, the confidence interval is given by relation (3.24) above. Limits H_1 and H_2 are points such that:

$$p = \widehat{p} \pm u_\alpha \sqrt{\frac{\widehat{p}(1 - \widehat{p})}{N}},$$

that is, the solutions of the quadratic equation:

$$(p - \widehat{p})^2 = u^2 \frac{\widehat{p}(1 - \widehat{p})}{N}.$$

Figure 3.9 displays the confidence interval versus the observed value, for a 95% confidence level (i.e. a 5% risk) and a sample size $N = 25$.

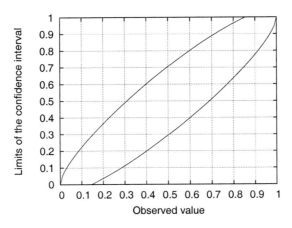

Figure 3.9. *Limits of the confidence interval for estimating a proportion ($N = 25$)*

3.4.2.4. *Estimating the parameter of a Poisson distribution*

Here, the problem is to estimate the parameter λ of the Poisson distribution, given by:

$$P(k) = \frac{\lambda^k}{k!} e^{-\lambda}. \tag{3.25}$$

A typical example could be in the observation of defective elements in the configuration of low rejection ratios, so that the Poisson distribution is a good approximation. Also, this is the distribution corresponding to the observation of the number of arrivals within a window of length T for a Poisson traffic with rate a: here, $\lambda = aT$.

The experiment consists of repeating the counting: observing m windows of size T, e.g., providing values $(k_1, k_2, \ldots, k_m)$. The maximum likelihood estimator is given by:

$$\widehat{\lambda} = \frac{k_1 + k_2 + \cdots + k_m}{m}. \tag{3.26}$$

The function H can be derived numerically, or by using tables.

3.5. Hypothesis testing

The goal of hypothesis testing is to help in deciding if a hypothesis made on a population can be retained, based upon the available observations. Depending on the nature of the hypothesis, and especially whether it can be formulated under a qualitative form or not, the parametric or non-parametric methods are used. For instance, testing that the instants of an arrival process obey the Poisson assumption or that the service durations are exponentially distributed is a non-parametric test. On the other hand, testing that they conform to the Poisson distribution with parameter m is a parametric test.

3.5.1. *Example: testing the mean value of a normal distribution*

This simple example provides a good introduction to the method. We have a population with a parameter X normally distributed with parameters m and σ. The standard deviation σ is known, and the test is related with m. For instance, the hypothesis is "m larger than 10". Such a test is called a "simple test".

We draw a sample size N, from which the sample mean is measured. Remembering that the sample mean is normally distributed, with mean m and standard deviation $\sigma/\sqrt{N}$, we can write: see (3.24):

$$P\left(\overline{X} < m - u_1 \frac{\sigma}{\sqrt{N}}\right) = \alpha_1, \quad \text{and} \quad P\left(\overline{X} > m + u_2 \frac{\sigma}{\sqrt{N}}\right) = \alpha_2. \tag{3.27}$$

Assume the sample has size $N = 100$, and the standard deviation is $\sigma = 5$. For a risk $\alpha = 0.01$, decomposed into two symmetric values $\alpha_1 = \alpha_2 = 0.005$, the normal law table gives $x_\alpha \simeq 2.32$ (see Table 2.1, Chapter 2). Thus, the above result gives: $P(\overline{X} < 10 - 1.16 = 8.84) = 0.01$.

Clearly, the hypothesis "m greater than 10" can be accepted if the measured $\overline{X}$ equals 12, for instance. Now, imagine that the result is $\overline{X} = 7.5$. According to the formula above the probability of observing such a value is low, if the hypothesis is true: this leads to a *rejection* of the hypothesis.

The procedure is rigorous, but there remains a risk of error in the decision, as any event can be observed, even if it is unlikely to occur. The following general scheme is intended to account for this risk.

Let X be the test variable. We have a first hypothesis H_0, e.g. $X = X_0$, or $X < X_0$, etc. As the experiment is of a statistical nature, there is a possibility of wrongly rejecting the hypothesis. A first risk α is thus introduced, the "*type I error*". This is the probability of rejecting H_0 although it is true.

Conversely, there is a risk of accepting the hypothesis while it is false. This introduces the "*type II error*", β. More precisely, we introduce a second hypothesis H_1, and the test is H_0 versus H_1. The type II error is the possibility of rejecting H_1 although it is true. Table 3.2 summarizes the procedure.

"Truth" Decision	H_0 true	H_1 true
Accept H_0	Correct decision	Type II error
Reject H_0 and accept H_1	Type I error	Correct decision

Table 3.2. *The procedure of the hypothesis test*

As a general rule, we associate these tests (as well as the others described below) with the notion of effectiveness, which accounts for the relevance of the procedure: this is referred to as the *power* of the test.

The power function of the test. The principle is as follows: we are given a population in which a character is subject to a test (a sample of N observations). The population conforms if the proportion of non-conforming values (for instance "greater than some limit") is lower than a boundary $P_{\max}$. A typical situation would be "the proportion of response time greater than $T_{\max}$ must be less than 5%" for a processing unit, otherwise the population is rejected. The power function gives the probability of accepting the test, given the sample size N, for a population having an actual but unknown

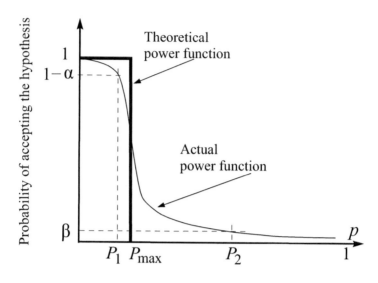

Figure 3.10. *The power function of the test*

parameter p. Figure 3.10 displays the general shape of the power curve. In the case of an exhaustive sampling, the test would yield a result with certainty:

– probability of acceptance = 1 if $p > P_{max}$,

– probability of acceptance = 0 if $p < P_{max}$.

This is symbolized by the theoretical curve. Now, the experiment introduces both a risk of erroneous acceptance β, and a risk of erroneous rejection α. This corresponds to the effective power function.

To summarize: a customer encounters a risk (type II) of making a wrong decision in accepting the product under test, although its actual ratio p of bad elements is higher than the threshold P_2 that has been agreed. Similarly, the provider encounters a risk (type I) that the product is rejected, although the actual ratio is lower than the limit P_1. Statisticians sometimes refer to these risks respectively as the buyer risk and the provider risk. In telecommunications, this would typically describe the relations between a network operator and an equipment manufacturer.

3.5.2. *Chi-2 test: uniformity of a random generator*

A discrete-event simulation makes use of random numbers, uniformly distributed in the interval $(0, 1)$ provided by a pseudo-random generator; see Chapter 8 for more details.

The problem arises of testing the quality of the generator, and more especially its uniformity. The Chi-2 test brings an answer to this problem. The interval $(0, 1)$ is divided in n sub-intervals of equal length (e.g., $n = 10$, each interval having a length 0.1). N numbers are drawn and are positioned in the intervals – i.e. we draw the histogram. If the generator conforms to the uniformity hypothesis, the probability that a number falls within any interval is simply $1/n$, so that an average of N/n elements are expected in each bin.

The hypothesis is "the generator is uniform". If this is true, the number of drawings in each bin conforms to the Bernoulli distribution:

$$P(k) = \binom{N}{k} p^k (1-p)^{N-k}, \quad \text{with} \quad p = \frac{1}{n}. \tag{3.28}$$

The mean is Np, the variance $Np(1 - p)$. Under the usual assumptions, the normal distribution is used as a convenient approximation. If k_j is the number of drawings in the interval j, then:

$$\frac{k_j - Np}{\sqrt{Np(1-p)}} = \frac{k_j - N/n}{\sqrt{\frac{N}{n}\left(1 - \frac{1}{n}\right)}}$$

is distributed according to the standard normal distribution. Thus, the variable:

$$Z = \sum \frac{\left(k_j - N/n\right)^2}{\frac{N}{n}\left(1 - \frac{1}{n}\right)} \simeq \frac{\sum_j \left(k_j - N/n\right)^2}{N/n} \tag{3.29}$$

is distributed as a Chi-2 with $n - 1$ degrees of freedom. A risk is adopted (for instance 5%) and the test is re-stated as $Z < u_\alpha$. For instance, with $\alpha = 5\%$ and $n = 10$, we can find on a Chi-2 table that with 9 degrees of freedom we obtain 16.92 as the limit: the hypothesis is accepted as long as Z is below 16.92.

3.5.3. Correlation test

The problem here is to test whether two variables are correlated or not. The sampling enables the estimation of the empirical correlation coefficient $\widehat{\rho}$ given by equation (3.7). Assume a trial on a sample of size n gives a value for $\widehat{\rho}$ near 0. How can we accept the independence property?

The hypothesis of the test is "no correlation", which translates to "$\rho = 0$". If the hypothesis is true, it can be shown that as the sample size increases, $\widehat{\rho}$ goes to a normal distribution with mean 0 and variance $1/n$: this is nothing more than the central limit theorem – and this illustrates once again its importance in statistics. The hypothesis is accepted, with a risk α, if:

$$|\widehat{\rho}\sqrt{n}| < x_\alpha \tag{3.30}$$

(x_α is naturally the quantile corresponding to α).

Chapter 4

Signal Theory

Signal theory and signal processing encompass all the operations performed on the signal, with the aim of modulating, filtering, performing spectral analysis, etc. In the case of digital processing, the original signal, which is generally analog and of continuous value, will be represented by a sequence of numbers and, for this, operations such as sampling, quantization and coding will be performed. The resulting signal will then be digitally processed, in order, for instance, to be filtered to retain its essential characteristics by eliminating parasitic frequencies when it comes to reproduce the initial signal, or to suppress negligible details for compressing data before storage or transmission.

In this chapter we introduce the mathematical bases involved in these operations, in the cases of deterministic as well as of random signals. First, the concepts of linear system and of filtering, and the representation of the signal in the frequency domain by means of Fourier transforms are discussed. Then we present several concepts specific to digital signal processing, such as sampling, quantization and discrete Fourier transform, in order to then introduce the basic principles of digital filtering, spectral analysis, prediction and adaptive filtering.

4.1. Concept of signal and signal processing

Generally speaking, the term *signal* refers to a quantity, a function of time (a sound signal for instance), or of spatial coordinates, as when an image or a video sequence is described as a series of pixels. This function may describe continuous variations of a physical parameter (e.g. the voltage issued from a microphone receiving vocal excitations) – we then speak of an *analog* signal. Also, it may describe a sequence of discrete values (the speech signal, *sampled* and *coded*, or the pixels of an image), and we then refer to *digital* signals. The terms of a continuous-time signal (the signal is a function continuously varying with time), and of a discrete-time signal (the variable takes values at specific instants only) are also used.

The concept applies to *deterministic* phenomena (e.g., a sinusoidal analog signal) as well as to *random* signals (the variable describes a random trajectory, e.g. the luminance of a video signal). Most often the measured signal is not perfectly predictable, and moreover it can be perturbed. It then needs some analysis in order to be identified, for instance by comparison to a *model*. Inversely, the goal could be to pilot a source so as to *build* a signal of specific characteristics, for transmission purposes, or for synthesis (speech, music, etc.). Processing a signal basically consists of performing various operations on available data, either measured or generated, in order to draw usable information from them. Figure 4.1 represents the general diagram of a system sending and receiving a signal.

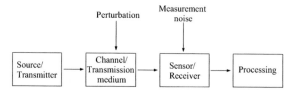

Figure 4.1. *Basic diagram of a system sending and receiving signals*

One (or several) source(s) sends a signal carrying some information, pre-processed or not, which is transmitted through a medium (air, water, optical fiber, wireline, etc.) referred to as the *channel*, as we will see in Chapter 5. The signal propagates under various forms, for instance, sound or electromagnetic waves. These waves may result from a composite of several signals, as when a carrier wave is modulated by the information signal. They may be subjected to distortions due to the transmission medium: time shifts, attenuations, reflections, etc. Most often detection in the receiver entails some degradation (measurement noise). Finally, for both transmission or storage operations we can attempt to minimize the volume of information, and thus to reduce the signal to its most significant components.

The need to retrieve the original signal, despite such impairments, and the need to extract its essential components have motivated the development of signal theory and signal processing through *analysis* and *filtering*. Thanks to the availability of powerful computing resources (software tools, DSP (digital signal processors), i.e. dedicated integrated circuits), digital processing has in most cases superseded the previously used analog devices, such as spectrum analyzers, discrete component filters, charge-transfer filters, etc. However, the theoretical foundations remain unchanged: linear system theory and probability theory. Signal sampling being generally the prerequisite to any digital processing, these mathematical tools will most often be applied to discrete-time signals. At last, we will be led to distinguish among two main signal types, namely deterministic and random signals, these latter calling for a specific statistical characterization.

4.2. Linear time-invariant systems and filtering

Filtering is the basic operation of signal processing. Indeed, as explained in the introduction, we may want to reduce the number of signal components, in order to minimize the volume of data to be processed; also, the signal can be associated with other signals, for transmission purposes (e.g., modulation); and, quite often, the signal is perturbed by parasitic noise during its transmission: we then want to eliminate these useless components to retrieve the initial information. At last, the filtering operation may help to build signal models and to predict its evolution over time. The goal of the filter, a linear system, is to perform all these operations.

4.2.1. *Linear time-invariant systems*

Signal and filtering theories are mainly based upon the concepts of linear time-invariant (LTI) systems.

Consider a system such that if $x(t)$ is applied at the input, the output is $y(t)$. The system is called *linear* if on entering $kx(t)$ the output is $ky(t)$. Similarly, inputting $x_1(t) + x_2(t)$ yields $y_1(t) + y_2(t)$ at its output. If a time shift of the input signal $x(t) \rightarrow x(t - \tau)$ now yields the same shift at the output, that is $y(t) \rightarrow y(t - \tau)$, then the system is called *time-invariant* (or *shift-invariant*).

LTI systems offer a realistic model for most processing systems, either hardware or software, dealing with signals. If $x(t)$ is the signal entering the system, then the output $y(t)$ is a new expression of the signal and the system can be characterized by a function, usually denoted as $h(t)$ and referred to as the *impulse response* of the system. This is the signal obtained on the output when a Dirac pulse $\delta(t)$ is entered. The Dirac delta function (unit impulse, or Dirac pulse for short) was introduced in Chapter 1.

4.2.2. *Impulse response and convolution function of an LTI system*

Due to its linearity and time-invariance properties, the effect of an arbitrary input $x(t)$ offered to a LTI system having $h(t)$ as impulse response is formally expressed by the following equation:

$$y(t) = x(t) \otimes h(t) \tag{4.1}$$

where the symbol $\otimes$ represents convolution, that is:

$$y(t) = \int_{-\infty}^{\infty} x(\tau)h(t - \tau)d\tau. \tag{4.2}$$

Now let us introduce the Dirac delta function (unit impulse, or Dirac pulse for short), already defined in Chapter 1 and of which we recall the definition (it shall be detailed further with the concept of distribution):

$$\int_{-\infty}^{\infty} x(t)\delta(t)dt = x(0)$$

and

$$\int_{-\infty}^{\infty} x(t)\delta(t - \tau)dt = x(\tau)$$

or, of course

$$\int_{-\infty}^{\infty} x(\tau)\delta(t - \tau)d\tau = x(t).$$

The Dirac delta function gives the function value at the origin, or at time τ when shifted by τ, etc.

Now let us assume that the input signal $x(t)$ is decomposed into an infinity of time-shifted Dirac delta functions, such that $x(t) = \int_{-\infty}^{\infty} x(\tau)\delta(t - \tau)d\tau$. For every shifted pulse $\delta(t - \tau)$, the system issues the shifted impulse response $h(t - \tau)$, due to its time invariance. The linear property of the system gives equation (4.2) for the system response. This justifies using the convolution product, and also the impulse response term for $h(t)$.

4.2.3. Filtering function

As already mentioned, filtering is a basic operation of signal theory. Under the assumptions of linearity and time-invariance, the filtering operation can be defined by the convolution product introduced just above:

$$y(t) = \int_{-\infty}^{\infty} x(\tau)h(t - \tau)d\tau, \quad \text{or} \quad y(t) = \int_{-\infty}^{\infty} x(t - \tau)h(\tau)d\tau. \qquad (4.3)$$

(due to the commutativity property of the convolution product).

In order to illustrate these points we take the low-pass filter as a simple example. Figure 4.2 symbolizes the role of the low-pass filter: the input signal is the sum of two sine signals, one of low frequency, called the fundamental, and another of higher

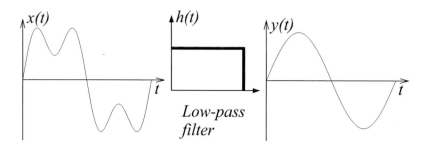

Figure 4.2. *Basic diagram of the low-pass filter*

frequency resulting from a perturbation, for instance at a frequency many times the original (a harmonic). The filter is intended to suppress the harmonic signal, so as to return the fundamental.

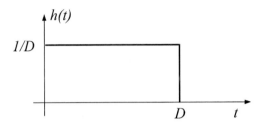

Figure 4.3. *Impulse response of a filter calculating the average*

To understand that relation (4.2) expresses a filtering operation, we take the simple case of a filter calculating the average value of a signal on a window D. Figure 4.3 represents the corresponding function.

We have:

$$t < 0 : h(t) = 0$$

$$0 \leq t < D : h(t) = 1/D$$

$$t \geq D : h(t) = 0$$

and equation (4.2) reads:

$$y(t) = \frac{1}{D} \int_{t-D}^{t} x(\tau) d\tau.$$

Obviously we have here a low-pass filter, as it integrates (i.e. takes the average) fast signal variations: we easily realize that, for a duration D correctly adjusted, the "sliding" window smoothes all these fast variations. We will come back to these operations and to their implementation in more detail in section 4.8, which is devoted to the study and realization of filters.

4.3. Fourier transform and spectral representation

Equation (4.3) directly expresses the actual filtering process. However, its practical application is not always easy, especially when we attempt to determine the impulse response providing the result we are looking for. To this end Fourier transforms have been introduced in signal theory. Indeed, the Fourier transform offers a frequency-domain (spectral) representation of a signal or a function and thus provides a natural approach, especially in domains where sound or electromagnetic waves, i.e. linear combinations of pure frequency components, are the physical reality.

For instance, moving from the time to the frequency domain allows us to clearly distinguish between the frequency components to be eliminated and those to be retained at the filtering stage. Moreover, as we have already seen in Chapter 1, these transforms replace the convolution product with an ordinary product between functions in the frequency domain.

The Fourier transform associates the frequency response of a linear system with its impulse response $h(t)$, and filtering then reduces to the product of this response by the transform – the *spectrum* – of the signal.

Thus, we study signal representation in the frequency domain, using Fourier transforms.

4.3.1. *Decomposing a periodic signal using Fourier series*

Recall first that, with complex plane notations, we have:

$$\cos \omega t = \frac{1}{2}\left(e^{j\omega t} + e^{-j\omega t}\right) \quad \text{and} \quad \sin \omega t = \frac{1}{2j}\left(e^{j\omega t} - e^{-j\omega t}\right).$$

A periodic signal $x(t)$, with period $T_0 = 2\pi/\omega_0$ may be written as:

$$x(t) = \sum_{n=-\infty}^{\infty} X(n\omega_0)e^{jn\omega_0 t}, \tag{4.4}$$

i.e. in the form of a sum of sine signals – the harmonics – the frequency[1] of which is a multiple of the fundamental, i.e.:

$$\omega_n = n\omega_0 \quad \text{where } \omega_0 = \frac{2\pi}{T_0},$$

and where the complex amplitude of each harmonic component is given by:

$$X(n\omega_0) = \frac{1}{T_0}\int_0^{T_0} x(t)e^{-jn\omega_0 t}\mathrm{d}t. \tag{4.5}$$

---

1. Strictly speaking ω is the "pulsation" and f the "frequency", which is the inverse of the period: $f = 1/T$. According to common use and to simplify, we denote here $\omega = 2\pi f$ as the frequency.

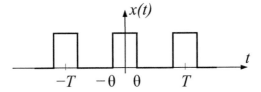

Figure 4.4. *Periodic sequence of rectangular pulses*

Indeed, we can verify, by importing equations (4.4) into (4.5):

$$\frac{1}{T_0} \int_0^{T_0} \sum_{m=-\infty}^{\infty} X(m\omega_0) e^{jm\omega_0 t} e^{-jn\omega_0 t} dt$$

$$= \frac{1}{T_0} \sum_{m=-\infty}^{\infty} X(m\omega_0) \int_0^{T_0} e^{j(m-n)\omega_0 t} dt = X(n\omega_0),$$

because $\int_0^{T_0} e^{j(m-n)\omega_0 t} dt = 0$, if $m \neq n$ and T_0 if $m = n$.

As an example, consider the expansion of a periodic series of rectangular pulses of width 2θ, of period T, as in Figure 4.4. This example is justified by the importance of this kind of signal in sampling theory, as we will see later on. Applying equation (4.5), with $\omega = 2\pi/T$, yields:

$$X(n\omega) = \frac{1}{T} \int_{-\theta}^{\theta} A e^{-jn\omega t} dt = \frac{A}{jn\omega T} \left(e^{jn\omega\theta} - e^{-jn\omega\theta} \right) = \frac{2A\theta}{T} \cdot \frac{\sin n\omega\theta}{n\omega\theta} \quad (4.6)$$

(where a $\sin x/x$ type function appears, referred to as cardinal sine, or sine cardinal). Hence we obtain the series expansion by applying (4.4):

$$x(t) = \frac{2A\theta}{T} \cdot \sum_{n=-\infty}^{\infty} \frac{\sin n\omega\theta}{n\omega\theta} e^{jn\omega t}. \quad (4.7)$$

Thus, the signals which appear in the expansion have frequency components which are integers many times the frequency of the original signal.

4.3.2. *Fourier transform of an arbitrary signal*

The previous decomposition can be extended to non-periodic functions, provided they remain absolutely convergent, or semi-convergent.[2] We then write:

$$x(t) = \frac{1}{2\pi} \int_{-\infty}^{\infty} X(\omega) e^{+j\omega t} d\omega, \quad (4.8)$$

---

2. In the following we consider the set of signals $x(t)$ called stable, belonging to the complete normed vectorial space $L_C^1(\mathcal{R})$ such that $\int_C |x(t)| dt < \infty$ (absolute convergence),

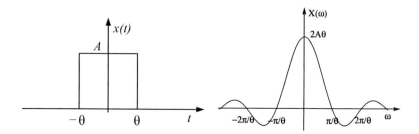

Figure 4.5. *Fourier transform of the rectangular pulse*

with

$$X(\omega) = \int_{-\infty}^{\infty} x(t)e^{-j\omega t}dt. \qquad (4.9)$$

$X(\omega)$ is the *Fourier transform* of $x(t)$, and $x(t)$ is called the inverse Fourier transform of $X(\omega)$.

As an example, let us calculate the Fourier transform of a rectangular pulse (or gate) of amplitude A and width 2θ (see Figure 4.5), centered on the time origin.

Applying (4.9) we obtain

$$X(\omega) = \int_{-\theta}^{\theta} Ae^{-j\omega t}dt = 2A\theta\frac{\sin \omega\theta}{\omega\theta}. \qquad (4.10)$$

The Fourier transform is also referred to as the signal spectrum. In this example the expression can be given an obvious meaning by making the analogy with the previous series expansion and its coefficients, given by formula (4.7).

Note also that the function cancels out for frequencies which are inverse multiples of the pulse duration.

Symmetrically, a rectangular gate in the spectral domain admits an inverse transform with the same shape (sine cardinal) in the time domain.

$$x(t) = \frac{1}{2\pi}\int_{-\omega_0}^{\omega_0} Ae^{j\omega t}d\omega = \frac{A}{2\pi}\frac{e^{j\omega_0 t} - e^{-j\omega_0 t}}{tj} = \frac{A}{t\pi}\sin \omega_0 t = \frac{2A}{T_0}\cdot\frac{\sin \omega_0 t}{\omega_0 t}.$$

---

but also those called of finite energy in the space $L_C^2(\mathcal{R})$ such that $\int_C |x(t)|^2 dt < \infty$ (semi-convergence). This is necessary in some cases, in order to justify writing (4.8), (4.9) (for instance $X(\omega)$ could not be absolutely convergent on $\mathcal{R}$, this last being valid almost everywhere in the Hilbert space of square-integrable functions).

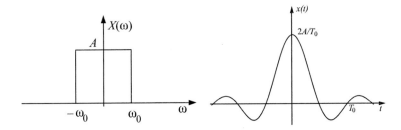

Figure 4.6. *Inverse Fourier transform of the pulse*

These results are applied hereafter in studying rectangular gates, and then for sampling and filter design.

4.3.3. *Dirac delta function and its Fourier transform*

The Dirac delta function, denoted as $\delta(t)$, is a function such that

$$\int_{-\infty}^{\infty} f(t)\delta(t)\mathrm{d}t = f(0). \tag{4.11}$$

However, strictly speaking no function matches the above definition and we must refer to the concept of distribution, as we will now present (see also [BEL 00, RUD 91, SCH 01]).

Concept of linear functional. If x is an integrable function on $\mathcal{R}$, and ϕ is another function on $\mathcal{R}$ that is infinitely derivable, identically zero outside a bounded set, then $\int x(t)\phi(t)\mathrm{d}t$ is a real number, depending continuously and linearly on ϕ. Function x is then said to be a linear functional, continuous on the test function space φ on $\mathcal{R}$. In a similar way, if μ is a measure on reals and ϕ a test function, then $\int \phi(t)d\mu$ is a real number, depending continuously and linearly on ϕ: measures can also be seen as continuous linear functionals in the test function space.

Concept of distribution. This concept of a "continuous linear functional in the test function space" is used as a definition of distributions: a distribution X is a continuous linear functional on the vector space of functions defined on $\mathcal{R}$, infinitely derivable and with bounded support.

Formally, a distribution X is defined by the relation:

$$\langle X, \phi \rangle = \int_{-\infty}^{\infty} x(t)\phi(t)\mathrm{d}t. \tag{4.12}$$

The Dirac distribution is defined as:

$$\langle \delta, \phi \rangle = \int_{-\infty}^{\infty} \delta(t)\phi(t)\mathrm{d}t = \phi(0), \tag{4.13}$$

valid for any signal ϕ continuous at 0.

In other words, the Dirac impulse $\delta(t)$ is an operator which extracts the value at the origin of a continuous function. More generally, for any function $\phi(t)$ continuous at $t = \tau$, we obtain:

$$\langle \delta(t - \tau), \phi \rangle = \int_{-\infty}^{\infty} \delta(t - \tau)\phi(t)\mathrm{d}t = \phi(\tau). \tag{4.14}$$

In particular, taking $\phi(t) = 1$ and $\tau = 0$, we derive

$$\int_{-\infty}^{\infty} \delta(t)\mathrm{d}t = 1. \tag{4.15}$$

Informally, we can visualize the Dirac distribution as a function from $\mathcal{R}$ on $\mathcal{R}$ which would be zero everywhere except the origin, and such that its integral on $\mathcal{R}$ would equal 1 (actually, no ordinary function obeys such properties).

Returning to a rectangular impulse with duration 2θ, as in the previous section, let us assume that its amplitude verifies $A = 1/2\theta$, so that its area is equal to 1.

This defines a distribution

$$\langle X, \phi \rangle = \frac{1}{2\theta} \int_{-\theta}^{\theta} x(t)\mathrm{d}t$$

which, for small enough values of θ, gives $\langle X, \phi \rangle \approx x(0)$, and so the Dirac distribution may be seen as its limit as θ tends to 0.

From the above properties we derive the conventional representation given in Figure 4.7, that is, a vertical arrow having a length proportional to the area.

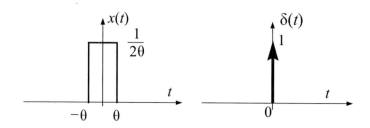

Figure 4.7. *Dirac pulse as a limit of a rectangular gate*

Dirac delta distribution transform. By definition the Fourier transform of a distribution X is a distribution such that for any integrable function ϕ:

$$\langle X(\omega), \phi \rangle = \langle X, \Phi(\omega) \rangle,$$

with $\Phi(\omega)$ the Fourier transform of ϕ. Applying the definition to Dirac delta distribution (see equations (4.13) and (4.15)) we obtain:

$$\langle \delta(\omega), \phi \rangle = \langle \delta, \Phi(\omega) \rangle = \Phi(\omega = 0) = \int_{-\infty}^{\infty} \phi(t)dt = \langle 1, \phi \rangle \qquad (4.16)$$

so that, by identification, $\delta(\omega) = 1$. For the pulse $\delta(t - T_0)$ shifted by T_0:

$$\delta_{T_0}(\omega) = e^{-j\omega T_0}. \qquad (4.17)$$

We can directly verify these results, by writing

$$\delta(\omega) = \int_{-\infty}^{\infty} \delta(t)e^{-j\omega t}dt = e^0 \int_{-\infty}^{\infty} \delta(t)dt = 1,$$

the Dirac pulse being defined only at $t = 0$. Then we proceed in the same way at T_0:

$$\delta_{T_0}(\omega) = \int_{-\infty}^{\infty} \delta(t - T_0)e^{-j\omega t}dt = \int_{-\infty}^{\infty} \delta(u)e^{-j\omega(u+T_0)}du$$

$$= e^{-j\omega T_0}\delta(\omega) = e^{-j\omega T_0},$$

where we have written $u = t - T_0$.

An important case that we will encounter in the study of sampling is the Dirac distributions series regularly shifted by T_e (the "Dirac comb"), and denoted as:

$$s(t) = \sum_{n=-\infty}^{\infty} \delta(t - nT_e). \qquad (4.18)$$

From the definition of the Dirac delta function given above, this series is a distribution of unit masses at abscissas nT_e. Its Fourier transform is thus a series (see (4.17)):

$$S(\omega) = \sum_{n=-\infty}^{\infty} e^{-j\omega n T_e}, \qquad (4.19)$$

and also:

$$S(\omega) = \frac{1}{T_e} \sum_{n=-\infty}^{\infty} \delta(\omega - n\omega_e).$$

We can verify this result by returning to the sequence of rectangular pulses displayed on Figure 4.4, where we take $T = T_e$, and making θ tend to zero in expression (4.7), normalized with $A = 1/2\theta$.

It follows:

$$s(t) = \lim_{\theta \to 0} x(t) = \lim_{\theta \to 0} \frac{1}{T_e} \sum_{n=-\infty}^{\infty} \frac{\sin n\omega_e\theta}{n\omega_e\theta} e^{jn\omega_e t} = \frac{1}{T_e} \sum_{n=-\infty}^{\infty} e^{jn\omega_e t}$$

and thus:

$$\sum_n S_{n\omega_e}(\omega) = \sum_n \frac{1}{T_e} \int_{-\infty}^{\infty} \frac{1}{T_e} e^{-j(\omega - n\omega_e)t} dt = \sum_n \frac{1}{T_e} \delta(\omega - n\omega_e).$$

This is an important result: the Fourier transform of the time distribution having an unit mass at points of abscissas nT_e is a frequency distribution having masses $1/T_e$ at abscissas n/T_e.

Convolution with a Dirac pulse. Convoluting a function $X(\omega)$ with a Dirac delta distribution shifted by ω_e corresponds to a translation of ω_e:

$$X(\omega) \otimes \delta(\omega - \omega_e) = X(\omega - \omega_e). \tag{4.20}$$

Indeed, the convolution product of two functions δ and X is written as $\int_{-\infty}^{\infty} \delta(v) \times X(\omega - v)dv$, which (by definition of the Dirac delta function) is the value $X(\omega)$ of the function at ω (i.e. for $v = 0$). The value at $v = \omega_e$ is thus obtained by a shifted Dirac delta function, that is: $\int_{-\infty}^{\infty} \delta(v - \omega_e)X(\omega - v)dv = X(\omega - \omega_e)$.

We will return to this result with the product of functions when introducing modulation.

4.3.4. *Properties of Fourier transforms*

We have already presented numerous properties of this type of operation, when introducing the Laplace transform in Chapter 1 (integration, differentiation, convolution). Here we develop the properties useful for signal processing.

4.3.4.1. *Time and frequency shifts*

Let us apply a delay τ to $x(t)$. The Fourier transform of the shifted function $x_\tau = x(t - \tau)$ is:

$$X_\tau(\omega) = e^{-j\omega\tau} X(\omega). \tag{4.21}$$

Indeed:

$$X_\tau(\omega) = \int_{-\infty}^{\infty} x(t - \tau)e^{-j\omega t} dt, \text{ and taking } u = t - \tau$$

$$X_\tau(\omega) = e^{-j\omega\tau} \int_{-\infty}^{\infty} x(u)e^{-j\omega(u+\tau)} du = e^{-j\omega\tau} X(\omega).$$

A translation in the time domain corresponds with a *phase shift* in the frequency domain.

4.3.4.2. *Convolution product and filtering*

Let $y(t)$ be the convolution product of two functions $x(t)$ and $h(t)$,

$$y(t) = \int_{-\infty}^{\infty} x(\tau)h(t-\tau)d\tau, \quad \text{denoted as } y(t) = x(t) \otimes h(t). \tag{4.22}$$

Its Fourier transform is $Y(\omega) = X(\omega)H(\omega)$, this operation being symbolically represented as:

$$y(t) = x(t) \otimes h(t) \longrightarrow Y(\omega) = X(\omega)H(\omega). \tag{4.23}$$

The Fourier transform of the convolution product of two functions is the product of the Fourier transforms of each function.

Indeed:

$$Y(\omega) = \int_{-\infty}^{\infty} \left(\int_{-\infty}^{\infty} x(\tau)h(t-\tau) \right) e^{-j\omega t} dt.$$

Taking as previously $u = t - \tau$, we obtain:

$$Y(\omega) = \int_{-\infty}^{\infty} x(\tau)e^{-j\omega\tau}d\tau \left(\int_{-\infty}^{\infty} h(u)e^{-j\omega u}du \right)$$

$$= \left(\int_{-\infty}^{\infty} x(\tau)e^{-j\omega\tau}d\tau \right) \left(\int_{-\infty}^{\infty} h(u)e^{-j\omega u}du \right),$$

that is,

$$Y(\omega) = X(\omega)H(\omega).$$

We realize the importance of this result, remembering that the output signal of a time-invariant linear system with $h(t)$ as impulse response, and to which $x(t)$ is applied, is given by the convolution product $y(t) = h(t) \otimes x(t)$. We have also seen that filtering operations provide an example of convolution. We will see in future sections that filtering operations and filter design are easily accomplished thanks to the Fourier transform and its product form. We then make use of the term *transfer function* to refer to $H(\omega)$, the Fourier transform of the system's impulse response.

4.3.4.3. *Product of functions and transform convolution*

This is in fact the reciprocal of the previous result.

$$x(t)h(t) \longrightarrow \frac{1}{2\pi}X(\omega) \otimes H(\omega). \tag{4.24}$$

The transform of a product of functions is the convolution product of their respective transforms.

Indeed, let us start from the convolution product in the frequency domain:

$$Y(\omega) = X(\omega) \otimes H(\omega) = \int_{-\infty}^{\infty} X(\nu)H(\omega - \nu)d\nu.$$

By the definition of the Fourier transform,

$$H(\omega - \nu) = \int_{-\infty}^{\infty} h(t)e^{-j(\omega-\nu)t}dt,$$

and thus

$$Y(\omega) = \int \int h(t)e^{-j\omega t}dt X(\nu)e^{j\nu t}d\nu.$$

Now the definition of the inverse Fourier transform tells us that:

$$x(t) = \frac{1}{2\pi} \int_{-\infty}^{\infty} X(\nu)e^{+j\nu t}d\nu,$$

and thus

$$Y(\omega) = 2\pi \int_{-\infty}^{\infty} h(t)x(t)e^{-j\omega t}dt,$$

where the Fourier transform appears as the product of the two functions, with an additional coefficient 2π.

4.3.4.4. *Product of functions and modulation*

We address here the specific and important case where a signal is multiplied by a sinusoidal waveform (thus expressed as a function of $e^{j\omega t}$).

We take the following product: $y(t) = x(t)e^{j\omega_0 t}$. Its Fourier transform is:

$$X_{\omega_0}(\omega) = X(\omega - \omega_0), \qquad (4.25)$$

since in fact:

$$X_{\omega_0}(\omega) = \int_{-\infty}^{\infty} x(t)e^{j\omega_0 t}e^{-j\omega t}dt = \int_{-\infty}^{\infty} x(t)e^{-j(\omega-\omega_0)t}dt.$$

This result is immediately applicable to the case of modulation. For instance, consider the linear amplitude modulation of a signal, which performs the product of a high frequency signal – the carrier – and of the information signal: the carrier is said to have been modulated by the information signal.

(We will see later on that sampling a signal can be interpreted as a special application of modulation.)

Let us focus on the typical example of amplitude modulation with a carrier. Assume that the signal to be modulated is given by

$$x_m(t) = M \cos \omega_m t.$$

It is modulated by a signal of much higher frequency

$$x_p(t) = P \cos \omega_p t.$$

The operation is realized through an addition (since the carrier signal is included in the resulting modulated signal) and a product. We obtain:

$$y(t) = x_p(t) + k x_p(t) x_m(t) = P \cos \omega_p t + mP \cos \omega_m t \cos \omega_p t,$$

where $m = kM$ is the *modulation index* (sometimes referred to as modulation depth). We simplify notations here by making $k = 1$.

We can write $\cos \omega_p t = \frac{1}{2}(e^{j\omega_p t} + e^{-j\omega_p t})$. Thus, by applying (4.25), the Fourier transform of $y(t)$ is:

$$Y(\omega) = X_p(\omega_p) + \frac{1}{2}MX_p(\omega_m + \omega_p) + \frac{1}{2}MX_p(\omega_m - \omega_p). \qquad (4.26)$$

In the frequency domain, the modulated signal in this example is thus the sum of three sine signals.

The original function is:

$$y(t) = P \cos \omega_p t + \frac{1}{2}PM \cos (\omega_m + \omega_p)t + \frac{1}{2}PM \cos (\omega_m - \omega_p)t. \qquad (4.27)$$

This result should also be obtained directly by applying Euler formulae:

$$\cos \omega_p t \cos \omega_m t = \frac{1}{2} \cos (\omega_m + \omega_p)t + \frac{1}{2} \cos (\omega_m - \omega_p)t.$$

The frequency spectrum is as shown in Figure 4.8.

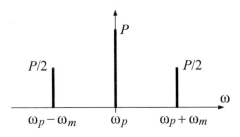

Figure 4.8. *Spectrum of the modulated signal*

To retrieve the initial components, the reverse operation of *demodulation* is performed (this is still a product of the modulated signal by a sine wave at the carrier frequency), and the useless frequencies are eliminated by low-pass filtering. In our example, we perform a product $y_0(t) = y(t)P_0 \cos(\omega_p t)$ – the reader may verify that it results in a signal with 5 components:

$$y_0(t) = \frac{P_0 P}{2}\left[1 + M\cos(\omega_m t) + \cos(2\omega_p t)\right.$$

$$\left. + \frac{1}{2}M\cos(2\omega_p + \omega_m)t + \cos(2\omega_p - \omega_m)t\right].$$

A pass-band filter allows us to retrieve ω_m only (see section 4.8).

Frequency modulation. Frequency modulation is another major modulation technique, having the appealing property of making the signal nearly impervious to additive noise, which affects amplitudes but not frequencies. The same principle holds, modifying the initial signal by another wave, which is formulated as:

$$y(t) = P\cos(\omega_p t + m\sin\omega_m t),$$

where again P is the amplitude and m the modulation index, but here only the frequency is subject to variation. Applying Euler formulae, we obtain:

$$y(t) = P\cos(\omega_p t)\cos(m\sin\omega_m t) - P\sin(\omega_p t)\sin(m\sin\omega_m t).$$

Now the Fourier expansions give:

$$\cos m\sin\omega_m t = J_0(m) + 2\sum_{n=1}^{\infty} J_{2n}(m)\cos 2n\omega_m t$$

and

$$\sin m\sin\omega_m t = 2\sum_{n=0}^{\infty} J_{2n+1}(m)\sin(2n+1)\omega_m t,$$

where we introduce the Bessel function of the first kind $J_n(m)$:

$$J_n(m) = \sum_{k=0}^{\infty} \frac{(-1)^k (m/2)^{n+2k}}{k!(n+k)!}.$$

Finally we obtain:

$$\frac{y(t)}{P} = J_0(m)\cos\omega_p t$$

$$- J_1(m)\left[\cos(\omega_p - \omega_m)t - \cos(\omega_p + \omega_m)t\right]$$

$$+ J_2(m)\left[\cos(\omega_p + 2\omega_m)t + \cos(\omega_p - 2\omega_m)t\right]$$

$$- J_3(m)\left[\cos(\omega_p - 3\omega_m)t - \cos(\omega_p + 3\omega_m)t\right] + \cdots$$

As previously, we find a spectrum centered on the carrier frequency, but with sidebands $\omega_p \pm n\omega_m$.

4.3.4.5. Energy conservation and Parseval's theorem

The energy of a signal is the quantity

$$E\left(|x|^2\right) = \int_{-\infty}^{\infty} |x(t)|^2 dt = \int_{-\infty}^{\infty} x(t)\overline{x(t)} dt \qquad (4.28)$$

where $\overline{x(t)}$ stands for the complex conjugate of $x(t)$.

The Fourier transform of $x(t)$ being denoted as $X(\omega)$, we have:

$$x(t) = \frac{1}{2\pi} \int_{-\infty}^{\infty} X(\omega)e^{+j\omega,t} d\omega$$

and so:

$$
\begin{aligned}
E\left(|x|^2\right) &= \int_{-\infty}^{\infty} \left[\frac{1}{2\pi} \int_{-\infty}^{\infty} X(\omega)e^{j\omega t} d\omega\right] \overline{x(t)} dt \\
&= \frac{1}{2\pi} \int_{-\infty}^{\infty} X(\omega) \left[\int_{-\infty}^{\infty} \overline{x(t)}e^{j\omega t} dt\right] d\omega \\
&= \frac{1}{2\pi} \int_{-\infty}^{\infty} X(\omega) \left[\overline{\int_{-\infty}^{\infty} x(t)e^{-j\omega t} dt}\right] d\omega \qquad (4.29) \\
&= \frac{1}{2\pi} \int_{-\infty}^{\infty} X(\omega)\overline{X(\omega)} d\omega \\
&= \frac{1}{2\pi} \int_{-\infty}^{\infty} |X(\omega)|^2 d\omega.
\end{aligned}
$$

Thus, Parseval's theorem can be written as:

$$E\left(|x|^2\right) = \int_{-\infty}^{\infty} |x(t)|^2 dt = \frac{1}{2\pi} \int_{-\infty}^{\infty} |X(\omega)|^2 d\omega. \qquad (4.30)$$

The energy of the signal has the same expression (except for a constant) in the time domain and in the spectral (frequency) domain. In other words, the power of the signal is equal to the power of its spectrum.

This result serves as a basis for spectral analysis, as we will see later (section 4.9.5).

4.4. Sampling

Sampling is a preliminary function mandatory to digital processing of signals in general, since the information we seek to manipulate must be in the form of a discrete sequence of finite values.

4.4.1. Sampling function

Sampling a signal consists of representing the continuous-time wave $x(t)$ with the values it takes at discrete instants, usually regularly spaced nT_e, and distributed as multiples of the sampling interval $T_e = 2\pi/w_e$.

Formally, the operation is described at each of the instants $t = 0, T_e, 2T_e, \ldots, nT_e$ by means of the Dirac delta function:

$$x(0) = \int_{-\infty}^{\infty} x(t)\delta(t)\mathrm{d}t, \quad \text{and} \quad x(nT_e) = \int_{-\infty}^{\infty} x(t)\delta(t - nT_e)\mathrm{d}t. \tag{4.31}$$

The sampled signal $y(t)$ can thus be viewed as a *series of Dirac pulses modulated in amplitude by the original signal* (we should obviously realize that the sampled signal is only defined at sampling epochs. This is by no means a step function). We then write:

$$y(t) = \sum_{-\infty}^{\infty} x(nT_e)\delta(t - nT_e) = x(t)\sum_{-\infty}^{\infty} \delta(t - nT_e) = x(t)s(t). \tag{4.32}$$

The distribution $s(t)$ is a *Dirac comb*, i.e. a sum of regularly spaced Dirac impulses, and the modulation is performed through the product of the function $x(t)$ by the series of pulses. Now we know that a product of functions in the time domain corresponds to a convolution in the frequency domain. Thus, by using equation (4.24):

$$Y(\omega) = \frac{1}{2\pi}X(\omega) \otimes S(\omega).$$

As we have seen in equation (4.19), $S(\omega)$ is a comb, too:

$$S(\omega) = \frac{1}{T_e}\sum_{n=-\infty}^{\infty} \delta(\omega - w_e).$$

Now, equation (4.20) tells us that the convolution with a Dirac pulse shifted by nw_e produces a translation by nw_e, and thus the sampled signal has the spectrum:

$$Y(\omega) = \frac{1}{T_e}\sum_{n=-\infty}^{\infty} X(\omega - nw_e). \tag{4.33}$$

The effect of sampling is to introduce a periodicity in the frequency space: the Fourier transform of the sampled signal is a periodic function of frequency (pulsation) w_e.

This result leads to several comments especially regarding the sampling theorem (due to Nyquist and Shannon).

4.4.2. *Shannon sampling theorem*

This sampling theorem explains the conditions under which a series of samples correctly represents the original signal, i.e. it allows us to restore this signal entirely. The previous result shows that sampling introduces a periodicity – and thus a replication – in the spectrum (see Figure 4.9), which we must eliminate to rebuild the signal. This will be performed (theoretically) by an ideal low-pass filter with a rectangular transfer function, such as that represented in Figure 4.10. Its impulse response, discussed in section 4.3.2, is obtained from its inverse Fourier transform:

$$h(t) = \frac{1}{2\pi} \int_{-\infty}^{\infty} H(\omega)e^{+j\omega t} d\omega = \frac{1}{2\pi} \int_{-w_e/2}^{w_e/2} \frac{2\pi}{w_e} e^{+j\omega t} d\omega = \frac{\sin w_e t/2}{w_e t/2}. \quad (4.34)$$

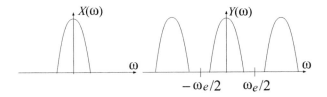

Figure 4.9. *Effect of sampling on the spectrum*

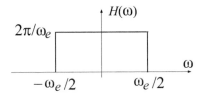

Figure 4.10. *Low-pass filter to rebuild a signal after sampling*

The signal $x_f(t)$ at the filter output is given by the convolution product of $y(t)$ and $h(t)$, as we have seen in section 4.2:

$$x_f(t) = \int_{\tau=-\infty}^{\infty} \sum_{n=-\infty}^{\infty} \left[x(\tau)\delta(\tau - nT_e) \right] \frac{\sin \pi(t-\tau)/T_e}{\pi(t-\tau)/T_e} d\tau,$$

i.e.

$$x_f(t) = \sum_{n=-\infty}^{\infty} x(nT_e) \cdot \frac{\sin \pi (t - nT_e)/T_e}{\pi (t - nT_e)/T_e}. \tag{4.35}$$

This relation allows us to re-evaluate the signal at the filter output for all instants between samples (right side of each sample), leaving the sample values unchanged (indeed the function is $x(nT_e)$ at the abscissa nT_e).

From these comments, it is clear that these operations restore the original signal only if it does not contain frequency components higher than $w_e/2$. Otherwise, the repeated spectra overlap, just as in Figure 4.11, giving rise to *aliasing*, and the restored signal will differ from the original one.

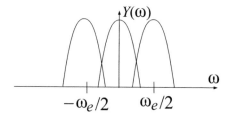

Figure 4.11. *Aliasing, due to a too slow sampling rate*

It can be stated in the form of the sampling (or Nyquist-Shannon) theorem: *a signal with frequency components strictly less than some value w_m can be entirely restituted provided that the sampling rate is at least $2w_m$.*

Note that, in practical cases, if the spectrum of the original signal spreads beyond the limit of half the sampling rate (which may be imposed), it can be limited by a preliminary pre-sampling (or anti-aliasing) low-pass filter.

Note also that the theorem expresses a sufficient but not always necessary condition for correctly restoring the signal. The minimum sampling frequency needed is known as the Nyquist frequency.

4.5. Quantization and coding

We now address issues related to the approximation of the original signal, in the *digitization* operation (which includes sampling). More precisely, we consider the following representation of the precision-limit problem, imposed by the finite number of values representing the initial signal related to the limited size of the words in which the values are coded.

4.5.1. *Quantization noise*

Quantization, naturally associated with the sampling operation, consists of representing each sample by a finite set of discrete values, each value being encoded into a binary number assumed to be b bits long. Thus, samples are represented by a set of intervals. Representing a continuous signal by a finite set of values raises several issues, including the effect of *rounding* on the precision, and optimum matching between the available intervals and the actual function shape to represent.

Indeed, let us consider a discrete-time signal $x(n)$ (actually, the sampled signal), taking values in an interval $[-A, +A]$. Defining a (scalar) quantizer with a resolution of b bits per sample consists of performing the following steps:

– Partition the interval $[-A, +A]$ into $L = 2^b$ distinct sub-intervals (possibly of different lengths).

– Attach to each of these intervals a value encoded on b bits, denoted as $\widehat{x}_1, \ldots, \widehat{x}_L$.

– Associate $x(n)$ with a value $\widehat{x}_n$ chosen among the possible values $\widehat{x}_1, \ldots, \widehat{x}_L$.

The procedure entails an unavoidable quantization error, which is denoted as $e_q(n) = x(n) - \widehat{x}_n$, and which is estimated, e.g. by $\sigma_q^2 = E[X(n) - \widehat{x}_n]^2$, that is the *mean square error* or the *error signal power*, $x(n)$ being assumed to represent the realization of the random process $X(n)$. Finding the optimal quantization thus consists of determining the partition and its representatives $\widehat{x}_1, \ldots, \widehat{x}_L$, so as to minimize σ_q^2.

We will not develop these techniques in more depth, so the reader is prompted to refer to specialized textbooks [SHE 95, MOR 97]. We present here only the main aspects of this topic.

The quantization operation is illustrated by Figure 4.12. The signal goes through a step function, the quantization step size q being possibly variable. When the quantization step size is constant, as represented in Figure 4.12, we speak of uniform quantization.

Rounding effects are a consequence of this operation. Their importance depends on the compared positioning of the step function and the signal. When the quantization step q is small enough, as compared with the signal variations, we can assume a uniformly distributed error in the interval $]-q/2, q/2[$, meaning that the error probability is constant within the interval. This is the *high resolution* assumption.

We can show that in this case the best representative is the average value in the interval (as in Figure 4.12). Any signal value between $(n - 1/2)q$ and $(n + 1/2)q$ is rounded to nq. The quantization error remains in the interval $[-q/2, q/2]$, and the error signal $e(t)$ corresponds to a segment, as shown in Figure 4.13.

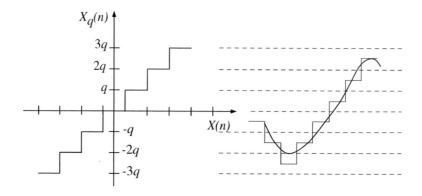

Figure 4.12. *Step function for signal quantization*

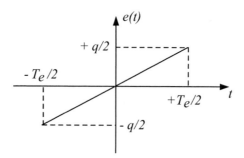

Figure 4.13. *The elementary error signal*

Its power, expressed by its variance, measures the degradation incurred by the signal:

$$\sigma_q^2 = \int_{-T_e/2}^{T_e/2} e^2(t) \frac{dt}{T_e} = \frac{1}{T_e} \int_{-T_e/2}^{T_e/2} \left(\frac{qt}{T_e}\right)^2 dt = \frac{q^2}{(T_e)^3} \int_{-T_e/2}^{T_e/2} t^2 dt = \frac{q^2}{12}. \quad (4.36)$$

In general, where L possible intervals have different lengths q_i, the mean square error is given by $\sigma_q^2 = \sum_{i=1}^{L} p(i) \frac{q_i^2}{12}$, where $p(i)$ is the probability that $X(n)$ belongs to interval i. We can prove, in accordance with our intuition, that the mean square error is minimized when choosing the smallest intervals for the areas with the highest probability of containing a signal value. In the case of uniform quantization (which is the optimal choice for a uniformly distributed source) we evidently obtain $\sigma_q^2 = \frac{q_i^2}{12} = \frac{A^2}{3} 2^{-2b}$. For a Gaussian source with variance (power) σ_X^2, we obtain $\sigma_q^2 = \frac{\sqrt{3}}{2} \pi \sigma_X^2 2^{-2b}$.

Finally, we can mention the technique of vector quantization, which consists of a single vector $\hat{x}(n)$ representing several samples of $X(n)$ simultaneously. This is especially useful in cases where resolution is low, but also when we intend to take account of correlations between successive signal values, or even between the parameters characterizing a signal (for instance, the spectrum coefficients). We do not detail these techniques, which lead to specific numerical procedures. However, we will develop a similar approach within the framework of information and coding theory, where they find their full justification.

4.5.2. Coding power

Representing initial data by a finite size binary number inevitably entails a certain level of inaccuracy. For instance, telephony uses an 8-bit fixed point encoding (the *PCM coding scheme*), leading to a maximum accuracy of 2^{-8}, while direct image coding generally also uses 8-bit encoding (i.e. 3×8 bits for each color pixel). With numbers b bits long, and q being the quantization step, we can at most distinguish between 2^b values, within the range $[q, 2^b q]$. Any amplitude larger than $2^b q$ is clipped. We define the *peak power* of the coder as the power of the maximum admissible unclipped sine wave amplitude. We then have:

$$P_{\text{peak}} = \frac{1}{2}\left[\frac{2^b q}{2}\right]^2 = 2^{2b-3} q^2. \tag{4.37}$$

Indeed, with the same notations as above, this signal has an amplitude between $-A$ and $+A = 2^b q/2$, and so its power is:

$$\frac{1}{T}\int_0^T (A\sin\omega t)^2 dt = \frac{1}{2}\left[\frac{2^b q}{2}\right]^2.$$

We can then define the *dynamic range* of coding as the signal-to-noise ratio (SNR), i.e. the ratio of peak power to quantization noise, for the sine wave with uniform coding. This gives:

$$P_{\text{peak}}/B = 2^{2b-3}/12 = 3/2.2^b, \quad \text{which gives in decibels} \quad \left(10 \cdot \log_{10} x\right)$$

$$P_{\text{peak}}/B = 6.02\, b + 1.76\, dB.$$

The formula links the code size (in number of bits) to the amplitude range we can encode without any clipping (or with a negligible clipping probability: for random signals we define a similar quantity depending on the amplitude statistics, the clipping level then being defined by reference to a negligible probability of being exceeded).

Finally, we can point out that the two representations of binary numbers are currently used: fixed-point representation for digitizing initial values, then floating-point representation to perform the following numerical computation with the expected accuracy (these techniques are developed within the framework of information and coding theory; see Chapter 5). Note that real-time computing in DSPs most often uses fixed-point representation.

4.6. Discrete LTI system

This is the same concept as for the continuous case, except with discrete signals. A discrete LTI system converts a data sequence $x(n)$ into another sequence $y(n)$. Just as for the continuous case with the Dirac delta function, we define the system's impulse response by the sequence $h(n)$, which is the output response to the *unit sample sequence* $u_0(n)$ such that:

$$u_0(n) = 1 \quad \text{for } n = 0,$$

$$u_0(n) = 0 \quad \text{for } n \neq 0.$$

For the unit sample sequence, often also called discrete time impulse or simply unit pulse, time-shifted by m, $u_0(n - m)$, the system issues $h(n - m)$ due to the time-invariance property.

Just as for the Dirac delta function in the continuous case, any sequence $x(n)$ can be decomposed into a sum of shifted unit pulses $x(n) = \sum_{m=-\infty}^{\infty} x(m)u_0(n - m)$, and thanks to linearity we obtain:

$$y(n) = \sum_{m=-\infty}^{\infty} x(m)h(n - m). \tag{4.38}$$

This is once again the fundamental convolution operation, and the system is fully characterized by its impulse response.

4.7. Transforms for digital signal processing

We introduce here the transforms which are specific to digital signal processing. As we have seen with Fourier transforms, they allow us to move from the time domain to the frequency domain in the case of sampled signals. We begin with the z-transform, then we introduce the Fourier transform of a discrete signal, then the discrete Fourier transform with the special case of cosine transform, and we end with the fast Fourier transform.

4.7.1. *The z-transform*

Several aspects of this transform have already been presented in Chapter 1. We now present it in the more general context of digital signal processing.

The z-transform is analogous to the Laplace transform. However, it is particularly well suited to the study of numerical series, such as time series formed by signal samples. It will be the specific reference tool for the study of discrete LTI systems we have just introduced.

4.7.1.1. *Definition*

Given a series $x(n)$, its *bilateral* (or two-sided) *z-transform* $X(z)$ is defined as:

$$X(z) = \sum_{n=-\infty}^{\infty} x(n)z^{-n}, \tag{4.39}$$

where z is a complex variable. $X(z)$ is generally defined only for certain values of z, such that the series is convergent: the domain of convergence is generally a ring centered on the origin, of radii r_1 and r_2, such that

$$r_1 < |z| < r_2.$$

If $x(n)$ is *anti-causal*, that is zero for $n = 0$ and for positive ns, then $r_1 = 0$. If $x(n)$ is *causal* (that is, zero for negative values of n), r_2 is infinite: this is the general case for most actual signals.

Taking causality into account leads us to introduce the *unilateral* (or one-sided) z-transform, which is written as:

$$X(z) = \sum_{n=0}^{\infty} x(n)z^{-n}. \tag{4.40}$$

Apart from a few peculiarities concerning time-shifts, as we now see, the one-sided and two-sided transforms enjoy the same properties, which we now present in the context of signal analysis.

4.7.1.2. *Time translation*

Moving a signal forward by n_0 samples corresponds to multiplying $X(z)$ by z^{n_0}, and similarly delaying by n_0 amounts to multiplying $X(z)$ by z^{-n_0}.

$$X_{n_0}(z) = z^{-n_0}X(z). \tag{4.41}$$

Indeed, let us denote as $x_{n_0}(n) = x(n - n_0)$ the version of $x(n)$ delayed by n_0. We then have, with $m = n - n_0$:

$$X_{n_0}(z) = \sum_{n=-\infty}^{\infty} x_{n_0}(n)z^{-n} = \sum_{n=-\infty}^{\infty} x(n - n_0)z^{-n} =$$

$$= \sum_{m=-\infty}^{\infty} x(m)z^{-(m+n_0)} = z^{-n_0}X(z).$$

This property will be used for instance in filter modeling. We should note that a causal signal of finite duration N is represented by a polynomial in z^{-1} of degree N.

For the one-sided transform the translation is expressed as:

$$X_{n_0}(z) = \sum_{n=0}^{\infty} x(n-n_0)z^{-n} = z^{-n_0}X(z) + \sum_{n=-n_0}^{-1} x(n)z^{-(n+n_0)}.$$

So, the initial conditions for the signal are taken into account, thus allowing us to study the transient behavior of the systems to which it is submitted. Moreover, we derive the limiting signal values: for the initial value $x(0) = \lim_{|z|\to\infty} X(z)$, and for the stationary state $x(\infty) = \lim_{z\to 1}(z-1)X(z)$.

4.7.1.3. *Discrete convolution*

We have already seen that convolution is a basic operation for signal processing, which characterizes LTI systems used in filtering. The z-transform allows us to extend it to discrete signals. Let us denote as $y(n)$ the sequence at the output of a discrete linear system, obtained by convoluting the series $x(n)$ and $h(n)$, as we have seen previously. We have

$$y(n) = x(n) \otimes h(n) \longrightarrow Y(z) = X(z)H(z). \qquad (4.42)$$

Indeed by definition:

$$y(n) = \sum_{m=-\infty}^{\infty} x(m)h(n-m),$$

or, by way of a commutativity property:

$$y(n) = \sum_{m=-\infty}^{\infty} x(n-m)h(m).$$

Its transform is thus:

$$Y(z) = \sum_{n=-\infty}^{\infty} \left[\sum_{m=-\infty}^{\infty} x(m)h(n-m) \right] z^{-n}$$

which we can write as:

$$Y(z) = \sum_{n=-\infty}^{\infty} \left[\sum_{m=-\infty}^{\infty} x(m)h(n-m)z^{-m}z^{m} \right] z^{-n}$$

$$= \sum_{m=-\infty}^{\infty} x(m)z^{-m} \left[\sum_{n=-\infty}^{\infty} h(n-m)z^{-(n-m)} \right].$$

or,

$$Y(z) = X(z)H(z).$$

We find this important result, already encountered in Chapter 1, and with the Fourier transform: *the transform of a convolution of two functions is the product of their transforms.*

Moreover, we deduce the expression of $H(z)$, of prime interest in filter design:

$$H(z) = \frac{Y(z)}{X(z)}. \tag{4.43}$$

$H(z)$ being the *transfer function* of the LTI system.

4.7.1.4. *Inversion*

Calculating the inverse transform returns us to the time domain. Such an operation is needed, as we will see later, to design a filter (we speak of filter synthesis), and also to analyze the characteristics of a signal in the time domain (after its modulation or filtering, for example).

From a mathematical standpoint, we again encounter the typical problem of the complex plane with the inverse z-transform (determining poles, computing residues, etc.). The reader is prompted to refer to Chapter 1, where these topics have been treated. The inverse z-transform is written:

$$x(n) = \frac{1}{2j\pi} \oint_C X(z) z^{n-1} \mathrm{d}z, \tag{4.44}$$

where C is a closed contour in the complex plane, containing the origin and all the singular points, or poles, of $X(z)$. We have seen in Chapter 1 how to perform the integration of this kind of *Cauchy integral* by applying the residues theorem (see formula (1.78)):

$$\frac{1}{2j\pi} \oint_C f(z) \mathrm{d}z = \sum R_i, \tag{4.45}$$

where R_i is the *residue* of $f(z)$. Most often the expressions for the z-transforms encountered in signal theory are rational fractions of the variable z, so that $X(z)$ has the form:

$$X(z) = \frac{P(z)}{Q(z)}.$$

The *poles* are the denominator roots, and the *zeros* the numerator roots.

z_i being a pole of order q, the residue at that pole is the coefficient of $(z - z_i)^{q-1}$ in the Taylor expansion of $\Psi(z) = (z - z_i)^q X(z) z^{n-1}$, i.e.:

$$R_i^q = \frac{1}{(q-1)!} \cdot \frac{\mathrm{d}^{q-1}}{\mathrm{d}z^{q-1}} \left[X(z) z^{n-1} (z - z_i)^q \right].$$

For single poles ($q = 1$), it is possible to write the transforms in the form of a partial fraction decomposition. The transform is then written as a sum of fractions having denominators of degree one (for functions with real coefficients) or two (functions with complex coefficients). Then we have:

$$X(z) = \frac{P(z)}{Q(z)} = \sum_{i=1}^{N} \frac{R_i}{z - z_i}, \qquad (4.46)$$

with

$$R = \lim_{z \to z_i} \frac{(z - z_i)P(z)}{Q(z)} = \left[\frac{P(z)}{Q'(z)}\right]_{z=z_i}.$$

(see Chapter 1, section 1.6.1.4). It is then an easy task to retrieve the original. Actually most often the original will be obtained by means of tables (see the Appendix). If we consider for instance the function $X(z) = \sum_{i=1}^{N} A_i/(1 - a_i z^{-1})$, we obtain (see the Appendix, or Chapter 1 and formula (1.92)): $x(n) = \sum_{i=1}^{N} A_i a_i^n$ for $n \geq 0$, $x(n) = 0$ otherwise. The stability condition is clear: the series $x(n)$ is bounded if and only if $|a_i| < 1$, i.e. the poles are inside the unit circle.

4.7.2. Fourier transform of a discrete signal

The Fourier transform of a discrete signal is analogous to the continuous case. Its expression is usually given as:

$$X(\omega) = \sum_{n=-\infty}^{\infty} x(n)e^{-jn\omega}. \qquad (4.47)$$

This is in fact a special case of the z-transform. Indeed, starting from the definition of the z-transform, $X(z) = \sum x(n)z^{-n}$, if $x(n)$ is the sample sequence, with period T_e, of the signal being studied, and taking $z = e^{j\omega T_e}$ we again find the Fourier transform. In the following, and in order to simplify the expressions, we take T_e as equal to 1. We then find the above expression for the Fourier transform $X(\omega) = \sum x(n)e^{-jn\omega}$.

Thus, the Fourier transform of the sampled signal is a periodic function, with period $\omega_e = 2\pi/T_e$, and its value is given by the z-transform value on the circle of radius 1, linearly graduated with $z = e^{j\omega}$. This is represented in Figure 4.14.

As with the z-transform, the Fourier transform of the discrete signal exists only if the series is convergent. We again find the same conditions as previously.

Inverse transform. The definition of the Fourier transform makes it a periodic function with period ω_e that can be decomposed into a Fourier series. Its coefficients are

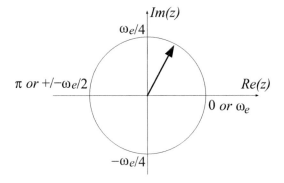

Figure 4.14. *Correspondance between Fourier and z-transforms*

obtained by the inverse transform, as in the previous sections.

$$x(n) = \frac{1}{2\pi} \int_{-\pi}^{\pi} X(\omega)e^{jn\omega} d\omega \qquad (4.48)$$

(as the function is periodic the integration occurs only in the main period, symmetric to the origin).

4.7.3. *Discrete Fourier transform*

Fourier transforms, as well as z-transforms, provide theoretical tools, which in turn require that formal expressions are provided for the signals and systems to be studied. Actual problems generally fail to fulfill this condition so consequently analytical tools are difficult to apply. Software tools and digital processing techniques allow us to overcome these problems. The discrete Fourier transform (DFT), with the attached software tools, is one of these basic tools.

4.7.3.1. *Definition*

In section 4.7.2 we defined the Fourier transform of a discrete signal:

$$X(\omega) = \sum_{n=-\infty}^{\infty} x(n)e^{-jn\omega},$$

and its inverse transform:

$$x(n) = \frac{1}{2\pi} \int_{-\pi}^{\pi} X(\omega)e^{jn\omega} d\omega.$$

Numerical evaluation of these expressions requires first that the summation is restricted to a finite number of samples N and also that the continuous variable ω is transformed into discrete values spaced by $\Delta\omega$. A simple solution is to consider the signal as periodic, with period N, and to make $\Delta\omega = \frac{\omega}{N} = \frac{2\pi}{N}$. This gives the following expression for the discrete Fourier transform:

$$X(k) = \sum_{n=0}^{N-1} x(n)e^{-2j\pi kn/N}. \tag{4.49}$$

This function is zero everywhere except for frequencies which are multiples of $2\pi/N$, and of period 2π. It gives the spectral value on the right of the pulsation $\omega_k = k\Delta\omega$.

The inverse transform is:

$$x(n) = \frac{1}{N}\sum_{k=0}^{N-1} X(k)e^{2j\pi kn/N}. \tag{4.50}$$

The validity of this expression is easy to verify:

$$x(m) = \frac{1}{N}\sum_{k=0}^{N-1} X(k)e^{2j\pi km/N} = \frac{1}{N}\sum_{k=0}^{N-1}\left[\sum_{n=0}^{N-1} x(n)e^{-2j\pi kn/N}\right]e^{2j\pi km/N}$$

$$= \frac{1}{N}\sum_{n=0}^{N-1} x(n)\sum_{k=0}^{N-1} e^{2j\pi k(m-n)/N}.$$

The last term makes use of the Nth *root of unity*, usually denoted as $w_N = e^{-2j\pi/N}$ and $w_N^k = e^{-2j\pi k/N}$. They verify the following properties:

- $w_N^{mN} = 1$;
- $w_N^{N/2} = -1$;
- $w_N^{m+N/2} = -w_N^m$;
- $w_N^2 = w_{N/2}$.

These properties are easy to verify on the unit circle, as in Figure 4.14, from which we also derive the orthogonal property:

- $\sum_{k=0}^{N-1} w_N^{kn} = N$ for $n = mN$, 0 otherwise.

Indeed, if $n = mN$ all the terms in the sum are equal to 1, while the sum is zero for the other values.

Given the orthogonal property, the last term of $x(m)$ is N if $n = m + iN$, so that finally:

$$x(m) = \sum_i x(m + iN). \tag{4.51}$$

The inverse transform returns us to the original sequence, but this is "periodicized" with period N. This is still a consequence of sampling, here performed on the signal spectrum. We will encounter this property again, as it will be applied in studying multirate filters.

4.7.3.2. *Properties*

DFT retains all the Fourier transform properties, as well as the z-transform, with however a few peculiarities related to the convolution product. We recall here the main properties.

Linearity. Let $x(n)$ and $y(n)$ be two periodic series with the same period N. The transform of their linear combination is also a linear combination of their transform:

$$u(n) = x(n) + \lambda y(n) \longrightarrow U(k) = X(k) + \lambda Y(k), \quad \text{with } \lambda \text{ a scalar.}$$

Translation. The DFT of $x_{n_0}(n) = x(n - n_0)$ is

$$X_{n_0}(k) = \sum_{n=0}^{N-1} x(n - n_0)e^{-jnk\Delta\omega} = X(k)e^{-jn_0 k\Delta\omega}. \tag{4.52}$$

Translating the signal by n_0 results in a phase shift of $n_0 k \Delta\omega$.

Circular convolution. The convolution product of two sequences of same period N is:

$$y(n) = \sum_{m=0}^{N-1} x(m)h(n - m). \tag{4.53}$$

This is a circular convolution: the index $n - m$ is calculated modulo N. This is also a series with period N. We obtain a result analogous to the Fourier transform:

$$Y(k) = H(k)X(k). \tag{4.54}$$

The discrete transform of the convolution product of two series is equal to the product of their transforms.

Indeed,

$$Y(k) = \sum_{n=0}^{N-1} \left[\sum_{m=0}^{N-1} x(m)h(n - m) \right] e^{-jnk\Delta\omega}$$

$$= \sum_{m=0}^{N-1} x(m) \left[\sum_{n=0}^{N-1} h(n - m)e^{-j(n-m)k\Delta\omega} \right] e^{-jmk\Delta\omega}$$

$$= \left(\sum_{m=0}^{N-1} x(m)e^{-jmk\Delta\omega} \right) \left(\sum_{n=0}^{N-1} h(n - m)e^{-j(n-m)k\Delta\omega} \right)$$

$$= X(k)H(k).$$

Periodicity and overlapping. By construction the discrete Fourier transform is a periodic function with period N, and so is its inverse transform.

If the initial signal $x(n)$ is of a non-periodic duration N, then its inverse transform yields an exact replica of it. For a periodic signal, the sum can obviously be limited to a single period. Note that the simple inspection of the transform cannot tell us whether the original signal is periodic or not.

If the initial signal has a duration larger than N, an overlap phenomenon occurs, similar to what we have already encountered for the sampling theorem. In the case of a signal of unlimited duration this leads us to limit it by way of a window of length N, the effect of which we will analyze in section 4.8.2.1 devoted to filters. At this point let us simply say that the duration limited by a window will generally provoke parasitic oscillations, and various techniques are then needed to attenuate their effect. The cosine transform we now present takes this problem into account by judiciously superimposing several shifted windows.

4.7.4. *Cosine transform*

The cosine transform is a special case of the Fourier transform. It is used in particular for audio and image encoding (MPEG and JPEG standards: DCT (discrete cosine transform)). We will see an example application in Chapter 5.

We are given a signal $x(n)$ with length N ($n = 0, 1, \ldots, N - 1$). Starting from the values of $x(n)$, we build a new signal $s(n)$, of length $4N$, with the following characteristics:

$$s(2n + 1) = s(-2n - 1) = x(n), \quad \text{and} \quad s(2n) = s(-2n) = 0.$$

This signal is symmetric, all its even rank values are zero, and it has only N distinct odd values.

Its DCT is, by definition, the DCT of $x(n)$:

$$X(k) = \frac{2}{N} c(k) \sum_{n=0}^{N-1} x(n) \cos\left[\pi k \frac{2n + 1}{2N}\right],\tag{4.55}$$

and the inverse transform:

$$x(n) = \frac{2}{N} \sum_{k=0}^{N-1} c(k) X(k) \cos\left[\pi k \frac{2n + 1}{2N}\right],\tag{4.56}$$

with $c(0) = 1/\sqrt{2}$ and $c(k) = 1$ for $k = 1, 2, \ldots, N - 1$.

4.7.5. *The fast Fourier transform (FFT)*

The algorithms known as FFT (standing for fast Fourier transform) have impacted considerably on the development of digital processing-based applications. Indeed, they offer a means to considerably reduce the complexity, by decomposing them into elementary problems. This approach, although generally associated with the names of J.W. Cooley and J.W. Tukey [COO 65], has been rediscovered time and again since the work of Gauss [GAU 66], and numerous FFT algorithms now exist, suited to various cases, such as N power of 2 or not, or a particular form of integer number. So, besides the Cooley-Tukey algorithm for powers of 2, we can quote Rader's algorithm, if N is prime, Good's algorithm when N decomposes in prime factors, Winograd's algorithm, which optimizes the number of products, etc. (see specialized papers, e.g. [DUH 90, KUN 93]). We here outline only the fundamental concepts, i.e. the decomposition into elementary transforms through the presentation of the Cooley-Tukey algorithm.

4.7.5.1. *Cooley-Tukey FFT algorithm*

Let us now use the notation $w_N^k = e^{-2\pi jk/N}$ (the Nth roots of unity) to express the Fourier transform (see (4.49)), we obtain:

$$X(k) = \sum_{n=0}^{N-1} x(n)w_N^{nk}, \tag{4.57}$$

which we can re-write, in matrix form:

$$X = W_N x, \tag{4.58}$$

where the vector $X = [X_0, \ldots, X_{N-1}]$ is the product of the vector $x = [x_0, \ldots, x_{N-1}]$ and the matrix W_N of elements w_N^{nk}, which represents N^2 products and $N^2 - N$ summations.

The idea behind the fast transform is to decompose the initial problem into auxiliary problems of reduced size, for instance using the prime factors of N, so that the sum of intermediate calculation costs remains smaller than the initial one. This can be achieved, thanks to the specific nature of the matrix W_N and its coefficients. Let us consider as an example a typical case where $N = 2^R$. The elementary operation consists of splitting into two transforms of order $N/2$. Separating even and odd indices, equation (4.58) can be written as:

$$X_k = \sum_{n=0}^{N/2-1} x_{2p}w_N^{2pk} + \sum_{n=0}^{N/2-1} x_{2p+1}w_N^{(2p+1)k}. \tag{4.59}$$

Now, $w_N^{2pk} = w_{N/2}^{pk}$ (see section 4.7.3.1) and so:

$$X_k = \sum_{n=0}^{N/2-1} x_{2p} w_{N/2}^{pk} + w_N^k \sum_{n=0}^{N/2-1} x_{2p+1} w_{N/2}^{pk}. \qquad (4.60)$$

This can be written as

$$X_k = Y_k + w_N^k Z_k \qquad (4.61)$$

where Y_k and Z_k are the discrete Fourier transforms of $y_p = x_{2p}$ and $z_p = x_{2p+1}$ respectively.

Moreover, we can observe that:

$$Y_{k+N/2} = Y_k, \quad Z_{k+N/2} = Z_k,$$

and also $w_N^{k+N/2} = -w_N^k$.

Relation (4.61) can thus be decomposed into two expressions:

$$X_k = Y_k + w_N^k Z_k \quad \text{for } 0 \le k \le N/2 - 1,$$

and

$$X_k = Y_k - w_N^k Z_k \quad \text{for } N/2 \le k \le N - 1. \qquad (4.62)$$

Finally we have replaced the calculation of a N-dimension discrete Fourier transform with two other calculations (Y and Z) with dimension $N/2$, and N additions. We can verify that the total number of operations is lower than for the direct calculation:

$$2\left(\frac{N}{2}\right)^2 + N < N^2.$$

(an exact comparison would take account of the different calculation costs of operations, as products are usually more time consuming than additions).

By iterations we end up with elementary transforms of order 2. The number of iterations is $\log_2(N/2)$ and the total number of operations is therefore $N/2 \log_2(N/2)$ products and $N \log_2(N/2)$ additions. This drastically reduces the complexity of the whole calculation when N is large.

4.8. Filter design and synthesis

We are now in a position to use all the mathematical apparatus presented up to now to undertake filter design – an operation referred to as *filter synthesis*.

4.8.1. *Definitions and principles*

Recall that a filter is basically a selective frequency function such that some frequency components of the signal are rejected and the others accepted. Figure 4.15 illustrates the most common types of filter: low-pass, band-pass, high-pass and band-stop (or band-rejection).

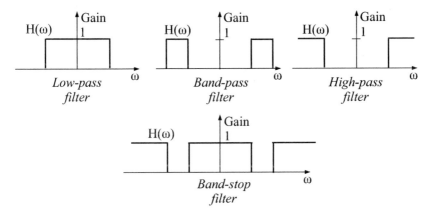

Figure 4.15. *Standard filters*

Digital signal processing has enabled us to greatly improve the design of linear filters, thanks to the use of computers, digital memories and programmable integrated circuits, performing the elementary additions and products at high speed.

4.8.1.1. *Principle*

Basically, a filter performs the discrete convolution of an input signal $x(n)$ with its impulse response $h(n)$, as has been presented above:

$$y(n) = \sum_{m=-\infty}^{\infty} x(m)h(n-m), \quad \text{or} \quad y(n) = \sum_{m=-\infty}^{\infty} h(m)x(n-m) \quad (4.63)$$

(practically the sum runs on a finite set, as we will see later).

Using the z-transform moves the problem to the frequency domain, and the previous relation becomes:

$$Y(z) = X(z)H(z), \quad \text{that is } H(z) = \frac{Y(z)}{X(z)}, \quad (4.64)$$

which, by using the conversion $z = e^{j\omega}$, returns us to the Fourier transform once again.

In order to filter out some of the frequency components of a signal, or to phase shift it, etc., it is simply a matter of determining the value of $H(z)$ for the result we are looking for, and then, in the time domain, to deduce the values of $h(n)$ which will be implemented for the actual realization of the filter.

This leads us to introduce two notions relative to physical filter realizations: causality and stability.

4.8.1.2. *Causality and stability*

A filter is said to be *causal* if its output $y(n)$ does not depend on future input $x(n + k)$ with $k > 0$: the effect does not precede the cause. The impulse response is therefore zero for $n < 0$.

$$h(n) = 0 \quad \text{for } n < 0. \tag{4.65}$$

This property is required for physical feasibility.

Concretely, causality problems typically arise when feedbacks from outputs to the inputs are introduced for filter realizations. It is also in these situations that we are confronted with stability issues.

A filter is said to be *stable* if, when a bounded input is applied, its output remains bounded. It can be shown that a necessary and sufficient condition for stability is that the impulse response verifies:

$$\sum_{n=-\infty}^{\infty} |h(n)| < B. \tag{4.66}$$

4.8.2. *Finite impulse response (FIR) filters*

FIR filters are systems with a finite length impulse response, meaning that the response to an impulse has a finite duration.

We have already encountered an example of an FIR system with the moving average filter. We have shown informally that its behavior is based on the convolution product of the input signal $x(n)$ by the filter response, $h(m) = 1/N$, giving the output signal $y(n)$.

From the results of the previous sections we are now in a position to describe the principle of the method for finding this function according to the targeted filter.

A FIR filter is defined by the following expression, which represents its output y resulting from a finite convolution with an input signal x:

$$y(n) = \sum_{m=0}^{N-1} h(m)x(n-m), \qquad (4.67)$$

where N is the filter length.

Following the classical methods of filter synthesis, we first determine the function $H(\omega)$, then, using the inverse discrete Fourier transform, we deduce $h(m)$. Filtering is realized by the convolution of the input signal $x(n)$ with $h(m)$.

Conventionally, the FIR filter is represented by a *block diagram* (functional diagram), as shown in Figure 4.16.

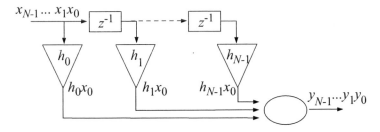

Figure 4.16. *Block diagram of a FIR filter*

Successive input samples $x_0, x_1, \ldots, x_{N-1}$ are convolved to give $y_0, y_1, \ldots,$ y_{N-1} at the output: the blocks represent the successive product operations followed by summation, the symbol z^{-1} conventionally representing the unit delay applied to a sample. In this way, we can illustrate the realization of a moving average filter with length three: we implement three blocks, performing a multiplication with a coefficient 1/3, followed by an adder block. Note that these realizations are either hardware or software, with possibly several computing units needed for higher execution speeds.

As a result of its design, a FIR filter is always stable. Such a property, evident for this type of structure, will not be so easily verified in the case of infinite response filters presented later on.

4.8.2.1. *Design methodology*

In reality, a filter is designed starting from an ideal frequency response with tolerated error bounds: we speak here of the *transition band* or *gabarit*.

Figure 4.17 displays an example: dotted lines limit the tolerance on the accepted frequencies, the *passband*, and the attenuated ones, the *stopband*.

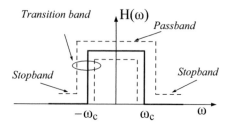

Figure 4.17. *Tolerance and transition band (gabarit) of a low-pass filter*

As we have indicated, the basic operating mode is first to define the ideal transfer function $H(\omega)$, and then to calculate the impulse response $h(n)$ by a Fourier expansion, obtained through the inverse transform. In reality, several runs are often needed in order to get the expected result. One reason is that the function $h(n)$ obtained this way generally has an infinite number of coefficients. A goal will then be to approximate the function by a limited number of coefficients. Another reason is that the coefficients in the implementation have finite precision, hence introducing some discrepancy vs. the ideal response of the filter. Moreover, the synthesized response is non-causal if appropriate phase constraints on $H(\omega)$ are not applied: therefore, implementing the filter needs a delay, called a *group delay*. It is often desirable in practice to achieve a constant group delay – we speak of *linear phase filters* in this case.

Let us examine how to approximate a low-pass filter with bandwidth ω_c. We have:

$$H(\omega) = 1 \quad \text{for } 0 \le \omega \le \omega_c,$$
$$H(\omega) = 0 \quad \text{otherwise.}$$

The impulse response is obtained by a series expansion, the coefficients of which are given by the inverse transform (see section 4.3.2):

$$h(n) = \frac{1}{2\pi} \int_{-\pi}^{\pi} H(\omega) e^{jn\omega} d\omega = \frac{1}{2\pi} \int_{-\omega_c}^{\omega_c} e^{jn\omega} d\omega = \frac{\sin n\omega_c}{n\pi}.$$

This is a non-causal function, having an infinite number of coefficients. We approximate it by first limiting n to a value N large enough so that the coefficients ranked above N can be considered negligible. Then we make the function causal by performing a time-shift $n \to n + N$.

Figure 4.18 represents the ideal response and its approximation.

In this particular case, as the function is symmetric with respect to N, the filter introduces a linear phase shift vs. frequency, and the delay is constant for all frequencies. In general, other rules for choosing N exist, based upon similar symmetry arguments we do not discuss here and which allow us to ensure a constant delay.

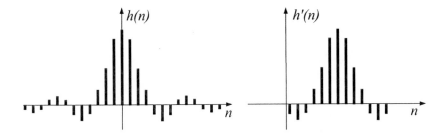

Figure 4.18. *Ideal response of the low-pass filter and its approximation*

Time windows and Gibbs phenomenon. The limitation operation just performed is actually the application of a rectangular *window* $2N$ unit samples in width, denoted as $w(n)$ (we will see why later on). We thus obtain a new filtering function $g(n) = h(n)w(n)$. We can formally study its impact on the signal: the frequency response of the resulting filter is given by the convolution product of $H(\omega)$ and $W(\omega)$, (see equation (4.23)) that is:

$$G(\omega) = \frac{1}{2\pi} \int_{-\pi}^{\pi} H(\omega')W(\omega - \omega')d\omega' = \frac{1}{2\pi} \int_{-\omega_c}^{\omega_c} W(\omega - \omega')d\omega' \qquad (4.68)$$

with $W(\omega) = \frac{\sin \omega N/2}{\omega N/2}$, see equation (4.10).

There is no explicit expression for this integral; however, we can visualize its value by considering the area under the curve shown in Figure 4.5 (limiting it between $\pm\omega_c$). We can see that the effect of the window is to generate parasitic oscillations ("ripples") in the frequency response: this is the *Gibbs phenomenon*. Also for low-pass, band-pass filters, etc., a transition band of positive width appears.

Figure 4.19 illustrates the phenomenon, where we can see $G(\omega)$ re-centered (application of $e^{j\omega N}$), and which shows the periodical nature of the frequency response.

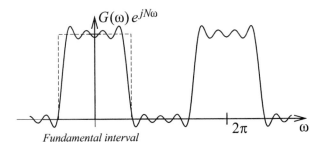

Figure 4.19. *Applying a window on a low-pass filter and Gibbs phenomenon*

In order to attenuate the amplitude of these oscillations, time windows, called *weighting windows* (w), have been defined, such as:

– Hamming window, defined as

$$n < -N/2 \longrightarrow w(n) = 0,$$

$$-N/2 \leq n < N/2 \longrightarrow w(n) = 0.54 + 0.46 \cos 2\pi n/N,$$

$$N/2 \leq n \longrightarrow w(n) = 0;$$

– Papoulis window, defined as

$$n < -N/2 \longrightarrow w(n) = 0,$$

$$-N/2 \leq n < N/2 \longrightarrow w(n) = \cos \pi n/N,$$

$$N/2 \leq n \longrightarrow w(n) = 0.$$

Various such window arrangements have been proposed, adapted to various situations. Generally, as we have already mentioned, several trials, with different window types and different values for N, will be needed to reach a satisfactory approximation. However, we can find less empirical approaches, derived from classical optimization methods such as the Remez algorithm. The reader may wish to refer to specialized textbooks [KUN 93].

Periodicity. Prior to addressing the actual filter realizations, it is important to recall here the periodical nature of the frequency response, with period 2π (for a sampling period taken as unity). This is clearly underlined in Figure 4.19 where we distinguish the fundamental interval (usually the only one displayed) and the other intervals, translated by $2k\pi$. So, strictly speaking, the digital low-pass filter does not exist: in order to obtain a real low-pass filtering effect in the sampled domain, the input signal spectrum must be limited to the lower half of the fundamental interval, i.e. between $-\pi$ and π. This limitation is usually achieved by using an analog anti-aliasing filter before signal sampling. Additional digital filters may be required as necessary. On the other hand this periodicity property will be useful to the realization of the other filter categories: high-pass and band-pass, as we see later on.

4.8.2.2. *FIR filter synthesis*

Direct form. Once determined $G(\omega)$, we obtain $g(n)$, as seen previously for $h(n)$, then we directly implement (*synthesis*) the convolution equation under the form of multipliers and adders:

$$y(n) = \sum_{m=0}^{N-1} g(m)x(n-m). \tag{4.69}$$

This type of realization is termed *canonical direct form*, and gives rise to a function diagram identical to that in Figure 4.16 (coefficients h simply being replaced by coefficients g).

Using z-transforms. Another method consists of using $G(z)$, the z-transform of $G(\omega)$, by factorizing its expression into second-order polymomials:

$$G(z) = \sum_{m=1}^{(N-1)/2} \left(1 + a_{1m}z^{-1} + a_{2m}z^{-2}\right) \tag{4.70}$$

for N odd, and with an additional degree if N is even. We are led to a kind of structure called *cascade* filters, made with second order cells, usually canonical, as illustrated in Figure 4.20.

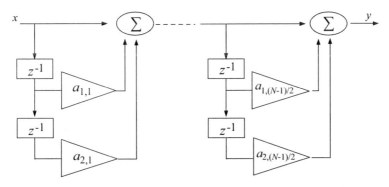

Figure 4.20. *Structure of cascade filters*

Choosing this approach is justified by a smaller sensitivity to the finite precision of the coefficients (we find again limitations related to the fixed- or floating-point representation of binary numbers, and to their addition and product).

Filter response in the frequency domain. In order to study the filter behavior, with its limitations in terms of number of stages, in the frequency domain we take $z = e^{j\theta}$ in order to again find Fourier transforms.

The frequency response value of the filter $G(z) = \sum_{m=1}^{(N-1)/2}(1 + a_{1m}z^{-1} + a_{2m}z^{-2})$ is given by the value of $G(e^{j\theta})$ on the unit circle, θ varying from $-\pi$ to π, which corresponds to a variation from $-\omega_e/2$ to $\omega_e/2$.

For instance, let us consider the case where $G(z)$ has complex coefficients (the transform is a fraction with a first degree numerator, see section 4.7.1.4): $zG(z)$ has a complex root on the unit circle, $z_0 = e^{j\theta_0}$, and $G(z)$ is zero for $\theta = \theta_0 + \pi$. Figure 4.21 displays the frequency response shape.

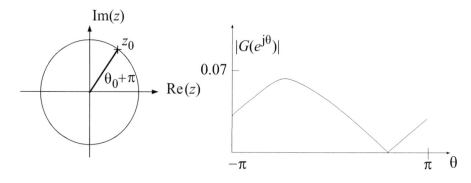

Figure 4.21. *Zero z_0 and response of a first-order FIR filter*

4.8.2.3. *Low-pass, high-pass and band-pass filters*

Up to this point we have mainly based our examples on low-pass filters: this is because an interesting relation exists between them and the other types, high-pass or band-pass filters, which will simplify their design. Indeed, the reader may easily verify (see Figure 4.15) that a high-pass filter can be deduced from a low-pass filter simply by inverting the passband and stopband, that is, by changing $H(\omega)$ into $1 - H(\omega)$. Note that the filter obtained this way possesses multiple attenuation bands, due to the periodicity of its transfer function, so it behaves as a band-pass filter with a symmetric pattern. The design of band-pass filters is inspired by this property, by proceeding in the reverse order: starting from the pattern imposed to the band-pass filter, we first determine the order and the transfer function of the appropriate low-pass filter, and then we apply the required substitutions (see [OSW 91]).

4.8.3. *Infinite impulse response (IIR) filters*

Studying infinite impulse response (IIR) filters is justified by the fact that FIR filters do not always provide a satisfactory answer to several filtering problems. For instance, in order to ensure a narrow transition band around the passband they need a large number of coefficients with two undesirable effects:

– an increase in the calculation time of the filtering algorithm;

– a large and unacceptable delay.

The principle of the IIR filter is given by the equation:

$$y(n) = \sum_{m=0}^{\infty} h(m)x(n - m). \tag{4.71}$$

Direct implementation of such a relation with an infinite number of terms is not possible. The solution to this problem consists of approximating the infinite sequence of filter response coefficients by the development of a rational function. In practice, this is obtained by re-injecting the filter output signal into the input, thus realizing an infinite impulse response with a finite number of stages. The filter is therefore said to be *recursive*.

The equation describing the operation is then a recurrence relation in the form:

$$y(n) = \sum_{m=0}^{q} b(m)x(n-m) - \sum_{k=1}^{p} a(k)y(n-k). \tag{4.72}$$

The z-transform of this equation is:

$$Y(z) = \sum_{n} y(n)z^{-n} = \sum_{n} \left[\sum_{m=0}^{q} b(m)x(n-m) - \sum_{k=1}^{p} a(k)y(n-k) \right] z^{-n}$$

$$= \sum_{n} \left[\sum_{m=0}^{q} b(m)z^{-m}x(n-m)z^{-(n-m)} - \sum_{k=1}^{p} a(k)z^{-k}y(n-k)z^{-(n-k)} \right],$$

that is:

$$Y(z) = \left[\sum_{m=0}^{q} b(m)z^{-m}X(z) - \sum_{k=1}^{p} a(k)z^{-k}Y(z) \right].$$

In this expression, $X(z)$ (resp. $Y(z)$) is the z-transform of $x(n)$ (resp. $y(n)$). We note $B(z) = \sum_{m=0}^{q} b(m)z^{-m}$ and $A(z) = \sum_{k=0}^{p} a(k)z^{-k}$ the z-transforms of the polynomials. Moreover, taking $a(0) = 1$, we obtain:

$$Y(z) = \frac{B(z)}{A(z)}X(z), \quad \text{i.e. } Y(z) = H(z)X(z) \quad \text{with } H(z) = \frac{B(z)}{A(z)}. \tag{4.73}$$

In the z-transform domain, the transfer function is a rational fraction which can be implemented using a finite number of elements.

However, one consequence is that a filter realized this way may be unstable.

Stability. Assuming a causal filter, the stability condition, as introduced in section 4.8.1.2, is that the sum of the moduli of the impulse response $h(n)$ is finite:

$$\sum_{n=0}^{\infty} |h(n)| < B,$$

$H(z)$ being the transform of $h(n)$, its modulus, calculated for $|z| > 1$, verifies the following inequality:

$$|H(z)| < \sum_{n=-\infty}^{\infty} |h(n)z^{-n}| < \sum_{n=-\infty}^{\infty} |h(n)|.$$

So, stability is ensured as long as the modulus of $H(z)$, evaluated for $|z| > 1$, is bounded, i.e. $H(z)$ does not possess any pole outside the unit circle. Knowing $H(z)$ we easily return to the frequency domain by a simple change of variables $z = e^{jn\omega}$. We then have:

$$H\left(e^{jn\omega}\right) = \frac{\sum_{m=0}^{q} b(m)e^{-jm\omega}}{\sum_{k=0}^{p} a(k)e^{-jk\omega}}. \tag{4.74}$$

(We will consider here the case where polynomials $A(z)$ and $B(z)$ have different degrees, the degree of $B(z)$ being higher than the degree of $A(z)$.)

4.8.3.1. *Filter design from models of the s plane*

As in the case of FIR filters, the first step consists of approximating the ideal transfer function $H(z)$ by a function $G(z) = N(z)/D(z)$ giving a frequency response as close as possible to the targeted gauge. Most often the resolution is done by means of numerical analysis software, as there is no simple analytical solution.

However, the design of IIR filters can also be inspired by that of analog filters, having a transfer function expressed by a Laplace transform in the variable s (see Chapter 1).

Indeed, we can go from the analog domain (s plane) to the digital domain (z plane), thanks specifically to the following affine transform (this is not the only transform, although it is the most commonly used), called a bilinear transform:

$$z = \frac{1 + s/2}{1 - s/2}. \tag{4.75}$$

This operation maps the imaginary s-axis on to the unit circle z and the left-side half-plane of s inside the unit circle of z. This is simply building an equivalence between the integration function of the continuous case and the discrete case. Recall that, in the continuous case, we have (see section 1.5.2.3):

$$y(t) = \int x(t)dt \iff Y(s) = \frac{1}{s}X(s). \tag{4.76}$$

Its discrete equivalent, obtained by applying the trapezoidal integration rule, is:

$$y(k) = y(k - 1) + \frac{T_e}{2}\left[x(k) + x(k - 1)\right], \tag{4.77}$$

T_e being the interval between samples, taken as unit time as usual, to simplify notations.

In the z plane, relation (4.77) becomes:

$$Y(z) = \frac{1}{2} \cdot \frac{1 + z^{-1}}{1 - z^{-1}}X(z). \tag{4.78}$$

Expressing the equivalence between these two operators, we have:

$$\frac{1}{s} = \frac{1}{2} \cdot \frac{1 + z^{-1}}{1 - z^{-1}} \quad \text{and thus} \quad z = \frac{1 + s/2}{1 - s/2}. \qquad (4.79)$$

It is then easy to verify that for $s = j\omega$, i.e. the imaginary axis, we find:

$$z = \frac{1 + j\omega/2}{1 - j\omega/2} = e^{2j \arctan(\omega/2)}, \quad \text{i.e.} \quad |z| = 1$$

$$\text{and} \ \arg z = 2 \arg (1 + j\omega/2). \qquad (4.80)$$

Hence, for s moving along the imaginary axis, ω traces out the real axis and z the unit circle. Moreover, if $Re(s) < 0$ we have $|z| < 1$: the left half-plane is mapped inside the unit circle of z-plane, so that the stability condition is fulfilled for s having its real part negative.

We can compare the gain in the continuous (analog) and digital cases: for the analog filter, it is obtained by making s trace out the imaginary axis, and these values are retrieved by tracing out the unit circle with $z = e^{2j \arctan(\omega/2)}$. For the digital filter, its gain is obtained by tracing out the unit circle with $z = e^{j\omega_n}$. Thus, the gains are equal for frequencies $\omega_n = 2 \arctan(\omega_a/2)$ – or yet $\omega_a = 2 \tan(\omega_n/2)$.

With this method, analog and digital filters have the same gains, but for different frequencies: there is a distortion on the frequency axis. For a low-pass filter this default is easily compensated by performing an *a priori* inverse pre-distortion.

To summarize, the design of this approach is to:
– from the specifications, determine the cutoff frequencies of the digital filter;
– derive from there the cutoffs belonging to a continuous filter (pre-distortion);
– choose a model of the continuous filter;
– calculate the transfer function of the continuous filter;
– move to the digital domain by way of the bilinear transform.

Among the classical models obtained by the analytic approximation in the s-plane, we can quote Butterworth and Chebychev filters (numerous others have been proposed). They are based upon a *polynomial* approximation. Their transfer functions have the following shape:

$$F(s) = \frac{1}{B(s)}, \qquad (4.81)$$

where $B(s)$ is a polynomial, and as for FIR filters we look for a polynomial such that $|F(s)| = |F(j\omega)|$ is as close as possible to the target gauge.

4.8.3.2. *Butterworth model*

In the case of Butterworth filters we write:

$$\left|F(j\omega)\right|^2 = \frac{1}{1+\epsilon^2\omega^{2n}}, \tag{4.82}$$

with n the filter degree, and ϵ a tuning coefficient of the passband. A simple expression for this function is:

$$\left|F(j\omega)\right|^2 = \frac{1}{1+\left(\frac{\omega}{\omega_c}\right)^{2n}}, \tag{4.83}$$

where ω_c is the cutoff frequency (the frequency for which the squared modulus of the function takes the value $1/2$).

Figure 4.22 displays the function for various values of n.

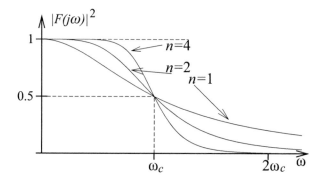

Figure 4.22. *Response of the Butterworth filter*

Such a filter has a flat response: there is no ripple on the totality of the passband. Moreover, the slope of the tangent of $F(j\omega)$ vanishes at the origin, and so do the other derivatives: we call this case a *maximally flat* response.

Taking $\omega_c = 1$ normalizes the expression. We then have in the s-plane:

$$\left|F(j\omega)\right|^2 = \left|F(s)F(-s)\right|_{s=j\omega} = \frac{1}{1+\omega^{2n}}, \tag{4.84}$$

and

$$F(s)F(-s) = \frac{1}{1+(s/j)^{2n}} = \frac{1}{1+(-s^2)^n}. \tag{4.85}$$

We derive the poles from the equation $1+(-1)^n s^{2n} = 0$, and we obtain the factorized and the expanded polynomial expressions for the transfer function:

$$F(s) = \frac{1}{B_n(s)} = \frac{1}{a_n s^n + a_{n-1} s^{n-1} + \cdots + a_1 s + a_0}. \tag{4.86}$$

We only retain polynomials $B_n(s)$ that have roots with a negative real part (left hand side of the imaginary axis), in order to obtain a stable filter.

In the simplest cases we can calculate the coefficients explicitly. For instance, in the case of a second order filter, we can write:

$$F(s) = \frac{1}{a_2 s^2 + a_1 s + a_0}, \quad \text{i.e.} \quad F(j\omega) = \frac{1}{-a_2 \omega^2 + j a_1 \omega + a_0},$$

and so, identifying (4.84) and (4.86):

$$|F(j\omega)|^2 = |F(j\omega)F(-j\omega)| = \frac{1}{a_2^2 \omega^4 - 2a_0 a_2 \omega^2 + a_1 \omega^2 + a_0^2} = \frac{1}{1 + \omega^4}.$$

From this expression we deduce, re-introducing the cutoff frequency ω_c:

$$a_0 = 1, \quad a_1 = \pm\sqrt{2}/\omega_c, \quad a_2 = 1/\omega_c^2,$$

or

$$a_0 = -1, \quad a_1 = \pm\sqrt{2}/\omega_c, \quad a_2 = -1/\omega_c^2.$$

In practice these values can be found in tables. Table 4.1 displays the first values of these polynomials, taken positive and for $\omega_c = 1$, for the first values of n.

n	$B_n(s)$
1	$s + 1$
2	$s^2 + 1.414s + 1$
3	$(s+1)(s^2 + s + 1)$
4	$(s^2 + 0.7654s + 1)(s^2 + 1.8478s + 1)$
5	$(s+1)(s^2 + 0.6180s + 1)(s^2 + 1.6180s + 1)$
6	$(s^2 + 0.5176s + 1)(s^2 + 1.414s + 1)(s^2 + 1.9318s + 1)$
7	$(s+1)(s^2 + 0.4450s + 1)(s^2 + 1.247s + 1)(s^2 + 1.8022s + 1)$
8	$(s^2 + 0.3986s + 1)(s^2 + 1.111s + 1)(s^2 + 1.6630s + 1)(s^2 + 1.9622s + 1)$

Table 4.1. *Coefficients of Butterworth filters*

The transfer function $G(z)$ of the corresponding digital filter is obtained at last by applying to $F(s)$ the change of variable $s = 2\frac{1-z^{-1}}{1+z^{-1}}$.

4.8.3.3. *Chebychev model*

The Chebychev model provides a solution with steeper transition zone, at the cost of a ripple in the passband. In this case, we write:

$$|F(j\omega)|^2 = \frac{1}{1 + \epsilon^2 T_n^2(\omega)}, \tag{4.87}$$

where $T_n(\omega)$ is the nth Chebychev polynomial defined as:

$$T_n(x) = \cos\left(n\cos^{-1}(x)\right) \qquad \text{for } |x| \le 1,$$
$$T_n(x) = \cosh\left(n\cosh^{-1}(x)\right) \quad \text{for } |x| > 1$$

and which is obtained by the following recurrence:

$$T_0(x) = 1, \quad T_1(x) = x, \ldots, T_{n+2}(x) = 2xT_{n+1}(x) - T_n(x). \tag{4.88}$$

As before, the corresponding transfer function is expressed by a polynomial:

$$F(s) = \frac{1}{E_n(s)} = \frac{1}{a_n s^n + a_{n-1}s^{n-1} + \cdots + a_1 s + a_0}. \tag{4.89}$$

As for the previous class of filters, the polynomial coefficients of $E_n(s)$ are calculated by identifying (4.88) and (4.89), or are found in tables. We should verify that their roots are distributed along a ellipse of semi-axes sinh and cosh, explaining our use of the term elliptic filter.

Figure 4.23 shows the shape of the transfer function, and Table 4.2 displays the first values of the coefficients.

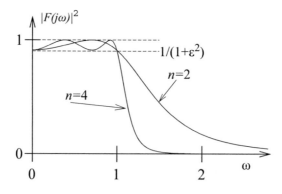

Figure 4.23. *Response of Chebychev filters*

n	$E_n(s)$
2	$s^2 + 0.9957s + 1$
3	$2.0353s^3 + 2.0116s^2 + 2.5206s + 1$
4	$3.628s^4 + 3.4568s^3 + 5.2749s^2 + 2.6942s + 1$

Table 4.2. *Coefficients of Chebychev filters*

4.8.3.4. *Synthesis of IIR filters*

Once a satisfactory transfer function has been obtained, we can, just as for FIR filters, implement the filter $Y(z) = G(z)X(z)$ according to various approaches. We have determined:

$$G(z) = \frac{N(z)}{D(z)} = \frac{\sum_{m=0}^{q} b(m)z^{-m}}{1 + \sum_{k=1}^{p} a(k)z^{-k}}. \tag{4.90}$$

We can return to the basic recurrence and implement it directly:

$$y(n) = \sum_{m=0}^{q} b(m)x(n-m) - \sum_{k=1}^{p} a(k)y(n-k), \tag{4.91}$$

yielding the realization illustrated in Figure 4.24, and called a *direct structure*.

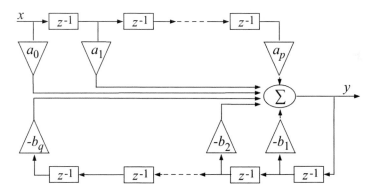

Figure 4.24. *IIR filter, direct structure*

We can also decompose the transfer function under another form, resulting in smaller delays, by writing:

$$Y(z) = N(z)W(z) \quad \text{and} \quad W(z) = \frac{X(z)}{D(z)}, \tag{4.92}$$

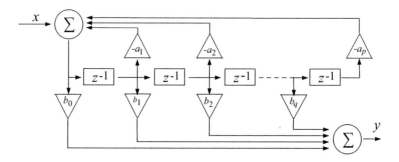

Figure 4.25. *Canonic structure of an IIR filter*

corresponding to the recurrences

$$y(n) = \sum_{m=0}^{q} b(m)w(n-m) \quad \text{and} \quad w(n) = -\sum_{k=1}^{p} a(k)w(n-k) + x(n). \quad (4.93)$$

Figure 4.25 depicts such a realization, called the *canonical form*.

Finally, just as for FIR filters, we prefer the use of *cascaded structures*, for the same reason of lower sensitivity to the limited precision on the coefficients. To this end we factorize $G(z)$ as a product of first or second degree rational fractions, that is:

$$G(z) = \prod_i G_i(z), \quad \text{with}$$

$$G_i(z) = \frac{b_{0i} + b_{1i}z^{-1}}{1 + a_{1i}z^{-1}}, \quad \text{or} \quad (4.94)$$

$$G_i(z) = \frac{b_{0i} + b_{1i}z^{-1} + b_{2i}z^{-2}}{1 + a_{1i}z^{-1} + a_{2i}z^{-2}}.$$

The implementation mimics these cascaded relations (Figure 4.26).

Note also that instead of the analytical approximations presented above, the Remez algorithm or numerical approximation tools can be used to provide the coefficients of the polynomials for IIR filters as well as for FIR filters.

4.8.3.5. *Low-pass, high-pass and band-pass filters*

As in the case of FIR filters, a simple relationship exists between transfer functions of low-pass and band-pass or high-pass filters. To go from a recursive low-pass filter to a recursive high-pass filter (or vice versa), it suffices to invert the roles of poles and zeroes in the rational fraction expressing the transfer function. For a recursive band-pass filter, we proceed as in the FIR case: starting from the gauge corresponding

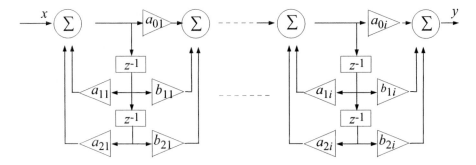

Figure 4.26. *Cascade structure of an IIR filter*

to the digital band-pass filter, we deduce the specifications of the associated analog low-pass filter, then we return to the digital filter by appropriate substitutions (see [OSW 91]).

4.8.4. *Non-linear filtering*

Linear filtering, as we have presented with FIR or IIR low-pass, band-pass and high-pass filters, allow us to remove unwanted bands and retain only useful frequency components. For efficiency, this presupposes a clear separation between the different bands. This is the case for most filtering applications: demodulation, noise removing, etc. However, we can find situations where the signal contains, in the same range of frequencies (generally high frequencies), both information (e.g. fast variation in an image) and parasitic impulse signals (noise). This will especially be the case for spectral analysis, as we will discuss later on.

Using a low-pass filter would be harmful, as it eliminates both the noise and the information. Non-linear filtering aims at overcoming these problems. Indeed, it consists of non-linear operations, referred to as "filtering", but which are more exactly a set of procedures, validated by simulation and without firm theoretical bases. Here we briefly present only one of these methods, median filtering, which finds particular use in image processing.

4.8.4.1. *Median filtering at rank N*

The principle is simply to replace the value of a sample by the median value (see Chapter 1) calculated on the set of $2N + 1$ values made of the sample value and the N values preceding and following it.

Formally, with our usual notations, if $x(n)$ is the input signal, $y(n)$ at the filter output is given by:

$$y(n) = \text{med}\left\{x(n - N), x(n - N + 1), \ldots, x(n + N)\right\}. \qquad (4.95)$$

This is the median value for window of width $2N + 1$ centered on n. Note that, if n refers to time, the filter is non-causal. In practice we take $x(-N) = \cdots = x(-2) = x(-1) = x(0)$. In the case of real-time processing, the operation should be performed with a delay of N time units. The same problem arises with the last samples of a limited duration signal L: we take $x(L + 1) = x(L + 2) = x(L + N) = x(L)$.

The particularity of median filtering, as compared with mean filtering is easily perceived. Assume for instance a window of size 3 ($N = 1$) with the respective sample values:

$$x(n - 3) = 4, \ x(n - 2) = 4, \ x(n - 1) = 4, \ x(n) = 1,$$
$$x(n + 1) = 1, \ x(n + 2) = 4, \ x(n + 3) = 4,$$

then the median yields:

$$y(n - 2) = 4, \ y(n - 1) = 4, \ y(n) = 1, \ y(n + 1) = 1, \ y(n + 2) = 4,$$

while with the mean:

$$y(n - 2) = 4, \ y(n - 1) = 3, \ y(n) = 2, \ y(n + 1) = 2, \ y(n + 2) = 3.$$

Median filtering does reproduce the signal variation around n, as opposed to the mean which smoothes the phenomenon.

More formally, we can verify the following properties:

– preserving steps: if a signal comprises a step at rank N, the median filter restores its output in the same step. A step at rank N is a sequence beginning with at least $N+1$ equal values, followed by a monotonic increasing or decreasing part and ending by at least $N + 1$ equal values;

– removing impulses: if the signal comprises an impulse at rank N, the median filter response to this impulse is constant and equal to the value surrounding it. An impulse at rank N is a sequence beginning and ending with at least the same $N + 1$ constant values surrounding a set of at most N arbitrary values.

Therefore, we can also verify that any signal composed of increasing or decreasing monotonic sequences separated by constant length sequences of at least $N + 1$ is invariant to a median filter at rank N.

4.8.5. *Filter banks and multirate systems*

Here we address an optimization problem, aimed firstly at reducing the processing power and run time required for the synthesis of digital filters, and also at making other functions possible, such as reducing the required bitrate for signal transmission. The basic principle is the reduction, under specific conditions, of the rate (frequency) at which signals are processed.

An immediate example of rate reduction is the subsampling of a signal filtered by a low-pass filter. Indeed, if the cutoff frequency is $2N$ times smaller than the signal sampling rate, the filtered signal can be sub-sampled at a rate N times smaller and thus the transmission rate as well as the calculating rate can be N times smaller. This shows clearly the gain this kind of operation (also called *decimation*) can bring. Upon receipt, this operation should be followed by an inverse over-sampling, corresponding to an *interpolation* function, so as to restore the original signal. Another application is the decomposition of a filter, say low-pass, into a bank of N filters, each running at a lower rate.

4.8.5.1. *Sub- and up-sampling*

Next we address the spectrum of the subsampled signal. We refer to the continuous case, but the translation to the discrete case is simple to perform, as we have shown above. Let $y_e(t)$ be the signal at the filter output. Subsampling (or downsampling) consists of taking one value among N on the output sequence.

Let $y_N(t)$ be the subsampled output sequence.

From the results previously obtained, we find for any sampling at the nominal rate, of period T_e (see equations (4.32) and (4.33)):

$$y_e(t) = \sum_{k=-\infty}^{\infty} y(kT_e)\delta(t - kT_e).$$

The Fourier transform gives the frequency response:

$$Y_e(\omega) = \frac{1}{T_e} \sum_{k=-\infty}^{\infty} Y(\omega - 2\pi k/T_e),$$

which can be written (where $T_e = 1$):

$$Y_e(\omega) = \sum_{k=-\infty}^{\infty} Y(\omega - 2\pi k),$$

and, if the signal is sampled with a rate N times smaller (i.e. with period NT_e):

$$y_N(t) = \sum_{k=-\infty}^{\infty} y(kN)\delta(t - kN).$$

The frequency response of the system is then:

$$Y_N(\omega) = \frac{1}{N} \sum_{k=-\infty}^{\infty} Y(\omega - 2\pi k/N). \tag{4.96}$$

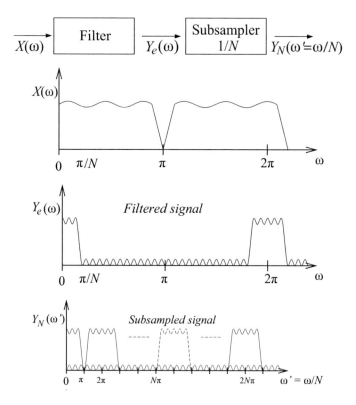

Figure 4.27. *Effect of subsampling and cadence change on the spectrum*

This underlines the fact that subsampling by a factor N divides the period of the signal spectrum by N. In the input signal the spectrum repeats with a rate multiple of the sampling frequency (i.e. 2π, if the period T_e is normalized at 1), while in the subsampled signal, the replicates, called *image bands*, occur for multiples of $2\pi/N$. This result is obviously in accordance with what was seen in section 4.4.2 on Shannon's theorem, here with a sampling period N times greater. This is illustrated schematically in Figure 4.27 for a signal initially filtered by a low-pass filter (the reader will notice the cadence change, from ω to $\omega' = \omega/N$).

Up-sampling. From what has just been explained above, it is clear that if we want to retrieve, at the receiver for instance, the original signal, with its original period and without the replicates, some process must be performed. That is the role of up-sampling followed by filtering.

Up-sampling (oversampling) increases the sampling frequency – in other words we reduce the sampling period. In order to do that we first increase the input signal rate

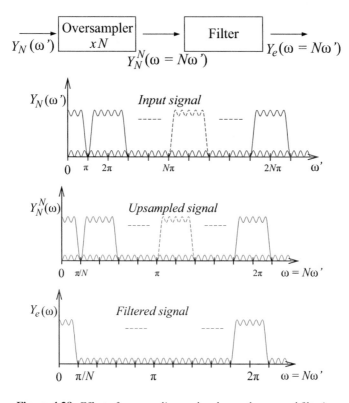

Figure 4.28. *Effect of up-sampling and cadence change and filtering*

by inserting $N - 1$ zeros between 2 successive samples. Then we perform a filtering operation at the new cadence, so as to retain only one spectrum image out of N.

The effect of up-sampling on the spectrum is analyzed as before: denoting as $y_e(t)$ the signal to be over-sampled by a factor N and as $y^N(t)$ the resulting signal, we have:

$$Y_N(\omega) = N \sum_{k=-\infty}^{\infty} Y(\omega - 2\pi k N). \qquad (4.97)$$

The replicated spectra are this time with periods N times smaller, that is, frequencies N times higher. However, the simple operation of inserting zeros does not change the spectrum, there is no information "added", and especially it does not eliminate the replicated spectra. That is why the operation is followed by a filtering at the new cadence. If the signal is subsampled first, the resulting signal would have a spectrum with the initial period as expected. However, even if the spectrum extends on the whole "baseband" 2π, clearly it cannot restore more than the information after subsampling, that is $2\pi/N$. This is illustrated in Figure 4.28 (the reader will notice the cadence change, from ω' to $\omega = N\omega'$).

4.8.5.2. *Multirate filtering and polyphase bank*

The goal is to decompose a filter into a cascade of elementary filters working at reduced rate, which is simpler to realize.

Assume we intend to realize a FIR filter, having a transfer function:

$$G(z) = \sum_{i=0}^{KN-1} a(i)z^{-i},$$

this function can be written as

$$G(z) = \sum_{n=0}^{N-1} z^{-n} G_n(z^N) \quad \text{with} \quad G_n(z^N) = \sum_{k=0}^{K-1} a(kN+n)z^{-kN}. \qquad (4.98)$$

Impulse responses of the elementary filters $G_n(z^N)$ are said to be polyphase components of the initial filter $G(z)$.

Let us then make the change of variables:

$$z \longrightarrow ze^{2j\pi m/N}, \quad \text{with} \quad m = 0, 1, \ldots, N-1.$$

This amounts to decomposing the initial filter in a series of filters, each with their rate reduced by N, *translated in the frequency domain* by $2\pi m/N$, and covering the whole initial band, as illustrated in Figure 4.29.

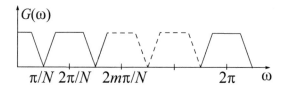

Figure 4.29. *Band coverage by frequency-shifted filters*

Each transfer function of the translated filter is written as:

$$G'_m(z) = \sum_{n=0}^{N-1} z^{-n} e^{-2j\pi nm/N} G_n(z^N) \qquad (4.99)$$

and the set of equation can be written in matrix form as follows:

$$
\begin{bmatrix} G'_0(z) \\ G'_1(z) \\ \vdots \\ G'_{N-1}(z) \end{bmatrix}
=
\begin{bmatrix}
1 & 1 & \cdots & 1 \\
1 & w & \cdots & w^{N-1} \\
\vdots & \vdots & & \vdots \\
1 & w^{N-1} & \cdots & w^{(N-1)^2}
\end{bmatrix}
\begin{bmatrix}
G_0(z^N) \\
z^{-1} G_1(z^N) \\
\vdots \\
z^{-(N-1)} G_{N-1}(z^N)
\end{bmatrix}
\qquad (4.100)
$$

where $w = e^{-2j\pi/N}$ (for the discrete transform, see section 4.7.3). Thus, we can recognize here an application of the DFT. Such a system, called a *polyphase filter*, is obtained by cascading a bank of filters and a DFT computer. It is important to note that each transform G'_m is a function of the whole set of the polyphase components via the DFT.

This technique can be applied to decompose a signal, or equally to rebuild it by inverting the sequence of operations, as we will now demonstrate.

4.8.5.3. *Signal decomposition and reconstruction*

We jointly apply the decomposition operation in filter banks and subsampling (oversampling) presented above, in order for instance to reduce the bitrate of a signal by decomposition before sending it, and then reconstructing it in the receiver.

To that end we first make use of a bank of N polyphase filters, each having bandwidth $2\pi/N$, so that they can be subsampled at a rate N times slower than the basic rate. Then, at the receiver, a symmetric system is used to reconstruct the signal (by performing a re-multiplexing).

Figure 4.30 displays a schematic representation of the system.

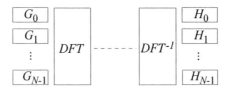

Figure 4.30. *Filter bank for signal decomposition and reconstruction*

This technique was first applied in transmultiplexers, systems which allow us to transform a time division multiplex of telephone channels to a frequency division multiplex, and vice versa. These systems are in use in certain compression techniques for image or audio signals, where sub-band signals are quantized with a resolution depending on the global available bitrate and on perceptive criteria (in the extreme case no signal is transmitted in a sub-band if it would not be perceptible). Sub-band filtering is also used for adaptive filtering, in order to provide an efficient processing of large size impulse responses.

From what we have just presented we can easily conceive that such a system offers a quasi-perfect reconstruction of the initial signal. However, it is necessary to formalize these decomposition and reconstruction operations to derive their design rules.

Let $x(k)$ denote the sequence of successive samples at the input of the sub-sampler:

$$x(k) = x_0, x_1, \ldots, x_{N-1}, x_N, x_{N+1}, \ldots, x_{2N-1}, x_{2N}, x_{2N+1}, \ldots, x_{kN-1}, \ldots$$

The sub-sampler decomposes the sequence into N interleaved sub-sampled sequences, denoted as:

$$x_i(kN) = x(kN + i) \text{ with } i = 0, 1, \ldots, N - 1 \text{ and } k = 0, 1, 2 \ldots, \text{ such that:}$$

$$x_0(kN) = x_0, x_N, x_{2N}, \ldots, x_{kN}, \ldots$$

$$x_1(kN) = x_1, x_{N+1}, x_{2N+1}, \ldots, x_{kN+1}, \ldots$$

$$\vdots$$

$$x_{N-1}(kN) = x_{N-1}, x_{2N-1}, x_{3N-1}, \ldots, x_{(k+1)N-1}, \ldots$$

These sequences are the polyphase components of $x(k)$. The z-transform of the signal $x(k)$ is then written:

$$X(z) = \sum_{k} \sum_{i=0}^{N-1} x(kN + i)z^{-(kN+i)},$$

or its equivalent:

$$X(z) = \sum_{i=0}^{N-1} X_i(z^N)z^{-i}, \quad \text{with} \quad X_i(z^N) = \sum_{k} x(kN + i)z^{-kN}. \tag{4.101}$$

This expression explicitly shows the transforms of the N sub-sampled sequences.

Conversely, given a sub-sampled sequence we can express its transform as a function of the initial signal:

$$X_0(z^N) = \frac{1}{N} \sum_{k=0}^{N-1} X(ze^{-2j\pi k/N}),$$

and for the rank i series

$$z^{-i}X_i(z^N) = \frac{1}{N} \sum_{k=0}^{N-1} e^{-2\pi jik/N} X(ze^{-2j\pi k/N}) \tag{4.102}$$

(in accordance with what we have seen for signal decomposition in the filter bank).

We can verify this, by inserting the last result in equation (4.101) that retrieves $X(z)$ exactly. We have:

$$X(z) = \sum_{i=0}^{N-1} X_i(z^N)z^{-i} = \frac{1}{N} \sum_{i=0}^{N-1} \sum_{k=0}^{N-1} e^{-2j\pi ik/N} X(ze^{-2j\pi k/N})$$

and, by denoting $z^{-i}X_i(z^N)$ by $X_i(z)$, it results that

$$X(z) = \sum_{i=0}^{N-1} X_i(z) = \sum_{i=0}^{N-1} \frac{1}{N} \sum_{k=0}^{N-1} e^{-2j\pi ik/N} X(ze^{-2j\pi k/N}). \tag{4.103}$$

This relation expresses the sub-sampling operation followed by a reconstruction operation by interleaving, and which restores the original signal. Also, this corresponds to the schematic representation in Figure 4.30.

The product of DFT multiplied by DFT^{-1} being 1, the transform of the reconstructed signal is:

$$X_R(z) = \sum_{i=0}^{N-1} G_i(z^N) H_i(z^N) X_i(z),$$

and by inserting the expression $X_i(z)$ given in (4.103) we obtain:

$$X_R(z) = \sum_{k=0}^{N-1} X(zw^k) \frac{1}{N} \sum_{i=0}^{N-1} G_i(z^N) H_i(z^N) w^{ik}, \qquad (4.104)$$

where $w = e^{-2j\pi/N}$ is the Nth root of unity, as usual.

This expression is the basis for the major types of realizations we now present. Equation (4.104) allows us to determine the functions $H_i(z)$ for a given set of functions $G_i(z)$. In the case of perfect reconstruction, for instance, we will attempt to obtain, at the price of some delay, $X_R(z) = X(z)$. This leads us to express $H_i(z)$ as a function of $G_i(z)$ in a specific way, as we show in the examples that follow.

4.8.5.4. Half-band filters

Frequently, "half-band" filters are used to design the previous systems. A half-band filter is such that its transfer function conforms to Figure 4.31. Its bandwidth is equal to half the useful band (at gain 0.5, i.e. -3 db), which explains its name.

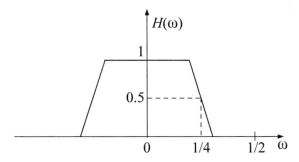

Figure 4.31. *Frequency response of a half-band filter*

This is a low-pass filter with a transfer function given by:

$$G(z) = \frac{1}{2}\left[z^{-2M} + z^{-1} \sum_{i=0}^{2M-1} a_{i+1} z^{-2i} \right]. \qquad (4.105)$$

Indeed, the reader should verify, with $z = e^{j\omega}$, that effectively $G(\omega_e/4) = 0.5$ and $G(\omega_e/4 + \omega) = 1 - G(\omega_e/4 - \omega)$, ω_e being taken as equal to 1. The function is said to be antisymmetric. Its decomposition is immediate:

$$G(z) = \frac{1}{2}\left[G_0(z^2) + z^{-1}G_1(z^2)\right],$$

with $G_0(z^2) = z^{-2M}$ and $G_1(z^2) = \sum_{i=0}^{2M-1} a_{i+1}z^{-2i}$.

Applying the results of (4.100), and taking into account the values of the roots of unity (see section 4.7.3), we obtain the matrix equation of a filter bank with $N = 2$ filters:

$$\begin{bmatrix} G_0'(z) \\ G_1'(z) \end{bmatrix} = \begin{bmatrix} 1 & 1 \\ 1 & -1 \end{bmatrix}\begin{bmatrix} z^{-2M} \\ z^{-1}G_1(z^2) \end{bmatrix}. \tag{4.106}$$

Note that we have thus obtained a low-pass and a high-pass filter, since a simple change in the sign of the second coefficient in (4.105) results in a high-pass filter (see section 4.8.2.3).

4.8.5.5. Quadrature mirror filters

This is an important case of using a two-filter bank to decompose and reconstruct the signal according to the principles of Figure 4.30.

The transform of the reconstructed signal is given by equation (4.104), taking $N = 2$:

$$X_R(z) = \frac{1}{2}\left[H_0(z^2)G_0(z^2) + H_1(z^2)G_1(z^2)\right]X(z)$$

$$+ \frac{1}{2}\left[H_0(z^2)G_0(z^2) - H_1(z^2)G_1(z^2)\right]X(-z)$$

The original signal is perfectly reconstructed if:

$$H_0(z^2)G_0(z^2) - H_1(z^2)G_1(z^2) = 0$$

and

$$\frac{1}{2}\left[H_0(z^2)G_0(z^2) + H_1(z^2)G_1(z^2)\right] = z^{-k} \tag{4.107}$$

In this case there is neither amplitude distortion nor aliasing. The reconstructed signal is simply delayed by k sampling periods.

These filters are termed *quadrature mirror filters* (QMF).

Obviously the two conditions are fulfilled if:

$$H_0(z^2) = G_1(z^2), \quad H_1(z^2) = G_0(z^2) \quad \text{and} \quad G_1(z^2)G_0(z^2) = z^{-k}. \tag{4.108}$$

In the common case where FIR filters with $2P$ real coefficients are used, equation (4.108) ensures that the two branches $G_0(z^2)$ and $G_1(z^2)$ have the same coefficients in reverse order: they are called mirror polynomials.

Let us apply this to a filter bank as defined in equation (4.106), and let us now consider the functions z^{-2M} and $\sum_{i=0}^{2M-1} a_{i+1} z^{-2i}$ as independent filter realizations, having transfer function respectively given by $G_0(z)$ and $G_1(z)$. We readily verify that the solution is given by:

$$H_0(z) = G_1(-z), \quad H_1(z) = -G_0(-z),$$

$$\frac{1}{2}\left[G_0(z)G_1(-z) - G_0(-z)G_1(z)\right] = z^{-k}.$$

From equation (4.105) we can also verify that the same kind of relation holds when using FIR filters with $2P + 1$ coefficients, i.e. such that $P = 2M - 1$, and if we take $G_1(z) = G_0(-z^{-1})z^{-P-1}$. We speak here of *conjugate quadrature filters* (CQF).

4.9. Spectral analysis and random signals

Up to now, all the signals we have considered have the property that they can be represented in analytic form. They can be models of audio or video signals, of signals coming from musical instruments, or synthesized sounds or images, radar signals, etc. On the other hand, natural signals in the real world, issuing from multiple and uncontrolled sources, rarely comply with deterministic models of that kind. It is then convenient (if not inevitable) to consider these real signals of complex nature, such as vocal or video signals, as random processes. We now study several problems related to random signals and to their analysis.

Analyzing random signals amounts to studying random variables by adopting a statistical approach, of which we have presented the main elements in the previous chapters (Chapters 1, 2 and 3). As presented in the introduction, signals are the physical support of information. Their analysis consists of extracting the most typical values related to the information they carry. The traditional approach aims at describing the signal by the energy at the different frequencies composing it: this constitutes *spectral* signal representation, and looking for the *energy* at frequencies of interest constitutes *spectral analysis*. Now we will demonstrate how to perform this analysis by means of statistical approaches.

We will first introduce the main notions in the case of continuous signals, then study the case of sampled signals.

4.9.1. *Statistical characterization of random signals*

Here we introduce the main characteristics and statistical properties used when analyzing random signals, especially the *power spectral density* (PSD).

4.9.1.1. *Average*

Let $x(t)$ be a stochastic process, weakly stationary (its average and covariance are independent of any time translation) and ergodic (the time average is equal to the ensemble average). Then we have:

$$m = E[x(t)] = \lim_{T \to \infty} \frac{1}{2T} \int_{-T}^{T} x(t)\mathrm{d}t \tag{4.109}$$

(see Chapter 1) and we can build an estimator for m from the N realizations x_n of $x(t)$ by:

$$\widehat{m} = \frac{1}{N} \sum_{n=0}^{N-1} x_n. \tag{4.110}$$

Most often it is convenient to work with variables of zero average; they are centered by the operation $x \to x - m$.

4.9.1.2. *Autocorrelation function*

Let $x(t_1)$ and $x(t_2)$ be the random values taken by $x(t)$ at epochs t_1 and t_2. The autocorrelation function of $x(t)$ is the function (see Chapter 1):

$$r(t_1, t_2) = E[x(t_1)x(t_2)]. \tag{4.111}$$

The autocorrelation function of a weakly stationary signal depends only on the difference $\tau = t_2 - t_1$, and we can then write:

$$r(\tau) = E[x(t)x(t + \tau)]. \tag{4.112}$$

The autocorrelation is a symmetric function:

$$r(\tau) = r(-\tau).$$

Indeed: $r(-\tau) = E[x(t)x(t - \tau)]$. If we take $t' = t - \tau$, it follows that $r(-\tau) = E[x(t' + \tau)x(t')] = r(\tau)$.

Generally, the autocorrelation function goes to zero as $\tau \to \infty$ for a centered and aperiodic signal.

Let us study the specific case of $r(0)$, by calculating the covariance:

$$c_x(\tau) = E[(x(t) - m_x)(x(t + \tau) - m_x)].$$

Developing this, we find:

$$r_x(\tau) = c_x(\tau) + m_x^2, \text{ or } c_x(0) = \sigma_x^2, \text{ hence } r_x(0) = \sigma_x^2 + m_x^2. \tag{4.113}$$

Special case: white noise. White noise is a signal such that the values at different epochs are independent of each other. Moreover, we generally consider it as centered, i.e. with a zero average. Hence:

$$\begin{aligned} \tau = 0 \longrightarrow r_x(\tau) = \sigma_x^2 \\ \tau \neq 0 \longrightarrow r_x(\tau) = 0 \end{aligned}$$

(4.114)

The autocorrelation function of a centered white noise is (up to a constant) a *Dirac impulse at the origin*, so that we can write:

$$r_x(\tau) = \sigma_x^2 \delta(\tau) \text{ where } \delta(\tau) \text{ is the Dirac delta function.}$$

Maximum of the autocorrelation function. Given $r_x(\tau) = E[x(t)x(t+\tau)]$, and taking account of the Cauchy-Schwarz inequality:

$$r_x^2(\tau) \leq E\left[x^2(t)\right] E\left[x^2(t+\tau)\right],$$

so that for a centered signal:

$$r_x^2(\tau) \leq E\left[x^2(t)\right]^2 = \left(\sigma_x^2\right)^2 = r_x^2(0),$$

and thus $r_x(\tau) \leq r_x(0)$.

The autocorrelation function has a maximum of $\tau = 0$.

Figure 4.32 depicts a typical example of a narrowband signal autocorrelation function.

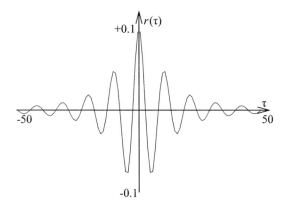

Figure 4.32. *Shape of the autocorrelation function of a narrowband random signal*

Cross-correlation function. This is simply an extension of the autocorrelation function to the case of two different signals. As for the autocorrelation, the signals being a weakly stationary cross-correlation depends only on τ:

$$r_{xy}(\tau) = E\big[x(t)y(t+\tau)\big], \quad \text{and} \quad r_{xy}(k) = r_{yx}(k).$$

In what follows, for homogenity, the autocorrelation will be denoted as r_{xx}.

4.9.1.3. *Power spectral density*

This is a central concept when studying frequency distribution of random signals. We attempt here to evaluate the average distribution of the energy as a function of the frequency of the signal.

Let $X(\omega)$ be the Fourier transform of $x(t)$, assumed to be weakly stationary, and $R_x(\omega)$ the Fourier transform of the autocorrelation function $r_{xx}(\tau)$, then $x(t)$ has a spectral density defined as:

$$E\big[|X(\omega)|^2\big] = R_x(\omega). \tag{4.115}$$

This is simply the Fourier transform of the autocorrelation function.

Indeed, let $\widehat{X}(\omega)$ be an estimate of $X(\omega)$ (as we generally cannot calculate the Fourier transform of a random signal, except in specific cases):

$$\widehat{X}(\omega) = \frac{1}{2T}\int_{-T}^{T} x(t)e^{-j\omega t}dt,$$

so that:

$$E\big[|\widehat{X}(\omega)|^2\big] = E\left[\frac{1}{2T}\int_{-T}^{T}\frac{1}{2T}\int_{-T}^{T} x(t)x(t')e^{-j\omega(t-t')}dtdt'\right].$$

By changing the order of summations and averages, and then making the autocorrelation function explicit, we obtain:

$$E\big[|\widehat{X}(\omega)|^2\big] = \frac{1}{2T}\left[\int_{-T}^{T}\frac{1}{2T}\int_{-T}^{T} E\big[x(t)x(t')\big]e^{-j\omega(t-t')}dtdt'\right]$$

$$= \frac{1}{2T}\int_{-T}^{T}\frac{1}{2T}\int_{-T}^{T} r(t-t')e^{-j\omega(t-t')}dtdt'.$$

We take $u = t - t'$ and $v = t + t'$, which gives:

$$E\big[|\widehat{X}(\omega)|^2\big] = \frac{1}{2T}\int_{-T}^{T}\frac{1}{2T}\int_{-T+v}^{T-v} r(u)e^{-j\omega u}dudv$$

or, denoting as $R(\omega)$ the Fourier transform of the autocorrelation function, assuming it exists:

$$E\big[|\widehat{X}(\omega)|^2\big] = \frac{1}{2T} \int_{-T}^{T} R_x(\omega)dv = R_x(\omega).$$

The average value of the energy distribution with frequency, called the power spectral density (or energy spectral density), is given by the Fourier transform of the autocorrelation function.

Figure 4.33 illustrates the typical shape of the power spectral density for a narrowband signal.

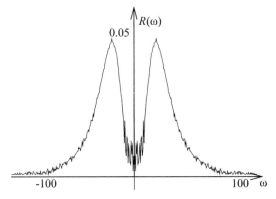

Figure 4.33. *Spectral density of a narrowband random signal*

The case of white noise. We still assume a zero average. As seen previously, the autocorrelation is then given by:

$$r_{xx}(\tau) = \sigma_x^2 \delta(\tau).$$

We have previously remarked that this is a Dirac pulse at the origin. Thus, its Fourier transform is given by:

$$R_x(\omega) = \sigma^2. \tag{4.116}$$

The spectral density of white noise is constant over the whole frequency range, and equal to the signal variance. This is an important result: when no other information is available, a white noise is often used to model the unknown, perturbed, signals.

Sum of uncorrelated random signals. We consider two uncorrelated signals $x(t)$ and $y(t)$. The autocorrelation function of their sum is:

$$r_{x+y}(\tau) = E\big[(x(t) + y(t))(x(t+\tau) + y(t+\tau))\big]$$
$$= r_{xx}(\tau) + r_{yy}(\tau) + r_{xy}(\tau) + r_{yx}(\tau),$$

and since the signals are uncorrelated this reduces to:

$$r_{x+y}(\tau) = r_{xx}(\tau) + r_{yy}(\tau).$$

Thus, the spectral density of the sum is the sum of the spectral densities:

$$R_{x+y}(\omega) = R_{xx}(\omega) + R_{yy}(\omega). \tag{4.117}$$

4.9.2. *Filtering a random signal*

We have seen that a random signal can be characterized by its autocorrelation function and by its spectral density. We now explore how filtering operates on these functions, which are essential tools for random signal analysis.

Filtering operations concentrate on these functions.

4.9.2.1. *Spectral density of a filtered signal*

Let $x(t)$ be a random signal submitted to an invariant linear filter with impulse response $h(t)$, and let $y(t)$ be the signal at the filter output. We denote as $R_x(\omega)$ (resp. $R_y(\omega)$) the spectral density at the input (resp. output), and $H(\omega)$ the filter frequency response:

$$R_y(\omega) = \left|H(\omega)\right|^2 R_x(\omega). \tag{4.118}$$

The spectral density at the output filter is equal to the product of the input spectral density multiplied by the squared frequency response module of the filter.

Indeed, $r_{xx}(\tau)$ (resp. $r_{yy}(\tau)$) being the autocorrelation function at the filter input (resp. at the output), the filtering operation is characterized by:

$$y(t) = \int_{-\infty}^{\infty} x(u)h(t-u)\mathrm{d}u, \text{ or also } y(t) = \int_{-\infty}^{\infty} x(t-u)h(u)\mathrm{d}u.$$

Thus, the autocorrelation function of $y(t)$ is

$$E\left[y(t)y(t')\right] = E\left[\int_{-\infty}^{\infty} x(t-u)h(u)\mathrm{d}u \int_{-\infty}^{\infty} x(t'-u')h(u')\mathrm{d}u'\right],$$

which can be written as

$$E\left[y(t)y(t')\right] = \int_{-\infty}^{\infty}\int_{-\infty}^{\infty} h(u)h(u')E\left[x(t-u)x(t'-u')\right]\mathrm{d}u\,\mathrm{d}u'$$

$$E\left[y(t)y(t')\right] = \int_{-\infty}^{\infty}\int_{-\infty}^{\infty} h(u)h(u')r_{xx}\left((t'-t)-(u'-u)\right)\mathrm{d}u\,\mathrm{d}u'$$

or, by putting $t' - t = \tau$:

$$E\big[y(t)y(t+\tau)\big] = r_{yy}(\tau) = \int_{-\infty}^{\infty} \int_{-\infty}^{\infty} h(u)h(u')r_{xx}\big(\tau - (u' - u)\big)\,du\,du'.$$

We should note that since the autocorrelation at the output depends on τ only, the process is thus stationary.

We now make the change of variable $w = u' - u$, yielding:

$$r_{yy}(\tau) = \int_{-\infty}^{\infty} \int_{-\infty}^{\infty} h(u)h(u+w)r_{xx}(\tau - w)\,du\,dw$$

$$= \int_{-\infty}^{\infty} \left[r_{xx}(\tau - w) \int_{-\infty}^{\infty} h(u)h(u+w)\,du \right] dw$$

This is a convolution. Actually, writing

$$r_{hh}(w) = \int_{-\infty}^{\infty} h(u)h(u+w)\,du,$$

we have:

$$r_{yy}(\tau) = \int_{-\infty}^{\infty} r_{xx}(\tau - w)r_{hh}(w)\,dw = r_{xx}(\tau) \otimes r_{hh}(w)$$

which can obviously be written as:

$$r_{yy}(\tau) = r_{hh}(\tau) \otimes r_{xx}(\tau). \tag{4.119}$$

The PSD of the filtered signal is given by the Fourier transform of the convolution product. This is the product of the individual transforms.

The Fourier transform of $r_{hh}(\tau) = \int_{-\infty}^{\infty} h(t)h(t+\tau)dt$ is:

$$R_h(\omega) = \int_{-\infty}^{\infty} \int_{-\infty}^{\infty} h(t)h(t+\tau)e^{-j\omega\tau}\,dt\,d\tau.$$

We introduce $h'(t) = h(-t)$ and $H'(\omega) = \overline{H}(\omega)$. This gives:

$$R_h(\omega) = \int_{-\infty}^{\infty} \int_{-\infty}^{\infty} h(t)h'(-t - \tau')e^{-j\omega\tau'}\,dt\,d\tau',$$

which is the transform of a convolution product and hence can be written:

$$R_h(\omega) = H(\omega)\overline{H}(\omega) = \big|H(\omega)\big|^2.$$

The transform of $r_{xx}(\tau)$ is $R_x(\omega)$, the spectral density of the signal (see equation (4.115)). At last we obtain the important result of equation (4.118):

$$R_y(\omega) = |H(\omega)|^2 R_x(\omega).$$

where $H(\omega)$ is the Fourier transform of $h(t)$, the filter impulse response.

Note that this result accords with equation (4.22) obtained when filtering deterministic signals:

$$Y(\omega) = H(\omega)X(\omega) \longrightarrow |Y(\omega)|^2 = |H(\omega)|^2 |X(\omega)|^2.$$

Another interesting point is that $r_{hh}(\tau)$ can be seen as the autocorrelation function of the impulse response $h(t)$ of the filter (which explains the notation).

Equation (4.119) can then be expressed as: *the autocorrelation function of the output signal is the result of filtering (convolution product) the input autocorrelation function by the "autocorrelation function" of the impulse response.*

4.9.2.2. *Filtering white noise*

The result of equation (4.118) is of prime importance for numerous practical applications. For instance, white noise with variance σ^2 filtered by a filter with transfer function $H(\omega)$ has the spectral density:

$$R_y(\omega) = |H(\omega)|^2 \sigma^2. \tag{4.120}$$

When the filter transfer function is non-flat (as here), the spectral density of the filtered signal is no longer constant: the signal is called a *colored noise*.

Reciprocally, this result tells us that, starting from an arbitrary[3] signal $y(t)$, we can process it through a filter $H^{-1}(\omega)$ to generate a white noise $b(t)$. We then speak of signal *whitening* and $b(t)$ is called the *innovation process* of $y(t)$.

4.9.3. *Sampled random signals*

As for deterministic signals, sampling and digital processing have given rise to powerful techniques for analyzing random signals. Essentially, the properties used are those of continuous signals presented previously, transposed to the discrete case of sequences of numbers, and expressed by means of the z-transform.

What follows are the main results, without the proofs already presented in the continuous case. We assume the Shannon conditions are fulfilled, and that we operate on stationary and ergodic signals.

---

3. Strictly speaking, the filter must be invertible, so the signal must not be completely arbitrary.

4.9.3.1. *Autocorrelation function*

With our usual notations for time averages and sample averages, we have

$$m_x = E\big[x(n)\big] = \lim_{n \to \infty} \frac{1}{N} \sum_{n=-N/2}^{N/2} x(n) \qquad (4.121)$$

and the autocorrelation function is:

$$r_{xx}(k) = E\big[x(n)x(n+k)\big] \qquad (4.122)$$

$$= \lim_{n \to \infty} \frac{1}{N} \sum_{n=-N/2}^{N/2} x(n)x(n+k). \qquad (4.123)$$

This is still a symmetric function.

As in the continuous case we have

$$r_{xx}(0) = \sigma_x^2 + m_x^2 \qquad (4.124)$$

and for white noise

$$r_{xx}(k) = \sigma_x^2 \delta(k). \qquad (4.125)$$

4.9.3.2. *Cross-correlation function*

Just as for the autocorrelation, if the two signals are stationary the cross-correlation depends only on k:

$$r_{xy}(k) = E\big[x(n)y(n+k)\big] \quad \text{and} \quad r_{xy}(k) = r_{yx}(k). \qquad (4.126)$$

4.9.3.3. *Power spectral density*

As for the continuous case the power spectral density is the Fourier transform of the autocorrelation function:

$$R_x(\omega) = \sum_{k=-\infty}^{\infty} r_{xx}(k)e^{-jk\omega} \qquad (4.127)$$

or again using the variable z:

$$R_x(z) = \sum_{k=-\infty}^{\infty} r_{xx}(k)z^{-k}. \qquad (4.128)$$

As in the continuous case we show that this is the average squared modulus of the Fourier transform $X(\omega)$ of a realization of the random process $x(n)$:

$$R_x(\omega) = E\left[|X(\omega)|^2\right].$$ (4.129)

From then on we again find the same properties as in the continuous case for white noise and for the sum of uncorrelated signals.

White noise. The PSD of a centered white noise is constant and equal to its variance:

$$R_x(\omega) = \sigma^2.$$ (4.130)

Sum of uncorrelated random signals. The spectral density of the sum is the sum of the individual spectral densities:

$$R_{x+y}(\omega) = R_x(\omega) + R_y(\omega).$$

Starting from this result we can address the case of a signal with a non-zero mean value.

Signal of non-zero mean. Consider a signal $x(n)$ of zero mean value to which a constant m is added. The autocorrelation function is (see (4.113)):

$$r_{(x+m)(x+m)} = E\left[(x(n) + m)(x(n + k) + m)\right] = r_{xx}(k) + |m^2|$$

and the spectral density:

$$R_{x+m}(\omega) = R_{xx}(\omega) + |m^2|\delta(\omega).$$ (4.131)

This is the spectral density of the initial signal to which a Dirac impulse is added.

4.9.4. *Filtering a sampled random signal*

Here again we give the main results directly, which are similar to those in the continuous case.

Let $x(n)$ be our weakly stationary input signal, with $h(n)$ the impulse response of the digital filter to which it is offered and $y(n)$ the output signal.

The digital filtering process, as seen in sections 4.6 and 4.8, is written:

$$y(n) = \sum_{m=-\infty}^{\infty} x(n)h(n - m).$$

4.9.4.1. *Spectral density of the filtered signal*

Let us denote as $R_x(\omega)$ (resp. $R_y(\omega)$) the input (resp. output) spectral density of the signal and $H(\omega)$ the frequency response of the filter. Just as in the continuous case we have (see equation (4.103)):

$$R_y(\omega) = |H(\omega)|^2 R_x(\omega). \tag{4.132}$$

The spectral density at the filter output is equal to the product of the input spectral density by the squared modulus of the frequency response of the filter.

Also (see (4.119)):

$$r_{yy}(k) = r_{hh}(k) \otimes r_{xx}(k). \tag{4.133}$$

The autocorrelation function of the output signal is the result of filtering the autocorrelation function at the filter input by the autocorrelation function of the impulse response.

4.9.4.2. *Correlation between input and output signals (cross-correlation)*

By definition, we have:

$$r_{xy}(k) = E\big[x(n)y(n+k)\big] = E\left[x(n) \sum_{i=-\infty}^{\infty} h(i)x(n+k-i)\right]$$

$$= \sum_{i=-\infty}^{\infty} E\big[x(n)x(n+k-i)\big]h(i),$$

hence

$$r_{xy}(k) = \sum_{i=-\infty}^{\infty} h(i)r_{xx}(k-i). \tag{4.134}$$

Filtering a random signal introduces a correlation between output and input signals. This actually corresponds to the previous result: the autocorrelation function at the output is the result of filtering the input autocorrelation function, so that the filter introduces a cross-correlation between input and output. The generation of "colored noise" is an application of this result, as already evoked and presented here in the discrete case.

4.9.4.3. *Colored noise*

Consider a signal $x(n)$ with independent samples, identically distributed, and with variance σ_x^2. This is the sampled equivalent of white noise. For the continuous signal, filtering gives:

$$R_y(\omega) = |H(\omega)|^2 \sigma_x^2 \quad \text{and} \quad \sigma_y^2 = R_{yy}(0) = \sigma_x^2 \int_{-1/2}^{1/2} |H(\omega)|^2 d\omega. \tag{4.135}$$

With an ideal band-pass filter with normalized passband B $(B < 1)$ we obtain:

$$\sigma_y^2 = \sigma_x^2 B.$$

The variance of the outgoing signal is lower than at the input, since a part of the spectrum has been eliminated. We then speak of colored noise, since the spectral density is no longer constant.

4.9.5. *Spectral estimation*

As we have remarked on several occasions, most of the time the engineer will have a limited number of realizations available (most often a single one) for a signal sequence $x_0, \ldots, x_{N-1}$ from signal $x(n)$. We present here the traditional methods for extracting the best estimation for the spectral density of the signal under study. We distinguish two types of approach.

The first, called non-parametric, evaluates the characteristics of interest directly from the available sample, namely the energy distribution as a function of frequency. This amounts to estimating the autocorrelation function directly on the available sequence. The estimation method is "neutral" with respect to data – i.e. there is no adjustment of the method with the data actually observed.

The second approach, called parametric, consists of adjusting a model in accordance with the data observed, considering the signal observed as the result of an original signal traveling through a system: in practice we consider it as the result of filtering a white noise. Generally simple linear models of the ARMA (*auto-regressive moving average*) family are used. The problem is then to find fast algorithms optimizing the parameters of the model. In this approach, as opposed to the previous one, there is *a priori* information added to the study (model chosen, criteria, etc.), even if the white noise assumption for the initial excitation proves to be relatively neutral.

It is the engineer's responsibility to make the most judicious choices, depending on the problem at hand. For speech analysis for instance, if we have no knowledge about the glottal signal, we do however have some information about the acoustic characteristics of the vocal tract. We will return to this example later on.

Estimating the autocorrelation function is the basic operation common to these approaches.

4.9.5.1. *Estimating the autocorrelation function*

As stated in the introduction to this section, we are given a series of N samples $x_0, \ldots, x_{N-1}$, that we consider as a realization of a signal $x(n)$. An estimator of its autocorrelation function $r_{xx}(k) = E[x(n)x(n+k)]$ (see equation (4.119)) is:

$$\widehat{r}_{xx}^k(k) = \frac{1}{N-|k|} \sum_{n=0}^{N-|k|-1} x(n)x(n+k). \tag{4.136}$$

This is an unbiased estimator: $E[\widehat{r}_{xx}^k] = r_{xx}(k)$, its value goes to the "true" value as N increases (see Chapter 3). However, its variance increases excessively with k, as k goes close to N (it varies as $N/(N-|k|)^2$), so that we prefer the following biased estimator, having a variance less dependent on k and decreasing significantly with N as it varies as $1/N$ (we do not give the proofs here):

$$\widehat{r}_{xx}(k) = \frac{1}{N} \sum_{n=0}^{N-|k|-1} x(n)x(n+k), \tag{4.137}$$

for which we have:

$$E[\widehat{r}_{xx}(k)] = \frac{N-|k|}{N} r_{xx}(k). \tag{4.138}$$

Above all, such an estimator is particularly suited to a fast calculation of the spectral density, as we see now.

4.9.5.2. *Non-parametric spectral estimation with periodogram*

This is the simplest method, directly drawn from the analysis of deterministic signals and classical estimation theory. It is called non-parametric as it does not refer to any analytical model (at least not explicitly).

Simple periodogram. The periodogram is the function

$$\widehat{R}_N(\omega) = \sum_{k=-(N-1)}^{N-1} \widehat{r}_{xx}(k)e^{-jk\omega}. \tag{4.139}$$

This is a spectral density estimation by means of the Fourier transform for a biased estimator of the autocorrelation function:

$$\widehat{r}_{xx}(k) = \frac{1}{N} \sum_{n=0}^{N-k+1} x(n)x(n+k).$$

Replacing $\widehat{r}_{xx}(k)$ with its expression in equation (4.139), we obtain:

$$\widehat{R}_N(\omega) = \frac{1}{N} \left| \sum_{k=0}^{N-1} x(k)e^{-jk\omega} \right|^2. \tag{4.140}$$

This expression is nothing but the basic formula to calculate fast Fourier transforms – see section 4.7.5.1, equation (4.57) – which gives N values of $\sum_{k=0}^{N-1} x(k)e^{-jk\omega}$ uniformly distributed between $\omega = -\pi$ and π (with $\omega = 2\pi/N$).

The periodogram, being based upon a biased estimator, is itself biased. In order to evaluate the bias we calculate its mean value. We have:

$$E\left[\widehat{R}_N(\omega)\right] = \sum_{k=-(N-1)}^{N-1} E\left[\widehat{r}_{xx}(k)\right]e^{-jk\omega}$$

$$= \sum_{k=-(N-1)}^{N-1} \frac{N-|k|}{N}\widehat{r}_{xx}(k)e^{-jk\omega} \neq R_N(\omega).$$

This expression corresponds to a convolution between the "true" spectral density and a triangular window of duration $2N - 1$.

We can also show that the variance is quite high: $\mathrm{Var}[\widehat{R}_N(\omega)] \sim |R_N(\omega)|^2$. Thus, the periodogram appears as an inconsistent estimator, needing to be modified to be of real help.

Modified periodogram. In this case we use, as seen in section 4.8.2.1, a weighting window applied to the calculation of the autocorrelation function, i.e. applied to the samples. Choosing the right type of window (such as a rectangular or Hamming window) is done according to the case, the main goal being to be able to distinguish between neighboring frequencies, the estimator remaining biased, however. The estimator has the form:

$$\widehat{R}_N(\omega) = \frac{1}{NP}\left|\sum_{k=0}^{N-1} x(k)w(k)e^{-jk\omega}\right|^2 \tag{4.141}$$

where P is a normalization factor, defined as $P = \frac{1}{N}\sum_{k=0}^{N-1} w(k)^2$.

Averaged periodogram. We have shown in Chapter 3 that we can reduce the variance of an estimator, by calculating and averaging several identical and independent estimators. The principle is thus to decompose the sequence of N samples into L shorter sequences of duration $M = N/L$. We then calculate L periodograms (possibly windowed) of which we calculate the average. That is:

$$\widehat{R}_i(\omega) = \frac{1}{M}\left|\sum_{k=0}^{N-1} x(i,k)e^{-jk\omega}\right|^2 \quad \text{and} \quad \widehat{R}(\omega) = \frac{1}{L}\sum_{i=0}^{L-1}\widehat{R}_i(\omega). \tag{4.142}$$

For a given N, as L increases the variance decreases, but as M decreases the bias increases, and the spectral resolution decreases. It is still a matter of finding a good compromise: N is often imposed by stationarity reasons (for instance, for speech processing N is taken between 80 and 160 for a signal sampled at 8kHz), and M is chosen as a function of the target spectral resolution.

Smoothed periodogram. The principle is to reduce the variance of the simple periodogram by weighting the estimation of the autocorrelation function (and not samples) by means of a window smoothing the calculation errors for its extreme values.

The estimator has the form:

$$\widetilde{R}_M(\omega) = \sum_{k=-M}^{M} w(k)\widehat{r}_{xx}(k)e^{-jk\omega}. \tag{4.143}$$

In this expression $w(k)$ is an even symmetric window of duration $2M + 1$ with $M < N$. Here too a compromise should be reached between a large M giving very selective results (close to a Dirac pulse) and a small M giving a low variance. A typical choice is $M = N/5$.

4.9.5.3. *Parametric spectral estimation: ARMA, AR, MA*

The periodogram provides a method which is simple to use. However, it suffers from a certain number of drawbacks, particularly its failure to discriminate spectral lines or contiguous peaks. Moreover, it yields poor estimations for small sample sizes N. Here we use parametric models corresponding to random signals resulting from filtering white noise. Various estimations are used, according to the attributes we are looking for in the unknown signal. We present only the ARMA, AR (*auto-regressive*) and MA (*moving average*) models, drawn – as their names indicate – from the filtering modes studied previously, with moving average (FIR) or recursive average (IIR).

The ARMA model. An ARMA process of orders p and q is a process generating a signal $y(n)$ by inputting a centered white noise $x(n)$ of variance σ^2 into a linear filter with P poles and Q zeros, i.e. with the form (see section 4.8.3):

$$y(n) = \sum_{m=0}^{q} b(m)x(n-m) - \sum_{k=1}^{p} a(k)y(n-k), \tag{4.144}$$

with the transfer function

$$H(z) = \frac{B(z)}{A(z)} = \frac{\sum_{m=0}^{q} b(m)z^{-m}}{1 + \sum_{k=1}^{p} a(k)z^{-k}}. \tag{4.145}$$

If $q = 0$ the filter has only poles and is purely recursive: the signal is called AR (*auto-regressive*), and $H(z) = \frac{1}{A(z)}$.

If $p = 0$ the filter has only zeros, and is of FIR type, the signal is called MA (*moving average*).

As we have seen in section 4.9.4.3, equation (4.135), the spectral density is given by:

$$R_y(\omega) = |H(\omega)|^2 \sigma_x^2.$$

Auto-regressive (AR) estimation. This kind of modeling is widely used, for spectral estimation, speech analysis, synthesis, coding, and for pattern recognition, etc., as it corresponds to solving a linear system, an operation that is usually simple. We will see examples of applications later.

Assume we intend to identify a AR signal with an unknown random signal. As we have seen, its spectral density has the form:

$$R_y(\omega) = \frac{\sigma^2}{|A(\omega)|^2} = \frac{\sigma^2}{|1 + \sum_{k=1}^{p} a(k)e^{-jk\omega}|^2}. \tag{4.146}$$

Thus, knowledge of parameters $a(k)$ is sufficient to obtain the PSD values. To that end we evaluate the autocorrelation function of the AR signal. By definition, we have (see equations (4.122) and (4.144)):

$$r_{yy}(i) = E\big[y(n)y(n+i)\big] \quad \text{and} \quad y(n) = x(n) - \sum_{k=1}^{p} a(k)y(n-k),$$

hence

$$r_{yy}(i) = E\left[y(n)\left(x(n+i) - \sum_{k=1}^{p} a(k)y(n-k+i)\right)\right]$$

$$= E\big[y(n)x(n+i)\big] - \sum_{k=1}^{p} a(k)r_{yy}(i-k).$$

Now, due to the property of independence, in the case of a white noise $x(n)$ at the input, between the realization $x(n+i)$ at time i, and the realization $y(n)$ at the output at past epochs

$$E\big[y(n)x(n+i)\big] = 0 \text{ if } i > 0 \quad \text{and} \quad \sigma^2 \text{ if } i = 0.$$

Finally we have the following relation, called the Yule-Walker equation:

$$r_{yy}(i) = -\sum_{k=1}^{p} a(k)r_{yy}(i-k) \quad \text{if } i > 0, \tag{4.147}$$

$$r_{yy}(i) = -\sum_{k=1}^{p} a(k)r_{yy}(-k) + \sigma^2 \quad \text{if } i = 0. \tag{4.148}$$

So, in order to adjust the AR model to the unknown signal, we have only to identify their autocorrelation functions for indices $0, \ldots, p$, and to calculate the coefficients a_k by means of the linear system (4.147). The variance is then adjusted using equation (4.148). Choosing an AR model amounts to imposing the p first values of the autocorrelation function, which corresponds concretely to impose the global shape of the power spectral density (the *spectral envelope*). We will see later how to solve this system, thanks to its special structure (Toeplitz matrix) and to the use of appropriate algorithms (Levinson algorithm).

Moving average (MA) estimation. We try to identify a MA model for the signal being studied. This can be done, just as before, by identifying the spectral densities using the autocorrelation function. We have (see relation (4.133)):

$$r_{yy}(k) = r_{hh}(k) \otimes r_{xx}(k),$$

or

$$r_{yy}(k) = \sum_{m=-\infty}^{\infty} r_{hh}(m) r_{xx}(k - m).$$

Now, as $x(n)$ is a white noise we find (see equation (4.125)):

$$r_{xx}(k) = \sigma_x^2 \delta(k),$$

hence

$$r_{yy}(k) = \sigma_x^2 r_{hh}(k),$$

and with (4.123) and (4.144):

$$r_{yy}(0) = \sigma_y^2 = \sigma_x^2 \sum_{i=0}^{q} b_i^2,$$

$$r_{yy}(1) = \sigma_x^2 \left(b_0 b_1 + b_1 b_2 + \cdots + b_{q-1} b_q \right),$$

etc., up to

$$r_{yy}(q) = \sigma_x^2 \left(b_0 b_q \right).$$

$r_{yy}(i)$ can then be identified with the $q+1$ autocorrelation function values of the signal studied. The set of equations is a system of $q + 1$ *non-linear* equations in the $q + 1$ variables, which can only be solved by using successive approximations.

4.9.5.4. *Toeplitz matrix and Levinson algorithm*

Solving the Yule-Walker set of equations (4.147) and (4.148) requires us to solve a linear system of p equations in p variables, which is generally expressed in its matrix form. Classical solutions, such as Gaussian elimination, could be used. However, in the present case the particular matrix structure allows us to deploy an efficient iterative method making the computational complexity from $O(p^3)$ to $O(p^2)$.

Returning to the Yule-Walker equations, expressed in their matrix form:

$$
\begin{bmatrix}
r_{yy}(0) & r_{yy}(-1) & \cdots & r_{yy}(-(p-1)) \\
r_{yy}(1) & r_{yy}(0) & \cdots & r_{yy}(-(p-2)) \\
r_{yy}(2) & r_{yy}(1) & \cdots & r_{yy}(-(p-3)) \\
\vdots & \vdots & \ddots & \vdots \\
r_{yy}(p-1) & r_{yy}(p-2) & \cdots & r_{yy}(0)
\end{bmatrix}
\begin{bmatrix}
a(1) \\ a(2) \\ a(3) \\ \cdots \\ a(p)
\end{bmatrix}
= -
\begin{bmatrix}
r_{yy}(1) \\ r_{yy}(2) \\ r_{yy}(3) \\ \cdots \\ r_{yy}(p)
\end{bmatrix}
$$

As the signal is real, the previous matrix can be written in a simpler form:

$$
\begin{bmatrix}
r_{yy}(0) & r_{yy}(1) & \cdots & r_{yy}(p-1) \\
r_{yy}(1) & r_{yy}(0) & \cdots & r_{yy}(p-2) \\
r_{yy}(2) & r_{yy}(1) & \cdots & r_{yy}(p-3) \\
\vdots & \vdots & \ddots & \vdots \\
r_{yy}(p-1) & r_{yy}(p-2) & \cdots & r_{yy}(0)
\end{bmatrix}
\begin{bmatrix}
a(1) \\ a(2) \\ a(3) \\ \cdots \\ a(p)
\end{bmatrix}
= -
\begin{bmatrix}
r_{yy}(1) \\ r_{yy}(2) \\ r_{yy}(3) \\ \cdots \\ r_{yy}(p)
\end{bmatrix}. \qquad (4.149)
$$

This is a symmetric matrix, with the property that the elements are constant along each of its diagonals, and is called a Toeplitz matrix. Once the p autocorrelation coefficients have been identified, the coefficients $a(p)$ can be obtained by matrix inversion (if this last is invertible).

The same type of matrix system is encountered in several applications, such as linear prediction and adaptive optimal filtering, which we present below. It is thus of interest to detail the corresponding resolution methods.

The particular structure of Toeplitz matrices has given birth to numerous specific algorithms: among them we can quote Levinson, Schur and Choleski algorithms and their improvements: *split Levinson* and *split Schur*. We now present the principles of the classical Levinson recursion. For more details on the whole set of these algorithms the reader is prompted to refer to specialized textbooks [KUN 93].

Levinson algorithm. This is a recursive algorithm, suggested by the particular matrix structure. Let us come back to the previous results. Taking into account the identical forms of the first row on the left and of the column on the right of the equation (4.149), and introducing (4.148), we obtain:

$$
\begin{bmatrix}
r_{yy}(0) & r_{yy}(1) & \cdots & r_{yy}(p) \\
r_{yy}(1) & r_{yy}(0) & \cdots & r_{yy}(p-1) \\
r_{yy}(2) & r_{yy}(1) & \cdots & r_{yy}(p-2) \\
\vdots & \vdots & \ddots & \vdots \\
r_{yy}(p) & r_{yy}(p-1) & \cdots & r_{yy}(0)
\end{bmatrix}
\begin{bmatrix}
1 \\ a(1) \\ a(2) \\ a(3) \\ \cdots \\ a(p)
\end{bmatrix}
= -
\begin{bmatrix}
\sigma^2 \\ 0 \\ 0 \\ 0 \\ \cdots \\ 0
\end{bmatrix}. \qquad (4.150)
$$

We write this system as:

$$
R_p A_p = \begin{bmatrix} \sigma_p^2 & 0 & \cdots & 0 \end{bmatrix}^T.
$$

We try to derive the values of the coefficients $a_p(1), \ldots, a_p(p)$ and σ_p^2. Assume a solution is available at rank m, given by the couple (A_m, σ_m^2) such that:

$$
\begin{bmatrix}
r_{yy}(0) & r_{yy}(1) & \cdots & r_{yy}(m) \\
r_{yy}(1) & r_{yy}(0) & \cdots & r_{yy}(m-1) \\
r_{yy}(2) & r_{yy}(1) & \cdots & r_{yy}(m-2) \\
\vdots & \vdots & \ddots & \vdots \\
r_{yy}(m) & r_{yy}(m-1) & \cdots & r_{yy}(0)
\end{bmatrix}
\begin{bmatrix}
1 \\
a_m(1) \\
a_m(2) \\
a_m(3) \\
\cdots \\
a_m(m)
\end{bmatrix}
= -
\begin{bmatrix}
\sigma_m^2 \\
0 \\
0 \\
\cdots \\
0
\end{bmatrix},
\qquad (4.151)
$$

that is:

$$
R_m A_m = \begin{bmatrix} \sigma_m^2 & 0 & \cdots & 0 \end{bmatrix}^T. \qquad (4.152)
$$

A solution at rank $m+1$ with the vector $\begin{bmatrix} A_m \\ 0 \end{bmatrix}$ is then:

$$
R_m \begin{bmatrix} A_m \\ 0 \end{bmatrix} = \begin{bmatrix} \sigma_m^2 & 0 & \cdots & \Delta_{m+1} \end{bmatrix}^T, \qquad (4.153)
$$

where

$$
\begin{aligned}
\Delta_{m+1} = \; & r_{yy}(m+1) + r_{yy}(m) a_m(1) \\
& + r_{yy}(m-1) a_m(2) + \cdots + r_{yy}(0) a_m(m).
\end{aligned} \qquad (4.154)
$$

Similarly, we have the solution

$$
R_{m+1} \begin{bmatrix} 0 \\ \tilde{A}_m \end{bmatrix} = \begin{bmatrix} \Delta_{m+1} & 0 & \cdots & \sigma_m^2 \end{bmatrix}^T \qquad (4.155)
$$

where $\tilde{A}_m$ is the vector A_m where the elements have been arranged in reverse order, i.e.:

$$
\tilde{A}_m = \begin{bmatrix} a_m(m) & a_m(m-1) & \cdots & 1 \end{bmatrix}^T. \qquad (4.156)
$$

Thus, a solution to (4.150) can be found, as a linear combination of these two solutions, such that all components of the right-hand side vector vanish. This is written:

$$
A_{m+1} = \begin{bmatrix} A_m \\ 0 \end{bmatrix} - k_{m+1} \begin{bmatrix} 0 \\ \tilde{A}_m \end{bmatrix}, \quad \text{with} \quad k_{m+1} = \frac{\Delta_{m+1}}{\sigma_m^2}. \qquad (4.157)
$$

This is the basic recurrence of the Levinson algorithm.

The coefficient k_{m+1}, of absolute value less than 1, is often referred to as *PARCOR* coefficients (partial correlation). We choose it so as to cancel the last element of the right-hand side vector.

We then obtain:

$$R_{m+1}A_{m+1} = \begin{bmatrix} \sigma_m^2 & 0 & \cdots & \Delta_{m+1} \end{bmatrix}^T - k_{m+1}\begin{bmatrix} \Delta_{m+1} & 0 & \cdots & \sigma_m^2 \end{bmatrix}^T$$

$$= \left[\left(\sigma_m^2 - \left[\frac{\Delta_{m+1}}{\sigma_m^2}\right]^2 \right) \quad 0 \quad \cdots \quad 0 \right]^T$$

hence:

$$\sigma_{m+1}^2 = \sigma_m^2 - \left[\frac{\Delta_{m+1}}{\sigma_m^2}\right]^2 = \sigma_m^2 \left(1 - k_{m+1}^2\right). \tag{4.158}$$

This last recurrence relation, both with equation (4.157), provides the solution of the Yule-Walker system of relation (4.150). The algorithm is initialized, at step $m = 0$, by $\sigma_0^2 = r_{yy}(0)$ and $A_0 = [1]$. We should note that, following equation (4.158), the input noise variance of the model decreases as its order m increases (we refer to it as the prediction error, as we see in section 4.10).

4.10. Linear prediction, coding and speech synthesis, adaptive filtering

We conclude this chapter by presenting the principles of linear prediction and optimal adaptive filtering, which are in fact application fields of the preceding section. This will be illustrated by the examples of speech synthesis, low bitrate coding and echo cancelation. Actually, all these signal processing techniques rely on a common approach: adjusting the parameters of a linear system (source and filter) to equalize the signal produced to the expected signal as effectively as possible. This approach is made particularly efficient thanks to the development of algorithms specifically suited to digital processing.

4.10.1. Linear prediction

The goal of linear prediction is to find the parameters of a system (here, a non-recursive filter) such that it predicts the future signal samples, from a combination of its past samples. This technique applies, for example, to low bitrate speech encoding, or to speech recognition and synthesis.

Formally, the linear prediction at order p of $x(n)$ is the value $\widehat{x}_n$ built from the p previous values of the process, an operation defined as:

$$\widehat{x}(n) = -\sum_{i=1}^{p} a^{(p)}(i)x(n-i). \tag{4.159}$$

By adjusting parameters p and $a^{(p)}$, we attempt to minimize the difference $\widehat{x}(n) - x(n)$ referred to as the prediction error, and denoted as $e^{(p)}(n)$.

Figure 4.34 illustrates the principle.

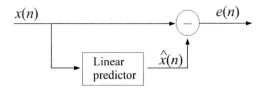

Figure 4.34. *Principle of linear prediction*

4.10.1.1. *Variance minimization*

The most common optimization criterion is the *variance minimization* (power) of the prediction error $e^{(p)}(n)$. We have:

$$e^{(p)}(n) = x(n) - \widehat{x}(n) = \sum_{i=0}^{p} a^{(p)}(i)x(n-i), \quad \text{with} \quad a^{(p)}(0) = 1, \quad (4.160)$$

and thus

$$V = E\big[e^{(p)}(n)\big]^2 = E\left[\sum_{i=0}^{p} a^{(p)}(i)x(n-i) \sum_{j=0}^{p} a^{(p)}(j)x(n-j)\right]$$

$$= \sum_{i=0}^{p} a^{(p)}(i) \sum_{j=0}^{p} a^{(p)}(j)E\big[x(n-i)x(n-j)\big],$$

that is:

$$V = \sum_{i=0}^{p} a^{(p)}(i) \sum_{j=0}^{p} a^{(p)}(j)r_{xx}\big(|i-j|\big). \quad (4.161)$$

This quadratic expression is positive definite, and its minimum is given by:

$$\frac{\partial E\big[\big(e^{(p)}(n)\big)^2\big]}{\partial a^{(p)}(i)} = 0, \quad \text{for } i = 1, \dots, p.$$

We denote as $a_0^{(p)}(i)$ the values obtained this way. We have:

$$\sum_{j=0}^{p} a_0^{(p)}(j)r_{xx}\big(|i-j|\big) = 0 \quad \text{for } i = 1, \dots, p$$

so, by transfering in (4.161):

$$V_{\min} = \sum_{j=0}^{p} a_0^{(p)}(j)r_{xx}(j). \quad (4.162)$$

We recognize a set of equations similar to those obtained in section 4.9.5.2 with the Yule-Walker equations: (4.150). The system, in its matrix form, is again a Toeplitz matrix:

$$\begin{bmatrix} r_{xx}(0) & \cdots & r_{xx}(p) \\ \vdots & \vdots & \vdots \\ r_{xx}(p) & \cdots & r_{xx}(0) \end{bmatrix} = \begin{bmatrix} 1 \\ a_0^{(p)}(1) \\ \vdots \\ a_0^{(p)}(p) \end{bmatrix} = \begin{bmatrix} V_{\min} \\ 0 \\ \vdots \\ 0 \end{bmatrix}$$

In the case where the signal $x(n)$ is actually a p order AR process, we have:

$$V_{\min} = \sigma^2.$$

Here again algorithms such as the Levinson algorithm are used to solve the system.

4.10.1.2. *Example of speech processing: coding and synthesis*

As we have already signaled in the introduction of this section, *speech encoding* is an important application of linear prediction. The voice signal results from modulation or fluctuations of air pressure generated by the lung, trachea and larynx, then filtered by the vocal tract. Thus, a source signal yields different sounds, according to the spectral shaping brought by the vocal tract. The source signal is represented by a white noise (non-voiced sound) or a periodic wave with many harmonics (voiced sound), and the vocal tract as an AR-like filter. The system is represented by the equation:

$$x(n) = -\sum_{i=1}^{p} a(i)x(n-i) + b(n)$$

where $b(n)$ represents the source signal and $x(n)$ the sound produced at instant n as a result of the AR filter.

This model is used for instance in linear predictive coding (LPC) for speech compression, according to the following principle:

– on a sequence of samples $x(1), x(2), \ldots, x(N)$ we estimate the filter $a(i)$ and source signal (average power of white noise and period if voiced sound) parameters;

– we transmit these parameters instead of the signal itself;

– the receiver reconstructs an approximation of the signal from the filtering equation.

Compression gain results from the ratio between the number of transmitted parameters ($p + 1$ or $p + 2$) and the sequence size N. The quality of restitution depends to a large extent on the precision of the model, and especially on the order p of the filter, and also on the precision of the binary representation of the parameters transmitted.

For telephony, the narrow bandwidth used, limited to frequencies below 3.5 kHz, and the characteristics of the speech signal allow us to limit the filters to orders around 10, while preserving a satisfactory quality with a reduced complexity. Note that state-of-the-art speech coders like CELP (Code Excited Linear Predictive coder) use additional parameters which describe the prediction error $e(t)$ in more detail – at the expense of an extra bitrate – and thus helps to enhance the quality of restitution vs. the basic LPC coder.

Speech synthesis is another application, used in answering machines or computer games. Its principle is to reproduce voice signals, starting from stored data resulting from speech analysis. In the case of direct storage of signal samples the volume of data rapidly becomes prohibitive for applications with limited storage capabilities, so that linear prediction techniques offer a judicious solution. As before, a source (periodic pulse or white noise) is applied to a recursive filter, the parameters of which are varied depending on the sound it must generate. Then these coefficients are stored with the type of source to use, depending on the type of sound (voiced or not) to generate. The digital signal issuing from the filter is then converted into an audio signal following a digital to analog conversion.

This last example, where we can vary filter parameters, leads us to present adaptive filtering techniques.

4.10.2. *Adaptive filtering*

Adaptive filtering is used when we have to build or model a system with time-varying characteristics so as to satisfy an optimality criterion. For example, we can vary the coefficients of a FIR filter modeling an unknown system. To that end the output is compared to the expected reference, and the parameters are adjusted depending on the deviation observed. The equations representing this operation are:

$$\widehat{y}(n) = -\sum_{i=1}^{p} a(i)x(n-i) \quad \text{and} \quad e(n) = y(n) - \widehat{y}(n).$$

Figure 4.35 outlines the principle of the operation.

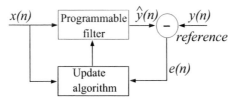

Figure 4.35. *Principle of adaptive filtering*

Least squares is often used as an optimization criterion. Its application takes various forms, as for instance least squares with exponential forgetting, moving window least squares, least squares with minimum absolute value, etc. [HAY 86, WID 85, KUN 93]. We present here the most used one, least squares with exponential forgetting, with which the gradient algorithm is associated.

4.10.2.1. *The least squares method with exponential forgetting*

Let us denote as $A(n) = \begin{bmatrix} a(1,n) \\ a(2,n) \\ \vdots \\ a(p,n) \end{bmatrix}$ the p coefficient vector of the programmable

filter at the index (instant) n and $X(n) = \begin{bmatrix} x(n) \\ x(n-1) \\ \vdots \\ x(n-p+1) \end{bmatrix}$ the vector of the p last samples

vector of the input signal.

The error signal is written as

$$e(n) = y(n) - A^T(n)X(n). \tag{4.163}$$

The optimization method consists of minimizing, for each index value, a weighted sum denoted as $J(n)$ of the square of the successive errors resulting from the filter updated at iteration n, that is:

$$J(n) = \sum_{i=1}^{n} w^{n-i}\left[y(i) - A^T(n)X(i)\right]^2 \tag{4.164}$$

with w a positive weighting factor less than 1, referred to as the *forgetting factor*.

As with linear prediction, we minimize the expression by canceling its derivative with respect to the filter coefficients: $\partial J(n)/\partial a(n) = 0$, which yields the solution, or normal equation: $\sum_{i=1}^{n} w^{n-i}[y(i) - A^T(n)X(i)]X(i) = 0$, or:

$$\sum_{i=1}^{n} w^{n-i}X(i)X^T(i)A(n) = \sum_{i=1}^{n} w^{n-i}y(i)X(i). \tag{4.165}$$

We take:

$$R(n) = \sum_{i=1}^{n} w^{n-i}X(i)X^T(i), \quad \text{and} \quad r(n) = \sum_{i=1}^{n} w^{n-i}y(i)X(i). \tag{4.166}$$

We obtain the so-called *Wiener-Hopf deterministic solution*:

$$A(n) = R^{-1}(n)r(n). \tag{4.167}$$

We now assume stationary signals, and we take the input autocorrelation matrix as:

$$R_{xx} = E[X(i)X^T(i)]$$

and the cross-correlation vector between the reference and the input as:

$$r_{yx} = E[y(i)X(i)].$$

It follows:

$$E[R(n)] = \frac{1-w^n}{1-w}R_{xx} \quad \text{and} \quad E[r(n)] = \frac{1-w^n}{1-w}r_{yx}, \tag{4.168}$$

indicating that $R(n)$ and $r(n)$ are asymptotically unbiased estimators of R_{xx} and r_{yx} respectively.

The optimal value is then obtained when $n \rightarrow \infty$, and we have the classical (statistical) *Wiener-Hopf solution*:

$$A = R_{xx}^{-1}r_{yx}. \tag{4.169}$$

4.10.2.2. *The stochastic gradient descent algorithm*

We start again from equations (4.166) and (4.167), from which we easily derive the following recurrences:

$$R(n+1) = wR(n) + X(n+1)X^T(n+1),$$
$$r(n+1) = w \cdot r(n) + X(n+1)y(n+1), \tag{4.170}$$

$$A(n+1) = R^{-1}(n+1)[w.r(n) + X(n+1)y(n+1)]. \tag{4.171}$$

Then, using (4.167) and (4.170):

$$wr(n) = wR(n)A(n) = [R(n+1) - X(n+1)X^T(n+1)]A(n) \tag{4.172}$$

and finally:

$$A(n+1) = A(n) + R^{-1}(n+1)X(n+1)[y(n+1) - X^T(n+1)A(n)] \tag{4.173}$$

this is the recurrence equation for updating the filter coefficients.

We should note that the term between brackets in the right member represents the *a priori* error signal, i.e. that calculated from the coefficient values at the present epoch, prior to coefficient update:

$$e(n+1) = y(n+1) - X^T(n+1)A(n).$$

Thus, equation (4.173) reads:

$$A(n+1) = A(n) + R^{-1}(n+1)X(n+1)e(n+1). \qquad (4.174)$$

The computational complexity is greatly decreased (at the price of a slower convergence of the algorithm) with the approximation: $R^{-1}(n+1) \approx \delta I_p$ where I_p is the $p \times p$ unit matrix and δ a coefficient called *adaptation step size*. The coefficient update equation thus becomes:

$$A(n+1) = A(n) + \delta X(n+1)e(n+1). \qquad (4.175)$$

The choice of δ results in a compromise: it must be small enough to ensure the convergence of the algorithm and its stability regarding noise, while keeping a large enough value to ensure a reasonable convergence speed.

In this case the optimization does not exactly correspond to the mean squares criterion, but rather to the average mean squares. The product $X(n+1)e(n+1)$ is proportional to the gradient of the squared error; indeed we have:

$$\frac{1}{2}\frac{\partial e^2(n+1)}{\partial a_i(n)} = x(n+1-i)e(n+1) \quad \text{for } i = 1, \ldots, p.$$

This explains the term LMS (least mean squares) given to the stochastic gradient descent algorithm.

Stochastic gradient descent is often used, because of its low computational cost and as it is well adapted to different filter structures, while offering a good robustness towards realization imperfections.

However, the initial convergence can be too slow in which case we should come back to the exact application of the mean squares approach: we can then make use of particular forms of algorithms, such as *fast least squares* (see [KUN 93]).

4.10.2.3. *Example: echo cancelation*

Echo cancelation on telephone transmission lines provides an important example of application of adaptive filtering techniques in telecommunications. The principle is given on Figure 4.36.

The problem arises at the boundary between analog (A) and digital (D) signals, typically between the subscriber's line and the network. Digital transmission makes use of two separate channels for sending and receiving speech signals, while the subscriber's line uses a bidirectional copper wire. The interface between these two modes is a differential transformer, working as a perfectly balanced bridge.

In practice, balancing is not perfect, and part of the received signal is re-injected on the "send" line: this is the echo phenomenon. The parasitic signal is canceled by

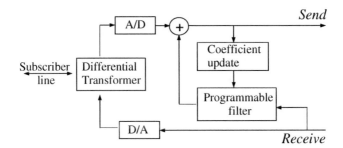

Figure 4.36. *Adaptive filtering for echo cancelation*

subtracting to the send signal another signal coming from a digital filter operating on the signal received, and which is an estimation of the echo signal on the sending line. The coefficients are calculated as a function of the signal sent $y(n)$ and of the received one $x(n)$ according to equation (4.175).

Chapter 5

Information and Coding Theory

In this chapter we present the basic concepts of information and coding theory. The role of a communication system is to reliably transport information, information which may originate in the form of an analog or digital flow but which always requires processing, so as to protect it against perturbations, and reduce it to a reasonable volume that is easier to transport and to store.

To this end, information theory provides the tools for modeling and *quantifying* information, while coding theory allows us to build reliable techniques for its transmission and compression.

As reflected throughout this book, probability theory plays a major role in the life of the engineer; not surprisingly, it constitutes the foundations of information theory. Indeed, the problem is here to build probabilistic models able to quantify the basic notion of uncertainty attached to any information, generally unknown, stored, transported, perturbed, etc. We present the bases of these models for multiple applications in the field of telecommunications, and computer science more generally (information storage, compression, transmission, coding and error correction).

5.1. Information theory

Information theory is usually considered to have been founded by Claude E. Shannon in the 1940s (*The Mathematical Theory of Communication*, 1948, see [SHA 48]). This work provides formal foundations to *quantify* information, enabling us to estimate limit properties such as the maximum compression ratio of digital data, the effective maximum bitrate of noisy channels, or the efficiency conditions of a code.

Coding, for its part, appears as an application of information theory, providing means to express information in such a way that it can be reliably transported and optimally stored.

To this end, we present the concepts of information measure, and the main theorems of the theory, initially established by Claude Shannon, and basically defining limits to storage and transmission capacity. Then, the following sections are devoted to the main applications, data or image compression, and coding for error detection and correction.

5.1.1. *The basic diagram of a telecommunication system*

Information theory aims to define the performance figures of a communication system, possibly in presence of perturbations. The basic diagram of the system conforms to Figure 5.1.

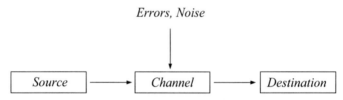

Figure 5.1. *The basic diagram of a communication system*

The source is designed to send a message to a receiver, in an optimal way, through a channel of given characteristics (language, bandwidth and error rate). To this end, the message coding scheme must be, as far as possible, adapted to the channel. Clearly the original message is not known by the receiver (or else there would be no need to transmit it). Moreover, the channel is subject to random perturbations (noise, transmission errors) so that the received message differs in an unpredictable way from the one which has been sent. We will see how coding rules derived from information theory may help in dealing with these constraints, and allow the receiver to regenerate an error-free message (or at least have a very high probability of doing so).

As the two main components of the communication system – the source and the channel – both have random behavior, we call on probability theory as the basic analysis tool. First of all we introduce the concept of *entropy*, which offers a way to measure the quantity of information.

5.2. Information measurement

The engineer engaged in system design has a constant concern, which is to estimate the resources that must be deployed in order to transport and store information as efficiently and reliably as possible. It is a matter of determining the format or message coding or data block containing the information. It amounts to estimating the *quantity* of information contained in the message and then to determining the resources to allocate (in terms of bitrate, storage capacity, etc.).

Obviously, the system is designed to work whichever message is sent and whatever information it carries. The distinction should be clearly established between the concepts of information and message: the message carries the information – unknown and thus random from the addressee's standpoint.

5.2.1. *Algebraic definition of information*

Let Ω be a finite set of messages, assumed to be equiprobable, and let $|\Omega|$ denote the cardinal of this set. Then the quantity of information contained in a message drawn from Ω is defined as:

$$\text{Info}_{\text{alg}}(\Omega) = \log\left(|\Omega|\right).$$

Indeed, the complexity of physical systems grows exponentially with the number of its elements. Obviously for a digital message built with 0s and 1s, the possible number of arrangements doubles for any additional bit, increasing by 1 its base-2 logarithm.

5.2.2. *Probabilistic definition of information*

Here we no longer consider all messages as equiprobable. Noting as $P(\omega_i)$ the occurrence probability of message ω_i, we then write:

$$\text{Info}_{\text{prob}}(\Omega) = -\sum_{1}^{|\Omega|} P(\omega_i) \log\left(P(\omega_i)\right). \tag{5.1}$$

The similarity with the mathematical form of the entropy in thermodynamics explains why the probabilistic definition of information is named entropy too.

Note that if all messages are equiprobable, then $P(\omega_i) = 1/|\Omega|$, and so

$$\text{Info}_{\text{prob}}(\Omega) = \log|\Omega| = \text{Info}_{\text{alg}}.$$

Finally, note that if a message is characterized by the quantity $i(\omega_i) = -\log P(\omega_i)$, then we can write:

$$\text{Info}_{\text{prob}}(\Omega) = E\left[i(\omega_i)\right]. \tag{5.2}$$

The quantity of information associated with the whole set of messages is the expectation of the random variable $i(\omega_i)$, this last being the information brought by the observation of message ω_i.

This leads us to the notions of self-information and mutual information.

5.2.3. *Self-information*

Let us denote as $A \subset \Omega$ an event, of probability $P(A)$. The *self-information associated with the event* A is the variable:

$$i(A) = -\log P(A). \tag{5.3}$$

This quantity has the following properties:

– it is always positive;

– it vanishes for the sure event;

– it goes to infinity as the probability of the event goes to 0;

– it is an additive quantity: observing two independent events A and B results in information which is the sum of the individual information:

$$i(A, B) = i(A) + i(B). \tag{5.4}$$

This last expression justifies using the logarithm function!

5.2.4. *Unit of information*

Information is a measure of the uncertainty related to the observation of a random event. The case of binary coding has naturally been used for its definition and its unit has been defined in the framework of binary coding of messages exchanged between a source and a destination in a communication network. In this context, the elementary uncertainty is related to the random event "arrival of a bit 0 or 1". Moreover, as we will see later on, the quantity of information then corresponds to the minimum number of bits needed for encoding the message.

We thus define the unit of information as the information obtained from the realization of one event among two of same probability, i.e.

$$\Omega = \{0, 1\}, \quad \text{with } P(0) = P(1) = 1/2,$$

and, choosing the base-2 logarithm we obtain:

$$i(A) = i(B) = -\log_2 P(1/2) = 1. \tag{5.5}$$

The unit of information here defined is the *bit* (abbreviation for *binary digit*), and is sometimes named the Shannon. In the following, and unless otherwise stated, the notation $\log x$ always stands for the logarithm to the base 2 of x.

Now we use the natural (Napierian) logarithm (base e) or the base-10 logarithm if it is easier. We then have $\log_e(e) = 1$, $\log_{10}(10) = 1$, and the following relations:

– $1 nit = \log_2(e) = 1/\log_e(2) = 1.44$ *bit*[1],

– $1 dit = \log_2(10) = 1/\log_{10}(2) = 3.32$ *bit*.

---

1. Some authors recommend the term *nat*, to avoid confusion with the unit of luminance.

5.2.5. *Conditional information*

Let us consider the realization of two events A and B, either independent or not.

The conditional information of A given B is the quantity:

$$i(A \mid B) = -\log P(A \mid B), \tag{5.6}$$

and (using the traditional notation):

$$i(A.B) = i(A) + i(B \mid A) = i(B) + i(A \mid B). \tag{5.7}$$

As a matter of fact,

$$i(A.B) = -\log P(A.B) = -\log P(A)P(B|A)$$
$$= -\log P(A) - \log P(B \mid A) = i(A) + i(B \mid A),$$

and also:

$$i(A.B) = -\log P(A.B) = -\log P(B)P(A \mid B)$$
$$= -\log P(B) - \log P(A \mid B) = i(B) + i(A \mid B).$$

The conditional information $i(A \mid B)$ is thus the information provided by A, and which was not already provided by B (and reciprocally for $i(B|A)$). Note for instance that if B is a sure event, conditional to the realization of A (that is, B is a consequence of A), then the information brought by the realization of both A and B is the same as that brought by A.

A typical transmission channel model consists of a conditional probability distribution: the addressee receives message B, given that the source has sent message A. The same model holds for prediction mechanisms.

5.2.6. *Mutual information*

Here again we consider two events (typically, at the input and output of a communication channel). The mutual information is the quantity:

$$i(A; B) = i(A) - i(A \mid B). \tag{5.8}$$

This quantity is symmetric:

$$i(A; B) = i(B) - i(B \mid A) = i(B; A).$$

Indeed:

$$i(A; B) = -\log P(A) + \log P(A \mid B)$$
$$= \log \frac{P(A \mid B)}{P(A)} = \log \frac{P(AB)}{P(A)P(B)} = i(B; A),$$

since $P(A \mid B) = \frac{P(AB)}{P(B)}$ (this is Bayes' theorem).

Notice that if the events A and B are identical (e.g. a noiseless communication), then $P(B \mid A) = 1$ and thus $i(A; B) = i(A) = i(B)$.

Now we can make the concept of *random source* information explicit. We have already noticed that from a qualitative viewpoint the concept of information can be considered as a measure of the *uncertainty* of observing an event. The more infrequent an event, the more information its realization brings. By observing the successive events the source generates, we actually measure the uncertainty associated with the source. As already noticed, the term *entropy* is attached to this notion, by analogy with thermodynamics. We now develop these points.

5.3. Entropy

In order to define entropy, let us consider a *memoryless* source, in its stationary state. That means that the successive symbols it sends are independent, obeying a common time-independent probability distribution.

5.3.1. *Entropy of a memoryless source*

We consider a memoryless source S, sending symbols s_i with probability p_i. The entropy $H(S)$ of the source is the average self-information it generates, that is:

$$H(S) = E\big[i(s_i)\big] = \sum p_i \log p_i. \tag{5.9}$$

More generally, given a discrete random variable $X = \{x_1, x_2, \ldots, x_n\}$ on Ω, its entropy is defined as:

$$H(S) = E\big[i(x_i)\big] = \sum p(x_i) \log p(x_i). \tag{5.10}$$

Clearly, this represents the *a priori* average uncertainty of the event (X).

5.3.2. *Entropy of a binary source*

A binary source is an important example. The corresponding random variable has a value 1 with probability $p_1 = p$ and a value 0 with probability $p_2 = 1-p$. Its entropy is thus given by:

$$H(X) = -p \log p - (1 - p) \log(1 - p) = H_2(p). \tag{5.11}$$

Let us consider in more detail the function $H_2(p)$:

– for $p = 0$ and $p = 1$, then $H_2(p) = 0$. Obviously in these two cases there is no uncertainty on the output;

– continuity: the entropy $H(X) = H_2(p_i)$ is a continuous function of p_i (sum of products of continuous functions – here the logarithm);

– the function is symmetric;

– it has a maximum for $p_1 = p_2 = 0.5$, where $H_2(p) = 1$.

Figure 5.2 represents the function $H_2(p)$. The properties of continuity and symmetry, and the existence of a maximum value still holds in the general case of the source with n symbols. Let us analyze the maximum value more closely.

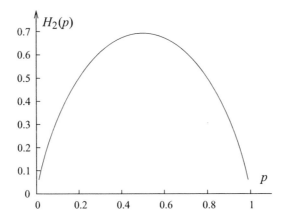

Figure 5.2. *Entropy function of a binary variable*

5.3.3. *Maximum entropy*

The maximum for the entropy is:

$$H_{\max} = \log n, \tag{5.12}$$

a value which is reached for $p_1 = p_2 = \cdots = p_n$. This result is obvious when we remember that uncertainty is highest when all events have the same probability, and thus the *a priori* knowledge is the smallest. Linking this with the thermodynamic concept of this entropy, corresponds to the case of maximum "disorder". This result can in fact be derived quite simply:

By the definition, $H(X) = -\sum p_i \log p_i$ with the condition $\sum p_i = 1$.

The Lagrange multipliers method allows us to write that:

$$\max \left[H(X) \right] \text{ happens for } \max \left[\Phi = -\sum_{i=1}^{n} p_i \log p_i + \lambda \left(\sum_{i=1}^{n} p_i - 1 \right) \right],$$

where λ is a constant.

The maximum of the function Φ is obtained by canceling its partial derivatives:

$$\frac{\partial \Phi}{\partial p_i} = 0 \quad \text{for } i = 1, \ldots, n, \text{ i.e.}$$

$\frac{\partial \Phi}{\partial p_i} = -\log p_i - \log e + \lambda = 0$, for all i, and thus $\log p_1 = \log p_2 = \cdots = \log p_n$.

Thus $p_1 = p_2 = \cdots = p_n$, and $H(X) = -\sum_{i=1}^{n} p_i \log p_i$ is then equal to $\log n$, so $H_{\max} = \log n$.

5.3.4. *Joint entropy of random variables*

Let $X = \{x_1, x_2, \ldots, x_n\}$ and $Y = \{y_1, y_2, \ldots, y_m\}$ be two random variables on Ω. The joint entropy of X and Y is the quantity:

$$H(X, Y) = -\sum_{i=1}^{n} \sum_{j=1}^{m} p(x_i, y_j) \log p(x_i, y_j). \tag{5.13}$$

Obviously, $H(X, Y) = H(Y, X)$.

The definition is readily extended to the case of an arbitrary set of random variables $X_p = \{x_1, x_2, \ldots, x_{n_p}\}$, with $p = 1, \ldots, k$:

$$H(X_1, X_2, \ldots, X_k) = -\sum_{i_1=1}^{n_1} \cdots \sum_{i_k=1}^{n_k} p(x_{1,i_1}, \ldots, x_{k,i_k}) \log p(x_{1,i_1}, \ldots, x_{k,i_k}).$$

5.3.5. *Average conditional entropy*

The entropy of X conditionally on Y is:

$$H(X \mid Y) = -\sum_{i=1}^{n} \sum_{j=1}^{m} p(x_i \mid y_j) \log p(x_i \mid y_j). \tag{5.14}$$

This is an average entropy, as we have:

$$H(X \mid y_j) = -\sum_{i=1}^{n} p(x_i \mid y_j) \log p(x_i \mid y_j),$$

and thus

$$H(X \mid Y) = -\sum_{j=1}^{m} p(y_j) H(X \mid y_j).$$

Note that, by its definition, the conditional entropy is no longer a symmetric quantity:

$$H(X \mid Y) \neq H(Y \mid X).$$

Instead of self-entropy or conditional entropy, the terms *a priori* and *a posteriori* are used. This leads to the following property.

5.3.6. *Additivity and joint entropy*

The additivity property is expressed as: the joint entropy of two random variables is the *a priori* entropy of the first added to the *a posteriori* entropy of the second. This property is a direct consequence of Bayes' theorem on conditional probabilities.

$$H(X,Y) = H(X) + H(Y \mid X) = H(Y) + H(X \mid Y). \tag{5.15}$$

Indeed,

$$H(X) + H(Y \mid X)$$

$$= -\left(\sum_{i=1}^{n} p(x_i) \log p(x_i) + \sum_{i=1}^{n} \sum_{j=1}^{m} p(x_i, y_j) \log p(y_j \mid x_i) \right)$$

$$= -\left(\sum_{i=1}^{n} \sum_{j=1}^{m} p(x_i, y_j) \log p(x_i) + \sum_{i=1}^{n} \sum_{j=1}^{m} p(x_i, y_j) \log p(y_j \mid x_i) \right)$$

$$= -\left(\sum_{i=1}^{n} \sum_{j=1}^{m} p(x_i, y_j) \log p(x_i) p(y_j \mid x_i) \right)$$

$$= -\left(\sum_{i=1}^{n} \sum_{j=1}^{m} p(x_i, y_j) \log p(x_i, y_j) \right) = H(X,Y),$$

as, from Bayes' theorem $p(x_i, y_j) = p(x_i) p(y_j \mid x_i)$.

More generally for several variables, we write

$$H(X,Y \mid Z) = H(X \mid Z) + H(Y \mid X, Z).$$

Indeed, the previous result for 2 variables allows us to write

$$H(X,Y,Z) = H(Z) + H(X,Y \mid Z),$$

and also

$$H(X,Y,Z) = H(X,Z) + H(Y \mid X, Z),$$

and

$$H(X,Z) = H(Z) + H(X \mid Z),$$

hence:

$$H(X, Y \mid Z) = H(X \mid Z) + H(Y \mid X, Z).$$

5.3.7. *Average mutual information*

The average mutual information is defined as:

$$I(X;Y) = \sum_{i=1}^{n} \sum_{j=1}^{m} p(x_i, y_j) \log \frac{p(x_i, y_j)}{p(x_i) p(y_j)}. \tag{5.16}$$

By its definition, average mutual information is a symmetric quantity:

$$I(X;Y) = I(Y;X).$$

We also have:

$$I(X;Y) = H(X) - H(X \mid Y) = H(Y) - H(Y \mid X)$$
$$= H(X) + H(Y) - H(X, Y).$$

5.3.8. *Conditional average mutual information*

Conditional average mutual information is defined as:

$$I(X;Y \mid Z) = \sum_{i,j,k} p(x_i, y_j, z_k) \log \frac{p(x_i, y_j \mid z_k)}{p(x_i \mid z_k) p(y_j \mid z_k)}. \tag{5.17}$$

By its definition this is a symmetric quantity:

$$I(X;Y \mid Z) = H(X \mid Z) - H(X, Y \mid Z).$$

All these expressions are readily generalized to an arbitrary number of variables.

5.3.9. *Extension to the continuous case*

Just as in probability theory, extension to the continuous case calls for the introduction of a new concept, namely *differential entropy* – to be compared with probability density. Indeed, if we go to the limit directly in the definition of entropy, this last goes to infinity since the probability of the elementary event goes to zero.

Differential entropy is defined as:

$$H_d(X) = - \int_{-\infty}^{\infty} p(x) \log \left[p(x) \right] \mathrm{d}x, \tag{5.18}$$

on condition that the integral exists. Similarly,

$$H_d(X, Y) = -\int\int p(x, y) \log\left[p(x, y)\right] dx dy,$$

$$H_d(X|Y) = -\int\int p(x|y) \log\left[p(x|y)\right] dx dy.$$

Consider, for instance, a uniformly distributed random variable on the interval $[0, a]$. It is such that the probability of a value within an interval being length dx is $f(x)dx = P(x < X \le x + dx) = dx/a$, and so $P(x) = 0, x < 0$; $P(x) = x/a$ for $x \le a$ and $P(x) = 1$, for $x > a$. Its differential entropy is given by:

$$H_d(X) = -\int_0^a \frac{1}{a} \log \frac{1}{a} dx = \log a.$$

In the same way, we could find that the Gaussian variable with mean m and standard deviation σ, and with cumulative distribution function given by:

$$P(X \le x) = \frac{1}{\sigma\sqrt{2\pi}} \int_{-\infty}^x e^{-(x-m)^2/2\sigma^2} dx, \quad -\infty < x < \infty$$

traditionally denoted as $N(m, \sigma^2)$, has the entropy:

$$H_d(X) = \frac{1}{2} \log\left(2\pi e \sigma^2\right) = \log\left(\sigma\sqrt{2\pi e}\right).$$

5.4. Source modeling

We now present various aspects of source modeling.

In what follows, we are exclusively concerned with discrete sources, i.e. sources which send information in the form of discrete symbols (samples, impulses, 0/1), as this corresponds to the general case in the telecommunications field. We distinguish the case of sources with memory and without memory. Emphasis will be placed in this context on the general model of the discrete Markov source (with memory). We show how we can approximate such sources with memoryless sources, by introducing the notions of *extension* and *adjoint* source. Then, as an example, we present the two main types of sources: images and texts.

5.4.1. *Concept of sources with and without memory*

A source is called memoryless when the occurrence probability of a symbol does not depend on the symbols previously observed. Denoting as $[S] = [s_1, s_2, \ldots, s_k]$ the set of source symbols, we then have $p(s_{i_n} \mid s_{i_{n-1}}, s_{i_{n-2}}, \ldots) = p(s_{i_n})$, index n standing for the rank of the symbol in the sequence.

On the other hand, a source is said to be with memory if the relation does not hold.

Studying this kind of source is mainly a matter of Markov graphs; these sources are called Markov sources. The source evolution is fully determined by its initial state and the conditional transition probabilities $p_{j|i}$ (in what follows we denote these probabilities by Π_{ij} too): $p_{j|i}$ is the probability that the source goes from state i to state j. It depends only on the present state, not on the previous ones (all the memory of the past history is summarized in the present state, and this is why we speak of a memoryless process). This is a very important model from a practical standpoint and we will develop its main features hereafter.

5.4.2. Discrete Markov source in discrete time

In this case, the source symbols are discrete random variables and are sent at discrete epochs (as opposed to a continuous process). Moreover, the alphabet of the source is assumed to be of finite size. This is naturally the situation commonly encountered in telecommunication systems.

The general model for that kind of source is a discrete-time discrete-random process, the evolution of which conforms to a Markov chain. Moreover, we assume *stationarity*, that is, the probability distributions are independent of the distance to the time origin, and *ergodicity*, that is, the expectation of an *arbitrary* random variable in the process, considered over a long enough period of time, goes to the time average (we return to these notions in greater detail in Chapter 6).

We denote as $X_i = \{1, 2, \ldots, q\}$ the set of states of the series $X_1, X_2, \ldots, X_n, \ldots$ of the random variable at times $(1, 2, \ldots, n, \ldots)$. The Markov chain which describes the process has q possible states. It is fully defined by the initial probability vector corresponding to the initial state X_1: $(\pi_1, \pi_2, \ldots, \pi_p)$, such that $\pi_i = P(X_1 = i)$, and by the transition probability matrix,

$$\Pi_{ij} = p(X_2 = j \mid X_1 = i) = p_{j|i}$$

with as usual $\sum_{j=1}^{q} \Pi_{ij} = 1$, for all $i \leq q$.

As a simple example we consider the case of a binary source. We assume it is a Markov source, which means that, observing a given symbol (0 or 1), we know the probability of observing 0 or 1 as the following symbol, as it is conditional to the previous symbol. The source is fully modeled by the set of conditional transition probabilities. In this simple case, we obtain a two-state Markov chain, with transition probabilities:

$$(p_{1|0}, p_{0|0} = 1 - p_{1|0}, \; p_{0|1}, p_{1|1} = 1 - p_{0|1}).$$

The Markov graph in Figure 5.3 highlights the evolution of the chain.

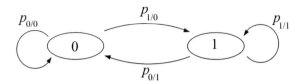

Figure 5.3. *Markov chain of a binary source*

In general, the models obviously tend to be more complex, but still completely defined by the set of transition probabilities from which we can derive the stationary state probabilities.

Markov models play a fundamental role in the fields of speech analysis, image processing, digital communications and numerous other domains, such as queueing theory, reliability, etc.: the following chapters will develop these models widely.

Stationarity. In all of what follows, we assume a stationary process, i.e. such that, observing the Markov chain for a long enough time, the distribution of the state probabilities goes to a limit distribution independent of the initial state, and such that:

$$\lim_{n \to \infty} P(X_n = i) = p_i,$$

and then we have (see Chapter 6):

$$p_j = \sum_{j=1}^{q} \Pi_{ij} p_i.$$

Returning to our simple example, the stationary behavior obeys the following set of equations:

$$p_1 = (1 - p_{0|1})p_1 + p_{1|0}p_0, \quad p_1 = 1 - p_0,$$

the solution of which is readily obtained:

$$p_1 = \frac{p_{1|0}}{p_{0|1} + p_{1|0}}; \quad p_0 = \frac{p_{0|1}}{p_{0|1} + p_{1|0}}.$$

Memory and entropy. On the whole, memory introduces a correlation between the successive states visited by the system. As a consequence, the model has to take account of the joint probabilities of a symbol series: $P(X_1, \ldots, X_n)$. For such a source we define the entropy of the message with length n (a sequence of n successive states): $H(X_1, \ldots, X_n)$, of which we take the average to define the source entropy. So:

$$H(S) = \lim_{n \to \infty} \frac{H(X_1, \ldots, X_n)}{n}. \tag{5.19}$$

This is the *entropy rate*, that is, the average entropy per symbol, if the limit exists. For a memoryless source, obviously $H(X_1, \ldots, X_n) = nH(X)$.

For a Markov source,

$$H(X_1, \ldots, X_n) = H(X_1) + H(X_2 \mid X_1)$$
$$+ H(X_3 \mid X_2) + \cdots + H(X_n \mid X_{n-1}),$$

with $H(X_2 \mid X_1) = H(X_3 \mid X_2) = \cdots = H(X_n \mid X_{n-1})$. Hence,

$$H(S) = \lim_{n \to \infty} \frac{H(X_1, \ldots, X_n)}{n}$$
$$= \lim_{n \to \infty} \left[\frac{1}{n} H(X_1) + \frac{n-1}{n} H(X_n \mid X_{n-1}) \right] \qquad (5.20)$$
$$= H(X_n \mid X_{n-1}).$$

That is,

$$H(S) = -\sum_{i=1}^{q} \sum_{j=1}^{q} p_i \Pi_{ij} \log \Pi_{ij}. \qquad (5.21)$$

This entropy is naturally lower than that of a memoryless source, for which we would have:

$$H_0(S) = H(X) = -\sum_{i=1}^{q} p_i \log p_i. \qquad (5.22)$$

Adjoint source. The source S' adjoint to the Markov source S is the memoryless source with the same stationary probabilities as the Markov source. Obviously,

$$H(S') = H_0(S) \geq H(S).$$

Concept of extension. The nth order extension of a source S, denoted as S^n, is the source such that its symbols are all possible sequences of length n of the source S. We can verify that its entropy is n times the entropy of S:

$$H(S^n) = nH(S). \qquad (5.23)$$

Clearly, working on the extension of a source decreases correlation, so that we have the important result:

$$\lim_{n \to \infty} \left| H(S^{n'}) - H(S^n) \right| = 0, \qquad (5.24)$$

meaning that *considering higher order extensions of the Markov source, we move closer to a memoryless behavior*. This result allows us to generalize the coding methods for memoryless sources to sources with memory, which we present in section 5.5.

5.4.3. *The main types of source*

We now illustrate these notions by presenting the major information sources as encountered in telecommunications.

5.4.3.1. *The binary source*

This is a source generating 0s and 1s as successive symbols, corresponding for instance to the black and white dots (*pixels*) obtained by scanning a document at constant speed, just as in a fax. If we make no assumption about the document to send, this is a memoryless source, the successive occurrences of 0s and 1s being independent, although they can have different probabilities.

As an example, consider that the probabilities of 0 and 1 are respectively $p_1 = 0.8$, $p_0 = 0.2$. The entropy of the source is, using equation (5.9):

$$H(S) = -(0.8 \log 0.8 + 0.2 \log 0.2) = 0.72.$$

However, real texts or images sent by fax obviously exhibit a correlation between symbols: the nature of the language itself, built from words, sentences, paragraphs, etc., introduces dependencies in the sequence of dots. A Markov model is well suited to study the behavior of such sources. Based on a large sample, we can estimate the transition probabilities. Assume for instance that we have observed $p_{1|0} = 0.4$ and $p_{0|1} = 0.1$. The symbol probabilities remain the same as those of the memoryless source:

$$p_1 = \frac{p_{1|0}}{p_{1|0} + p_{0|1}} = 0.8, \quad p_0 = \frac{p_{0|1}}{p_{1|0} + p_{0|1}} = 0.2,$$

but its entropy is given this time by equation (5.21):

$$H(S) = -\sum_{i=1}^{q}\sum_{j=1}^{q} p_i \Pi_{ij} \log \Pi_{ij},$$

that is, here

$$H(S) = p_1 \left[-p_{0|1} \log p_{0|1} - (1 - p_{0|1}) \log (1 - p_{0|1}) \right]$$
$$+ p_0 \left[-p_{1|0} \log p_{1|0} - (1 - p_{1|0}) \log (1 - p_{1|0}) \right].$$

The numerical application gives $H(S) = 0.568$, which is indeed lower than 0.72, reflecting the effect of the correlation.

Let us now consider the second order extension of this source; this means that we are concerned with word sequences of two symbols: $(00, 01, 10, 11)$. The probabilities corresponding to this case are:

$$p_{00} = p_0 p_{0|0}, \quad p_{01} = p_0 p_{1|0}, \quad p_{10} = p_1 p_{0|1}, \quad p_{11} = p_1 p_{1|1}.$$

The entropy of this adjoint source is $H(S') = -\sum\sum p_{ij} \log p_{ij}$, and the numerical application yields $H(S') = 1.288$, that is, 0.644 per symbol. Clearly we get closer to the memoryless case; third order extensions would again increase the entropy.

For actual applications, such as a fax machine, an image or text is transmitted by sending 2,623 black or white dots per line. By observing a large sample, we can build statistics on the number of consecutive black (white) dots, and we encode the corresponding sequences. In the 1-dimension G31D standard, this statistic is performed for each line, and lines are encoded one at a time, but more sophisticated versions take account of correlations between successive lines.

A colored image is another example of this kind of source (and more generally a sequence of images, e.g. television). Here too the image is a sequence of symbols representing the three primary colors of each pixel, obtained by browsing each line of each image of the sequence to transmit. This mechanism is referred to as *raster scanning*.

We will discuss the compression techniques for these images later. Their characteristics will lead us to develop a large variety of these techniques.

5.4.3.2. *Text, or alphabetic source*

The source produces a sequence of symbols drawn from the *alphabet of a given language*. Numerous examples can be imagined, from telegraph to emails or signaling messages exchanged in telecommunication networks, etc. In the general case, the initial source *symbols* $[S] = [s_1, s_2, \ldots, s_k]$ are transformed in the same number of *codewords*, best suited to the transmission channel. Codewords are built from the channel alphabet, generally made of binary characters $\alpha = (0, 1)$. They are the *letters* of the code.

Most often it is a matter of transforming a source file, already in a binary form, into another binary file, better suited to the channel. Several encoding schemes are possible. As an elementary example, for a source able to generate four symbols, we could have the following encoding of $[S] = [s_1, s_2, s_3, s_4]$ into $[C] = [c_1, c_2, c_3, c_4]$:

$$\text{Code 1}: c_1 = 00, \quad c_2 = 01, \quad c_3 = 10, \quad c_4 = 11;$$

or

$$\text{Code 2}: c_1 = 0, \quad c_2 = 10, \quad c_3 = 110, \quad c_4 = 111.$$

Naturally other codes could be considered, which will be more or less optimal, as we show later.

A source of that kind usually exhibits memory properties, depending on the correlation of the symbols (the letters of the text) generated by the source. The simplest model assumes independence between successive letters, but these letters are no longer equiprobable (in English, as well as in French, "e" is by far the most frequent letter, for instance). A more precise model takes account of various correlations, such as those related to grammatical rules (on that subject, we should note that Markov developed his theory in the context of linguistics).

It will then be necessary to operate on symbol blocks, via techniques such as extension, or others discussed later, in the case of images for instance.

5.4.4. *Information rate of the source*

Here, we attempt to associate the quantity of information with its transmission speed. The information rate of the source is defined as the product of its entropy (i.e. the average information per symbol) and the average number of symbols sent per time unit. This concept adapts perfectly to the case of actual communication networks, where symbols are sent at a constant rate.

Let $\bar{\tau}$ be the average duration to transmit a symbol, the information rate is then:

$$H_t(S) = \frac{H(S)}{\bar{\tau}}, \quad \text{with} \quad [S] = [s_1, s_2, \ldots, s_k]. \tag{5.25}$$

It is usually expressed in bits per second (b/s).

5.5. Source coding

We now present the basic principles of source coding, from the standpoint of information theory – and specifically the notions of code efficiency and redundancy. Here we restrict ourselves to the case of memoryless sources, keeping in mind that the notions of adjoint source and extensions, already presented, allow us to extend these principles to sources with memory, such as Markov sources.

5.5.1. *Code efficiency*

We have seen previously that the source symbols s_i are translated into codewords c_i. Naturally, the main goal of this coding is to reach the maximum efficiency in the transport of information.

In order to quantify this efficiency, we associate a cost with the message, corresponding to its length. Actually, we can consider that the longer the message, the higher its transmission cost.

Let us denote as l_i the length of the codeword c_i, i.e. the total number of letters (drawn from an alphabet of l letters) composing the word. We assume that all the letters of the alphabet $[\alpha] = [\alpha_1, \alpha_2, \ldots, \alpha_l]$ in the codewords $[C] = [c_1, c_2, \ldots, c_k]$ are transmitted at the same speed (e.g., the 0s and 1s are transmitted with the same speed on a digital link). We assume that the codewords and source symbols have the same occurrence probability (there is a direct correspondence between a symbol and its codeword). Then we have the following properties:

– The source or code entropy is:

$$H(S) = H(C) = -\sum_{i=1}^{k} p(s_i) \log p(s_i),$$

where $H(C)$ is the entropy of the codewords (average information).

– The average length of a codeword is

$$\bar{l} = \sum p(s_i) l_i. \tag{5.26}$$

The average information of a codeword is the product of its average number of letters by the average information per letter, that is:

$$i(C) = H(S) = H(C) = \bar{l} H(\alpha), \tag{5.27}$$

with, for $H(\alpha)$, the entropy of the code alphabet:

$$H(\alpha) = -\sum_{i=1}^{l} p(\alpha_i) \log p(\alpha_i),$$

the maximum of which is $\log l$.

Thus, we have the following important relation:

$$H(S) = H(C) = \bar{l} H(\alpha) \leq \bar{l} \log l. \tag{5.28}$$

Capacity of a code. The *capacity* of a code is the maximum entropy value of its alphabet:

$$C = \max H(\alpha) = \log l. \tag{5.29}$$

Minimum length. Taking account of the above inequality, the minimum length for a code is:

$$\bar{l}_{\min} = \frac{H(S)}{\log l}. \tag{5.30}$$

This allows us to define the efficiency.

Efficiency. The efficiency of the code is the ratio of its minimum to its average length.

$$\eta = \frac{\bar{l}_{\min}}{\bar{l}} = \frac{H(S)}{\bar{l} \log l} = \frac{H(\alpha)}{\log l}, \tag{5.31}$$

which we can write as:

$$\eta = \frac{H(\alpha)}{H_{\max}(\alpha)}. \tag{5.32}$$

5.5.2. *Redundancy of a code*

From all these notions, we can define the redundancy of the code as the difference between the maximum entropy of its alphabet and its actual value:

$$R_s = H_{\max}(\alpha) - H(\alpha),$$

and the *relative redundancy*:

$$\rho = 1 - \frac{H_{\max}(\alpha)}{H(\alpha)} = 1 - \eta, \tag{5.33}$$

which can be written as:

$$\rho = \frac{\log l - H(\alpha)}{\log l}.$$

As an example, we consider again code (1), with four two-letter codewords, presented above:

$$[S] = [s_1, s_2, s_3, s_4] \longrightarrow \text{code (1)} \ [C] = [c_1 = 00, c_2 = 01, c_3 = 10, c_4 = 11],$$

with which we associate the set of probabilities $[p_1 = 0.5, p_2 = 0.25, p_3 = 0.125, p_4 = 0.125]$.

The average codeword length is $\bar{l} = \sum p(s_i) l_i = 2$. The efficiency is

$$\eta = \frac{H(S)}{\bar{l} \log l} = \frac{-\sum p(s_i) \log p(s_i)}{\bar{l} \log l} = 0.875,$$

and the redundancy:

$$\rho = 0.125.$$

On the other hand, considering code (2), with the same set of probabilities,

$$[S] = [s_1, s_2, s_3, s_4] \longrightarrow \text{code (2)} \ [C] = [c_1 = 0, c_2 = 10, c_3 = 110, c_4 = 111],$$

we obtain:

$$\bar{l} = 1.75, \quad \eta = 1, \quad \rho = 0.$$

As we will see later, minimizing the redundancy, so as to optimize the transmission resources, is an essential goal of coding – but not the only one.

5.5.3. *Instantaneous and uniquely decipherable codes*

Up to now we have concentrated on code length. We can end by addressing their *nature*. We can conceive that a desirable property of a code is that each codeword has a precise meaning, i.e. each source symbol corresponds with one and only one codeword, so that it can be identified without ambiguity. Such a code is said to be *uniquely decipherable*. Moreover, if we attempt to optimize the decoding speed, the order in which the letters appear in the codewords is of interest.

For instance, with

$$[S] = [s_1, s_2, s_3, s_4] \longrightarrow \text{code (2')} \; [C] = [c_1 = 0, c_2 = 10, c_3 = 110, c_4 = 1110],$$

each word can be identified, *without any ambiguity*, upon arrival of the letters 0 and 1 (the reader should note that 0 plays the role of separator between successive words). We can compare this with the previous codes which do not enjoy such a property.

The feature of the code is that no codeword can serve as a prefix for another longer word: it is said to possess the prefix property or to be *irreducible*.

5.6. Shannon's first theorem

We present here Shannon's first theorem, which concerns optimal source coding and the transmission of its information on a non-perturbed channel, while also giving limits to the compression rate which can be expected. We first introduce several basic concepts.

5.6.1. *Optimal coding*

Here, we attempt to determine the conditions of existence required for an optimal coding scheme, i.e. a code having maximum efficiency.

Let S be a memoryless stationary source $[S] = [s_1, s_2, \ldots, s_k]$, generating k codewords $[C] = [c_1, c_2, \ldots, c_k]$, of average length $\bar{l}$.

We have seen previously that efficiency is maximized when $\bar{l} = \bar{l}_{min} = H(S)/\log l$, and is obtained when $H(\alpha)$ is maximum, i.e. $H(\alpha) = \log l$. This value is reached when all the l letters of the alphabet have the same occurrence probability:

$$p(\alpha_1) = p(\alpha_2) = \cdots = p(\alpha_l) = \frac{1}{l}.$$

Assuming these letters are independent, we have:

$$p(s_i) = p(c_i) = \left(\frac{1}{l}\right)^{l_i}.$$

Now, $\sum_{i=1}^{k} p(s_i) = 1$, and so:

$$\sum_{i=1}^{k} \left(\frac{1}{l}\right)^{l_i} = 1. \tag{5.34}$$

From here we can conclude that, given an alphabet, with a known number of letters and words, an *optimal coding scheme* can be designed, provided relation (5.34) holds.

This result is only a special case of the McMillan inequality, which states:

$$\sum_{i=1}^{k} \left(\frac{1}{l}\right)^{l_i} \leq 1, \tag{5.35}$$

and which expresses a necessary and sufficient condition for the existence of *irreducible codes*.

McMillan inequality. We consider a code with k words of increasing lengths l_i, $i = 1, \ldots, j$, such that n_i words have length l_i. Clearly we have $\sum_{i=1}^{j} n_i = k$, thus McMillan inequality (5.35) can be re-written in the form:

$$\sum_{i=1}^{j} n_i \left(\frac{1}{l}\right)^{l_i} \leq 1. \tag{5.36}$$

Let us first verify that this condition is necessary for irreducibility.

The maximum possible number of words with length l_j with an alphabet of l letters is l^{l_j}. As already explained, the condition required for the code to be irreducible is that none of its codewords should be obtained from another shorter word serving as a *prefix*. Now, beginning with a word of length l_i, $i = 1, \ldots, j - 1$, $l^{l_j - l_i}$ words of length l_j can be formed using this word of length l_i as prefix. Thus, with n_i words of length l_i, $n_i l^{l_j - l_i}$ can be formed, and on the whole $\sum_{i<j} n_i l^{l_j - l_i}$ words of length l_i, which must be excluded in an irreducible code.

Thus, the *maximum* number n_j of possible words forming an irreducible code (we speak here of a maximum absolute code) is:

$$n_j = l^{l_j} - \sum_{i<j} n_i l^{l_j - l_i},$$

which can be written as:

$$n_j l^{-l_j} + \sum_{i<j} n_i l^{-l_i} = \sum_{i=1}^{j} n_i (l)^{-l_i} = 1.$$

This is precisely the McMillan condition:

$$\sum_{i=1}^{j} n_i \left(\frac{1}{l}\right)^{l_i} \leq 1.$$

This condition is sufficient, too. Indeed, consider again a l-letter alphabet, from which we draw n_1 words of length l_1 among the l^{l_1} words possible, i.e. $n_1 \leq l^{l_1}$. So $l^{l_1} - n_1$ words remain as possible prefixes for the other codewords. Using these prefixes we can form $(l^{l_1} - n_1)l^{l_2 - l_1} = l^{l_2} - n_1 l^{l_2 - l_1}$ words of length l_2, and so on until l_j, which gives the condition.

This is actually the previous expression, which therefore happens to give sufficient conditions for the existence of an irreducible code.

5.6.2. Shannon's first theorem

We now take into account the fact that the symbols to be encoded appear with probability $p(s_i)$.

We have already established that the minimum average length of the codewords, i.e. the maximum efficiency of the code, is obtained when codeword lengths obey the relation:

$$p(s_i) = p(c_i) = \left(\frac{1}{l}\right)^{l_i},$$

or:

$$l_i = \frac{-\log p(s_i)}{\log l}.$$

The above ratio is generally not an integer, and the condition becomes (by simply rounding to the nearest integer):

$$\left\lfloor \frac{-\log p(s_i)}{\log l} \right\rfloor \leq l_i \leq \left\lfloor \frac{-\log p(s_i)}{\log l} \right\rfloor + 1. \qquad (5.37)$$

This gives:

$$- \log p(s_i) \le l_i \log l = \log l^{l_i},$$

or $(1/l)^{l_i} \le p(s_i)$, and thus $\sum_{i=1}^{k}(1/l)^{l_i} \le 1$. That means that the McMillan inequality is satisfied and thus an irreducible code with words of length l_i exists, as defined above. Equation (5.37) gives, by summing on indices i:

$$\frac{H(S)}{\log l} \le \bar{l} \le \frac{H(S)}{\log l} + 1.$$

Now, instead of considering the symbols individually, we can associate and encode them in groups of size n. The source being memoryless, we have for the new source, which is the *extension* denoted as S^n already introduced:

$$\frac{H(S^n)}{\log l} \le \bar{l_n} \le \frac{H(S^n)}{\log l} + 1,$$

and

$$H(S^n) = nH(S),$$

where $H(S^n)$ stands for the joint entropy of the messages composed of n successive symbol strings.

So:

$$\frac{H(S)}{\log l} \le \frac{\bar{l_n}}{n} \le \frac{H(S)}{\log l} + \frac{1}{n},$$

and going to the limit:

$$\lim_{n \to \infty} \frac{\bar{l_n}}{n} = \frac{H(S)}{\log l} = \bar{l}. \tag{5.38}$$

We again find the condition for an optimal coding, $\bar{l}_{\min} = H(s)/\log l$.

This is Shannon's first theorem, related to source coding on noiseless channels: *for any stationary source it is possible, through appropriate coding, to reduce the average entropy per letter as close as desired to the code capacity $\log l$ – i.e. to come to the minimal average codeword length.*

Actually, the value of n remains finite, and moreover $n = 1$ often provides satisfactory results, as larger values improve the efficiency for memoryless sources only marginally. The problem is then to build a *simply optimal* code, the one closest to the really optimal code.

This is the goal of source coding, as well as data compression algorithms (as an appropriate encoding reduces the volume needed to store data). We now address these issues.

5.7. Coding and data compression

Source encoding is a natural constraint, due to the need to adapt to transport support or information storage. The goal is then to translate from one symbol to the other so as to make the best possible use of the resource (transmission channel or storage medium), assumed to be error-free. Moreover, as will become clear for images, various kinds of redundancy make it possible to associate coding with specific compression techniques.

In light of what we have seen previously, we can understand that the goal of source coding is to obtain another source of maximum entropy. Here, we look for a method yielding the optimal code regardless of the source symbol probabilities. As we have seen, for an optimal code the shortest words should be associated with the most probable source symbols. It follows that, given codewords of known lengths, encoding consists of sorting these according to increasing lengths so as to match the longest words with the source symbols that occur least. This is *entropy coding*. It should be recalled that only codewords enjoying the prefix property can be taken into account (they are sometimes also called prefix-free); thus, the source alphabet must be used to build codewords of increasing length obeying this property.

These are the bases on which various encoding algorithms have been developed. We first illustrate the principle, through the presentation of the fundamental Huffman coding. Then we address the general issue of compression, for which a large variety of encoding and redundancy reduction techniques can be deployed.

5.7.1. *Huffman coding algorithm*

The Huffman algorithm is adapted to binary codes, i.e. codes relying on binary alphabets: the alphabet has two symbols, for instance 0 and 1. Obviously this is well suited to telecommunications.

Let us introduce the concept of a *tree*. We can represent the set of source symbols $[S]$ as S leaves of a tree. Then, we can build a binary tree as follows. To each leaf the probability $p(s_i)$ of a symbol s_i is attached, and then we propagate towards the root, by attaching a weight to each internal node, equal to the sum of the probabilities of its children. The following diagram gives an example of a binary tree corresponding to a source with 4 symbols $[S] = [s_1, s_2, s_3, s_4]$, with which the probabilities $[p(s_1) = 0.5, p(s_2) = 0.25, p(s_3) = 0.125, p(s_4) = 0.125]$ are associated.

The Huffman algorithm builds an optimal tree, in that it leads to an optimal code, starting with the leaves and grouping symbols according to their probabilities. This is achieved through the following steps:

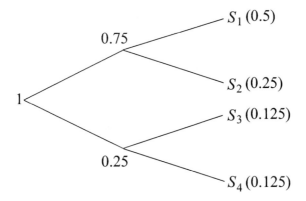

Figure 5.4. *Binary tree of a 4-symbol source*

– sorting the set of symbols by probability in decreasing order:

$$p(s_1) \geq p(s_2) \geq p(s_3) \geq \cdots \geq p(s_S)$$

– grouping the symbol couples with the lowest probability (thus necessarily $p(s_S)$ and $p(s_{S-1})$) into one new element g_1 with which is associated the weight $p(g_1) = p(s_S) + p(s_{S-1})$; the new element is introduced in the list, which is sorted again so that:

$$p(s_1') \geq p(s_2') \geq p(g_1) \geq \cdots$$

– the process is iterated with the two elements at the end of the list, and then iterated until the last two elements g_n and g_{n-1} are obtained;

– now, starting from the root (probability 1), the set $[S]$ may be described by a tree, the first two branches of which are g_n and g_{n-1}, having probabilities as close as possible $p(g_n)$ and $p(g_{n-1})$, themselves split into two sub-branches of close probability, etc., until reaching the leaves, which are the symbols $s_1, s_2, s_3, \ldots, s_S$.

The codewords are built by associating a 0 (or 1) and a 1 (or 0) with each step:

$$g_n \longrightarrow 0 \quad (\text{or } 1)$$
$$g_{n-1} \longrightarrow 1 \quad (\text{or } 0),$$

and so on. Applying this procedure to our previous example yields the diagram in Figure 5.5, from which we obtain the following code:

$$[S] = [s_1, s_2, s_3, s_4] \longrightarrow \text{code: } [C] = [c_1 = 0, c_2 = 10, c_3 = 110, c_4 = 111]$$

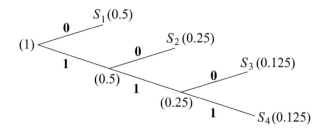

Figure 5.5. *Binary tree according to the Huffman algorithm*

The way 0s or 1s are chosen at each step leads to several codes, all of which are optimal.

We can verify the efficiency of the example; here we have:

$$\bar{l} = \sum p(s_i)l_i = 1.75 \quad \text{and} \quad \eta = \frac{H(S)}{\bar{l}\log l} = \frac{1.75}{1.75\log 2} = 1.$$

The code is directly based upon the occurrence probability of the symbols, explaining the term *entropic*, or *statistic*, attached to it.

5.7.2. *Retrieval algorithms and decision trees*

The algorithm just described can also serve to optimize the time needed to retrieve items in a database. Knowing the probability attached to each object, we can store them optimally using the Huffman algorithm.

The same approach can be applied to build optimal questionnaires, and more generally to the problems related to *decision trees*, as we now show.

The medical diagnosis will serve as an example. We assume the physician has the knowledge of the conditional probabilities of some diseases, given the symptom S_i the patient describes. More precisely, if the answer to the question S_i "does this organ hurt you?" is "yes", then he knows that the probability of disease D_i is $P(D_i \mid S_i)$.

The problem is then to design a questionnaire leading to a diagnosis in the smallest possible number of questions.

To that end, the questionnaire is built in the form of a decision tree. This is exactly the coding diagram we have already introduced. Figure 5.6 displays the typical structure. The practitioner asks the first question, and depending on the answer asks another one, etc., so as to review the different symptoms, until he reaches the leaf

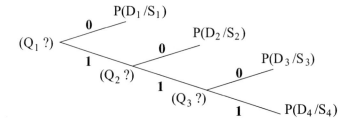

Figure 5.6. *Decision tree of a diagnosis*

with the lowest residual uncertainty. Knowing the set of probabilities attached to the branches, the sequence of questions can be arranged, just as for the design of the optimal coding.

The set of variables – symptoms, diseases, diagnosis – and the corresponding conditional probabilities form a typical *Bayesian network*.

5.7.3. *(Reversible) data compression*

Here we address the following problem: from a binary source file T, we must obtain another binary file C, which is shorter but carries the same information.

The compression ratio is defined as the ratio of the file lengths $l(T)$ and $l(C)$ (usually expressed in number of bits or bytes). Here we are mainly concerned with reversible compression, such that we can retrieve the totality of the original file when decompressing.

We distinguish the case of real time compression (the content of T is received as a data flow) from the case where the whole source file is already available.

At last, we limit the presentation to the so-called *zero order methods*, in which the successive symbols are considered as independent. In the higher order methods this assumption is relaxed; however, they use the same approach, based upon conditional probabilities (for instance, we will use the notion of extension, by considering symbol clusters).

The principle is first to define a set of words (symbols) $S = \{s_1, s_2, \ldots, s_S\}$ in the source file T, and then to replace each word s_i by a codeword c_i in the compressed/encoded file C.

The first step concerns the definition of the words of T; this is referred to as parsing the file. In most of the methods the set of the words is such that it verifies the important *strong parsing property* (SPP) a list of symbols $S = \{s_1, s_2, \ldots, s_S\}$ (binary words) is said to verify the SPP if and only if every binary text can be represented in the form of a unique concatenation of some of the words and of a suffix (possibly empty) with no other word as prefix, and shorter than the maximum word length.

To understand this condition we need to remember that a prefix-free code (that is, such that no word is a prefix for another word) is uniquely decipherable. So, if we build a text T by the concatenation of an arbitrary sequence of words from this code, it will be impossible to build the same text using another sequence. Thus, the decoding can be performed on the fly (as soon as the symbols are received: this is called an *instantaneous* code).

It can be shown that if $s_1, s_2, \ldots, s_S$ is a string of binary words, then it verifies the SPP property if and only if it is prefix-free and it verifies the so-called Kraft-McMillan inequality (we do not give the proof here):

$$\sum_{s_i \in S} 2^{-l(s_i)} \leq 1.$$

S is then said to be a complete prefix-free code.

Although this can seem rather complex, the reader should not worry. Indeed, we can verify that such conditions can be met simply by using an alphabet $S = \{0,1\}^8$ for the text (i.e. a source file encoded in bytes – this is the commonly used solution). More generally, any alphabet of the kind $S = \{0,1\}^L$, with L the (fixed) word length, is a solution.

Once we have solved the problem of defining source symbols, we can address coding issues, so as to compress the text as much as possible, i.e. so as to reduce its length to the minimal value without any information loss.

Needless to say, in the light of the previous considerations, the shortest codewords must be associated with the most frequent source symbols, and this naturally returns us to the Huffman algorithm.

5.7.3.1. *The Huffman method*

This is by far the most popular method. Here again, it consists of building a binary tree, starting from the smaller probability leaves and moving to the root by grouping them.

To this end, we assume we know the sequence $T = s_3 s_2 s_5 \ldots$, built with the symbols $(s_1, s_2, \ldots, s_S)$ and their relative frequencies $f_1, f_2, \ldots, f_S$, and we assume they have been numbered in such a way that $f_1 \geq f_2 \geq \cdots \geq f_S$. We should however note that while this implies having the whole text at our disposal, the method could work from a probabilistic *model* of the source.

Let us give an elementary example.

Assume we are given a source text made with symbols $(s_1, s_2, s_3, s_4, s_5)$, of which the relative frequencies have been estimated: $f_1 = 0.41$, $f_2 = 0.17$, $f_3 = 0.15$, $f_4 = 0.14$, $f_5 = 0.13$. The tree is built as previously, shown in Figure 5.7, with a slightly different presentation, intended to bring out the grouping process from the "extreme" leaves to the root.

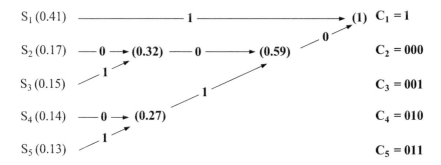

Figure 5.7. *Coding tree for compression, Huffman method*

By convention the bit 0 is associated with the branch of higher weight (but choosing bit 1 would work as well). Going from the root to the leaves we find the various codewords. We know this procedure leads to an optimal code.

The average code length is 2.18 bits, to be compared with a code using fixed-length words 3 bits long.

It is important to note that this method also works for streams of data. In this case the frequencies are modified on the fly while reading data and the decision tree is correlatively updated. This method is referred to as *adaptive Huffman encoding*. Decoding raises no difficulty as long as the decoder updates its tree synchronically with the encoder.

Other methods were designed earlier, notably by Fano and Shannon, the principles of which are briefly presented now.

5.7.3.2. *Fano method*

The Fano method is close to the Huffman method. It differs by proceeding in the reverse order, that is, journeying from the root to the most distant leaves. The *ordered sequence* is split into two groups (1 to k and $k+1$ to S) of closest cumulated frequency. As before, they are associated with bits 0 and 1 respectively, then the process is repeated until all leaves are reached.

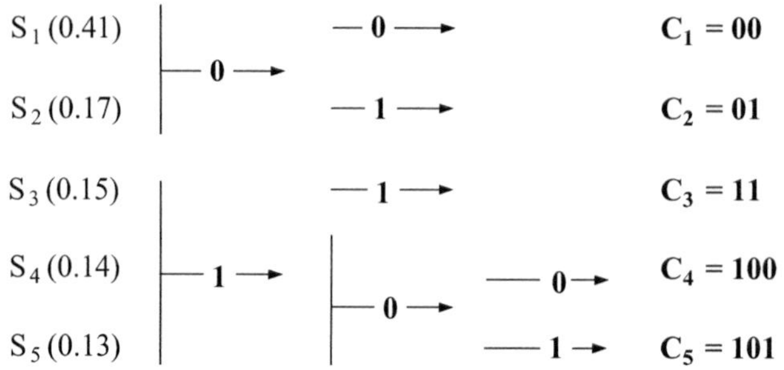

Figure 5.8. *Coding tree for compression, Fano method*

We can apply the method to our example, ending up with the diagram in Figure 5.8.

The average code length is 2.27 bits, slightly greater than in the previous solution, but with different codewords, and still smaller than 3 bits.

5.7.3.3. *Shannon's method*

We briefly outline this method, as its interest lies in its principles, re-used in the arithmetic coding described hereafter. Given the set of symbols $s_1, s_2, \ldots, s_S$ and their relative frequencies $f_1, f_2, \ldots, f_S$ (possibly rearranged and renumbered so as to verify $f_1 \geq f_2 \geq \cdots \geq f_S$), the idea is to calculate the cumulated frequencies (F_i), and then to take as code c_i the l_i initial bits of the binary expansion of the number F_i, with $l_i = -\log(f_i)$.

Remember that the binary expansion of a real number r is defined by the series (a_i), such that $r = \lim_{n \to \infty} \sum_{j=1}^{n} a_j 2^{-j}$, with $a_i \in \{0, 1\}$.

This method generates prefix-free codes. The interested reader may find more details in specialized textbooks [WEH 03].

5.7.3.4. *Arithmetic coding*

In circumstances where the fixed length L of source codes is high (for instance source encoded in bytes), thus corresponding to a large number of symbols, the previous methods require the processing of a large number of frequencies, and may lead to poor performance for these algorithms, due to the exponential growth in the related combinatorics. In such a case, arithmetic coding provides a more efficient approach.

Instead of encoding characters of the source file one by one, the algorithm processes strings of characters, of length depending on the capacity of the machine to code large real numbers. In this method, we make use of the probability of each symbol (given *a priori* or estimated according to some model) to determine an interval for the probability of the string. To this interval is allocated a unique number between 0 and 1, which encodes the whole string.

Let us consider a block t of text (or the entire text). It appears as a particular symbol string from the source alphabet.

Arithmetic coding takes up the basic idea of Shannon's method. We first calculate the relative frequencies $f_1, f_2, \ldots, f_S$ of the symbols $s_1, s_2, \ldots, s_S$ (possibly rearranged and renumbered so as to verify $f_1 \geq f_2 \geq \cdots \geq f_S$) and the cumulated frequencies F_j. Each symbol is then assigned an interval $]F_{j-1}, F_j]$ on the distribution function. From this it is possible to calculate a probability level $]F_{t-1}, F_t]$ for each specific sequence of t symbols, and a real number belonging to this interval is chosen for encoding the string.

Let us make this clearer through a simple example. We consider the string corresponding to the word IRIS (the divine messenger of the gods in the Greek mythology). It uses 3 symbols, here arbitrarily numbered from 1 to 3: $s_1 = I$, $s_2 = R$, $s_3 = S$. The relative frequencies are here $f_1 = 0.5$, $f_2 = 0.25$, $f_3 = 0.25$, and thus the cumulated frequencies are:

$$F_0 = 0; \quad F_1 = 0.5; \quad F_2 = 0.75; \quad F_3 = 1.$$

Thus, each symbol is associated with the following interval:

$$(I)s_1 \longrightarrow 0 \leq r < 0.5,$$

$$(R)s_2 \longrightarrow 0.5 \leq r < 0.75,$$

$$(S)s_3 \longrightarrow 0.75 \leq r < 1.$$

The text is encoded progressively, starting with the first letter. For I the value is between 0 (strict) and 0.5. Then for the string IR, with the symbols assumed to be independent (the zero order assumption), the value is between $0 + (0.5 - 0) \times 0.5 = 0.25$ and $0 + (0.5 - 0) \times 0.75 = 0.375$, this is the joint probability interval of I and R.

Similarly for IRI we obtain a value between $0.25 + (0.375 - 0.25) \times 0 = 0.25$ and $0.25 + (0.375 - 0.25) \times 0.5 = 0.3125$. Finally, for $IRIS$ the interval between $0.25 + (0.3125 - 0.25) \times 0.75 = 0.296875$ and $0.25 + (0.3125 - 0.25) \times 1 = 0.3125$. To summarize, the probability distribution of the "function" IRIS is

$$I \longrightarrow 0 \leq P < 0.5$$

$$IR \longrightarrow 0.5 \leq P < 0.375$$

$$IRI \longrightarrow 0.25 \leq P < 0.3125$$

$$IRIS \longrightarrow 0.296875 \leq P < 0.3125.$$

The code for the message "IRIS" is the lower limit of the last interval: 0.296875 – or any value between the two limiting values.

We should note that *the width of the interval is naturally the probability (frequency) of occurrence of the sequence "IRIS"*, that is:

$$P(IRIS) = p(s_1)p(s_2)p(s_1)p(s_3) = 0.5 \times 0.25 \times 0.5 \times 0.25 = 0.015625,$$

which will be denoted as $f_t = 0.015625$. This example highlights the power of that kind of method, which encodes the whole text into a single real number – then translated into its binary form, as we will see later on.

Finally we note that the code is optimal by construction (in a known text, or in a model if the source conforms to a probabilistic model), since it associates with the text a number (the code) having a value proportional to its probability.

Decoding is performed by the reverse procedure, yielding a unique solution. Naturally, the intervals for each symbol are known, and so is the length of the whole text. The cost of carrying such information is negligible if the text is long enough. If f_i keeps a constant value from one text to another they are provided only once to the decoder (they can be permanently wired in it).

Let us describe the decoding technique: 0.296875 being between 0 and 0.5, the first symbol of the message is I. The lower bound of interval is subtracted, here 0, keeping 0.296875, and the quantity is divided by the interval length, i.e. 0.5, which gives 0.59375, a value between 0.5 and 0.75.

The second symbol is thus R. Then, we subtract 0.5, the lower bound of R, and divide by 0.25, its length. This gives 0.375, a value between 0 and 0.5, indicating that the third letter is I. Lastly, subtracting 0 and dividing by 0.5, the length of I, we obtain 0.75, between 0.75 (included) and 1, indicating that the last letter is S.

In practice these quantities are binary coded. To this end we here recall the rules for writing a real number in binary form. Two representations must be distinguished, called fixed-point or floating-point. These basic techniques are assumed to be well known and will not be discussed; we simply summarize their main features to concretize the arithmetic coding method.

Fixed-point number representation. The method is analogous to the definition of binary numbers.

For instance, the number 2.625 is the decimal representation of the sum: $2.625 = 2 + 0.5 + 0.125$, that is $2 + 0 + 1/2 + 0/4 + 1/8$.

Thus, its binary representation is $1 \times 2^1 + 0 \times 2^0 + 1 \times 2^{-1} + 0 \times 2^{-2} + 1 \times 2^{-3}$, which we write as 10.101.

It can be proved that each positive real number can be written this way. As for the sign, we may use a specific bit (the "sign bit") or a convention such as two's complement. Numerous variants have been devised in computer systems. The sought-after precision conditions the number of representation bits.

As we have seen in Shannon's method, the size in bits is taken as $l_t = -\log f_t$. In the previous example, $f_t = 0.015625$, and thus $l_t = 6$, and the code is finally $0 \times 2^0 + 0 \times 2^{-1} + \cdots + 0 \times 2^{-5} + 1 \times 2^{-6} = 0.000001$.

This kind of representation can be costly in number of bits, if high precision is required. The floating-point representation is then preferred.

Floating-point number representation. We recall here the floating-point scientific notation for real numbers.

For instance, 0.006234 is written as $6.234e - 3$, or $6.234E - 3$. This notation is equivalent to 6.234×10^{-3}:

– the integer part (here, 6) is a number between 1 and 9 (0 being excluded);

– the decimal part (here, 234) is separated from the integer part either by a "." (US/UK) or a "," (EU);

– an integer, the decimal exponent, follows the letter "e" or "E", $E - 3$ standing for 10^{-3}.

Moreover, the number is preceded by its sign, if needed.

The binary representation obeys the same principles: successively a sign bit, the bits coding the exponent, then the bits for the *mantissa* (or significand). We can evoke here the 32-bit long "single-precision" format, standardized by IEEE, which uses 1 sign bit, 8 bits for the exponent and 23 for the mantissa. The 64-bit long double-precision format uses 1 sign bit, 11 for the exponent and 52 for mantissa.

5.7.3.5. *Adaptive and dictionary methods*

As a conclusion to this section, it is worth mentioning the principles of several other methods, well suited to specific situations.

Adaptive methods. Consider the case where the text to be processed does not exhibit stationarity properties. This should be for instance a postscript file, in which there are mixed elements of different nature, such as text and pictures. In this case a statistical frequency analysis on the whole source is meaningless.

A solution consists of dynamically calculating the relative frequencies of the symbols as they vary locally. While browsing the text, we continuously update a counter for the number of each symbol type encountered. The instantaneous value of the counter is used to estimate frequencies and to code the next symbol encountered. This being encoded we process the next, and so on. The decoding algorithm proceeds the same way, by counting the symbols already encountered.

This principle of incrementally building f_i during the text processing is well suited to the Huffman method as well as to arithmetic coding.

In the case of the Huffman algorithm, this naturally leads us to modify the coding tree at each step. Also, encoder and decoder should agree on the convention for affecting 0s and 1s. Various methods, such as that of Knuth and Gallager [KNU 85, HAN 03, WEH 03], provide efficient tree management.

Arithmetic coding is even better suited to this adaptive approach, as there is no need to update any coding tree, since the computing procedure does not rely on any probabilistic model. In fact it appears perfectly adapted to "intelligent" source models (intelligence being understood as artificial intelligence).

Dictionary methods. Here, instead of considering a probabilistic model for source symbol occurrence, we make use of the addresses of a list of source words: the *dictionary*. Thus, the text is encoded as a series of pointers to words in the dictionary. In order to process texts with variable content it is necessary to adapt the content of the dictionary as we go through the text – the dictionary thus being built on the fly.

Among the methods which have been proposed for that goal, we can quote the Lempel and Ziv algorithm [WEH 03]. These methods appear quite efficient, from the perspective of runtime and algorithmic complexity. However, as they make no *a priori* use of the probabilistic source characteristics, they cannot guarantee an optimal coding, and reach their best performance only for very long texts. Typical applications are the graphical format GIF, and the ZIP compressed file format.

5.7.4. *Image compression*

The importance of images in the communications domain need not be labored: digital photography, television, mobile and multimedia services, etc. Their raw volume is somewhere between mega- and giga-bytes, so that compressing them is mandatory.

Although the methods previously presented could work as well, image compression makes use of specific techniques, better suited to the particular nature of their structure.

5.7.4.1. *Describing an image: luminance and chrominance*

We generally describe images by a function $f(x, y)$ representing the color in each sample point (*pixel*, for picture element) with coordinates x, y: x stands for the vertical axis (the row index, counted from top to bottom), and y for the horizontal axis (the column index, from left to right). We refer to the spatial representation of the image, to which a specific data structure is attached. The dataset describing each pixel is stored in a matrix; for instance, a black and white image is described by a matrix, the elements of which are simply 0s and 1s (a *bitmap* format). An image with colors can be stored as a superposition of three monochrome images, one for each primary color: red, green and blue for video, yellow, magenta and cyan for printing purposes. A pixel with coordinates (x, y) is characterized by the value of the sum $Z = rR + gG + bB$: this way any color can be coded as a combination of these primary colors.

However, as we will see, colors tend to be obtained from another reference, instead of the simple primary sources. For instance, the components RGB can be transformed into YIQ: Y for *luminance* – or *brightness*, and I and Q for *chrominance* (*color scale*).

These changes find their justification in the properties of the human eye, which is more sensitive to light intensity variations than to the color scale, as Figure 5.9 shows. Clearly, the eye is most sensitive to brightness, then to green, red and blue to respectively lower extents. From these observations, several "spaces" have been defined: RGB and UVW by the CIE (International Lighting Committee), YIQ space by the NSTC (National Television Standard Committee), etc.

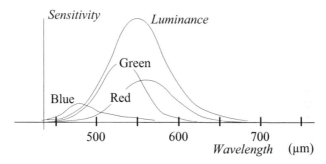

Figure 5.9. *Comparative eye sensitivity to luminance and chrominances*

Thus, an RGB coded image will be converted into an image coded by its luminance (Y) and its chrominance, for instance I and Q. This provides a new expression for Z: $Z = yY + iI + qQ$, corresponding to a change of coordinates, while keeping an orthogonal basis, as illustrated in Figure 5.10.

For instance, the NSTC has adopted the following transformation formulae, first on the basis of the measured relative influences of the various RGB components on luminance (Y), then for chrominance:

$$Y = 0.30R + 0.59G + 0.11B, \quad I = 0.60R - 0.28G - 0.32B,$$

$$Q = 0.21R - 0.52G + 0.31B$$

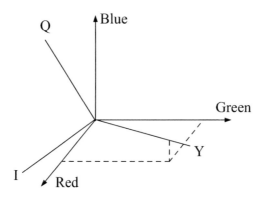

Figure 5.10. *Changing RGB basis to YIQ basis*

Not only does this change of variables offer an optimized use of transforms, as we see in the next sections, but it also offers a first step of "mechanical" compression.

A luminance value is first attached to each pixel. This value, the most significant data, encoded on one byte for instance, is defined by the light intensity per emission area and integrates the effect of the three primary colors.

Then pixels are processed in blocks to which are attached only one component I and Q instead of generating data for each pixel and each of the colors R, G and B, the eye being less sensitive. For instance, taking blocks of 4 pixels (2×2), to each block are attached 4 informations for luminance and 2 for chrominance (I and Q), that is only 6 data (e.g. bytes), instead of 12: ($4R + 4V + 4B$).

However, a complete image still represents a huge amount of data: think of the TV screen, with 720 pixels per lines and 576 lines in total. Fortunately, the specific redundancy characteristics of video images help to decrease these figures.

5.7.4.2. *Image redundancy*

We can define three forms of redundancy:

– *Spatial redundancy* (inter-pixel) refers to a set of identical pixels, in the case of a uniform area. In this case a single element will be encoded, along with the number of its replications. Compression techniques of that kind (e.g. RLC run length coding) provide compression rates of 8 to 10. In fact, we will show that this kind of technique is best suited to images already transformed by operations described hereafter.

– *Subjective redundancy* (visual redundancy) exploits imperfections of the human eye, as it cannot distinguish between pixels of close characteristics (especially for chrominance, the eye being more sensitive to luminance). So, the corresponding pixels can be identically encoded. This corresponds to going from the spatial to the frequency domain by using appropriate transforms which bring possible approximations to the fore, just as for signal processing. Gains of 100 or more can be reached this way! We should note that this kind of compression is irreversible.

– *Statistical redundancy* corresponds to a more frequent repetition of certain data (e.g., some color levels): here again this is a matter of optimization, shorter codes being allocated to the more frequent elements. The previously presented techniques (Huffman, etc.) are used here. This provides compression ratios between 2 and 3.

Using all of these techniques, we can build a complete image compression system, such as the one illustrated in Figure 5.11, which represents the well known standardized system JPEG.

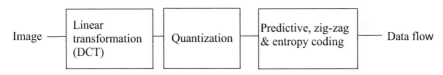

Figure 5.11. *The JPEG encoding procedure*

The first step executes the image transformation. The second weakens the precision of its output, for instance by rounding, and grouping close values together: the quantization step. The third step completes the process by performing an optimal coding, based first upon redundancy and also on the relative symbol frequency values, as already presented for Huffman coding.

We first give a deeper attention to the first step of the processing. This is a quite important application of the transforms introduced in signal theory. We next give a quick survey on quantization and coding, following the JPEG approach.

5.7.4.3. *The discrete cosine transform (DCT)*

Generally speaking, and just as for signal processing, transforms allow us to work in the spectral (frequency) domain, so as to be able to profit from the different spectral characteristics of useful and useless signals by means of filtering operations.

Formally, the *transform* of an image with size $N \times N$, described by function $f(x, y)$ is the new $N \times N$ image described by the function $T(u, v)$ obtained using the kernel $g(x, y, u, v)$ by the operation:

$$T(u, v) = \sum_{x=0}^{N-1} \sum_{y=0}^{N-1} f(x, y) g(x, y, u, v). \qquad (5.39)$$

The transformation is reversible: for any $f(x, y)$, its transform $T(u, v)$ possesses an inverse transform of kernel $h(u, v, x, y)$.

We will be mainly concerned in what follows by *DCT (discrete cosine transform)*, as it is the most commonly used transform, and because it has been standardized in the Joint Photographic Experts Group (JPEG).

In concrete terms, applying DCT transfers the information of the image from the spatial domain to the spectral domain (see Chapter 4). As we have observed, redundancy occurs between neighboring pixels: their value varies continuously, in a normal image. Conversely, rapid changes in intensity are generally infrequent except for contours. This transform makes this continuity explicit: low frequencies reflect continuities while high frequencies reflect rapid changes.

Thus, we can represent the totality of information contained in the image with a small number of coefficients, corresponding to rather low frequencies, the continuous component (i.e. the average brightness of the image) being of major importance for the human eye.

Principles. In order to illustrate the principle of transforms such as DCT for the purposes of image processing, we first take as an example the elementary case of an "image" made of a single line with 8 pixels (see below). Reading the line from left to right results in a 2D signal: the value varies with time, just as for sound amplitude[2]. Assume we then obtain a sequence of 8 values spaced from 0 to 255 (encoded on 8 bits), corresponding to the luminance of each pixel. A visual representation of the sequence would resemble the following picture, considering 255 as coding white and 0 for black.

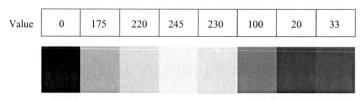

Value	0	175	220	245	230	100	20	33

Figure 5.12. *Analysis of an elementary "image"*

We have considered here a single value for each point. Indeed, the transform is applied separately to each characteristic Y, I and Q. Because the function Z is linear, the expression $Z(Y, I, Q)$ will be conserved by the transform. Figure 5.13 gives an approximate representation of $f(x)$ in an orthogonal basis.

2. Indeed, MP3 encoding used for compressing a sound sequence follows the same kind of approach.

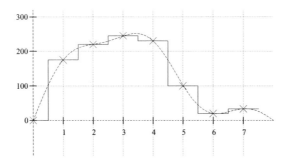

Figure 5.13. *Luminance of the pixels in the previous image*

By applying the DCT, or another transform of the same family (see Chapter 4), we obtain the frequency spectrum shown in Figure 5.14 (here with the Fourier transform).

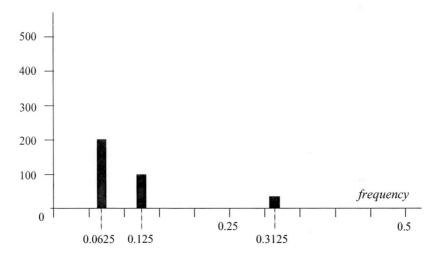

Figure 5.14. *Frequency spectrum obtained from $f(x)$*

This spectrum corresponds to the following function:

$$f(x) = 200 \sin(2\pi 0.0625x) + 100 \sin(2\pi 0.125x) + 30 \sin(2\pi 0.3125x),$$

where the coefficients represent the amplitude of the components, the parameters of which are the frequencies displayed on the spectrum. Using Figure 5.15 below, we can verify that this function corresponds to the initial image and to the values displayed in Figure 5.13. Returning to spectral representation, we easily realize the importance of this transformation, as the spectrum highlights the relative importance

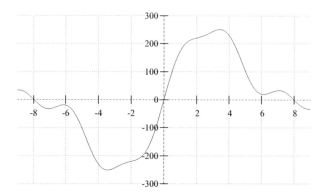

Figure 5.15. *Original signal rebuilt by inverse transform*

of the different frequencies. The compression then consists of ignoring the less significant frequencies, thus reducing the amount of data needed to describe the signal. For instance, in our example, conserving only the lower two frequencies would yield the result described below (the original image is just above).

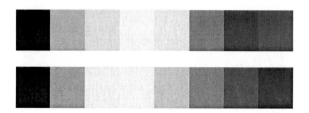

Figure 5.16. *Rebuilding compressed image*

The difference is clearly visible; however, it retains the general shape of the signal, even for this very simplistic example.

Fourier and Walsh 2D transforms. We give only a quick sketch of these transforms as, for reasons we will develop later, they have actually been superseded by another transform.

We introduce the 2D Fourier transform first. It is based on the following kernel:

$$g(x, y, u, v) = \frac{1}{N} \exp\left(\frac{-2j\pi(xu + yv)}{N}\right), \qquad (5.40)$$

the image being of size $N \times N$. The kernel associated with the inverse transform is:

$$h(x, y, u, v) = \frac{1}{N} \exp \left(\frac{+2j\pi(xu + yv)}{N} \right). \tag{5.41}$$

The Walsh transform relies upon a set of basis functions with only two possible values $\pm 1/\sqrt{N}$. It is defined only for $N = 2^n$, with n integer. Its kernel is

$$g(x, u) = h(x, u) = \frac{1}{\sqrt{N}} \prod_{i=0}^{n-1} (-1)^{b_i(x)b_{n-1}(u)},$$

where $b_k(z)$ corresponds to the kth bit of the binary representation of z. This kind of transform only works for discrete cases.

The DCT. We describe here in more detail the DCT as it has been retained in the JPEG standard.

The DCT belongs to the same class of tools as the Fourier transform. Both offer a way to represent information on another basis: the cosine basis (or "Fourier basis"). However, the Fourier basis has several drawbacks: if the image contains discontinuities, then the coefficients of the Fourier transform decay at $1/k$, k being the index of the coefficient. As a result, a large number of coefficients are needed, as they decay too slowly to neglect those with high indices. The DCT does not suffer this drawback.

Moreover, the truncation may entail Gibbs phenomenon (see Chapter 4), provoking oscillations in the vicinity of discontinuities. Finally, the original function must be periodic, in order to apply the Fourier transform: with a period N, $f(x, y)$ should have the same value for $x = 0$ and $x = N - 1$, otherwise the jump results in artificial-high frequency components. Decomposing on the basis of cosine functions makes the function symmetric around $1/2$.

As we have explained, the DCT operates by transforming a set of dots in the spatial domain into an equivalent representation in the frequency domain. In the present situation we apply the DCT on a 3D signal. Indeed, the signal is a graphical image, the x and y axes being the screen coordinates and the z-axis representing the signal amplitude, i.e. the pixel value at each point on the screen: $z = f(x, y)$. It operates a transformation of a discrete bidimensional amplitude signal (each value of the signal gives the amplitude, here the luminance) into a bidimensional frequency information.

The DCT function is defined as:

$$\text{DCT}(u, v) = \frac{2}{N} c(u) c(v) \sum_{x=0}^{N-1} \sum_{y=0}^{N-1} f(x, y) \cos \left[\pi u \frac{2x+1}{2N} \right] \cos \left[\pi v \frac{2y+1}{2N} \right], \tag{5.42}$$

with $c(0) = 1/\sqrt{2}$ and $c(l) = 1, l = 1, 2, \ldots, N - 1$.

The inverse transform is:

$$f(x, y) = \frac{2}{N} \sum_{u=0}^{N-1} \sum_{v=0}^{N-1} c(u)c(v) \, \mathrm{DCT}(u, v) \cos \left[\pi u \frac{2x + 1}{2N} \right] \cos \left[\pi v \frac{2y + 1}{2N} \right]. \quad (5.43)$$

It is usually impossible to calculate the DCT on a full image, first due to the amount of calculations this entails, and also because the transform must operate on a square matrix. Thus, the JPEG standard proceeds by decomposing the image in blocks of 8×8. The method is applied on each block separately – the incomplete blocks on the border needing an adjustment.

The transformation is applied to each 8×8 pixel matrix yielding another 8×8 matrix of the frequency coefficients $\mathrm{DCT}(u, v)$ (coefficients of the periodical functions composing the signal, as we have shown in the simplistic example before).

When working with the signal $f(x, y)$, the x and y axes are associated with the vertical and horizontal dimensions of the image. On the other hand, when working with the transforms the axes represent in two dimensions the *frequencies* of the signal.

The $(0, 0)$ element of the matrix gives the average value of the component (e.g. luminance) on the block, while the other elements give the spectral power for each spatial frequency. Moving towards the elements on the right and/or on the bottom of the 8×8 matrix gives information about the higher frequencies, which are the image areas of highest contrast.

The matrix can then be used to "neglect" several details of the image without altering its quality as perceived by human eyes. This is the *quantization* operation: we now present its principle.

5.7.4.4. *Quantization and coding*

Quantization

The discrete cosine transform is conservative: it entails no information loss, except that related to rounding effects. On the other hand it does not offer any significant compression. This is the goal of the quantization step, which reduces the values of the matrix elements, and thus their size, and the difference between them.

The principle is first to decrease the matrix elements by dividing each of them by a given factor, and then by rounding them to the nearest integer. We readily appreciate the effect of the operation on the magnitude of the figures and thus the compression carried out.

However, an excessive reduction would strongly damage the image, and the JPEG standard has limited this factor to a maximum value equal to 25. Moreover, a uniform reduction would reduce the role of the lowest frequencies, which happen to be of prime importance. So, as the transformation stores data from the lowest to the highest frequencies from left to right and from top to bottom, the *quantization factor* varies according to the coordinates in the matrix. This coefficient increases as we move toward the right and the bottom of the matrix. A typical relation is as follows:

$$\text{Quantization } (u, v) = 1 + (u + v + 1) \times \text{Quality}. \tag{5.44}$$

We finally obtain a table where all the coefficients lower than the quantization factor are set to 0, canceling a large part of the highest frequencies.

The decompression step simply performs the reverse operation by multiplying each matrix element by the corresponding factor. However, as several coefficients have been forced to 0 (those of the bottom right corner), the whole process inevitably *destroys* a part of the information. The methods to estimate the tolerable degradation level differ with the applications; however, they remain subjective, and inevitably related with a compromise between cost and quality. Most generally for video, different images are compared with an image taken as reference (similarly, in audio applications we compare different sequences, the reference being hidden).

Encoding. In the JPEG standard the first step is the predictive encoding, which makes use of differential modulation and adaptive encoding. Differential modulation takes advantage of the similarity between adjacent blocks. So, instead of transmitting the absolute value attached to a pixel, the difference between its value and the preceding one is used, reducing the number of bits needed. Adaptive coding allows us to anticipate, by predicting a pixel value from preceding pixel values, while the differential modulation will transmit the difference – if any exists – between the predicted and actual values. We should note that all these operations are lossless.

The next steps are the so-called zig-zag and entropy encoding. The quantized coefficients of the DCT matrix are ordered in a specific way: the values are read in 45° "zig-zag" order, beginning from the left upper corner (the lowest frequencies) to the right bottom corner (high frequencies), according to the principle of Figure 5.17.

As we have mentioned, the quantized matrix contains a large amount of identical and zero values, and so the zig-zag scan will result in identical and long sequences of 0s, which simplifies the subsequent steps. Run length coding (RLC), as mentioned before in relation to redundancy, reduces the number of bits for encoding, by coupling value with the number of identical values. Lastly, a statistical encoding (e.g., Huffman) will operate efficiently by coding the most frequent values with the smallest number of bits.

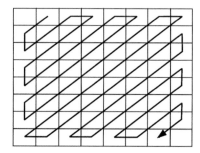

Figure 5.17. *Zig-zag scan of a 8 × 8 quantized block*

5.7.4.5. *Recent methods: wavelets*

Up to now, we have considered the image as a set of pixels. Another approach consists of describing its components by their contours and textures, something closer to the actual process of visual perception. Contours are defined as sudden changes of luminance. Defining the texture precisely can be difficult – unless we take as "texture" all the image except its contours.

The image is described by decomposing it into several textured areas surrounded by contours, and then by encoding these areas. Several techniques have been developed to this end, and this remains a field of research, for which no unified theory exists.

However, a very efficient technique is emerging among these new approaches, with an elaborated formalism: the technique of *wavelet transforms*.

A wavelet-based analysis is similar to the Fourier analysis, as it transforms the signal into its main components in order to process it. However, it differs specifically by the principle of *multiresolution* analysis.

The multiresolution analysis. The multiresolution (or multiscale) analysis consists of using a large range of scales to analyze the image, just as for cartographic purposes. Starting with a given scale, the image is replaced by a first approximation, which we associate with detailed information, then a second approximation, etc., going from the most detailed to the least detailed scales leading to increasingly coarse representations associated with more and more details.

The analysis proceeds by computing both the "trend" and the differences between successive scales, i.e. the details by which a rough image can be corrected to produce another one of better quality. So, in order to recreate the signal with a given precision, we simply need to know the trend and the details corresponding to the targeted precision level, neglecting all other details.

In order to proceed to the analysis the same kind of *wavelet transform* is applied to the different resolutions, from the finest scale to the coarsest one. We start from a *mother wavelet*, a sequence of shifted and expanded wavelets, differing only by their size will be applied. At each step, to distinguish the general trend from the details, a couple of filters are used instead of a single one: a low-pass and a high-pass filter. The low contrasted areas (regular areas) are considered as low frequency areas, and inversely the areas with high contrast are seen as high frequency. To that end two wavelets from the same family are used: a high scale one (also called "large", i.e. a wavelet with high amplitude) and a low scale (or "thin") one.

So, wavelets offer greater accuracy in signal analysis: the technique allows us to compress the different image areas differently, according to the quantity of information they contain. While the DCT gives information on the frequency amplitude, the wavelets transform provides information on this amplitude for a given location, something more in accordance with human vision. Note also that wavelets operate on the full image, avoiding the mosaic phenomenon typical of JPEG technique (which proceeds by blocks), as soon as the compression ratio becomes too high.

In order to give a more precise account of the method we rely on the simplest and more frequent type, known as the Haar wavelet.

Haar wavelets. Haar wavelets are the simplest wavelets and the first to have been used for signal analysis. They are defined by:

$$\phi(x) = \begin{cases} 1 & x \in [0,1] \\ 0 & \text{elsewhere,} \end{cases} \qquad \Psi(x) = \begin{cases} 1 & x \in \left[0, \frac{1}{2}\right[\\ -1 & x \in \left[\frac{1}{2}, 1\right[\\ 0 & \text{elsewhere,} \end{cases} \tag{5.45}$$

and $\Psi_{n,k}(x) = 2^{n/2}\Psi(2^n x - k)$ with $k = 0, 1, \ldots, 2^n - 1$.

Signal analysis. Analyzing the signal amounts to representing it by basis functions through transforms for different resolutions. The decomposition consists of successively dividing the image into two, four, etc., i.e. proceeding progressively on the intervals $[0, 1[$, then $[0, 1/2[$ and $[1/2, 1[$, then again $[0, 1/4[$, $[1/4, 1/2[$, $[1/2, 3/4[$ and $[3/4, 1[$, etc. Wavelets are the multiscale basis functions that ensure a coherent progression through all the resolutions.

Let us consider a signal (i.e. the image), regularly sampled on the interval $[0, 1]$ into 2^n points (we speak of discretization into *dyadic* intervals). The points are referred to as $x_k = k/2^n$, and the model consists of a discrete signal represented by the functions f such that $f(x) = f_k$ if $x \in [x_k, x_{k+1}[$, 0 otherwise. As k varies the function f traces out the set of the functions constant on each of the intervals $[x_k, x_{k+1}[$, and zero outside the interval $[0, 1]$. We denote as E_n the set of these functions. E_n is a vector space, subspace of the vector space $R^{[0,1]}$ of the real functions defined on the interval [0,1] (for this section the reader is referred to the Appendix).

Orthonormal basis. Just as for Riemann integrals, every function $f(x)$ of E_n may be decomposed in an unique way in the form of a function series such that:

$$f(x) = \sum_{k=0}^{2^n-1} f_k \phi_{n,k}(x), \tag{5.46}$$

where the f_k are scalars and the functions $\phi_{n,k}(x)$ are a basis of E_n.

In our case the functions $\phi_{n,k}(x)$, which are zero everywhere except on $[x_k, x_{k+1}]$ provide an obvious basis, that is:

$$\phi_{n,k}(x) = \begin{cases} 1 & \text{if } x \in [x_k, x_{k+1}[\\ 0 & \text{elsewhere.} \end{cases} \tag{5.47}$$

These functions are written, starting from the "mother function" $\phi(x)$, by the relation:

$$\phi_{n,k}(x) = \phi(2^n x - k). \tag{5.48}$$

Since all these functions have finite energy, E_n can be given a scalar product defined by $\langle f, g \rangle = \int_0^1 f(x)g(x)$.

Thus, E_n constitutes euclidian spaces with orthogonal basis $\Phi_{n,k}$, since we can verify that the basis functions check $\langle \phi_{n,k}, \phi_{n,k'} \rangle = 0$ if $k \neq k'$.

Moreover, we should note that $\langle \phi_{n,k}, \phi_{n,k} \rangle = \frac{1}{2^n}$: we retrieve an orthonormal basis by using $2^{n/2}\phi_{n,k}$ instead of $\phi_{n,k}$.

Multi-scale analysis. In multi-scale analysis, we proceed by varying the parameter n. This results in a sequence of spaces E_i such that $E_0 \subset E_1 \subset \ldots \subset E_n \ldots$. The union of all these spaces is still a subspace of the vector space of real functions, such that:

$$f(2^i x) \in E_i \implies f(2^{i+1} x) \in E_{i+1},$$
$$f(2^i x) \in E_i \implies f(2^{i-1} x) + f(2^{i-1} x + 2^{i-1}) \in E_{i-1} \tag{5.49}$$

Each of these spaces has its own basis:

$$E_0 \longrightarrow \phi(x - k)$$

$$\vdots$$

$$E_i \longrightarrow \phi(2^i x - k)$$

The function ϕ is referred to as a *scaling function*

Detail spaces. Now, let F_n the orthogonal complement of E_n. We can then build a new vector space E_{n+1} composed with E_n and F_n. In a similar way the orthogonal complements of the E_i are denoted as F_i, they verify $E_{i+1} = E_i \oplus F_i$ for each i and thus:

$$E_n = E_0 \oplus F_0 \oplus \cdots \oplus F_{n-1}$$

This decomposition allows us not only to determine the rough trend of the signal, inside the spaces E_i up to E_0, but also its details with increasing precision, in the spaces F_0, F_1, etc.

We thus have two signals to analyze. The analysis proceeds in the spaces F_n just as for E_n, by using the wavelet transform Ψ defined as:

$$\Psi(x) = \begin{cases} 1 & x \in \left[0, \dfrac{1}{2}\right[\\ -1 & x \in \left[\dfrac{1}{2}, 1\right[\\ 0 & \text{elsewhere,} \end{cases} \tag{5.50}$$

and $\Psi_{n,k} = \Psi(2^n x - k)$ using the same notations as introduced for ϕ.

The function obeys the following properties: $\langle \Psi_{n,k}, \Psi_{n,k'} \rangle = 0$ if $k \neq k'$, as previously, and also $\langle \phi_{n,k}, \Psi_{n,k'} \rangle = 0$ for all k.

From this, we can deduce that the set combining $\phi_{n,k}$ and $\Psi_{n,k}$ is an orthogonal basis for E_{n+1}. Thus, $\Psi_{n,k}$ are an orthogonal basis for F_n, the orthogonal complement of E_n in E_{n+1}.

Calculating the coefficients for signal decomposition. We now write the signal being studied in the basis E_{n+1} in the form:

$$s_{n+1}(x) = \sum_{k=0}^{2^n - 1} s_{n+1,k} \phi_{n+1,k}(x).$$

As $E_{n+1} = E_n \oplus F_n$, then s_{n+1} decomposes into $s_{n+1} = s_n + d_n$, with

$$s_n = \sum_{k=0}^{2^n-1} s_{n,k}\phi_{n,k}, \quad \text{and} \quad d_n = \sum_{k=0}^{2^n-1} d_{n,k}\Psi_{n,k}.$$

Thanks to the orthogonality argument previously introduced,

$$\langle \phi_{n+1,k}\phi_{n,k'} \rangle = \frac{1}{2^n} \quad \text{if} \quad \left\lfloor \frac{k}{2} \right\rfloor = k', \text{ and } 0 \text{ otherwise,}$$

$$\langle \phi_{n+1,k}\Psi_{n,k'} \rangle = \frac{(-1)^k}{2^n} \quad \text{if} \quad \left\lfloor \frac{k}{2} \right\rfloor = k', \text{ and } 0 \text{ otherwise.}$$

$\lfloor x \rfloor$ denotes the largest integer lower than x.

Now, since $s_{n+1} = s_n + d_n$, the orthogonality allows us to write

$$\langle s_{n+1}, \phi_{n,k} \rangle = \frac{s_{n,k}}{2^n} \quad \text{and} \quad \langle s_{n+1}, \Psi_{n,k} \rangle = \frac{d_{n,k}}{2^n}.$$

The decomposition $s_{n+1} = \sum_{k=0}^{2^n-1} s_{n+1,k}\phi_{n+1,k}$ using the value of the scalar products then gives:

$$\langle s_{n+1}, \phi_{n,k} \rangle = \frac{s_{n+1,2k} + s_{n+1,2k+1}}{2^{n+1}}; \quad \langle s_{n+1}, \Psi_{n,k} \rangle = \frac{s_{n+1,2k} - s_{n+1,2k+1}}{2^{n+1}},$$

thus

$$s_{n,k} = \frac{s_{n+1,2k} + s_{n+1,2k+1}}{2}; \quad d_{n,k} = \frac{s_{n+1,2k} - s_{n+1,2k+1}}{2}. \tag{5.51}$$

We finally obtain two "sub-signals": the main one containing the lowest frequencies of the original signal, and providing the "rough" (overall) description of the image (the average of two successive samples), and a second one made with the higher frequencies, corresponding to the details (difference between successive samples).

The method proceeds in this way iteratively on all the spaces, up to F_0 and E_0, with a component with a single coefficient. Once transformed, the signal is thus made of $n+1$ sub-signals or sub-bands. The original signal is easily retrieved by performing the same operations in the reverse order.

Compression. For a relatively smooth signal, the values of successive coefficients are close to each other. The detail coefficients stemming from the difference between two successive values of the sample are thus small. So, once a given precision is fixed for d, only the coefficients of the wavelets larger (in absolute value) than this threshold are retained, giving a first compression of the signal.

Several wavelets. We will now present several of the main kinds of wavelets in use.

– Haar wavelets (reminder):

$$\phi(x) = \begin{cases} 1 & x \in [0, 1] \\ 0 & \text{elsewhere,} \end{cases}$$

$$\Psi(x) = \begin{cases} 1 & x \in \left[0, \dfrac{1}{2}\right[\\ -1 & x \in \left[\dfrac{1}{2}, 1\right[\\ 0 & \text{elsewhere} \end{cases}$$

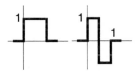

– Gabor wavelet (and the real part of its discrete representation)

$$\Psi(x) = \pi^{-\frac{1}{4}} e^{-\frac{x^2}{2}} e^{-2i\pi\nu x}$$

with ν the scale factor.

– Morlet wavelet (and the real part of its discrete representation)

$$\Psi(x) = \frac{1}{\sqrt{2\pi}} e^{-\frac{x^2}{2}} e^{-i\omega_0 x}$$

ω_0 being the scale factor.

– Daubechies wavelet (imaginary part)

$$\Psi(x) = \sum_{k=-(2N-1)}^{2N-1} \frac{k}{5} [\cos kx + i \sin kx]$$

N being the scale factor.

– Spline wavelet

$$\Psi(x) = 1 \text{ if } x \in \left] -\frac{1}{2}, \frac{1}{2} \right], \quad 0 \text{ otherwise}$$

$$\Psi_{n+1}(x) = \int_{x-1/2}^{x+1/2} \Psi_n(x) \mathrm{d}x$$

5.7.4.6. *JPEG2000*

As an example application, we now present the JPEG2000 standard. The standard does not, strictly speaking, specify an encoding scheme, as it is rather concerned with the techniques for decoding and for the organization of information flows. However, it provides a basic set of techniques and a general approach, as we have already seen with cosine transform and JPEG. Figure 5.18 gives the mechanism, which consists of the following steps:

1) Wavelet transform.

2) Quantization: the details of the image below a given threshold are suppressed, depending on the targeted efficiency. Information loss occurs during this step.

3) Encoding of the remaining values.

4) Bandwidth allocation.

This overall picture leaves a high degree of freedom for designing an effective encoding system. However, the compressed data flow issuing from the encoder must comply with the format specified in the JPEG standard *(codestreams)*. To this end the rate allocation algorithms have the goal of building data blocks (packets) conforming to the standard.

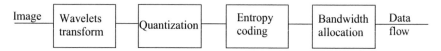

Figure 5.18. *The successive steps of JPEG encoding*

Wavelet transforms. The JPEG2000 format makes use of two types of wavelet transforms:

– the "CDF 9/7" transform (Cohen-Daubechies-Fauvaue) in the case of an irreversible transform;

– the "spline 5/3" conforming to Le Gall's scheme, which is much simpler and allows a reversible operation.

Numbers 9 and 5 correspond to the number of low-pass filter elements; numbers 7 and 3 correspond to the number of high-pass filter elements. The JPEG2000 standard uses these transforms to carry out a dyadic decomposition of the full picture (actually, of each of its components) into sub-bands according to the *recursive Mallat algorithm.*

Recursive Mallat algorithm. The principle of the algorithm is to divide the image in four parts at each of the iterations: three blocks are devoted to the details of the image (higher frequencies), the fourth one contains the most important information for the eye – the lower frequencies – and is the basis for the next operation (see Figure 5.19).

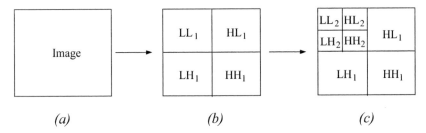

Figure 5.19. *Dyadic division of the image in sub-bands*
(a) after one (b) and two (c) decomposition steps

The first step corresponds to the first layer of wavelets. Each following step refines by processing the space LL_i to obtain the next spaces LL_{i+1}, HL_{i+1}, and so on. Each step leads to coarser images associated with more and more details.

JPEG format limits the number of iterations between 0 and 32, default values most often being between 4 and 8.

The decomposition makes use of 2 filters (a high-pass and a low-pass) derived from the chosen wavelet.

Quantization. The decomposition algorithm concentrates the energy of the image in the LL blocks of higher level decomposition. Then, all the other blocks are only details of the image. As already seen with the cosine transform, compression is achieved by quantization, forcing several matrix coefficients to 0 in the blocks of higher level decomposition.

This method provides strong compression for smooth areas, while keeping all discontinuities, by following the contours of the image, as high-pass filters are applied to all directions: vertical, horizontal and diagonal (a combination of the two).

Coding. We again find here the techniques already presented. Entropy coding is recommended in the JPEG2000 standard. The quantized values previously obtained are coded in a context-adaptive arithmetic coder. The quantized coefficients are first grouped, in each sub-band, in a rectangular block *(code-blocks)* with a typical size of 64×64 or 32×32. Then each code-block is encoded, each bit plane at a time, beginning with the most significant ones. In each plane the bits are first organized into three groups depending on their neighborhood, then encoded in three successive *coding passes*.

5.8. Channel modeling

We now address the issue of transmitting the information through a perturbed medium. Just as for the source, we will rely on the concept of entropy, and more specifically here on conditional and mutual entropy, from which we can define the *information capacity* of a noisy channel. Then the following sections introduce the second Shannon's theorem and the methods for detecting and correcting errors, so as to increase the information capacity of the channel.

5.8.1. *Definition of the channel*

Generally, we mean by channel any physical or logical entity used for carrying and processing information (transmission channel in a network, bus in a computer, data processing system, etc.). Formally, noisy channels operate a transformation between the set of input symbols and the set of output symbols.

We concentrate on *discrete* (binary), *memoryless* (the transformation of one input symbol into another does not depend on previous transformations) and *stationary* channels (the transformation does not depend on the time origin).

$[X]$ denotes the set of all possible input symbols, and $[Y]$ the set of possible symbols at the output. We associate each input symbol x_i with its occurrence probability $p(x_i)$, and similarly $p(y_j)$ is associated with output symbol y_j. Due to the perturbations, sets $[X]$ and $[Y]$ may differ, and so do $p(y_j)$ and $p(x_i)$.

The channel behavior is fully specified by the transition matrices $[P(X|Y)]$ giving the conditional probabilities $p(x_i|y_j)$ and $[P(Y|X)]$ giving the $p(y_j|x_i)$.

The matrix $[P(X|Y)] = \begin{bmatrix} p(x_1|y_1)\cdots p(x_n|y_1) \\ \vdots \\ p(x_1|y_m)\cdots p(x_n|y_m) \end{bmatrix}$ defines the *uncertainty* about the input field, given the output symbols observed: without any perturbation, receiving y_j implies x_i has been sent, so $p(x_i|y_j) = 1$: the uncertainty on the original symbol vanishes.

Similarly, the matrix $[P(Y|X)] = \begin{bmatrix} p((y_1|x_1)\cdots p(y_m|x_1) \\ \vdots \\ p((y_1|x_n)\cdots p(y_m|x_n) \end{bmatrix}$ is referred to as the *noise matrix*: it gives the uncertainty on the output symbols, when the input field is known. The name refers to the fact that in numerous cases the uncertainty is brought by the noise on the channel.

5.8.2. *Channel capacity*

We now introduce the concept of *information transfer capacity* for a noisy channel, as introduced by Shannon, which provides a limit for transmission efficiency through a channel.

As previously, let $[X]$ (resp. $[Y]$) stand for the set of input symbols x_i (resp. the set of output symbols y_j at the receiver).

The channel capacity C is defined as:

$$C = \max I(X;Y) = \max \left[H(X) - H(X \mid Y) \right] = \max \left[H(Y) - H(Y \mid X) \right].$$

It represents the maximum of the average mutual information, introduced in section 5.3.7, and of which we recall the definition:

$$I(X;Y) = \sum_{i=1}^{n} \sum_{j=1}^{m} p(x_i, y_j) i(x_i; y_j) \quad \text{with} \quad i(x_i; y_j) = \log \frac{p(x_i, y_j)}{p(x_i) p(y_j)},$$

and is called *transinformation* in this context. Indeed, it defines the quantity of information actually transferred through the channel.

$H(X \mid Y)$ is said to measure ambiguity (*equivocation*), while $H(Y \mid X)$ measures the average error. If there is no perturbation, then $p(x_i \mid y_j) = 1$ and $i(x_i; y_j) = -\log p(x_i)$ and thus mutual information is equal to self-information. We then have $H(X \mid Y) = H(Y \mid X) = 0$, the equivocation and average error are zero, and $I(X;Y) = H(X) = H(Y)$: transinformation is maximum. On the other hand, if y_j becomes independent of x_i due to strong perturbations on the channel, then the ambiguity is equal to the entropy at the channel input, while the average error is equal to the entropy at channel output: transinformation becomes zero. Obviously, to be significant for the receiver, the information at the output should depend on the information sent – in case of independence, the information received is of no use for any decision about the information delivered by the sender.

Now, just as for the source, we define the channel redundancy:

$$R = C - I(X;Y),$$

and the efficiency of its usage:

$$\eta = \frac{I(X;Y)}{C}.$$

Finally, the capacity can be estimated as a rate in bits per second, just as for the entropy. We define $C_\tau = \frac{C}{\bar{\tau}}$, where $\bar{\tau}$ is the average duration of a symbol (this amounts to taking it as time unit).

5.8.3. *Binary symmetric channel*

We illustrate these concepts by considering a binary symmetric channel (BSC). Although quite simplistic, this is quite an important case, as it represents numerous actual situations.

A channel is said to be *symmetric* when the conditional error probability is the same for all symbols. It is fully defined by its noise matrix channel $[P(Y \mid X)]$. For a *binary symmetric* channel, with p the error probability per symbol, we have:

$$[P(Y|X)] = \begin{bmatrix} p(y_1 \mid x_1) & p(y_2 \mid x_1) \\ p(y_1 \mid x_2) & p(y_2 \mid x_2) \end{bmatrix} = \begin{bmatrix} 1-p & p \\ p & 1-p \end{bmatrix}.$$

Let us calculate the information capacity of this channel:

$$I(X;Y) = H(Y) - H(Y \mid X) = H(Y) - \sum_X P(X)H(Y \mid X)$$

$$= H(Y) - \sum_X P(X)H_2(p),$$

and thus $I(X;Y) = H(Y) - H_2(p)$.

Now Y is a binary variable and so $\max H(Y) = 1$ (see section 5.3.2). Thus:

$$C = 1 - H_2(p).$$

We should note that the function is symmetric. It vanishes for $p = 0.5$, and it equals 1 for $p = 0$, corresponding precisely to the case of a noiseless channel.

With such a channel, it is not possible to determine if an error occurred or not when a symbol is received. This is precisely the goal of the following sections: to show how to reliably transmit on a channel, by using extensions of the input sequences.

5.9. Shannon's second theorem

We address here the problem of coding on a noisy channel. The goal is to encode information in order to protect it against transmission errors. We consider a source that is optimally or near optimally encoded as we have explained above. We add additional control symbols to the symbols generated on the channel, allowing the receiver to detect, or even to correct possible transmission errors. We then speak of error-detecting and error-correcting codes. Shannon's second theorem, or the noisy-channel coding theorem (1948), guarantees the existence of such codes.

5.9.1. *The noisy-channel coding theorem (Shannon's second theorem)*

The theorem, also called the fundamental theorem, is formulated as follows:

Consider a source with information rate R bits/s, and a channel with capacity C bits/s. Under the condition $R < C$, there exists a code with words of length n such that the maximum error probability at the decoder P_E is $P_E \leq 2^{-nE(R)}$.

In the expression, $E(R)$ is a non-negative function decreasing with R, called the *random-coding exponent* of the channel.

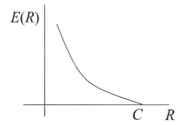

We do not give any proof of the theorem here, as it would not be of any use for engineers. We nevertheless illustrate its meaning, then in the following sections we will develop its applications.

In accordance with definition (5.25) the code rate R (the information rate) is equal to the entropy per symbol at channel input, when these symbols are equally likely. So, if M is the number of codewords, then $R = (\log M)/n$. Generally, in the applications in the communication field, codewords are encoded on n bits, with k information bits, giving thus $M = 2^k$ codewords. The code rate is then simply given by $R = k/n$, the *coding rate* of the channel.

Obviously, the goal of the coding scheme is to maximize this code rate, given the two following factors: error probability p on the channel and decoding error P_E, intended to be as low as possible. The theorem asserts that, whatever the perturbation level on the channel (more generally, on any transmission support), it is always possible to transmit with an error probability as low as required, provided that $R < C$. This property is by no means obvious, and for instance the elementary method consisting of repeating the messages to correct transmission errors leads to reduce the useful rate, which can even decrease to 0 as the number of retransmissions increases.

The following considerations should help to make the meaning of Shannon's limit explicit.

Consider a binary symmetric channel with error probability p: according to section 5.8.3, its capacity is $C_p = 1 - H_2(p)$. Also, consider a binary code, for which the decoding error P_E has been evaluated (by calculation or simulation): its maximum bitrate (the limit for long messages), also called distortion rate, is $R_d = 1 - H_2(P_E)$. We can then calculate the ratio C_p/R_d, which is the maximum coding rate for the whole system source-channel. So we have the following inequality:

$$R \leq \frac{C_p}{R_d}, \quad \text{i.e.} \quad R \leq \frac{1 - H_2(P)}{1 - H_2(P_E)}.$$

The inequality expresses the meaning of the Shannon limit, corresponding to the optimal coding: the higher R, the more efficient the coding; however, this is limited to C_p/R_d. So, if the decoding error probability is zero, the code rate R is limited by channel capacity C. In practice, given a code with parameters k and n, and with known P_E, the inequality indicates its performance as compared with Shannon's limit, given by C_p/R_d, or inversely provides the minimum error probability we can expect for a code of given rate k/n.

The fundamental importance of Shannon's theorem leads quickly to the development of error-detecting and correcting theory [HAM 50, PET 72], and numerous codes have subsequently been proposed. However, the constant search for a better efficiency (reducing the size of decoding tables, increasing bitrates) demonstrates that the theory remains a domain of active research.

Moreover, it should be emphasized that, while bidirectional packet networks make it possible to efficiently transport information by associating coding and message repetition, unidirectional systems such as those encountered in space communication or data storage (CD, DVD, etc.) require error-correcting codes with quite a high performance level.

5.10. Error-detecting and error-correcting codes

The effect of errors is to decrease the information each message carries. If the source rate is lower than the channel rate, redundant coding can be used to protect against their negative effect. We consider here a source of maximum entropy, that is, a source for which all symbols are equally likely. To protect it from errors, we send additional symbols, called control symbols – this introduces some redundancy.

The number of available sequences (words) will be increased, but only a limited number of them will be meaningful (the codewords). An appropriate decoding algorithm allows the receiver to distinguish the right words from the erroneous ones (error-detection) and possibly to correct them (error-correction).

We can distinguish three main classes of coding:

– algebraic coding;

– convolutional coding;

– composite coding.

5.10.1. *Algebraic coding*

This highly structured mathematical approach has lead to two types of code: group codes and cyclic codes. These are called block codes, as they operate on strings which are blocks of n symbols. Hamming codes belong to this category [HAM 50], work which forms the basis of numerous fundamental results, as do the more recent Reed-Solomon codes.

Group codes are built on a vector space over a finite field. By definition, this is a group (hence the name). We develop these properties later on (the reader is prompted to refer to the Appendix for this section).

5.10.1.1. *Principles*

Vectorial representation. The n symbols of the string (a word) are seen as the component of a n-dimension vector. The set V of the 2^n possible sequences can be represented by the row vectors $\nu_i = [a_{i1}, a_{i2}, \ldots, a_{in}]$ with elements 0 and 1 for our types of applications. They can be written $\nu_i = a_{i1}\alpha_1 + a_{i2}\alpha_2 + \cdots + a_{in}\alpha_n)$, where $(\alpha_1, \alpha_2, \ldots, \alpha_n)$ is a basis of the vector space V (that is, a set of n linearly independent vectors, for instance the canonical basis $\alpha_1 = (1, 0, 0..)$, $\alpha_2 = (0, 1, 0..)$, etc.).

The usual linear operations can be performed on these vectors (transposition, product, etc.) by matrix operators, whose elements are those $(0, 1)$ of the field K (finite field, or Galois field with two elements; see the Appendix).

Polynomial representation. The word can also be represented as a polynomial $\nu_i(x) = a_{i1} + a_{i2}x + \cdots + a_{in}x^{n-1}$.

On this set of polynomials the rules of sum and product modulo 2 are defined. With this representation, we have for instance $(x+1)^2 = x^2 + 1$. We use this representation mainly for the cyclic codes presented below.

Principle of algebraic coding. As explained in the introduction, the idea is to associate with each source symbol one and only one codeword (using the channel alphabet, here a binary one). The basic way to detect errors is to distinguish meaningful (i.e. belonging to the set of words which have been sent) and nonsensical words.

The set V is split in two subsets T and F. Only those $\nu_i \in T$ are codewords $\nu_i = [a_{i1}a_{i2} \cdots a_{in}]$, while the words of F are meaningless. This is the basic criterion to detect the presence of an error in the receiver.

In the following, we denote as ν_i' the words received. If an error occurred, then $\nu_i' \neq \nu_i$. In this case we must detect the word as belonging to the meaningless ones, and then correct the error or errors by retrieving the original word ν_i. To this effect we now introduce the notion of Hamming distance.

5.10.1.2. *Hamming distance*

The Hamming distance $d(\nu_i, \nu_j)$ between two words ν_i and ν_j is the number of positions for which ν_i and ν_j differ, for example, $d(011, 001) = 1$, and $d(011, 100) = 3$. This is written as:

$$d(\nu_i, \nu_j) = \sum_{k=1}^{n} (a_{ik} + a_{jk}), \qquad (5.52)$$

where the "+" stands for the addition modulo 2 and $\sum$ for the usual addition of integers. This is really a distance, as it verifies the three axioms:

$$d(\nu_i, \nu_j) = d(\nu_j, \nu_i) \geq 0,$$

$$d(\nu_i, \nu_j) = 0 \quad \text{if and only if } \nu_i = \nu_j,$$

$$d(\nu_i, \nu_j) \leq d(\nu_i, \nu_k) + d(\nu_k, \nu_j) \quad \text{(triangular inequality)}.$$

The Hamming geometric model, illustrated in Figure 5.20, is of frequent use. In a n-dimension space representation, the words ν correspond to the vertices of a hypercube with a unit edge, and only some of them are codewords (for instance those circled in black in the figure). The distance between two words is the minimum number of edges connecting them.

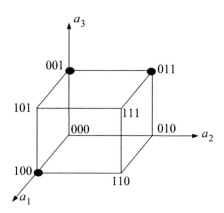

Figure 5.20. *Hamming geometric model for three dimensions and eight words (vectors)*

We now show the importance of the concept of distance between codewords.

Minimum distance of a code. The minimum distance of the code is the smallest distance between two different codewords:

$$d_m = \inf d(\nu_i, \nu_j), \quad \nu_i \neq \nu_j. \qquad (5.53)$$

Neighborhood and decision criterion. We can generally assume that a single or double error in a word is the most likely situation. So, in the usual case of one or two errors, the output sequence is close, in terms of the Hamming distance, to the codeword. This is the basis of the method for retrieving the original codeword. Moreover, in order to distinguish it from any other codeword, the coding will be such that it increases the distance between codewords. This emphasizes the importance of the minimum distance between codewords. Intuitively, the distance is a measure of similarity, and the codewords should be as dissimilar as possible.

Consider for instance a memoryless binary channel with error probability $p < 1/2$. When a word ν_i' is received the probability it comes from the codeword ν_i is $p(\nu_i \mid \nu_i') = p^{d_i}(1-p)^{n-d_i}$, with $d_i = d(\nu_i', \nu_i)$.

The probability it comes from another word ν_j is, in the same way $p(\nu_j \mid \nu_i') = p^{d_j}(1-p)^{n-d_j}$, with $d_j = d(\nu_i', \nu_j)$. Thus:

$$\frac{p(\nu_i \mid \nu_i')}{p(\nu_j \mid \nu_i')} = \left(\frac{1-p}{p}\right)^{d_j - d_i} > 1 \quad \text{if } d_j > d_i \text{ and } p < \frac{1}{2}. \tag{5.54}$$

This can be stated as follows: *upon the receipt of a word, if the distance between it and some codeword is smaller than the distance to any other one then the probability that this codeword is the right one is larger than for any other codeword.* This decision criterion is said of maximum conditional probability. It amounts to say that the original word is the most likely conditionally to the observation at the output, which is intuitively satisfying.

Concept of a sphere. We consider a codeword ν_0 (for instance, placed on the hypercube). The sphere $S(\nu_0, e)$ with center ν_0 and radius e is the set of all words with a distance to ν_0 less than or equal to e.[3]

Now consider a linear code with a minimum distance d_m. Then the closed spheres with radius e, $S(\nu_i, e)$ and $S(\nu_j, e)$ centered on codewords ν_i, ν_j are disjoint if and only if:

$$e \leq \left\lfloor \frac{d_m - 1}{2} \right\rfloor.$$

The following properties are a consequence of this result.

---

3. We use the term "sphere" to conform to universal usage, although the term "ball" would be more appropriate from a mathematical perspective.

5.10.1.3. *Detection and correction capability*

Detection. In order to *detect* e errors the minimum distance between codewords must be:

$$d_m = e + 1.$$

Indeed, if at least 1 and *at most* e errors occurred then the word received is not a codeword, which indicates the presence of error(s).

Correction. A linear code with minimum distance $d_m = 2e + 1$ may correct up to e errors, e being the largest integer such that:

$$e \leq \left\lfloor \frac{d_m - 1}{2} \right\rfloor. \tag{5.55}$$

Indeed if $d_m = 2e + 1$ all the spheres with radius e are disjoint. A sphere $S(\nu_i, e)$ contains strings ν_i' of distance to ν_i at most e. If the number of errors is less than or equal to e, then the received word ν_i' is inside the closed sphere centered on the sent word ν_i with radius e. The principle of minimal distance decoding, i.e. the criterion maximizing the conditional probability leads us to decide that the origin word was ν_i thus correcting the errors introduced by the channel.

On the other hand, a code with minimum distance $d_m = 2e$ allows us to detect up to e errors but only correct at most $e - 1$. In fact, if $d_m = 2e$, several spheres $S(\nu_i, e)$ can have common sequences at distance e of each of the centers. This allows us to detect e errors, but only to correct $e - 1$, using the same principle as before.

To summarize:

– a necessary and sufficient condition under which a binary code operating on equal length words ensures the correction of e errors is:

$$d_m \geq 2e + 1,$$

– a necessary and sufficient condition to detect e errors is:

$$d_m \geq e + 1,$$

– a condition to correct e errors and detect d errors is:

$$d_m \geq 2e + 1 + d. \tag{5.56}$$

Here we can introduce a quantitative result giving an upper bound on the number of words corresponding to a code ensuring the correction of e errors. Each word having length n, combinatorics show that each sphere with radius e contains $N_e = \sum_{k=0}^{e} \binom{n}{k}$ sequences among the 2^n possible sequences. The number S_e of disjoint spheres is such that $N_e S_e \leq 2^n$ and so:

$$S_e \leq \frac{2^n}{\sum_{k=0}^{e} \binom{n}{k}}.$$

5.10.1.4. *Additional definitions and properties*

We have seen that encoding provides efficient protection against errors, at the price of some redundancy, and that according to Shannon's theorem the impact of errors can be made as small as required, as long as the information bitrate remains lower than the channel capacity.

The analysis presented, based upon the notions of spheres and distance, leads us to build the decoding process on the comparison between received and acceptable sequences. As the length n of the words increases the number of acceptable sequences grows exponentially – showing the limits of this approach. In order to overcome the difficulty we now make use of the structure of the vector space of our codes, the main features of which are recalled here (see also the Appendix).

As we have mentioned above, the codes are built from the vector space structure on a finite field denoted K.

The components of a word i of n elements are represented as $\nu_i = [a_{i1}, a_{i2}, \ldots, a_{in}]$. In the applications we have in mind, these elements belong to a Galois field with two elements $(0, 1)$, where the operations are the addition modulo 2 and the scalar product.

We introduce the following definitions:

The weight of the word is:

$$w(\nu_i) = \sum_{x=1}^{n} a_{ix}. \tag{5.57}$$

So, $d(\nu_i, \nu_j) = w(\nu_i + \nu_j)$.

Note that $w(\nu_i) = \sum a_{ix}$ gives the distance to the origin. The word is said to be of even weight if $w(\nu_i) = 0 \pmod 2$, otherwise it is said to be odd:

– The *addition* of two words is given by $\nu_k = \nu_i + \nu_j$, with $a_k = a_i + a_j \pmod 2$.
– The *identity element* is the word "0" (all its components are 0).
– Each word is its own *inverse*, as $\nu_i + \nu_i = 0 \pmod 2$.
– The *complement* to 1 of the word ν_i is $\overline{\nu_i}$ such that $\overline{a_i} = a_i + 1 \pmod 2$.
– The *product* by a scalar is $\lambda \nu_i = \nu_i$ if $\lambda = 1$, and 0 for $\lambda = 0$.

These are just the properties of the vector space V built on the field K.

The set of S meaningful words – i.e. the codewords – with $S = 2^k$, $k < n$, is a subspace of V.

5.10.1.5. *Linear block codes, group codes*

Block codes are those where error-detection and correction are processed in strings (codewords) of n symbols. Group codes are block codes where the n symbols of a block are the components of a n-dimension space. The term "group code" is justified by the structure of (Abelian) group induced by the vector space.

Parity code, parity control. This is a special case of linear group codes. The principle of the parity control consists of inserting an additional bit to a block of size $n-1$ bits so that the weight of the resulting n bits is defined (even, for instance). At the receiver the parity of the word weight received indicates the possible presence of errors: an even number $(2, 4, \ldots)$ – but also no error – if the weight has even parity, and an odd number $(1, 3, 5, \ldots)$ otherwise. This is a simplistic procedure, having a limited efficiency; however, numerous cases are such that the probability of more than a single error is negligible so that the method works satisfactorily. An elementary probability analysis shows that for an error probability p assumed small compared to 1:

$$\frac{P(\text{undetected error with parity control})}{P(\text{error without parity})} \approx \frac{\binom{n}{2}p^2(1-p)^{n-2}}{1-(1-p)^{n-1}}. \qquad (5.58)$$

Codes $C(n, k)$. We now consider the general case of linear codes using m control bits. We have $n = k + m$. The code generates strings made of k information bits and $m = n - k$ so-called control bits. These codes are denoted as $C(n, k)$.

In the following we assume that the $n - k$ control bits are put (for instance) behind the k useful bits. This type of code, where control bits are added before or after the information data, is referred to as systematic. We make this assumption as it simplifies the discussion, and moreover we can show that it is always possible to return to such a code.

In its vector form a codeword is written as:

$$\nu = \left[a_1, a_2, \ldots, a_k, a_{k+1}, \ldots, a_n\right],$$

where the first k symbols are for the data, the $n - k$ others being redundant control symbols.

The codeword is represented in the synthetic form of a row vector $\nu = [i\ c]$ where i stands for the information data and c the control symbols.

Generating codewords. The principle of linear encoding consists of building codewords by a linear application on the information symbols. *The redundant symbols are, just like codewords, a linear combination of the information symbols.*

The 2^k vectors built this way generate the set E_k of codewords. This is a subspace of E_n.

Let us denote as g the linear application, and i the information block, with codewords given by $\nu = g(i)$.

The simplest structure for the operator is the univocal linear transformation such that:

$$
\begin{aligned}
a_1 &= g_{11}a_1 + g_{21}a_2 + \cdots + g_{k1}a_k \\
a_2 &= g_{12}a_1 + g_{22}a_2 + \cdots + g_{k2}a_k \\
&\vdots \\
a_n &= g_{1n}a_1 + g_{2n}a_2 + \cdots + g_{kn}a_k
\end{aligned}
\tag{5.59}
$$

where the g_i are k linearly independent vectors forming a basis of E_k. This is written, under matrix form:

$$
\nu = iG.
\tag{5.60}
$$

G, a matrix with k rows and n columns, is the *generating matrix* of the code $C(n, k)$:

$$
G = \begin{bmatrix}
g_{11} & g_{12} & \cdots & g_{1n} \\
g_{21} & g_{22} & \cdots & g_{2n} \\
\vdots & & & \vdots \\
g_{k1} & g_{k2} & \cdots & g_{kn}
\end{bmatrix}
\tag{5.61}
$$

and i the row matrix

$$
i = \begin{bmatrix} a_1 a_2, \ldots, a_k \end{bmatrix}.
\tag{5.62}
$$

Note that the matrix G is not unique: any permutation or addition of rows or columns yields equivalent codes where the respective positions of redundant and information bits are simply modified.

An elementary transformation allows us to write G as:

$$
G = [I_k \ P],
\tag{5.63}
$$

where I_k is the k order unit matrix and P a $(k, n - k)$-matrix, giving the $n - k$ redundant elements.

$$
G = \begin{bmatrix}
1 & 0 & \cdots & 0 & p_{11} & p_{12} & \cdots & p_{1,n-k} \\
0 & 1 & \cdots & 0 & p_{21} & p_{22} & \cdots & p_{2,n-k} \\
\vdots & & & \vdots & & & & \\
0 & 0 & \cdots & 1 & p_{k1} & p_{k2} & \cdots & p_{k,n-k}
\end{bmatrix}
\tag{5.64}
$$

Indeed, we have:

$$\nu = iG = i\left[I_k\ P\right] = [i\ iP],$$

or, with the notations already introduced:

$$c = iP.$$

The control symbols are a linear combination of information blocks.

This code structure, systematic with the form $\nu = [i\ c]$, where k arbitrarily chosen information symbols are put consecutively at the beginning or end of the word, makes the correction of errors more straightforward, as we see now.

Let us give an example. We assume a 6-letter code, such that the information is encoded into 8 codewords of 3 bits long, $i = [a_1\ a_2\ a_3]$, to which we intend to add 3 control bits $c = [a_4\ a_5\ a_6]$ obtained by $a_4 = 1a_1 + 1a_2 + 0a_3$, $a_5 = 0a_1 + 1a_2 + 1a_3$, $a_6 = 1a_1 + 0a_2 + 1a_3$.

The corresponding matrix is: $G = \begin{bmatrix} 1\ 0\ 0\ 1\ 0\ 1 \\ 0\ 1\ 0\ 1\ 1\ 0 \\ 0\ 0\ 1\ 0\ 1\ 1 \end{bmatrix}$, which, once multiplied by the 8 information vectors, gives the codewords (equation (5.60)):

$$i \rightarrow \nu = iG$$

0 0 0	$\longrightarrow$	0 0 0 0 0 0		1 0 0	$\longrightarrow$	1 0 0 1 0 1
0 0 1	$\longrightarrow$	0 0 1 0 1 1	and	1 0 1	$\longrightarrow$	1 0 1 1 1 1
0 1 0	$\longrightarrow$	0 1 0 1 1 0		1 1 0	$\longrightarrow$	1 1 0 0 1 1
0 1 1	$\longrightarrow$	0 1 1 1 0 1		1 1 1	$\longrightarrow$	1 1 1 0 0 0

Error-detection and correction. We take advantage of the vector space properties. With each vector-codeword is associated an orthogonal vector of E_n, which is a vector such that their scalar product is 0. This produces a code, called the dual of the original one.

Let us denote as H the $(n - k$ rows, n columns) matrix generating this code, and u the words of the dual code. We have:

$$\langle u, \nu \rangle = 0, \quad \text{i.e.} \quad \nu u^T = 0 \quad \text{and} \quad \nu(iH)^T = 0, \quad \text{or} \quad \nu H^T i^T = 0,$$

the relation should hold for any i, hence: $\nu H^T = 0$ or $H\nu^T = 0$.

The geometric interpretation is as follows: the condition required for a n-dimension vector to belong to the vector subspace of the code is that it is orthogonal to the orthogonal subspace, just as in the euclidian space R^3 a vector belongs to a plane if and only if it is orthogonal to the normal to the plane.

From here the principle of *error-detection* immediately follows.

Upon receipt of a word ν' with components $a_1', a_2', \ldots, a_n'$, we calculate the matrix product $H\nu'^T$. If $H\nu'^T \neq 0$ then an error has occurred, as the product is zero if and only if $\nu' = \nu$ (recall that ν is the codeword sent). In other words, a vector ν' is a codeword of $C(n, k)$ if and only if it is orthogonal to the words of its dual code, i.e. if $\langle \nu', \nu \rangle = 0$.

Note however that the condition can be fulfilled even if an error has occurred: *the corrupted codeword can correspond to another codeword* (recall we have clearly stated in the introduction: detection and correction *with high probability!*).

Matrix H is described as the *control matrix*, or *parity matrix*.

In the case of a systematic code, the relation between H and G is easily obtained. We have $\nu = iG$ and $\nu H^T = 0$ and thus $iGH^T = 0$ for any i so that:

$$GH^T = 0.$$

With the previous notations, $G = [I_k \ P]$, which gives $[I_k \ P]H^T = 0$, implying:

$$H = \begin{bmatrix} P^T & I_{n-k} \end{bmatrix}. \tag{5.65}$$

In our previous example:

$$H = \begin{bmatrix} 1 & 1 & 0 & 1 & 0 & 0 \\ 0 & 1 & 1 & 0 & 1 & 0 \\ 1 & 0 & 1 & 0 & 0 & 1 \end{bmatrix}$$

We now focus on error-correction, and introduce the notion of *syndrome*. The syndrome of the word ν' is defined as:

$$s(\nu') = \nu' H^T. \tag{5.66}$$

It represents the vector projection ν' on the subspace orthogonal to the code, with $n - k$ dimensions. In the absence of error, $\nu' = \nu$ (ν is the word sent) and $s(\nu') = 0$.

We set $\nu' = \nu + e$, any component of e different from 0 reveals the occurrence of an error, and:

$$s(\nu') = s(\nu + e) = s(\nu) + s(e) = s(e). \tag{5.67}$$

The syndrome depends only on error, and not on the codeword. This property greatly simplifies error-correction.

So, we are given ν' such that $s(\nu') \neq 0$: ν' is not a codeword. The decoding rule consists of determining the most plausible word ν, that is the word which minimizes the Hamming distance $d(\nu', \nu)$. In principle, this is just a matter of building a table of all possible sequences and allocating the minimum distance codeword to each one.

However, calculating the minimum distance can be difficult and time-consuming, especially for a large number of words. The following comments concerning syndromes can help in this task. We note by $\nu' = \nu + e$ the word received (it differs from the codeword sent by the word e). As above, we have $s(\nu') = s(e)$. We have seen that:

$$d(v', v) = w(v' + v).$$

Now, $v' + v = v + e + v = e$ (every vector is its own opposite). Thus,

$$d(v', v) = w(e). \tag{5.68}$$

Therefore, finding the minimum distance word amounts to determining the sequence e of minimum weight that has $s(e) = s(\nu')$ as syndrome, and the codeword we are looking for is simply $\nu = \nu' + e$ (addition and substraction are the same modulo 2 operation).

In practice, we build a decoding table giving all possible syndromes, which we then associate with the minimum weight sequence having the same syndrome value. Due to the independence property between codewords and syndromes, such a list is easily obtained.

The syndrome of a sequence being the product of a vector ν' of length n and the $n - k$-column matrix H^T, the syndromes are the 2^{n-k} possible sequences of length $n - k$. Returning to our example,

Matrix H^T has 3 columns:

$$H^T = \begin{bmatrix} 1 & 0 & 1 \\ 1 & 1 & 0 \\ 0 & 1 & 1 \\ 1 & 0 & 0 \\ 0 & 1 & 0 \\ 0 & 0 & 1 \end{bmatrix}$$

The list of syndromes is the series of the 2^3 possible binary combinations. We then easily derive (cf. equation (5.66)) the associated string set of length 6 with minimum weight. This gives Table 5.1.

Such a code is able to correct all single errors and to detect a 2-error configuration. Inspecting the 8 codewords, we verify that their minimum distance is 3, allowing us to correct a single error and detect a double error.

Syndrome	Minimum weight sequence
000	000000
001	000001
010	000010
011	001000
100	000100
101	100000
110	010000
111	010001 (for instance)

Table 5.1. *The 2^3 possible syndromes*

Hamming code. The Hamming code provides a classical example of this kind of code. Its feature is that the control matrix columns are binary representations of numbers 1 to n. For example:

$$H = \begin{bmatrix} 1 & 1 & 1 & 0 & 1 & 0 & 0 \\ 1 & 1 & 0 & 1 & 0 & 1 & 0 \\ 1 & 0 & 1 & 1 & 0 & 0 & 1 \end{bmatrix}$$

The minimum distance of a code is the smallest number of linearly independent control matrix columns. In the case of a Hamming code, the columns being the binary numbers, any column is the sum of two other columns. Hence, there are a minimum of three dependent columns.

We can recall the result established above:
- a necessary and sufficient condition to correct e errors is $d_m \geq 2e + 1$;
- a necessary and sufficient condition to detect d errors is $d_m \geq d + 1$.

Thus, Hamming codes correct at least 1 error and detect 2. As an illustration, the standard Bluetooth makes use of a Hamming code ($n = 15$, $k = 10$) and thus operates at rate $R = 0.66$.

5.10.1.6. *Cyclic codes*

Cyclic codes are linear code-blocks, such that any cyclic permutation of the symbols of a codeword gives another codeword. Such a property makes their design more straightforward, and also simplifies error-detection and correction.

For the analysis of cyclic codes, a polynomial representation is generally preferred. The n symbols of a word are the coefficients of a polynomial of degree $n - 1$:

$$\nu(x) = a_0 + a_1 x + a_2 x^2 + \cdots + a_{n-1} x^{n-1}.$$

In what follows the representations of the words successively obtained by the right shifts are denoted as $\nu_0(x)$, $\nu_1(x)$, etc., with:

$$\nu_0(x) = a_0 + a_1 x + a_2 x^2 + \cdots + a_{n-1} x^{n-1},$$
$$\nu_1(x) = a_1 + a_2 x + a_3 x^2 + \cdots + a_0 x^{n-1}.$$

The set of words defined in this way is formally considered as an *algebra*, of which the words form an *ideal*, that is, the subset comprising the multiples of a given element (see the Appendix, and also [SPA 87]); we take advantage of its properties to detect and correct errors.

We have the following property:

$$x^{-1} \nu_0(x) = a_0 x^{-1} + a_1 + a_2 x + \cdots + a_{n-1} x^{n-2},$$

which can be written as:

$$x^{-1} \nu_0(x) = a_0 x^{-1}(x^n + 1) + \nu_1(x).$$

Thus multiplying a codeword by x gives a codeword modulo $x^n + 1$. So we write:

$$x^{-1} \nu_0(x) = \nu_1(x) \bmod (x^n + 1).$$

The result extends to any power of x:

$$x^{-i} \nu_0(x) = \nu_i(x) + \left(a_0 x^{-i} + a_1 x^{-i+1} + \cdots + a_{i-1} x^{-1} \right) (x^n + 1),$$

and

$$x^{-i} \nu_0(x) = \nu_i(x) \bmod (x^n + 1). \tag{5.69}$$

As the code is linear by assumption, the sum of two codewords gives another codeword, the property being generalized to any linear combination of the form $(\lambda_0 + \lambda_1 x + \cdots + \lambda_i x^i + \cdots) \nu_0(x) \bmod (x^n + 1)$.

Now, let $g(x)$ be a polynomial dividing $x^n + 1$, then any multiple of $g(x)$ is still a codeword. Indeed, given such a polynomial $g(x)$ of degree $n - k$, i.e. $g(x) = g_0 + g_1 x + \cdots + x^{n-k}$ and $h(x)$ of degree k being the quotient of $x^n + 1$ by g, we can write:

$$g(x)h(x) = x^n + 1,$$

and, according to (5.69):

$$\nu_i(x) = x^{-i}\nu_0(x) + a_i(x)(x^n + 1) = x^{-i}\nu_0(x) + a_i(x)g(x)h(x).$$

Thus, *if $\nu_0(x)$ is a multiple of $g(x)$* then $\nu_i(x)$ is a multiple of $g(x)$, and so are all the words generated this way. The set of the code polynomials, multiples of the same polynomial modulo $x^n + 1$, form an *ideal* in the algebra of polynomials with degree n built on the field K.

Now let us denote as $i(x)$ a block of k binary elements, represented as a polynomial of degree $k - 1$:

$$i(x) = i_0 + i_1 x + \cdots + i_{k-1} x^{k-1}$$

The associated codeword is:

$$\nu_i(x) = i(x)g(x).$$

Given the set of information words i, all the words ν of the cyclic code can be obtained by the product ig of the polynomial associated with the information bits by the polynomial g.

The polynomial $g(x)$, dividing $x^n + 1$, is referred to as the *generator polynomial*.

Several polynomials may be used. For instance, for 4 bit information words, a code on 7 bits can be defined, denoted as $C(7, 4)$ with $g(x) = 1 + x + x^3$, or $1 + x^2 + x^3$, both dividing $x^7 + 1$.

Just as for linear code blocks, the code is called systematic when the redundant elements are separated from the payload. Codewords are then associated with polynomials of the type:

$$\nu(x) = c(x) + x^{n-k}i(x)$$

where $c(x)$ is the polynomial of degree $n - k - 1$ associated with the redundant elements. As $\nu(x)$ is a multiple of $g(x)$, we also have:

$$x^{n-k}i(x) = q(x)g(x) + c(x),$$

indicating explicitly that $c(x)$ is the rest of the quotient of $x^{n-k}i(x)$ by $g(x)$.

The method for building the codeword associated with a string of k binary elements follows: this last is multiplied by x^{n-k}, to which the rest of the division of $x^{n-k}i(x)$ by $g(x)$ is added.

Returning to the example of $C(7,4)$, the previous expression $\nu(x)$ becomes:

$$\nu(x) = c(x) + x^3 i(x).$$

Consider for instance the string $i = [1101]$. This is associated with $i(x) = 1 + x + x^3$. Taking $g(x) = 1 + x + x^3$, the quotient of $x^3 i(x)$ by $g(x)$ is 1, so that the polynomial associated with the codeword is $\nu(x) = 1 + x^3 + x^4 + x^6$. Thus, the codeword for $i = [1101]$ is $\nu = [1001101]$.

A similar process is used for decoding. We first divide the word received by the generator polynomial, and the rest of the division gives the syndrome $s(x)$. Error-detection and correction follow the same principle as linear codes (does the word received belong to the code, and what is the nearest one), using the appropriate algorithms. In the general case of a linear code, the condition for the word to belong to the code was that the projection in the orthogonal subspace is zero. Here the criterion is that the rest of the division of the polynomial associated with the word received by the generator polynomial is zero.

Among the most famous families of cyclic codes we should note the BCH codes (Bose, Chaudhuri and Hocquenghem) and the Reed-Solomon codes.

These codes are not built from the generator polynomial, but from its roots, which is equivalent. Indeed, we can verify that a polynomial of degree $n - 1$ is a codeword if and only if its roots are those of the generator polynomial (this is equivalent to the previous conditions, as a polynomial having the same roots as $g(x)$ is a multiple of it).

Moreover, as $g(x)$ divides $x^n + 1$, *its roots are also roots of $x^n + 1$ and of the codewords.*

Consequently, the procedure to find the generator polynomial for a code with length n is: determine a number r of roots $(\beta_i, i = 1, \ldots, r)$ of $x^n + 1$, and build the generator polynomial from these roots. We can prove that the roots $(\beta_i, i = 1, \ldots, r)$ are the elements α^i of a Galois field $\mathrm{GF}(2^\nu)$, generated by an irreducible primitive polynomial $q(x)$, such that $q(\alpha^i) = 0$, of degree ν, written as $q(x) = 1 + x + \cdots + x^\nu$, with $n = 2^\nu - 1$.

Therefore, factorizing $x^n + 1$ yields a product in the form $(x - \alpha^1)(x - \alpha^2) \times (x - \alpha^3) \ldots$, that is, a product of minimum polynomials (i.e. of the lowest possible degree) in the form $q_1(x) q_2(x) q_3(x) \ldots$, with the α^i as roots.

In practice, the development will be performed by reference to tables of primitive and irreducible polynomials $q(x)$, such as those given in [PET 72] (see also the Appendix).

BCH codes. For a BCH code correcting e errors, we can prove that:

$$\beta_1 = \alpha, \quad \beta_2 = \alpha^3, \ldots, \beta_r = \alpha^{2e-1}$$

(with naturally $r = e$). We can also show that the degree k of $g(x)$ is at most $r\nu$.

As an example, in order to correct 3 errors the roots of the generator polynomial are α, α^3, α^5. We thus factorize the generator polynomial with the corresponding 3 minimum polynomials. The degree of $g(x)$ is at most 3ν.

If $n = 15$, then $\nu = 4$. The roots are thus generated by an irreducible polynomial $q(x)$ of degree 4.

That means that the irreducible factors in the decomposition of $x^{15} + 1$ have at most a degree of 4, and there exists at least one which is primitive with degree 4. The degree of $g(x)$ is at most 12. Referring to Peterson's tables, to find the decomposition of $x^{15} + 1$, we obtain:

$$x^{15} + 1 = (1 + x)(1 + x + x^2)(1 + x + x^4)(1 + x^3 + x^4)(1 + x + x^2 + x^3 + x^4).$$

Once we have chosen a primitive polynomial of degree 4, for instance $q_1(x) = 1 + x + x^4$, corresponding to α ($q_1(\alpha) = 0$), we obtain $\alpha^4 = 1 + \alpha$ and $\alpha^5 = \alpha + \alpha^2$. We then derive the other polynomials of $g(x)$, such that $q_3(\alpha^3) = 0$ and $q_5(\alpha^5) = 0$. We have $q_3 = 1 + x + x^2 + x^3 + x^4$ and $q_5 = 1 + x + x^2$. The generator polynomial of a $C(15, 5)$ code is thus:

$$g(x) = (1 + x + x^4)(1 + x + x^2)(1 + x + x^2 + x^3 + x^4).$$

The reader can refer to specialized books for a deeper investigation on the rules for deriving these polynomials (see [PET 72, OSW 91, SPA 87]).

Reed-Solomon codes. These are a special case of BCH codes: instead of choosing the minimum irreducible polynomial with root α within $GF(0, 1)$, we choose it in a finite field of any size. Most of the time they will be extension fields of the binary field with 2^q different symbols, represented by binary vectors of length q. This kind of code has the appealing property of correcting error bursts. A quite common Reed-Solomon code has been standardized in numerous applications, referred to as $RS(255, 239)$: it encodes a payload (information) of 239 bytes into a 255 bytes word. This allows us to correct 8 errors in a word, being possibly 8 consecutive erroneous bytes, or only one erroneous byte having even all its bits in error. In this configuration the code is thus able to correct a erroneous packet of 64 consecutive bits.

Interleaving. We conclude the section by mentioning methods based upon interleaving of cyclic codes: a string of length jk is decomposed into j blocks of k symbols, each block being separately encoded and the blocks then being interleaved (instead of simply concatenating them). This multiplies the detection and correction capability of a $C(n, k)$ by a factor j. We return to this technique in section 5.10.3.

Applications. Cyclic codes have found numerous applications, such as error-detection in X.25, Ethernet protocols (such as cyclic redundancy check (CRC)), where correction is achieved by retransmitting the message, and also for correcting multiple errors with the BCH or Reed-Solomon codes in packet switching cellular networks, in cable video broadcast, in CD/DVD players, etc.

5.10.2. *Convolutional codes*

In convolutional codes the block of n elements at the coder output (information and control data) depends not only on the present block of k elements but also on the $m - 1$ previous blocks. This introduces an m order memory effect. The value m is the *constraint length* of the convolutional code.

The principle of encoding is to temporarily memorize groups of information words (by using a register with depth mk) to which a combinatorial logic is applied in order to produce the output elements. This can be seen as a continuous process on a sliding window of width mk.

If the input information elements can be found explicitly in the output elements, the code is said to be systematic. This kind of code, as with other linear codes, performs a linear combination of its input data. It is called convolutional, since it actually performs a convolution between the input sequences and the generating sequences of the coder.

Figure 5.21 presents the principle of convolutional coding: at each time the encoder transforms the n symbols in the register into n other symbols, resulting from the parallel combination between the input symbol and the ones already present in the register. At each time a new symbol is sent, by a parallel-series conversion. Indeed, this is a sliding window operation.

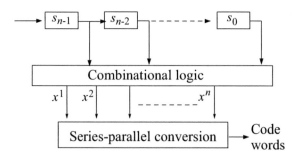

Figure 5.21. *Principle of the convolutive coding*

5.10.2.1. *D-transform*

An appropriate notation, based upon the position of binary elements with time (ie. in the register), allows us to formalize the encoding operation in a similar manner to that of the codes previously studied: the convolution is an algebraic operation between the input data sequence and the coefficients of the generator polynomial.

As in system theory, the D-transform ("D" as delay) can been used; the variable D stands for the unit delay operator (a shift of one time unit in a register).

A sequence of input symbols is represented as

$$s(D) = s_0 + s_1 D + \cdots + s_k D^k + \cdots$$

The symbol with index 0 arrives at t_0, the symbol with index k arrived k time units ago.

The generating sequence of the output element x^i is denoted as $h^i(D)$ and referred to as the impulse response of the system, because it is analogous with signal processing operations (see Chapter 4). For instance, we should have $h^i(D) = 1 + D^{k-i} + \cdots + D^k$, meaning simply that at time t the output symbol of index i ($i = 1, 2, \ldots, k$) is obtained by adding the input symbol with the symbols entered at times $t - k, t - k + 1, \ldots, t - k + i$. The encoding operation is then represented by the product:

$$x_i(D) = h^i(D)s(D).$$

An example of functional diagram is presented hereafter.

The memory effect greatly increases the complexity of any formal manipulation in this kind of modeling. It will generally be completed with graphical representations, in the form of trees, trellis diagrams or state diagrams.

5.10.2.2. *Graphical representation, graphs and trellis*

The encoding algorithm can be represented by a state machine (just as the state diagram of a Markov chain), where the transitions depend on the symbols (randomly) sent by the source.

Markov model. The Markov model provides the most synthetic representation. Here we develop an elementary example, corresponding to the functional diagram in Figure 5.22. We assume $k = 1$ (a block with a single binary element) and $m = 2$ (a register with two binary elements). The encoding operation is defined by the two polynomials $h^1(D) = 1 + D^2$ and $h^2(D) = 1 + D + D^2$.

We start from the initial state (00) in registers at time t_0. If a "0" enters the system at time t_1 nothing happens, while if a "1" enters, the register state becomes (10) and

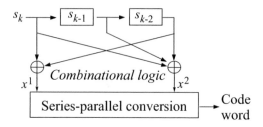

Figure 5.22. *Functional architecture of convolutional coding*

the following sums are calculated: $x^1 = 1 + 0 = 1$ and $x^2 = 1 + 0 + 0 = 1$. If another "1" arrives in the system we have $x^1 = 1 + 0 = 1$ and $x^2 = 1 + 1 + 0 = 0$, the register state moves to (11), etc.

The corresponding Markov diagram is displayed in Figure 5.23.

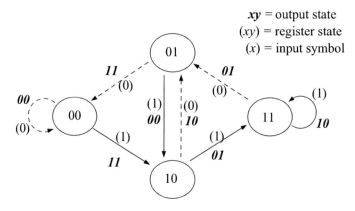

Figure 5.23. *Markov model for convolutional coding by* $h^i(D) = 1 + D + D^{2-i} + D^2$

Trellis diagrams. The trellis representation is of most common use. In order to simplify the diagram, dotted lines will indicate transitions related to the arrival of a "0", and plain line transitions related to "1". With each binary sequence entering the encoder is associated a unique path through the trellis, built by edge concatenation, each one reflecting the transition associated with the ingoing binary element of the incoming sequence.

Figure 5.24 illustrates this kind of model applied to the previous example. We now start from this representation to address the decoding step. Indeed, these models lead to powerful algorithms, such as Viterbi's.

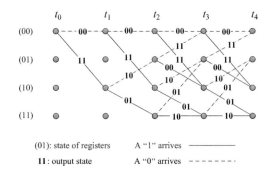

Figure 5.24. *Trellis diagram of the convolutional coding*

Decoding. Just as for block codes, we search the binary sequence (a path in the trellis), called the *most likely sequence* conditional to the observation – that is the one closest to the received sequence. Here again, as for block codes, the most likely sequence (remember, the correction is done with a certain probability!) is the one at shortest distance of the received one.

To avoid a complex search, algorithms such as those of Fano and Viterbi have been developed. The powerful Fano sequential algorithm is rather suited to sequences of long constraint lengths ($m > 8$). The Viterbi algorithm, adapted to lower lengths, is the most commonly employed.

5.10.2.3. *Viterbi's algorithm*

The problem is the following: find the valid sequence S as close as possible to the received one, the closeness being expressed by their Hamming distance. The weight of a given path is the sum of its edge metrics, the edge metric being defined as the sum modulo 2 of its associated binary elements and the corresponding bits actually received (see the example below). Thus, the search for the most likely sequence amounts to finding the shortest path in a trellis.

Viterbi's algorithm exploits the fundamental additivity property of the metrics: the weight of a path is the sum of the weight of its edges, so that once given the path of minimum weight $S(i, k)$ going to node i at instant k, if the most likely path we are looking for goes through i at instant k, necessarily $S(i, k)$ is part of this path (this is the principle of *dynamic programming*). This opens the way to a method of sequential search, at the basis of Viterbi's algorithm.

For each node in the trellis, we only keep track of the most likely path leading to it, that is the path at minimum distance of the received sequence, and referred to as the *survivor path*.

Let us take our previous coder/decoder, with its trellis, as an example. Assume an input sequence (1001), then the output sequence is (11 10 11 11). Assume that, in the course of transmission, an error occurred at the third position, so that the sequence we receive is (11 00 11 11). This sequence is clearly not a codeword, as it does not correspond to any possible path in the trellis.

We correct as follows: at the first instant, block (11) is compared with the two edges 00 and 11 leaving the node 00 (the initial state is assumed to be 00). The distances are respectively 2 for the edge 00 leading to the internal state 00 and 0 for the edge 11 which leads to internal state 10. At the next instant the following block received (00) is compared with the edges leaving states 00 and 10. From the state 00 the distance of 00 with edge 00 is 0, while it is 2 with the edge 11. Similarly at node 10 the distance of 00 with 10 is 1, and 1 with 01. The additivity property of the metrics gives the following figures for these paths:

$$(00\ 00)d = 2; \quad (00\ 11)d = 4; \quad (11\ 10)d = 1; \quad (11\ 01)d = 1.$$

This example shows that we can discard the path (00 11). We proceed similarly with all the next blocks received. The reader can easily continue the exercise, and find that the most likely path at instant 4 is (11 00 11 11) with a cumulated distance $d = 1$. From the diagram, we conclude that the most likely sequence is indeed (1001).

Note however that the distances along two different paths can conceivably be the same, and the decision has to be taken at random. It is not certain that we will reach a decision about the correct path in finite time. We can even show that the probability of more than a single path after a certain time is never zero. In practice, we choose a given decision depth D, that is the decision on the element a_k will be delayed until time $k + D$. In the case where more than one possibility remains, the decision is taken at random.

Interestingly enough, note that Viterbi's algorithm is in fact a special case of probabilistic inference from graphic models, which are an active research field. Indeed, decoding has been performed by searching in a graph (the trellis) for the most probable path leading to a given state. The general problem of maximum *a posteriori* likelihood remains a fundamental domain of study.

Applications. Convolutional codes are used for satellite communication (Voyager program as well as commercial or defence systems), and also for cellular telephony (such as GSM, where a code of constraint length 6, with efficiency 1/2 is used).

5.10.3. *Combined codes and turbo codes*

It is impossible to present here all the coding schemes which have been developed. As we have already noticed, their study remains an active research field, and the reader should have realized the diversity of the solutions, starting from a relatively limited basic principles, such as minimum distance.

Thus, we conclude this section by briefly describing the main features of codes built by combining several techniques, especially *turbo codes*, which are a typical composite use of the basic techniques we have already presented.

The idea is that, by combining several codes which are easy to encode and decode, we can expect to derive new codes, which are more powerful while remaining easy to decode.

We have already evoked the interleaving, products, concatenation and parallelization of codes as available tracks. The reader should notice the analogy with the techniques developed for generating random numbers (see Chapter 8).

5.10.3.1. *Interleaving*

We recall here the main characteristics. The goal of interleaving is to allow the correction of error bursts using a simple code. To that end the symbols of several codewords are interleaved.

So, interleaving two codewords (with the usual notations, the words being distinguished by upper indices):

$$a_0^{(1)}, a_1^{(1)}, \ldots, a_{n-1}^{(1)} \quad \text{and} \quad a_0^{(2)}, a_1^{(2)}, \ldots, a_{n-1}^{(2)}$$

leads to a new sequence

$$a_0^{(1)}, a_0^{(2)}, a_1^{(1)}, a_1^{(2)}, \ldots, a_{n-1}^{(1)}, a_{n-1}^{(2)}.$$

Each sequence is represented by polynomials:

$$v^{(1)}(x) = a_0^{(1)} + a_1^{(1)}x + a_2^{(1)}x^2 + \cdots + a_{n-1}^{(1)}x^{n-1}$$
$$v^{(2)}(x) = a_0^{(2)} + a_1^{(2)}x + a_2^{(2)}x^2 + \cdots + a_{n-1}^{(2)}x^{n-1},$$

and the new sequence is represented as:

$$V(x) = a_0^{(1)} + a_0^{(2)}x + a_1^{(1)}x^2 + a_1^{(2)}x^3 + \cdots + a_{n-1}^{(1)}x^{2n-2} + a_{n-1}^{(2)}x^{2n-1}.$$

In general, the *degree of interleaving* is the number j of interleaved codewords. From the previous example we see that two consecutive symbols of a given codeword are at distance l greater than the length of the error bursts, as long as $l < j$. The burst does not then affect several symbols of the word, so that even for error burst each stream suffers from independent errors only.

We can verify that the codewords $\nu(x)$ being multiple of a generator polynomial $g(x)$ dividing $x^n + 1$, the interleaved codewords $V(x)$ are multiple of the generator polynomial $G(x) = g(x^j)$, dividing $x^{jn} + 1$.

Thus, a word $V(x)$ is obtained by encoding a block of jk symbols according to the generator polynomial $g(x^j)$ using the usual method.

We can also verify that if the non-interleaved code is able to correct bursts of length l, then the interleaved version corrects bursts of length jl.

Interleaving is used for instance on radio channels, where fading can affect a large number of consecutive symbols. Once de-interleaved, the consecutive binary elements of the transmitted sequences are therefore separated.

5.10.3.2. Product codes

Given two codes $C_1(n_1, k_1)$ and $C_2(n_2, k_2)$, we consider a block of $k_1 k_2$ source symbols, encoded first according to C_1, resulting in k_2 vectors of length n_1.

These vectors are then stored in a matrix with k_2 rows and n_1 columns. Then the n_1 columns are encoded using C_2, yielding n_1 blocks of length n_2.

We can prove that the resulting code has, for minimum distance, the product of minimum distances of the two origin codes. This shows that a significant increase in the minimum distance, and thus of the correction capability, can be obtained by combining two codes of poor performance, according to this criterion.

Decoding will be performed symmetrically.

5.10.3.3. Concatenation

The concatenation technique is a variant of the previous one. After a first encoding, we perform a second encoding starting from the symbols generated by the first.

5.10.3.4. Parallelization

The source word is encoded several times using several schemes in parallel, and the results are multiplexed and transmitted. After decoding, the words received should be identical. This technique is used in turbo codes, as we will now see.

5.10.3.5. Turbo codes

The principle of turbo codes is to make use of two parallel encoders, usually of the RSC type (recursive systematic convolutional coder) since the recursivity results in interesting properties of pseudo-randomness. It is the combination of two such encoders that allows us to approach Shannon's limiting capacity, that is, *to make the error transmission probability as low as required, for a given bitrate and a given noise*

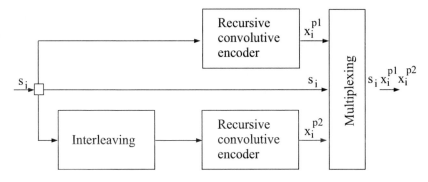

Figure 5.25. *Principle of the turbo encoder*

level, without indefinitely increasing code length. The name "turbo" is associated with a specific decoding scheme, making use of two decoders, as we show hereafter.

The diagram in Figure 5.25 gives the typical organization of a turbo encoder. The encoder multiplexes three sequences $x_i^{p_1}$, $x_i^{p_2}$ and s_i. Encoding n input bits yields $3n$ output bits, the rate of this code is thus $R = 1/3$. The encoding is systematic as the input symbols are found unchanged in the outgoing sequence. The two other sequences $x_i^{p_1}$ and $x_i^{p_2}$ are parity control sequences built by two identical recursive convolutional encoders, one of them receiving as input a permutation of the input data performed by an permuter/interleaver.

A convolutive encoder is said to be recursive when it receives in input the content of the registers through feedback loops.

A simple example of a recursive encoder is provided in Figure 5.26.

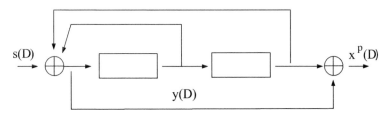

Figure 5.26. *Principle of the recursive encoder*

It is easy to derive its impulse response $h(D)$. We have:

$$y(D) = s(D) + Dy(D) + D^2y(D)$$

hence

$$s(D) = y(D) + Dy(D) + D^2y(D)$$

(remember that the additions are "modulo 2", i.e. $1 + 1 = 0 + 0 = 0$, $1 + 0 = 1$, and consequently addition and subtract on are the same operation). Then:

$$s(D) = \left(1 + D + D^2\right)y(D)$$
$$x^p(D) = \left(1 + D^2\right)y(D)$$

so that:

$$x^p(D) = \frac{1 + D^2}{1 + D + D^2}s(D)$$

and thus

$$h(D) = \frac{x^p(D)}{s(D)} = \frac{1 + D^2}{1 + D + D^2}$$

Multiplying each term by $1 + D$ we obtain:

$$h(D) = \frac{1 + D^2}{1 + D + D^2} = \frac{(1 + D)^3}{1 + D^3}$$
$$= \left(1 + D + D^2 + D^3\right)\left(1 + D^3 + D^6 + D^9 \cdots\right).$$

This highlights the infinite nature of impulse response, but also its periodicity: we verify that, just as in a treillis diagram, the same pattern reproduces after a number of transitions. This limits the ability of the code to distinguish between different input sequences. Any attempt to improve this should lead us to increase the encoder size, albeit at the price of increasing decoding complexity.

The *permuter-interleaver* performs pseudo-random permutations (see Chapter 8) on the input sequence of the second encoder (identical to the first one), thus making it generate codewords resembling those issued for a random coding, and *a priori* quite different from the codewords of the first encoder.

However, a direct decoding of the Viterbi kind is no longer possible, as the depth of the corresponding trellis would be prohibitive. The solution is to decode the received message iteratively, by means of successive simple decoders exchanging information at each step. This is a fundamental characteristic of turbo codes. Figure 5.27 describes the principle.

We naturally assume that the receiving end is aware of the interleaving algorithm. The two decoders work iteratively. Once the signal is demultiplexed, at each step

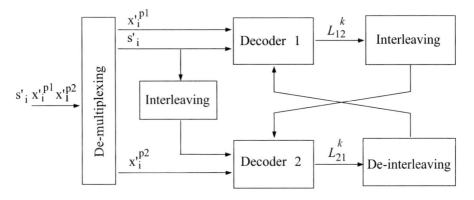

Figure 5.27. *Iterative turbo code decoder*

k a decoder receives at its input *a priori* information L_{21}^k or L_{12}^k (L stands for *Log likelihood ratio*) about source symbols s_k, in the form of a partial likelihood ratio calculated by the preceding decoder. They are logarithmic ratios, of the form $L(s_k) = \log[P(s_k = 1|y_1, \ldots, y_N)/P(s_k = 0|y_1, \ldots, y_N)]$, estimated on the basis of conditional transition probabilities, and indicating the confidence level we should opt for, either 0 or 1.

The calculation can be efficient when it is performed on a limited zone: the systematic part s_i', and a single control sequence, for instance $x_i'^{p1}$ (the exponent $'$ indicates that we refer to the symbols received). At the beginning, and in the absence of data, *a priori* information can be elaborated from a model of the source.

This principle of reinjecting the result of one decoder into the other explains the term "turbo" (by analogy with turbo engines). As indicated by their inventors, we should also notice the analogy with crosswords solving [BER 93].

We then progressively evaluate the transition probabilities between states and the most likely paths. In fact, we build a Viterbi diagram, recursively. The updating process of the decoders stops after a certain number of iterations (usually specified) and this is then the last decoder, which decides, for each of the symbols received, if it is a 0 or 1.

The BCJR algorithm (Bahl, Cocke, Jelinek, Raviv) is often quoted for decoders. It evaluates the *a posteriori* probabilities of source symbols s_i, given the symbols received s_i' and x_i' on the noisy channel. The reader is prompted to refer to specialized literature [BER 93].

Applications. Turbo codes have realized a major improvement in the domain of coding, as they allow us to approach Shannon's limit. They can, for instance, provide error rates around 10^{-5}, for a signal/noise level of 0.7 dB.

They are deployed in modern mobile communication systems, such as UMTS, terrestrial or satellite digital video broadcasting, local loop radio, and communication satellite networks like Immarsat and Intelsat. Finally, they are essential for deep space exploratory missions due to their high performance level.

5.11. Cryptology

We present here the major techniques aiming at guaranteing the confidentiality and authenticity of messages.

We distinguish between *ciphering* and *signature* algorithms. Ciphering is the basic operation in cryptology. It consists of transforming a message (*plaintext*) into a hidden, encrypted message (*ciphertext*), only readable by its legitimate addressee. This is called a *cryptogram*. The transformation is performed by using a key (the *ciphering key*). The technique associated with ciphering systems is referred to as *cryptography*. Only the receiver possessing the key should be able to decipher the message. This system is reliable only if a third party cannot retrieve the message, i.e. cannot retrieve the key. Deciphering a message without possessing the key is called *cryptanalysis*. The term *cryptology* encompasses all the techniques for cryptography and cryptanalysis.

This discipline has a long history (examples are found in antiquity, with substitution ciphers), and initially found its justification in military and diplomatic areas. Today, the development of communications and commercial transactions on the Internet ("e-business") makes it an essential operation, in order to guarantee confidentiality of the exchanged data. New functions are now employed, such as *signatures*, the goal of which is to authenticate messages (both their content and their sender).

5.11.1. *Encryption*

We distinguish between symmetric-key and public-key encryption. Symmetric-key encryption relies on the sharing of a secret-key between the sender and the receiver. Public-key algorithms do not have this weakness, but being slower they do not always allow on-line encryption.

5.11.1.1. *Symmetric-key encryption*

The basic principle of symmetric-key encryption is to process the initial binary message (plaintext) using an operation "parameterized" by another, secret, block k bits long, referred to as the key. Most often this is an *exclusive OR* operation.

Let us denote as M the set of messages $m_1, m_2, \ldots$ to be encrypted and C the cyphertext space (the set $c_1, c_2, \ldots$ of cryptograms). For the cryptanalyst, who does not possess the key, any message m_i should have been translated into a cryptogram

c_j, and the encryption system is seen as a strongly perturbed channel. Here again, Shannon has elaborated the mathematical bases of the discipline, in the framework of his information theory [SHA 49].

According to the definitions already introduced in sections 5.3.7 and 5.8.2, the efficiency of the encryption system can be estimated by calculating its transinformation content.

We have:

$$I(M;C) = H(M) - H(M \mid C),$$

where $H(M|C)$ represents the equivocation:

$$H(M \mid C) = -\sum_i \sum_j p(m_i, c_j) \log p(m_i \mid c_j).$$

Thus, if $p(m_i \mid c_j) = p(m_i)$, then:

$$H(M \mid C) = H(M) \quad \text{and} \quad I(M;C) = 0,$$

meaning that the cryptanalyst does not obtain any information on the original message: secrecy is absolute. The condition $p(m_i \mid c_j) = p(m_i)$ means that any cryptogram can be issued from any of the possible messages with the same probability. Furthermore, it also implies that $p(c_j \mid m_i) = p(c_j)$ which means that any message can be translated into any cryptogram, i.e. that all keys are equally likely. A perfect system thus has a single key, a single cryptogram per message and all the keys are equally likely.

The system does not depend on the *a priori* probabilities of the messages. Modern cryptology is inspired by these principles.

The robustness of symmetric-key systems depends both on the encryption procedure and on the difficulty of retrieving the key. Recent experience with new applications (e.g. mobile phones) has made it clear that it is impossible to keep the procedure secret, so that the security relies only on the key being kept secret, and then on the size of the key space.

The most well known symmetric-key systems are DES (standardized in 1977 and 1991) and AES (adopted as a new standard in 2000).

DES (*data encryption standard*) operates on 64-bit blocks, and uses a key 56 bits long. This has been superseded by AES, as the computing power now available is such that DES codes become vulnerable to brute force (systematic) attacks. A systematic attack consists simply of enumerating all the possible keys, that means with k bit keys, testing 2^{k-1} combinations. As early as 1998 a systematic attack was successfully undertaken against a DES, lasting 56 hours on a dedicated computer. This explains why DES has been modified by three successive encryptions with two keys (giving a key 112 bits long): a first encryption is performed with the first key, followed by a decryption using the second key, and finally a new encryption with the first key.

AES (*advanced encryption standard*) operates on 128 bit blocks and can make use of three key sizes: 128, 192 or 256 bits. Encryption consists of repeating the same permutation operation ten times, parameterized by a secret sub-key changing at each iteration. More precisely, during each iteration:

– on each of the 16 bytes of the message we perform first the same permutation S (inverse function in a finite field with 2^8 elements); then on the resulting 128 bits long word, a second permutation P is applied (also made with the simple operations on the same finite field);

– lastly we calculate the exclusive OR (XOR) between the result and the subkey of the iteration.

The process is iterated ten times. At each iteration a new 128-bit subkey is derived from the previous one. The zero order subkey is the secret key. The i order subkey is derived from the order $i - 1$ one, by first applying a permutation on its 4 last bytes, then applying function S and adding a constant, and by performing a XOR between the result and the 4 last bytes of order $i - 1$ key. The next 4 bytes are obtained by a XOR between the result just obtained and the 4 following bytes of the $i - 1$ subkey, and so on.

5.11.1.2. *Public-key encryption*

The issue is to avoid sharing a secret between several parties (all those knowing the code of a safe can access its content, which is not really confidential!). Here the sender encrypts the message by means of a public-key (broadcast in a directory, for instance, so accessible to anyone), and decrypted by the recipient using a private key he alone possesses (everybody may deposit a message in the mailbox, but only its owner possesses the key).

This kind of encryption relies on the concepts of *trap-door*, and *one-way function*. A one-way function is easy to calculate, but difficult (or impossible) to invert (to retrieve $x = f^{-1}(y)$). It becomes a trap-door if the knowledge of an additional information (the trap) makes it easy to invert. These are very specific functions, which can be obtained for instance from factorizing integers, and also from the problem of finding discrete logarithms.

Rivest, Shanin and Adelman (RSA) algorithm. RSA algorithm is probably the most well-known public-key system (from its authors, Rivest, Shanin and Adelman [RIV 78]). It is based on the fact that while it is easy to calculate the product of two prime numbers, it is on the other hand quite difficult to factorize the result. Formally, the method relies on the following arithmetic theorem:

Let n be an integer, the product of two prime numbers p and q, i.e. $n = pq$. Euler's theorem states that if a is an integer such that

$$a \bmod \left((p - 1)(q - 1)\right) = 1$$

then, for any positive $0 < x < n$, we have:

$$x^a (\bmod\, n) = x.$$

The principle of the RSA algorithm is then as follows: the message is split into blocks which can be considered as integers between 0 and $n - 1$. The public-key of the user is formed by a number $n = pq$ and an integer e prime with $(p - 1)(q - 1)$. Values of n and e are published in some directory. The secret key is an integer d verifying $ed(\bmod(p - 1)(q - 1)) = 1$. Message block m is encrypted into message c by the operation $c = m^e (\bmod\, n)$. Upon receipt, the addressee retrieves the original text by the operation:

$$c^d (\bmod\, n) = m.$$

Indeed by definition we have $ed(\bmod(p - 1)(q - 1)) = 1$ and so:

$$c^d (\bmod\, n) = \left(m^e\right)^d (\bmod\, n) = m^{ed} (\bmod\, n) = m.$$

A cryptanalyst who wishes to attack the RSA system should retrieve the plaintext m from the only knowledge of e, n, and $c = m^e (\bmod\, n)$. Up to now, no efficient algorithm is known to solve this problem. A systematic attack would consist of finding the secret key d starting from e and n, but examining 2^d numbers of d bit length is presently out of reach, as soon as d is around 512 bit long. This leads to factorize n: the RSA system generally employs numbers n with 1,024 bits, and it has not been possible up to now to go beyond factorizing numbers around 600 bits long (155 digits in 1999, consuming 224 hours of a Cray C916, 200 digits in 2005).

Discrete logarithms. The method is based upon the solution of the discrete logarithm problem: given a number x ciphered by the operation $\beta = g^x$, where g is the generator of a finite group G and β an element in G, and starting from β we are required to retrieve x (extracting the logarithm). This approach is the basis of the El Gamal cryptosystem and of the Diffie-Hellman key exchange protocol for instance. In El Gamal's method, the first party takes a random number $1 \leq a \leq n - 1$ where $n = |G|$ (the cardinal of G), then calculates the number A such that $A = g^a$. His/her public-key is G, g, n, A. A second party, wanting to send him/her a message M also chooses randomly $1 \leq b \leq n - 1$ and sends (B, C), with $B = g^b$ and $C = M.A^b$. This corresponds to the exchange of a secret-key $K = g^{ab} = A^b = B^a$ and to the ciphering $C = M.K$. Deciphering is performed by calculating $M = C.K^{-1}$. On the other hand, the cryptanalyst will have to retrieve K knowing G, g, n, A, B. The only known general solution stems from solving the discrete logarithm problem.

The method, originally applied to multiplicative groups G, has been extended to other groups, such as the additive elliptic curve groups: we then speak of *cryptosystems elliptic curves*. The reader should consult specialized references [SCH 96, STI 06].

In practice, mixed encryption methods are often used. So, confidential data will be exchanged through a symmetric-key encryption algorithm, because of its speed, but after first having exchanged the secret-key using a public-key algorithm. Generally, public-key systems are reserved for short messages.

5.11.2. *Digital signature*

Digitally signing a document consists of adding several additional bits to a plaintext, depending both on the message and on its author. We must be able to verify the signature, but not to forge it. Any modification of the plaintext modifies and thus invalidates the signature. So, the digital signature simultaneously guarantees the author identity (authentication), the integrity of the message received and its non-repudiation by the author. A digital signature is now legally accepted in most countries.

Calculating the signature depends on a secret key. On the other hand, its verification does not need any secret information. We will quote two techniques for digital signature: RSA and DSA.

RSA signature. The sender applies the RSA deciphering algorithm to his message using his own secret key d. The addressee verifies the signature by applying the ciphering function with public-key (e, n): the result should correspond to the plain (deciphered) received message. Smart cards (credit cards) provide an example application of the RSA scheme: the signature, initially written in the chip by the bank authority, is verified at each transaction by the trader's terminal. Fraud may happen if malevolent users are able to build forged cards, by retrieving the signature (this has been done already!).

DSA signature. We apply a ciphering scheme based upon the discrete logarithm extraction, as presented above.

5.11.3. *Signature and hashing*

In practice, prior to applying the algorithms we have described, a preliminary *hash function* is applied, the description of which is public, with the goal of transforming a binary string of arbitrary length into a word of fixed reduced length (generally, 128, 160 or 256 bits). This greatly simplifies the process of computing the signature: the "hashed" (digital fingerprint) message is signed instead of the message itself, which is much longer. However, the hash message must be long enough to avoid *collisions*, that is, two different messages resulting in the same hashed string. We can mention some of the most well known hash-functions: MD4, MD5 (*message digest*), SHA 256, 384, 512 (*secure hash algorithm*) used with the RSA signature, and also RIPEMD-160 (*race integrity primitive evaluation* MD).

We will not detail the hash function here. We simply mention the principle, taking the MD5 process as an example: the message is broken up into fixed-size blocks 512 bits long. The blocks are processed sequentially by an irreversible compression function, having as inputs the 512-bit block and an auxiliary 128-bit vector, and returning a 128-bit "hash". For the first block we use a 128-bit initialization vector (defined in the standard) and the hash is used as auxiliary input for the following step. The blocks are processed successively, the last one yielding the final hash (also called the *message digest*).

It is admitted today that hashed strings at least 256 bits long are needed to foil collision attacks.

Clearly, the resistance of all the techniques presented in this section to cryptanalysis depends strongly on the processing power of computing equipment available. Consequently, both key sizes and algorithms should evolve, at the pace of processor power.

Chapter 6

Traffic and Queueing Theory

In the design and analysis of information processing systems, the concept of "traffic" plays a central role, especially when it comes to assessing their performance level. The mathematical methods related to these points are based upon the results of queueing theory, which this chapter will detail.

Communication networks, as well as the services they provide, make use of a large variety of mechanisms: connection set-up in a circuit-switched network, transport of IP packets in the IP world, organization of operators in a call center, task sharing in the processor of multimedia systems, etc. However, as far as performance analysis is concerned, all these phenomena come under the rule of a small number of fundamental concepts, initially established by the pioneers of *teletraffic*, and which are presented hereafter. The phenomena to take account of are rejection probabilities and response delays of transport protocols or control processors, examples of which are to be found in [FIC 04].

6.1. Traffic concepts

In any real-time system, the concept of *traffic* accounts for the volume of tasks it has to process, and of the resulting load. The traffic of a telecommunications network is the volume of information transported or processed by the network. In the computing unit of an information system, the traffic is made of all software tasks generated by customer demand. In a network control server, it is made of signaling data, routing information to be processed, administration and maintenance routines, etc.

6.1.1. *The Erlang concept*

Clearly, the more frequent and the longer the exchanges between two elements, the more resources are needed to carry them with acceptable quality. For example, if a network receives over a given period permanent demand of 1 call per second, with each call lasting for 3 seconds, the network will continuously have $N = 3$ calls coexisting. After a transient state, corresponding to the time needed to reach the expected load level, each end of call (corresponding to the outgoing process) will be replaced by a new start of call (corresponding to the incoming process), thus maintaining a constant load level in the network during the period considered. The phenomenon is described in Figure 6.1.

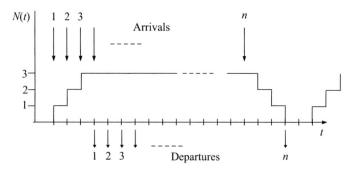

Figure 6.1. *Simultaneous calls and the Erlang concept*

To simplify, we have represented regular incoming flows and constant holding times, but the phenomenon remains the same with arrivals and service times which vary around average values. The average number N of demands simultaneously in progress is termed *traffic intensity*. The measurement unit is the *Erlang*, denoted E, from the name of the distinguished Danish engineer A.K. Erlang (1878-1929) who established the first fundamental laws of traffic theory.

This concept is of course fundamental, as it defines the basis for system dimensioning. So, if a resource (a circuit, a frequency in radio access network, a virtual circuit, bitrate, etc.) is associated with each of the N demands, a capacity of at least N resources will be required to process the whole traffic. The precise number of elements to be provided will depend on the stochastic laws governing arrivals and services. This is exactly what enables the calculation of the famous Erlang formula in the case of Poissonian arrivals, i.e. arrivals conforming to a Poisson law. More generally, in order to be able to extend this concept to all types of telecommunication services, and all types of resources used, the following definition has been adopted: *a set of identical resources is said to carry at a given instant a traffic of N Erlangs when N of its units are busy.* This definition covers a number of circuits in traditional telephony, as well as a volume of memory, a capacity in bit/s for a transmission support, or the number of simultaneous tasks in the processing unit of multimedia servers.

Formally, traffic in Erlangs is denoted A, and if the number of busy resources is noted as $n(t)$, this gives the following for a period of observation T (assuming a stable behavior – we speak of stationary processes):

$$A(T) = \frac{1}{T} \int_0^T n(t)\mathrm{d}t, \quad A = \lim_{T \to \infty} A(T). \tag{6.1}$$

In more concrete terms, if we assume a sufficient number of resources to carry out all the requests presented, and if we call λ the mean number, constant, of requests per time unit and t_m the average occupation time of the resource by each request, this gives:

$$A = \lambda t_m. \tag{6.2}$$

Erlang demonstrated the following fundamental result, called the *Erlang loss formula*, which gives the rejection probability (B) of a new request, because of a lack of resources, for a traffic A offered to N resources:

$$B(A, N) \equiv B = \frac{\frac{A^N}{N!}}{\sum_{j=0}^N \frac{A^j}{j!}}. \tag{6.3}$$

These demands which are accepted form the so-called *handled traffic* (also named *carried traffic*), denoted as A_h. This is thus the average number of busy servers. We also have:

$$A_h = A(1 - B). \tag{6.4}$$

This formula also expresses the system capacity considered necessary to handle the traffic offered to it. As the reality of a network is far more complex than this basic model, we will also have to deal with phenomena such as waiting, jitter, etc. However, it will always be a matter of evaluating the resources necessary to handle traffic offered in acceptable conditions (loss, delay, etc.).

6.1.2. *Traffic modeling*

Optimal resource sizing, i.e. the ability to provide a correct processing of the demands, is the main goal of traffic theory. Here *queueing theory* is called into play as the modeling tool allowing the specialist to estimate state probabilities of the system under the load level (the offered traffic) and given the quantity of available resources.

Here the *customers*, or *clients*, are the requests presented to a set of *servers* which process them. Demands for bandwidth in a communication system are an example of such customers; circuits, IP links, processors, etc., most often organized in clusters, are the servers. When several customers simultaneously attempt to access a server, some of them may be rejected, or stored in *queues*, or *buffers*. Estimating the probability of these events, loss or waiting, forms the basis of resource dimensioning, and is the subject of *teletraffic*. Indeed, Quality of Service standards define maximum values for these quantities, and it is up to the teletraffic engineer to determine the correct number of servers so as to process the traffic in accordance with the standards in use. We will show how to estimate such probabilities.

Generally, the systems studied are represented using *models* which conform to Figure 6.2.

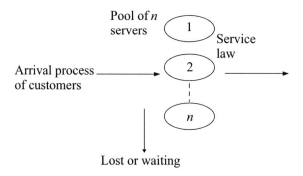

Figure 6.2. *The basic client-server system*

6.2. The concept of processes

The state of the system changes, according to external (e.g. arrival demands) or internal events (end of service, failure, etc.). These events occur according to random processes, which are characterized by probability laws, such as the number of events per time unit, or the delay between events. Besides the probability function itself, the first moments, namely mean and variance as presented in Chapter 1, are important parameters.

6.2.1. *Arrival process*

The arrival process aims at giving a mathematical description of the way "customers" enter the system. A direct characterization is given by the duration between successive arrivals, or else the number of arrivals per time unit: during the interval T, $n(T)$ customers arrive and the arrival rate λ is defined as

$$\lambda = \lim_{T \to \infty} \frac{n(T)}{T}. \tag{6.5}$$

6.2.1.1. *Renewal process*

In the most favorable case, the statistical description of the time between arrivals is very simple. Let us assume that the situation can be described as follows:

Each time an arrival takes place, the interval until the next arrival is drawn according to a given law, in such a way that durations of successive intervals are independent of each other. This is in fact the special case of a *renewal process*. It is essential to understand the value of this concept, but also what is rare about it. For example (in Figure 6.3) let us observe the arrival process resulting from the superimposition of two independent renewal processes.

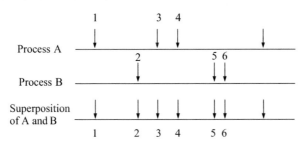

Figure 6.3. *Superimposing processes A and B does not result in a renewal process:
the arrival of "4" is related to "3", but "5" is related to "2"*

Clearly, this is a very common situation, but the superimposition process is not a renewal process. To predict the arrival of the 4th client, reference must be made to the 3rd, by using the inter-arrival time. However, the arrival of the 5th client can only be predicted by reference to the 2nd client, and not to the 4th.

6.2.1.2. *Poisson arrivals*

The Poisson arrival process is by far the most frequent we can encounter, as it is a fairly good model for a common situation where the customer source actually results in the superimposition of a very large number of elementary customers. We explain its properties and briefly justify its use.

Let us assume that the arrival process complies with the following rules:

– the probability of an arrival in an interval $[t, t + \Delta t[$ does not depend on what happened before the instant t. This is the so-called *memoryless property* (a concept already introduced in Chapter 5 for characterizing an important type of source of information),

– the probability of client arrival is proportional to Δt, and the probability of more than one event is negligible (in the upper order of the infinitely small, in mathematical language – we denote it as $o(\Delta t)$). The proportionality factor is rated λ (process intensity).

These classical assumptions lead to the Poisson process. How can the probability distribution of the number of arrivals in a given time be estimated on the basis of the above axioms? The reasoning applied is typical of the theory.

Let us denote as $P_k(t)$ the probability of k arrivals in the interval $[0, t[$. We can describe how this probability varies over time: k clients will be observed in the interval $[0, t + \Delta t[$ if:

– k clients have been observed in $[0, t[$, and no arrival has been observed in $[t, t + \Delta t[$;

– $k - 1$ clients have been observed in $[0, t[$, and one arrival occurred in $[t, t + \Delta t[$;

– $k - n$, $n > 1$ arrivals have been observed in $[0, t[$, and n arrivals in $[t, t + \Delta t[$, etc.

Gathering these observations into an equation (noting that the events are mutually exclusive):

$$P_k(t + \Delta t) = P_k(t)\big[1 - \lambda\Delta t + o(\Delta t)\big] + P_{k-1}(t)\big[\lambda\Delta t + o(\Delta t)\big]$$
$$+ P_{k-2}(t)\big[(\lambda\Delta t)^2 + o(\Delta t)\big]^2 + \cdots$$

For $k = 0$, the terms $k - 1$, etc., disappear:

$$P_0(t + \Delta t) = P_0(t)\big[1 - \lambda\Delta t + o(\Delta t)\big].$$

The development of the previous equation (making $\Delta t \to 0$, etc.) leads to:

$$\frac{d}{dt}P_0(t) = -\lambda P_0(t),$$

that is, $P_0(t) = ae^{-\lambda t}$, where a is a constant, still unknown at this point.

The general equation will be developed following the same approach. It should be noted that in the passage to the limit that leads to the derivative (that is, $\Delta t \to 0$), all terms in $o(\Delta t)/t$ disappear:

$$P_k(t) + \frac{d}{dt}P_k(t)\Delta t = P_k(t) - \lambda P_k(t)\Delta t + \lambda P_{k-1}(t)\Delta t + o(\Delta t),$$

and thus

$$\frac{d}{dt}P_k(t) = -\lambda P_k(t) + \lambda P_{k-1}(t).$$

The basic resolution method proceeds using a recurrence:

$$\frac{d}{dt}P_1(t) = \lambda P_1(t) + \lambda ae^{-\lambda t}, \text{ and thus } P_1(t) = \lambda ate^{-\lambda t} + be^{-\lambda t}.$$

The obvious condition $P_1(0) = 0$ leads to $b = 0$; the reader will be able to write the second iteration, which gives the intuition of the general solution:

$P_k(t) = a\frac{(\lambda t)^k}{k!}e^{-\lambda t}$. This can be verified with the general equation. It can now be noted that since 0, 1, 2, etc. arrivals have occurred in the interval, it is essential that:

$$\sum_{k=0}^{\infty} P_k(t) = 1,$$

this is the *normalization condition*, and it gives $a = 1$. We finally obtain the probability of observing k arrivals in an interval of length t:

$$P_k(t) = \frac{(\lambda t)^k}{k!}e^{-\lambda t}.$$

This discrete distribution is the Poisson law, which is sometimes written by noting $A = \lambda t$, with t being the time unit:

$$P_k = \frac{A^k}{k!}e^{-A}. \tag{6.6}$$

A is then the mean traffic offered during the period considered. The average number of arrivals observed in any interval of length t and its variance are:

$$m = \lambda t, \quad \sigma^2 = \lambda t. \tag{6.7}$$

Indeed, using equation (6.6):

$$\overline{X} = \sum kp_k = 0 \cdot e^{-A} + 1 \cdot Ae^{-A} + 2\frac{A^2}{2}e^{-A} + \cdots + k\frac{A^k}{k!} \cdot e^{-A} + \cdots$$

$$\overline{X} = Ae^{-A}\left(1 + A + \frac{A^2}{2} + \cdots + \frac{A^{k-1}}{(k-1)!} + \cdots\right) = A.$$

For the variance, using $\sigma^2 = \overline{X^2} - (\overline{X})^2$:

$$\overline{X^2} = \sum k^2 p_k = 0.e^{-A} + 1 \cdot Ae^{-A} + 2^2\frac{A^2}{2}e^{-A} + \cdots + k^2\frac{A^k}{k!} \cdot e^{-A} + \cdots$$

Now, a simple transformation gives the result, already presented in Chapter 2:

$$\sigma^2 = A = m.$$

The probability distribution function of the interval between successive arrivals is derived from the distribution: the probability of an interval between arrivals greater than t is the probability that no arrival occurs between 0 and t:

$$A(t) = 1 - e^{-\lambda t}, \tag{6.8}$$

of probability density function (by derivation of the distribution):

$$a(t) = \lambda e^{-\lambda t}. \tag{6.9}$$

We again find the exponential law: in the Poisson process interarrival times are exponentially distributed.

At this point it is worth remembering our initial assumption about the lack of memory in our process: the probability of an event in a time interval $[t, t + \Delta t[$ does not depend on what happened prior to t, and is proportional to Δt, that is $\lambda \Delta t$. Thus, the exponential distribution enjoys this important property: it is memoryless.

The following section clarifies and justifies the success of the assumption of Poisson arrivals: not only does it lead to a relatively simple calculation, but it is often an accurate model for traffic issuing from a large number of independent sources.

6.2.1.3. *The use of the Poisson process*

When we know nothing about an arrival process, it is tempting to ascribe to it the two properties set out above, which lead to the Poisson process formulae, as they are both generally applicable and reasonable for many systems. In fact this is not the case – and verifying these hypotheses will usually be a difficult task. In most cases, the justification for using the Poisson hypothesis is based on the following result.

THEOREM 6.1 ([FEL 71, CIN 75]). *Let us assume k independent renewal processes, not necessarily Poissonian, with arrival rates $(\lambda_i, \ i = 1, \ldots, k)$. We denote as $\lambda = \sum \lambda_i$ the global arrival rate of the process resulting from their superimposition.*

If the previous sum has a limit λ^* when k increases indefinitely, then the superimposition process tends towards a Poisson process with the rate λ^*.

(Note: the use of the notation λ_i and of the concept of arrival rate does not in any way mean that a Poisson assumption is adopted for individual processes.)

6.2.2. *Service process*

The service process may be extremely complex, but we usually limit ourselves to assuming that each service time is independent of the others, and that all of them comply with the same distribution function: we speak of independent and identically distributed variables. This service law is described by its probability distribution:

$$B(x) = P\{\text{service time} \leq x\}.$$

The assumption concerning the independence and identity of distribution between successive services, although a simplification, in fact represents a good assumption in most actual cases, such as call duration or independent session times, etc. We will however need to deal with systems handling clients whose service laws obey different distributions. This is the case, for example, with multi-service systems, in which each type of service has its own characteristic.

6.2.2.1. *Exponential distribution*

The most popular service law is the exponential distribution, which is traditionally written:

$$B(x) = P\{\text{service time} \le x\} = 1 - e^{-\mu x}, \quad b(x) = \mu e^{-\mu x}, \qquad (6.10)$$

where μ is the *service rate* and $b(x)$ the density function. Just as for the Poisson process, the exponential distribution accounts for the memoryless property: the probability of an end of service in the coming instant (in the interval $[t, t + \Delta t[$) is $\mu \Delta t$, whatever the age of the service, as presented in the discussion about the residual service time below.

The exponential distribution is characterized by its moments – mean and variance. From definitions (1.25) and (1.27), we easily obtain:

$$m = \overline{X} = \int_0^\infty x f(x) \mathrm{d}x; \quad \mu_2 = \sigma^2 = \int_0^\infty (x - m)^2 f(x) \mathrm{d}x = \overline{X^2} - (\overline{X})^2$$

$$\text{mean value } m = 1/\mu, \quad \text{variance } \sigma^2 = 1/\mu^2. \qquad (6.11)$$

Its coefficient of variation i.e. the ratio of standard deviation to mean service time is $c = \sigma/m = 1$.

6.2.2.2. *Residual service time*

This concept will enable us to clarify the "memoryless" property of some processes. The following question is asked: if a service is observed which has already reached the "age" y, what is the distribution of time X still to elapse before the service end?

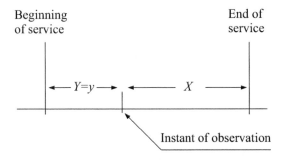

Figure 6.4. *Distribution of the residual service time*

The answer is very simple: stating that $X > x$ seconds are still to be accomplished is the same thing as stating that the total time will be greater than $y + x$, and as $Y = y$

this corresponds to calculating the conditional probability *knowing that* the total time is larger than y. For the distribution of X, this generates:

$$P(X > x|Y = y) = P(\text{whole service} > x + y|Y = y)$$

$$= \frac{P(\text{whole service} > x + y)}{P(\text{whole service} > y)} = \frac{1 - B(x + y)}{1 - B(y)}. \qquad (6.12)$$

In an equivalent way, the density will be:

$$P\big(X \in [x, x + \mathrm{d}x[|\ Y = y\big) = \frac{b(x + y)\mathrm{d}x}{1 - B(y)}. \qquad (6.13)$$

Applying this result to the exponential law shows that the conditional event density is:

$$b(x \mid y) = \frac{\mu e^{-\mu(x+y)}}{e^{-\mu y}} = \mu e^{-\mu x} = b(x),$$

independently of y. This is once again the "memoryless" property, in other words the probability of an end of service in the coming instant (in the interval $[t, t + \Delta t[$) is $\mu \Delta t$, whatever the age of the service.

This result is apparently paradoxical (it is mentioned in the literature as the "taxi (or bus) paradox"), as compared with the intuition which would lead to the erroneous conclusion of an average residual time that is half the average inter-arrival. The paradox vanishes if we remember that the arrival rate of the bus is constant, independent of the observer, and thus from the observer standpoint we still have the exponential distribution. So, the distribution of the remaining time is identical to the initial distribution for an exponential law, and thus also its mean value. It can also be shown that "age" (time Y in the diagram) has the same distribution and the same average, and finally that the total interval observed has an average duration of twice that of the mean value of the law! So, for an external observer who would not know the arrival law, it could be deduced from this, erroneously, that the inter-arrival time has an average duration of twice the correct value!

The same exercise, reproduced with a constant length service, would give a result which is more in line with naive intuition: the remaining duration being half the inter-arrival time. This result stresses the difficulty, and the traps, related to sampling measurements. Indeed, sampling for observing the inter-arrivals introduces a bias: let us take the example of a colleague who wants to talk to you when you are taking part in a phone call. When he arrives in your office by chance, the risk is greater that he will arrive during a long conversation (as this interval is long). The *sample* of the conversation durations he observes no longer conforms to the true distribution. The engineer will often be faced with this kind of problem during observations or measurements on systems as well as during simulations (see section 8.3.1).

6.2.2.3. *Erlang distribution*

The Erlang distribution provides an important set of models for more complex service time distributions.

Let us assume that the service process is composed of a cascade of k elementary exponential servers, which are identical (i.e. have the same parameter μ) and independent of each other. The service time is the sum of the times spent in each server. There is indeed only one server, with k stages (only one client at a time is authorized to enter the compound server). The service time is distributed as the sum of k exponential variables, which are independent and with the same parameter: This law is called the Erlang-k law whose form has already been given in Chapter 1:

$$B(x) = P\big(X_1 + X_2 + \cdots + X_k \le x\big) = 1 - e^{-\mu x} \sum_{j=0}^{k-1} \frac{(\mu x)^j}{j!}. \qquad (6.14)$$

As this is a sum of independent random variables, the mean and variance are easily obtained, as sum of the mean and variance of each exponential variable:

$$\text{Erlang mean} - k \text{ variable} : k/\mu, \ \text{ variance} : k/\mu^2. \qquad (6.15)$$

The coefficient of variation is:

$$c = 1/\sqrt{k}. \qquad (6.16)$$

The coefficient of variation is thus always less than 1, and it is used as a typical representative of laws less variable than the exponential. The limit case will be, for a very large k, a constant service time.

6.2.2.4. *Hyperexponential distribution*

The hyperexponential distribution is another model of interest. The service mechanism is here provided by two exponential servers with different rates, between which the client chooses (Figure 6.5). On entering the server, the client "chooses" service 1 (average duration $1/\mu_1$) with probability α, or server 2 (average $1/\mu_2$) with probability $1 - \alpha$. Only one client at a time resides in the server. For example, the client is a task in a processor, which according to a given criterion will run either

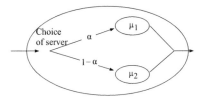

Figure 6.5. *The hyperexponential server*

one program or another. The situation can be enriched on the same principle, by proposing a choice between n servers. The corresponding distribution for the two servers has the following form:

$$P(\text{Service} \le x) = \alpha\left(1 - e^{-\mu_1 x}\right) + (1 - \alpha)\left(1 - e^{-\mu_2 x}\right). \tag{6.17}$$

Calculating the mean and variance gives:

$$\text{Mean: } m = \frac{\alpha}{\mu_1} + \frac{1 - \alpha}{\mu_2}, \quad \text{Variance: } \frac{\alpha}{\mu_1^2} + \frac{1 - \alpha}{\mu_2^2} - m^2, \tag{6.18}$$

$$\text{Coefficient of variation: } c^2 = 2\frac{\frac{\alpha}{\mu_1^2} + \frac{1-\alpha}{\mu_2^2}}{\left[\frac{\alpha}{\mu_1} + \frac{1-\alpha}{\mu_2}\right]^2} - 1. \tag{6.19}$$

This factor is always greater than 1: a service with a *supervariant* distribution (i.e. such that its standard deviation is larger than the mean) may be represented by a hyperexponential law.

The example of two components is easily generalized to the case of a choice between n exponential services. The probability distribution is given by:

$$P(\text{Service} \le x) = \sum_k \alpha_k\left(1 - e^{-\mu_k x}\right), \quad \text{with} \quad \sum_k \alpha_k = 1. \tag{6.20}$$

The moments are:

$$\text{Mean value: } \sum_k \frac{\alpha_k}{\mu_k}, \quad \text{variance: } 2\sum_k \frac{\alpha_k}{\mu_k^2} - \left(\sum_k \frac{\alpha_k}{\mu_k}\right)^2. \tag{6.21}$$

$$\text{Coefficient of variation: } c^2 = 2\frac{\sum_k \frac{\alpha_k}{\mu_k^2}}{\left[\sum \frac{\alpha_k}{\mu_k}\right]^2} - 1. \tag{6.22}$$

The Cauchy-Schwarz inequality asserts that $(\sum a_i b_i)^2 \le \sum a_i^2 \sum b_i^2$. Applied to the previous expression, with $a_i = \sqrt{\alpha_i}$, $b_i = \sqrt{\alpha_i}/\mu_i$, this shows that the coefficient of variation is always greater than 1. This justifies using this law for distributions more bursty than the exponential distribution.

The couple (Erlang-k, hyperexponential) provides a means of approximating any law whose mean and variance are known. The generalization of this approach is known as the "Cox laws" which enable the representation of any probability distribution of a service law by a combination of exponential servers, as presented below.

6.2.3. *General arrival and service processes*

Although Poisson arrivals and exponentially distributed services are in common use, engineers can be confronted with arrivals and services obeying more complex probability distributions. In particular, calculating the distribution of waiting times requires taking account of the actual distributions of inter-arrival and service time distributions. As already mentioned, a first technique consists of building complex distributions by combining exponential servers: Erlang-n, hyperexponential laws, etc., and their generalization, the *Coxian distribution*, as presented in Chapter 2.

Recall that the n-phase Coxian distribution is obtained by a combination of n exponential servers, in a way which generalizes the hyperexponential scheme in Figure 6.5. As for this case, only one customer may reside in the network of servers, recalled in Figure 6.6 for completeness: the rule is the same as for the Erlang-k or hyperexponential schemes: upon arrival in front of server k, of service rate μ_k, the client chooses to enter the server (probability α_k) or leave the system (probability $1 - \alpha_k$).

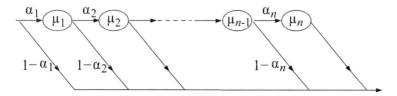

Figure 6.6. *The Coxian distribution*

The Laplace transform of the resulting distribution is:

$$B(s) = 1 - \alpha_1 + \sum_{i \leq n} \prod_{j=1}^{n} \frac{\alpha_j \mu_j}{s + \mu_j} \left(1 - \alpha_{i+1}\right). \qquad (6.23)$$

However, Coxian distributions rapidly lead to complex models, with a large number of branches – and thus a large number of state variables. In such complex cases, other techniques, and especially Laplace transforms, z-transforms or the characteristic function are often more appropriate for describing service laws. We show in section 6.6 how to make use of characteristic functions, in relation with the embedded Markov chains and the Pollaczek method.

6.3. Markov and birth/death processes

Markov processes play an important role in numerous engineering fields, and their study goes far beyond the scope of the present book. Actually, we are here concerned with the Markov property: it conveys the idea of the independence between the past and future in the evolution of a phenomenon, as already mentioned in Chapter 5.

Here, we develop the so-called *Markov chain* technique, which is of constant use in traffic and queueing theory, and also in reliability theory, as we will explain in Chapter 7.

6.3.1. *State concept*

The state concept has an intuitive basis: describing the state of a system means giving a list of the characteristics it possesses, and also providing elements which enable predictions about how it will change. In mechanics, for example, a point particle is described by its coordinates (x, y, z) and by its velocity (v_x, v_y, v_z). Once these quantities are known, it is possible to describe the position of the point, and via the mechanics equations and given the initial state, the trajectory it must follow.

The same is true of a stochastic system, except that the forecast of the trajectory takes on a probabilistic character: it is not possible to predict the exact state within a few seconds, but only its probability distribution.

6.3.2. *Markov chains*

Let us consider a random variable X, with discrete state space (it only takes its values in a discrete space). X may represent the number of clients in a buffer: $X = 1, 2, 3, \ldots$ These states may be noted as $E_1, E_2, \ldots, E_k, \ldots$. Let us note as $t_1, t_2, \ldots, t_n$ the successive instants of X state changes, and as $x_1, x_2, \ldots, x_n$ the sequence of the states visited. The t_n could be for example the instants of arrival in or departure from the buffer. In general, the study of the evolution of X is very difficult. There is however one capital circumstance, which is the basis of all the following developments.

In the general case, the value of X at instant t_{n+1} depends on the whole of the past, that is on $X(t_1), X(t_2)$, etc. X is said to be obeying the Markov property if:

$$P\big[X(t_{n+1}) = x_{n+1} \mid X(t_n) = x_n, \ X(t_{n-1}) = x_{n-1}, \ldots\big]$$
$$= P\big[X(t_{n+1}) = x_{n+1} \mid X(t_n) = x_n\big].$$

In short, only the current state at instant t_n influences the future evolution of the process, and the earlier states may be forgotten. This is another form of the *memoryless property* already encountered in Chapter 5 and in sections 6.2.1.2 and 6.2.2.2.

Let us also assume that the process is homogenous, i.e. invariable by translation over time. This enables the introduction of the notation:

$$p_{j,k} = P\big[X(t_{n+1}) = E_k \mid X(t_n) = E_j\big]$$

(without homogenity, it would have been necessary to introduce a notation of the type $p_{j,k}^{(n)}$). The Markov property is translated as:

$$P\big[X(t_{n+1}) = E_k\big] = \sum_j p_{j,k} P\big[X(t_n) = E_j\big]. \tag{6.24}$$

This is the elementary form of a fundamental result, known as the Chapman-Kolmogorov equation. The process studied is a *Markov chain*.

6.3.3. *Birth and death processes*

The study of the most general Markov processes is one of the main concerns of probability theory. Considering the very specific needs of this section we will limit our interest to the very special and very useful case in which the process can only make "jumps" to its direct neighbors. For simplification and without loss of generality we say that the state of the system can change from E_k to E_{k+1} or E_{k-1}. The rate of passage from E_k to E_{k+1} is conventionally denoted as λ_k: this is the *birth rate*. The rate of passage from E_k to E_{k-1} is the *death rate* μ_k. The birth and death rate concept has been introduced into the study of population trends, where the state refers to the size of the population. In accordance with this provenance, and to simplify the writing, the states will be named simply $1, 2, \ldots, k$, with no loss of generality.

The problem is simple: we are aiming to derive the probability distribution of the state, i.e. the function $P_k(t) = P[X(t) = k]$, with the initial state being supposed to be known.

Establishing the equation is relatively intuitive. In fact, the aim is simply to rediscover the dynamics of the Chapman-Kolmogorov equations, and resembles the analysis of the Poisson process (see section 6.2.1.2). Let us examine the possible evolutions from instant t. At instant $t + \Delta t$, our process will be observed in state k if:

– the state was k at instant t, *and* nothing happened in the elementary interval $[t, t + \Delta t[$;

– the state was $k-1$ at instant t, *and* a birth occurred during the interval $[t, t+\Delta t[$;

– the state was $k+1$ at instant t, *and* a death occurred during the interval $[t, t+\Delta t[$.

The interval $[t, t+\Delta t[$ is assumed to be "small": other more complex events (2 arrivals, one arrival and one departure) will take place with probabilities of the order $o(\Delta t)$. We can therefore write:

$$P_k(t + \Delta t) = P_k(t)\big[1 - \lambda_k \Delta t - \mu_k \Delta t\big]$$
$$+ P_{k-1}(t)\lambda_{k-1}\Delta t$$
$$+ P_{k+1}(t)\mu_{k+1}\Delta t$$
$$+ o(\Delta t).$$

This equation accurately transcribes the description of the possibilities given above. Based on this form, we write a differential equation with the classical analytical methods:

$$\frac{P_k(t + \Delta t) - P_k(t)}{\Delta t} = -\big(\lambda_k + \mu_k\big)P_k(t) + \lambda_{k-1}P_{k-1}(t) + \mu_{k+1}P_{k+1}(t).$$

One special case: at 0 the death transition will not exist, as there is no state numbered -1. Finally, the passage to the limit leads to the fundamental differential system:

$$\frac{\mathrm{d}}{\mathrm{d}t}P_k(t) = -\left(\lambda_k + \mu_k\right)P_k(t) + \lambda_{k-1}P_{k-1}(t) + \mu_{k+1}P_{k+1}(t), \quad k > 0,$$

$$\frac{\mathrm{d}}{\mathrm{d}t}P_0(t) = -\lambda_0 P_0(t) + \mu_1 P_1(t).$$

(6.25)

This *state equation* takes us back to the analogy with point particle mechanics. If the initial state is known, we can predict the distribution for any instant in the future. The necessity of knowing the initial state seems a cumbersome need! Fortunately, a class of systems exists, whereby it is not necessary to know this initial state. The analysis of this process leads to a distinction being drawn between two cases:

– Case 1. When the time increases, probabilities tend towards a limit that is independent of the initial state. We then speak of systems that have reached their statistical equilibrium – or their steady-state condition.

– Case 2. No equilibrium is achieved, the $P_k(t)$ have no asymptote. This will in particular be the case for overloaded systems (intuitively, for such a system, the number of clients present increases indefinitely, and no stationary condition could exist). Furthermore, in practice, congestion combined with rejection mechanisms will occur and will result in the abandonment of requests, and in general a behavioral dynamic modification of the whole system.

We will limit ourselves to the study of the systems in case 1, of which we will study the equilibrium state. For a dynamic system at equilibrium, a *steady-state* condition exists, such that the state probabilities are equal to the asymptotic value and thus do not depend on time. We will simply rewrite the above system, canceling all the derivatives. The stationary distribution will be denoted P_k.

$$\left(\lambda_k + \mu_k\right)P_k = \lambda_{k-1}P_{k-1} + \mu_{k+1}P_{k+1}, \quad k > 0,$$

$$\lambda_0 P_0(t) = \mu_1 P_1(t).$$

(6.26)

This system is solved by recurrence: P_1 as a function of P_0, and then P_2 as a function of P_1, and so on. The calculation is completed by the normalization condition, which simply stipulates that the system must exist somewhere: $\sum_k P_k = 1$.

The set of equations (6.26) is open to a very fruitful interpretation, illustrated in Figure 6.7. The left hand term $(\lambda_k + \mu_k)P_k$ can be interpreted as a probability flow that is leaving state k. A term such as $\lambda_k P_k$ measures the probability flow rising from k to $k + 1$. This flow is the product of the probability of reaching the state by the rising departure rate (given the present state). The same interpretation applies to the other terms. The equation says that, for the probabilities to retain constant values, the incoming probability flow must be equal to the outgoing flow, for each of the states.

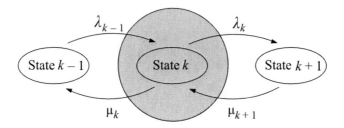

Figure 6.7. *Evolution of the states in the birth and death process*

This interpretation is used to write the equations very rapidly, from a diagram similar to that in Figure 6.7 above. A particularly effective method consists of noticing that the conservation principle applies for any group of states. In particular, the outgoing probability flow of the set of states $0, 1, 2, \ldots, k$ must be equal to the one which enters from state $k + 1$: Figure 6.8.

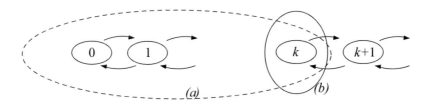

Figure 6.8. *Conservation flow around boundaries (a) or (b) makes the writing state equations possible*

The application of approach *(b)* is extremely effective: compare the two sets of (equivalent) equations:

(a)

$$\left(\lambda_k + \mu_k\right) P_k = \lambda_{k-1} P_{k-1} + \mu_{k+1} P_{k+1}, \quad k > 0,$$
$$\lambda_0 P_0 = \mu_1 P_1.$$

(b)

$$\lambda_k P_k = \mu_{k+1} P_{k+1}, \quad k \geq 0. \tag{6.27}$$

Indeed, we can easily check that the sum, member by member, of equations *(a)* yields system *(b)*.

6.4. Queueing models

6.4.1. *Introduction*

As each theory already proposed, queueing theory offers a schematic and simplified vision of the real world. Actually, the theory will be applied on *models*, abstract views of real objects, which are assumed to capture the spirit of the phenomenon under study.

Obviously, the theory is unable to account for all the diversity of reality – or rather cannot deal with its complexity. So, we have to make use of approximate results or sophisticated methods, according to the situation. In the most difficult cases, we will be led to associate it with methods such as simulation.

Essentially, queueing theory works on the basic model depicted in Figure 6.9, which recalls the theory's vocabulary.

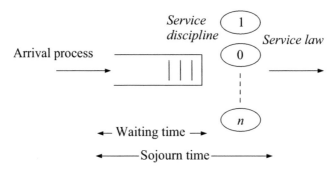

Figure 6.9. *The basic service station*

The system is composed of a queue (buffer) of finite capacity or otherwise, emptied by one or several server(s) and fed by a flow of customers. Its features are:

– the arrival law: the probability distribution the arrival process does comply with;

– the service time distribution (i.e. the probability distribution of its duration);

– the service discipline (when a server becomes idle, which client should it choose, and in what order of which priority).

We aim to determine:

– the *waiting time* distribution (time spent waiting in the queue);

– the *sojourn time* distribution (total time spent in the system, waiting or being served);

– the distribution of the number of customers in the queue or in the system.

KENDALL NOTATION. To identify a queueing system, the following formal expression has been proposed and unanimously adopted:

$$A/B/n/K/N.$$

The first letter identifies the arrival process distribution, the second the service process, with the following conventions in both cases:

- M: memoryless law (Poissonian arrivals or exponential service);
- D: deterministic law;
- Ek: "Erlang-k" law;
- Hk: "hyperexponential" law of order k;
- GI: general law, with the successive variables being independent;
- G: general law, without any assumption of independence.

The parameter n gives the number of servers, the following letters (optional) identify the size of the queue, and the size of the source population (if these values are omitted, they are supposed to be infinite).

For example, M/M/1 refers to the basic model: Poisson arrivals, exponential service, a single server, non-limited queue length. $M/D/R/R$ indicates a constant duration service, R servers and R positions on the whole (i.e. no waiting: Erlang model, see below).

The load offered to the server. We can always define the offered traffic, as in equation (6.2): $A = \lambda E[s]$. When dealing with single server systems, we usually denote this quantity as ρ.

Before dealing with the main kinds of queues, we now introduce two fundamental results, which are based upon quite general considerations of means and stationary limits: the Little formula and the PASTA property.

6.4.2. *A general result: the Little formula*

In a client-server system such as the one introduced above, average numbers and waiting times are linked by the celebrated Little formula (John D.C. Little, 1961): $E[N_x] = \lambda_x E[W_x]$. The index x indicates that any possible interpretation can be given to these values: the average waiting time and the number of waiting customers, or the sojourn time and the number of clients in the system, etc.

This happens to be quite an important result, especially due to its independence from the probability distributions of the processes involved. We can give an intuitive proof of it, based on very simple graphic reasoning.

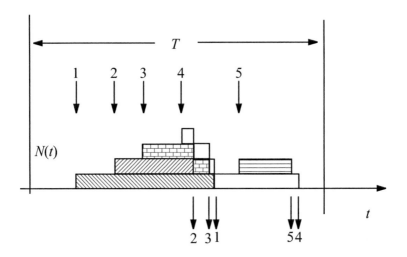

Figure 6.10. *Little formula*

Let us observe the system occupation (number of clients in the system). No assumption is made about the system, or about the state of the clients, waiting, in service or otherwise. Each time a client enters or leaves, the number of individuals present is updated, and the evolution in $N(t)$, the number of clients present, resembles the diagram in Figure 6.10. To estimate the average number of clients in the system, we measure the total surface area intercepted by $N(t)$: this is the sum of the surface areas contributed by each client: $\sum D_k$, D_k being the duration of the sojourn in the system for client k. The average number will then be:

$$E[N] = \lim_{T \to \infty} \frac{\sum D_k}{T}$$

(actually, this is simply the definition of the mean). Now the sum can be rewritten, by introducing the number n of clients concerned in time T:

$$\frac{\sum D_k}{T} = \frac{\sum D_k}{n(T)} \times \frac{n(T)}{T}.$$

Under relatively general conditions, the product limit is equal to the product of the limits. The term $n(T)/T$ is simply the arrival rate of the process, and is noted λ. The first term is nothing other than the mean time that each client spends in the system. If the system analyzed is the queue in front of a server, we obtain the classical form of the Little formula:

$$E[N] = \lambda E[W]. \tag{6.28}$$

More generally, it may also be noted that, interpreting the system as a pool of resources, we simply find the concept of traffic in Erlangs as presented at the beginning of the chapter. $E[N]$ is the mean number of clients (calls, sessions, etc.) simultaneously occupying the pool of resources, i.e. the traffic A generated by an arrival rate λ and a service time $E[s]$.

It is possible to arrive at a greater degree of client particularization (in a system with priorities, the formula links up the number and waiting time of priority clients, non-priority clients, etc.).

6.4.3. PASTA property (Poisson arrivals see time averages)

We return to the Poisson process properties. It has quite an attractive property known as the PASTA property, which is particularly useful in calculations relating to Quality of Service.

Imagine a system that evolves in such a way that it has been possible to evaluate its state probabilities. Rigorously speaking, we will speak of *stationary state probabilities*, to indicate the fact that they do not depend on time (note the passage to the limit carried out to establish state equations, and note that the existence of stationarity is a property to be verified, as a given system will not necessarily have a stationary state).

The intuitive significance of these stationary probabilities is as follows: the system is observed for a relatively long period Θ. The system runs through, in accordance with its logic, a series of states (noted $0, 1, 2, 3, \ldots$). We record the duration of passage in each state, and we take their aggregate: $\theta(n)$. The state probability is defined as

$$P_n = \lim_{T \to \infty} \frac{\theta(n)}{\Theta}$$

so that if the observation time is relatively long: $\frac{\theta(n)}{\Theta} \approx P_n$.

We often speak in the case of stationary probabilities of *time averages*, to recall the formula. Now, we can imagine another method for observing the system. We observe the clients who arrive in front of the system. Each client arriving will note an instantaneous state. We add up the number of clients observing the system in state $0, 1, 2, 3, \ldots$; let us call $q(n)$ the number of arrivals finding n clients, and N the total number of clients taking part in the experiment. It is possible to calculate the ratio $Q_k = q(k)/N$, which is also a set of probabilities (because $0 \leq Q_k \leq 1; \sum Q_k = 1$): probabilities at arrival epochs. In general, the two sets of probabilities are different. However, *if arrivals occur in accordance with a Poisson process, then $P_k = Q_k$: Poisson arrivals see time averages*. This is the PASTA property. For a single server, for instance, we have:

$$P_W = \sum_{n \geq 1} P_n.$$

The sum accounts for the stationary probability (time average) that the server is busy, as would be noticeable to an external observer. Thanks to the PASTA property, this is also the waiting probability as observed by customers arriving according to a Poisson process. We will see later counter-examples to this result, when the arrivals do not conform with the Poisson assumption, and which can be interpreted as a certain correlation between the system and the arrivals. The PASTA property signifies, or rather confirms, that the Poisson process is carrying out a "pure chance" process.

6.4.4. The elementary queue: the M/M/1 system

We consider a system made of an infinite capacity queue, served with an exponentially distributed time with parameter μ. The arrival process of the clients obeys a Poisson process with parameter λ. We introduce the parameter $\rho = \lambda/\mu$ – the offered load. It also represents the utilization rate of the server, as we show below.

6.4.4.1. Resolution of the state equations

When $n > 0$ clients are in the system (one in service, $n - 1$ waiting) at instant t, the end of service for the client in progress occurs in the interval $[t, t + \Delta t[$ with a probability $\mu \Delta t$: the basic property of the exponential service law. Similarly, an arrival will occur in the interval with a probability $\lambda \Delta t$. To this system is applied the formalism and results obtained earlier in the birth and death process. The state is described by n, which this time represents the total number of clients in the system. It evolves in accordance with a very simple birth and death process shown schematically in Figure 6.11.

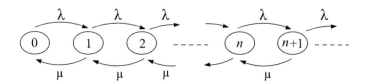

Figure 6.11. *Evolution of the state of the M/M/1 queue*

From the diagram, the following results can be deduced. This will take the form of a detailed demonstration. For the other systems presented later, the exercise will be left to the reader.

The system analysis, in accordance with the application of Chapman-Kolmogorov equations, leads to the following equations already presented in section 6.3.3, equation

(6.26):

$$\lambda P_0 = \mu P_1$$

$$\vdots \tag{6.29}$$

$$(\lambda + \mu)P_n = \lambda P_{n-1} + \mu P_{n+1}.$$

Summing up, term to term, the equations of ranks 0 to n (according to approach (b), see Figure 6.8), leads to the particularly simple expression $\lambda P_n = \mu P_{n+1}$, i.e. $P_{n+1} = \rho P_n$, with $\rho = \lambda/\mu$, and by recurrence $P_n = \rho^n P_0$. The normalization condition completes the processing, and finally:

$$P_n = \rho^n(1 - \rho) \quad n \geq 0, \; \rho = \lambda/\mu. \tag{6.30}$$

The parameter ρ is the offered traffic, as here $E[s] = 1/\mu$. For the infinite-capacity single server system, we should have $\rho < 1$; this is the *stability condition*: intuitively, the offered work should not enter the system faster than the server can process it, in order to guarantee system stability. As a consequence, ρ is here equal to the *server utilization rate*.

The distribution of the number of clients is a geometric distribution of parameter ρ, from which the mean and the variance are deduced. We leave this exercise to the reader. Starting from:

$$E[n] = \sum nP_n, \quad E[n^2] = \sum n^2 P_n, \quad \text{and} \quad \sigma^2 = E[n^2] - E[n]^2,$$

we obtain:

$$E[n] = \frac{\rho}{1 - \rho}, \quad \sigma^2(n) = \frac{\rho}{(1 - \rho)^2}. \tag{6.31}$$

With regard to waiting time, a distinction is drawn between queueing proper, or waiting in short (time spent between arrival in the queue and the start of the service) and sojourn time (time elapsed up to departure from the system). These quantities are noted W (waiting in the queue) and S (sojourn time).

In the same way, a distinction is drawn between clients in the system and clients waiting in the queue. There are 0 clients waiting if the server is inactive or if a single client is present; n are waiting if there are $n + 1$ in the system:

$$P(n \text{ waiting clients}) = \rho^{n+1}(1 - \rho), \quad n \geq 1, \; \rho = \lambda/\mu,$$

$$P(0 \text{ waiting client}) = (1 - \rho) + \rho(1 - \rho) = 1 - \rho^2. \tag{6.32}$$

By operating as in the previous case, the mean number of waiting clients is obtained:

$$E[n_W] = \frac{\rho^2}{1 - \rho}, \quad \sigma^2(n_W) = \frac{\rho^2(1 + \rho - \rho^2)}{(1 - \rho)^2}. \tag{6.33}$$

From this we can deduce the mean waiting (denoted as W) and sojourn times (denoted as S), by way of the Little formula:

$$\overline{W} \equiv E[\text{waiting}] = \frac{E[n]}{\lambda} = \frac{\rho}{1-\rho} \times \frac{1}{\mu},$$

$$\overline{S} \equiv E[\text{sojourn}] = \frac{E[n]}{\lambda} = \frac{1/\mu}{1-\rho}.$$

(6.34)

In many queue sizing problems, the issue is the probability of exceeding a certain queueing threshold, or a certain system threshold. The probability sought is therefore $P(\geq n)$.

For the whole system, this is written as follows:

$$P(\geq n) = \sum_{i=n}^{\infty} P_i = \sum_{i=n}^{\infty} \rho^n (1-\rho) = \rho^n$$

(6.35)

and for the queue only (excluding service): $P(\geq n_W) = \rho^{n_W+1}$.

6.4.4.2. *Using generating functions*

The direct resolution of state equations by substitution is immediately comprehensible, but it leads to fastidious calculations, as soon as the expressions become a little more complex. In this case it may be advisable to use generating functions – see Chapter 1 for their definition and main properties.

The generating function of a probability distribution $(P_k, \ k = 0, 1, \ldots)$ is the complex variable function $P(z) = \sum_k z^k P_k$.

It is necessary to place ourselves in the domain $|z| < 1$, so that the function $P(z)$ exists: $|P(z)| < P(1) = 1$ when $|z| < 1$; this is an analytical function of the complex variable. Its appeal comes from the properties of its derivatives, which will directly give the moments of the variable.

We now show how to apply the formalism of generating functions to these analyses. We consider the elementary case of the queue M/M/1: again writing the system of equations (6.29):

$$\lambda P_0 = \mu P_1,$$

$$\vdots$$

$$(\lambda + \mu) P_n = \lambda P_{n-1} + \mu P_{n+1}.$$

we can, from the set of equations, calculate the generating function by application of the definition: in this extremely simple example, each of the k rank equations is multiplied by z^k, and the sum is then calculated member by member:

$$\lambda P_0 + \sum_{k \geq 1} (\lambda + \mu) P_k z^k = \mu P_1 + \sum_{k \geq 1} (\lambda P_{k-1} + \mu P_{k+1}) z^k,$$

i.e.,

$$\lambda P(z) + \mu \big(P(z) - P_0 \big) = \lambda z P(z) + \frac{\mu}{z} \big(P(z) - P_0 \big).$$

A simple algebraic manipulation leads to the result:

$$P(z) = \frac{\mu P_0}{\mu - \lambda z} = \frac{P_0}{1 - \rho z}. \tag{6.36}$$

The normalization condition translates here as $P(1) = 1$, and thus $P_0 = 1 - \rho$.

From this highly synthetic expression the first and second derivatives are deduced, and thus the first two moments, and the variance of the number of clients in the queue; the reader is left to find the results already given. The Taylor series expansion of the fraction yields the state probabilities by identification.

For instance, the average number of clients in system is obtained from equation (6.36):

$$E[n] = \big| P'(z) \big|_{z=1} = \frac{\rho}{(1 - \rho)^2}.$$

In this simplistic case, the justification for the calculation may appear to be fallacious. However, we will see how, with this method, we can obtain certain fundamental results in the important case of the M/G/1 queue. The references, such as [KLE 74], should also be consulted. Finally, we should stress the fact that transforms are only being used here to resolve a previously established system of equations. We will see subsequently how to make use of the transforms, and more exactly the characteristic function, for the resolution of complex problems, which are impossible to describe using a system of state equations as before.

6.4.4.3. *Waiting time distribution*

Even if the calculation of the mean or the variance of the waiting time is an important result, it is often essential to have the distribution of the waiting time, or at least its quantiles, e.g. for the purposes of QoS characterization. In the case of the M/M/1 system, it is possible to deduce this distribution from the state probabilities.

We assume the clients are processed using the *first-in, first-out* discipline. A new client, arriving as n clients are already in the system, has to wait for n service times. As these n service times are independent and distributed in accordance with the same exponential law (even the service in progress, which according to the results of section 6.2.2.2 has the same exponential distribution), their total time is given by their convolution product (see section 6.2.2.3). In fact we have already demonstrated that this results in the Erlang-n distribution.

The probability density for n service times with rate μ is:

$$f(t) = \mu e^{-\mu t} \frac{(\mu t)^{n-1}}{(n-1)!}.$$

Denoting as W the waiting time in the queue, this gives:

$$P(W \le t | N = n) = \frac{\mu^n}{(n-1)!} \int_0^t x^{n-1} e^{-\mu x} dx. \tag{6.37}$$

According to the theorem of total probabilities (see Chapter 1):

$$P(W \le t | n > 0) = \sum_{n=1}^{\infty} P(W \le t \mid N = n) P_n,$$

hence:

$$P(W \le t \mid N = n) = \sum_{n=1}^{\infty} \frac{\mu^n}{(n-1)!} \int_0^t x^{n-1} e^{-\mu x} P_n dx \tag{6.38}$$

with, as seen previously in equation (6.30): $P_n = \rho^n (1 - \rho)$. So:

$$P(W \le t \mid n > 0) = \sum_{n=1}^{\infty} \frac{\mu^n}{(n-1)!} (1 - \rho) \rho^n \int_0^t x^{n-1} e^{-\mu x} dx,$$

i.e.

$$P(W \le t \mid n > 0) = \int_0^t \lambda e^{-\mu x} (1 - \rho) \sum_{n=1}^{\infty} \frac{(\lambda x)^{n-1}}{(n-1)!} dx.$$

Now, we have:

$$\sum_{n=1}^{\infty} \frac{(\lambda x)^{n-1}}{(n-1)!} = e^{\lambda x},$$

hence:

$$P(W \le t | n > 0) = \int_0^t \lambda e^{-(\mu - \lambda)x} (1 - \rho) dx$$

which after integration gives:

$$P(W \leq t \mid n > 0) = \frac{\lambda}{\mu}\left(1 - e^{-(\mu-\lambda)t}\right)$$

$$= \rho\left(1 - e^{-(\mu-\lambda)t}\right) \tag{6.39}$$

$$= \rho\left(1 - e^{-t/\overline{S}}\right).$$

This is the probability of waiting for less than t, for those clients who are waiting because n has been taken to be strictly greater than zero.

Thus also:

$$P(W \leq t) = P(W = 0) + P(0 < W \leq t)$$

$$= 1 - \rho + \rho\left(1 - e^{-\mu(1-\rho)t}\right)$$

$$= 1 - \rho e^{-\mu(1-\rho)t}.$$

Noting that ρ represents the waiting probability, we can also directly derive the distribution of the total time spent in the system (sojourn time S) from this result. At last, the following important expressions give the distribution of the waiting and sojourn times:

$$P(W \leq t) = 1 - \rho e^{-\mu(1-\rho)t},$$
$$P(S \leq t) = 1 - e^{-\mu(1-\rho)t}. \tag{6.40}$$

From these expressions, the means and variances are easily obtained (for mean values, the reader can verify the identity with (6.34)):

$$E[W] = \frac{\rho}{1-\rho} \times \frac{1}{\mu}, \quad \sigma^2(W) = \frac{2\rho - \rho^2}{(1-\rho)^2} \times \frac{1}{\mu^2},$$

$$E[S] = \frac{1}{1-\rho} \times \frac{1}{\mu}, \quad \sigma^2(S) = \frac{1}{(1-\rho)^2} \times \frac{1}{\mu^2}. \tag{6.41}$$

(The reader will remember that, for the exponential distribution $F(x) = 1 - e^{-\lambda x}$, we have $E[x] = 1/\lambda$, and $E[x^2] = 1/\lambda^2$.)

Now let us show how to derive these results directly by using Laplace transforms.

Let $P(S \leq t|n)$ denote the probability distribution function of the time S spent in the system by a new client finding n clients ahead of him.

In that case, the time it resides in the system is the sum of the n service times of the n preceding clients plus its own service time, as already observed.

The distribution of the total time spent is then given by the convolution product of the $n + 1$ service time probability densities, as they are independent (recall that the client in service has its remaining service time exponentially distributed, as a consequence of the memoryless property). In view of the properties already recalled, the Laplace transform of this convolution product is simply the product of their Laplace transform.

Each of the service times obeys the exponential distribution. If we denote its parameter as μ, their Laplace transform is written:

$$T^*(s) = \frac{\mu}{\mu + s}.$$

The Laplace transform of $P(S \leq t|n)$ is then simply

$$S^*(s|n) = \left(\frac{\mu}{\mu + s} \right)^{n+1},$$

and thus for the set of all possible n:

$$S^*(s) = \sum_{n=0}^{\infty} \left(\frac{\mu}{\mu + s} \right)^{n+1} (1 - \rho)\rho^n = \frac{\mu(1 - \rho)}{s + \mu(1 - \rho)}.$$

By inspection we find the original, as it is the classical form of an exponential function, and the probability density of the time spent in the system:

$$s(t) = \mu(1 - \rho)e^{-\mu(1-\rho)t}, \quad S(t) = \int_0^t s(u)\mathrm{d}u,$$

and so for the distribution function:

$$S(t) = 1 - e^{-\mu(1-\rho)t}.$$

To find the time spent waiting, it is just a matter of excluding the service time of the client himself, and thus limiting the convolution product to n and no longer to $n + 1$. We thus obtain:

$$W^*(s) = \sum_{n=0}^{\infty} \left(\frac{\mu}{\mu + s} \right)^n (1 - \rho)\rho^n = 1 - \rho + \rho \frac{\mu(1 - \rho)}{s + \mu(1 - \rho)}.$$

The original of $1 - \rho$ is necessarily the Dirac pulse function at the origin, i.e. $u_0(t)$, with the factor $1 - \rho$ simply expressing the fact that the probability of no waiting is equal to the probability that the server is free and therefore:

$$w(t) = (1 - \rho)u_0(t) + \rho\mu(1 - \rho)e^{-\mu(1-\rho)t},$$

and

$$W(t) = (1 - \rho) + \rho\left(1 - e^{-\mu(1-\rho)t}\right) = 1 - \rho e^{-\mu(1-\rho)t}.$$

We find the preceding result again, as expected.

6.4.5. *The M/M/R/R model (Erlang model)*

This is one of the most popular models, and the first to have been studied. Let us consider a group of R servers, operated in pool mode (i.e. each of the servers can serve any of the clients presenting themselves.) The clients arrive in front of the group of servers in accordance with a Poisson process, of rate λ. Upon arrival, the client is served immediately as long as at least one server is free; if all the servers are busy, the client that arrives is rejected, and is assumed to disappear definitively. We speak of a "loss" model.

Let us consider the system in the state $k < R$. This means that k clients are present, and occupy k servers (the other servers are inactive). In the coming interval Δt, each of the services in progress may end with probability $\mu\Delta t + o(\Delta t)$ (the services are exponentially distributed). The probability of one and only one end of service is the sum of probabilities that any of the services ends, after deducing the probability of two or more ends of service: event of probability $o(\Delta t)^2$, and thus negligible in the operation of passage to the limit.

The service rate is thus $k\mu$ in this state, while $k \leq R$, and zero beyond (there cannot be any state beyond the limit $k = R$). The traffic offered is noted A ($A = \lambda/\mu$) and we can define a traffic offered per server $\rho = A/R$. Here, there is no stability condition (i.e. we may have $A \lessgtr R$): intuitively when the traffic increases the number of customers in the system cannot grow indefinitely. Indeed, in this case A/R no longer stands for the occupancy rate, due to the loss process.

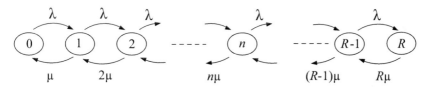

Figure 6.12. *State diagram of the Erlang model*

Based on the diagram, we find the distribution of state probabilities:

$$P_k = \frac{\frac{A^k}{k!}}{\sum_{j=0}^{R} \frac{A^j}{j!}}, \tag{6.42}$$

$$E(A, R) \equiv B(A, R) \equiv P_R = \frac{\frac{A^R}{R!}}{\sum_{j=0}^{R} \frac{A^j}{j!}}. \tag{6.43}$$

The notations $E(A, R)$ and $B(A, R)$ are relatively traditional (we also find $E_1(A, R)$ to distinguish it from the M/M/R system, see below) and they give the probability of finding the system full (all the servers active); in view of the nature of the arrivals, this is also the rejection probability. It is possible to prove that the preceding result is valid even for a service of any type (M/G/R/R system). We refer to this fundamental result as the Erlang-B formula.

When the number of servers becomes large, the denominator of the above formulae tends towards the exponential of A, and in these conditions the state probabilities are given by $P_k \approx \frac{A^k}{k!} e^{-A}$. They are governed by a Poisson law (but this is an approximate limit, valid only for low loss probabilities, k close to R and large R).

The effective calculation of the loss formula can raise a problem in the form given above: it would be pointless to evaluate a factorial by a direct method, for a relatively large R. It is best to use a recurrence method, based on the relationship (derived directly from the above formula):

$$B(A, R+1) = \frac{A \cdot B(A, R)}{R + A \cdot B(A, R)}, \tag{6.44}$$

which leads to the recurrence:

```
X:= 1
for j going from 1 to R do
X:= 1 + X*j/A
End for
B(A,R):= 1/X
```

It is also often possible to use an approximation (to replace the sum in the denominator by the exponential, and use the Stirling formula for the factorials: $R! = R^R e^{-R} \sqrt{2\pi R}$), which gives quite spectacular precision:

$$B(A, R) = \left(\frac{A}{R}\right)^R e^{R-A} / \sqrt{2\pi R}. \tag{6.45}$$

Going back to the definition of offered and handled traffics (see equation (6.4)), the calculation of carried traffic confirms the concordance between the definitions:

$$A_h = \sum j P_j = A[1 - B(A, R)]. \tag{6.46}$$

The Erlang model is usually referred to as a *loss model*. We now turn to *queueing models*.

6.4.6. *The M/M/R queue and the Erlang-C formula*

Let us consider again a system with R servers, this time with a queue of infinite size. We are in the situation of the previous case, except that in this case when a client arrives and finds the R servers occupied, it joins the queue.

What happens to service rates? As long as $k < R$, nothing changes compared with the previous example: the service rate is $k\mu$. As soon as k reaches the value R, the servers are saturated and the service rate remains equal to $R\mu$. The traffic offered is noted A and the traffic per server is $\rho = A/R$. The stability condition here is $A < R$, that is $\rho < 1$, as will be obvious from the solution.

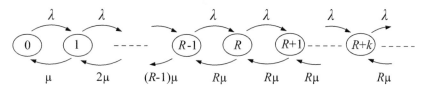

Figure 6.13. *State transition diagram of the M/M/R queue*

The exercise of writing and solving the equations is left to the reader. We finally obtain:

$$P_k = P_0 \frac{A^k}{k!} \quad k < R,$$

$$P_k = P_0 \frac{A^R}{R!} \rho^{k-R}, \quad k \geq R,$$

$$(6.47)$$

with:

$$P_0 = \left[\sum_{k<R} \frac{A^k}{k!} + \frac{A^R}{R!} \cdot \frac{1}{1-\rho} \right]^{-1}.$$

The probability of having to wait is:

$$E_2(A, R) \equiv C(A, R) \equiv P_W = \frac{A^R}{R!} \cdot \frac{P_0}{1-\rho} = \frac{\frac{A^R}{R!} \cdot \frac{R}{R-A}}{\sum_{k<R} \frac{A^k}{k!} + \frac{A^R}{R!} \cdot \frac{R}{R-A}}. \quad (6.48)$$

This is simply the stationary probability that R clients or more are in the system. This formula is called "Erlang-C".

After a few calculations, we deduce from the above results the average number of waiting clients:

$$E[N] = C(A, R) \cdot \frac{R}{R-A}. \quad (6.49)$$

The mean waiting time is obtained using the Little formula: $E[N] = \lambda E[W]$:

$$E[W] = \frac{C(A, R)}{R-A} \cdot E[T], \quad (6.50)$$

where $E[T] = 1/\mu$ is the average duration of the time spent being served.

This formula makes it possible to obtain the mean waiting time, *as seen by the clients who are actually waiting*. Calculating the distribution of the number of clients actually waiting is carried out using the conditional probabilities theorem:

$$P(\text{waiting} \le t \mid \text{the client waits}) = \frac{P(\text{waiting} \le t)}{P(\text{the client waits})} = \frac{P(\text{waiting} \le t)}{P_W}.$$

The transition to mean values directly gives:

$$E[W'] = \frac{E[T]}{R - A},$$

where W' is the mean waiting time experienced by clients actually waiting. The comparison between the two expressions is instructive: the existence of a waiting delay is not perceptible, except by clients who are actually waiting, and the mean waiting time calculated on all clients is only slightly representative of the QoS actually perceived.

Relationship with the Erlang formula. It is useful to link up the preceding formulae with those of the Erlang loss system. The Erlang formula is easily calculated by means of the recurrence given above, which can also supply $C(R, A)$. A simple manipulation gives:

$$C(A, R) = \frac{R \cdot B(A, R)}{R - A + A \cdot B(A, R)}.$$

For low probability values, the following approximate form may be given:

$$C(A, R) \simeq \frac{R}{R - A} B(A, R).$$

Waiting time distribution. When all the servers are busy, the interval until the next end of service is exponentially distributed, with a rate $R\mu$. The probability that no end of service will occur for a time t is $(e^{-\mu t})^R = e^{-R\mu t}$ (this is the probability that no service will stop, and thus the product of the probabilities for each of the servers). As soon as a server is released, and if there is at least one client waiting, the server is immediately busy.

We assume here that clients are served in the order of their arrival (the so-called first-in, first-out discipline. Upon arrival of a client, if there are $i \ge 0$ other clients already waiting, the client will wait for a time longer than t, if and only if there are fewer than i ends of service during t. This probability is given by the Poisson law in view of the preceding remark:

$$\sum_{j=0}^{i} \frac{(\mu Rt)^j}{j!} e^{-\mu Rt}$$

and conditioning to the state of the queue on the arrival of the client:

$$P(\text{waiting} > t) = 1 - F(t) = \sum_{i=0}^{\infty} P_{R+i} \sum_{j=0}^{i} \frac{(\mu R t)^j}{j!} e^{-\mu R t}$$

$$= \sum_{j=0}^{\infty} \frac{(\mu R t)^j}{j!} e^{-\mu R t} \sum_{i=j}^{\infty} P_{R+i}$$

(the latter relation is obtained by reversing the order of summations). We develop the state probabilities, expressed in terms of the waiting probability $C(R, A)$, and we obtain:

$$1 - F(t) = C(A, R) e^{-\mu R t} \left(1 - \frac{A}{R}\right) \sum_{j=0}^{\infty} \frac{(\mu R t)^j}{j!} \sum_{i=j}^{\infty} \left(\frac{A}{R}\right)^i.$$

The second sum is rewritten as $(A/R)^j / (1 - A/R)$, and thus:

$$1 - F(t) = C(A, R) e^{-\mu R t} \sum_{j=0}^{\infty} \frac{(\mu R t)^j}{j!} \left(\frac{A}{R}\right)^j = C(A, R) e^{-\mu(R-A)t}. \qquad (6.51)$$

6.4.7. The M/M/∞ queue and the Poisson law

There are situations in which arriving clients are always served immediately, without waiting, because the number of servers is always greater than the level of demand – the image used for this situation is that of an infinite number of servers. The arrival rate of the Poisson input process is λ, and the service rate is $k\mu$, for any value of k.

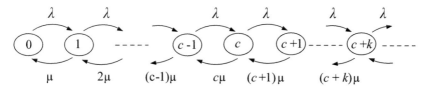

Figure 6.14. *The queue with infinitely many servers M/M/∞*

This is a simple modification of the M/M/R diagram and of the corresponding equations. The state probabilities can easily be derived:

$$P_k = P_0 \frac{A^k}{k!}, \quad k > 0, \quad \text{and thus } P_0 = \left[\sum_k \frac{A^k}{k!}\right]^{-1} = e^{-A}, \text{ i.e. } P_k = \frac{A^k}{k!} e^{-A}.$$

This system is quite special, in the sense that no client will ever wait. The term sometimes used for this system is *pure delay*.

We should note that the state probabilities are governed by a Poisson law with parameter A. It is in accordance with the result obtained for the Erlang problem, of which the Poisson law is the limit. Indeed, the M/M/∞ system is the limit of the M/M/R/R system, as R going to infinity. Moreover, we will see below another configuration, the Engset problem, of which the Erlang and Poisson distributions can be seen as special cases, which all have the Poisson law as a limit.

6.4.8. The M(n)/M/R/R queue and the Engset formula

The Poisson assumption, which enables analysis of the preceding mechanisms, amounts to postulating a constant client arrival flow. A particularly interesting counter-example of this assumption is the case where the flow stems from a population of finite size, each of the sources having a very simple behavior, and governed by memoryless laws. This is the *Engset problem*.

We assume that the behavior of each source is as follows: a source remains inactive for a random time with an exponential distribution with parameter λ. When it becomes active again, it requests a service, which will last for a time exponentially distributed with parameter μ. In the Engset problem, a limited number of servers is provided and if all are busy when a request arrives, the request is rejected and the source begins another inactivity period. The following diagram (Figure 6.15) shows the behavior of a source in schematic form.

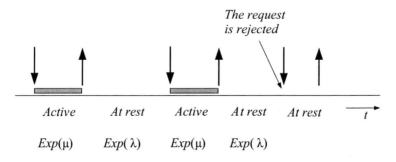

Figure 6.15. *Evolution of the source activity*

Let us consider a population of N sources with identical behavior, served by a group of R servers with no waiting capability. To make the problem significant, we assume that $R \leq N$. This configuration is noted "M(n)/M/R/R".

The key to dealing with this problem can be found in the following statement: *the arrival process depends on the instantaneous state of the system*. In fact, "active sources do not generate new requests". Assumptions on the behavior of the sources make it possible to perform the same kind of analysis again: the system is characterized by the number n of active clients. On this occasion, however, the elementary events are:

– the arrival of a new client, which causes a move from n to $n + 1$ if $n < R$. In state n, only $N - n$ sources are inactive and likely to become active again: the corresponding birth rate is $(N - n)\lambda$;

– the end of a service, with the rate $n\mu$, which moves from n to $n - 1$, as in the system with several ordinary servers.

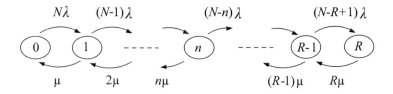

Figure 6.16. *State transition diagram for the M(n)/M/R/R system*

The set of equations giving the stationary probability of observing n busy servers is written (here form (*b*) illustrated in equation (6.27) takes on its full importance):

$$(N - n)\lambda P_n = (n + 1)\mu P_{n+1}, \quad 0 \le n < R,$$

the solution of which is:

$$P_n = \frac{\binom{N}{n}\alpha^n}{\sum_{0 \le k \le R}\binom{N}{k}\alpha^k}, \quad \alpha = \frac{\lambda}{\mu}. \tag{6.52}$$

In this equation, parameter α represents the behavior of the elementary source. However, it does not play the role of the offered traffic (the total offered traffic is not $N\alpha$). The traffic offered by a source is $a = \lambda/(\lambda + \mu) = \alpha/(1 + \alpha)$. This is also the occupancy factor of the source; it will also be noted as p ($p = a$), to emphasize the analogy with the binomial distribution; see equation (6.53). The correspondence is $a = p = \alpha/(1 + \alpha)$, and $\alpha = p/q$, with $q = 1 - p$.

P_R is the proportion of time during which all servers are busy. However, this is not the rejection probability, as here customers do not arrive independently of the system state – their arrival rate is lower as the system fills up. This system provides an example where the PASTA property does not hold.

The average number of clients arriving in a duration Θ is $\sum(N - n)\lambda P_n\Theta$. The clients rejected are those who arrive in state R, so that $(N - R)\lambda P_R\Theta$ are rejected in the long run. The rejection probability will be the quotient of these two values. Thus,

$$\Pi = \frac{(N - R)\lambda P_R}{\sum(N - n)\lambda P_n}.$$

After a moderate amount of algebraic gymnastics, we obtain:

$$\Pi = \frac{\binom{N-1}{R}\alpha^R}{\sum_{0 \le n \le R} \binom{N-1}{n}\alpha^n}, \quad \text{or} \quad \Pi = \frac{\binom{N-1}{R}p^R q^{(N-1)-R}}{\sum_{0 \le n \le R} \binom{N-1}{n}p^n q^{(N-1)-n}}. \tag{6.53}$$

This expression is known as the *Engset formula*.

In the special case where $N = R$, it follows that

$$P_n = \frac{\binom{N}{n}\alpha^n}{(1+\alpha)^N}, \quad \text{and} \quad P_R = P_N = \left[\frac{\alpha}{1+\alpha}\right]^N \ne 0.$$

This is the binomial (Bernoulli) distribution. We sometimes refer to Bernoulli traffic as the configuration, which perfectly illustrates the case where the PASTA property does not hold. Indeed here the rejection probability is obviously zero, and different from P_R: this is because the total offered traffic is not Poissonian.

As for the Erlang formula, the numerical evaluation of the loss probability is simplified using the following recurrence:

$$\Pi_j = \frac{\alpha(N-j)\Pi_{j-1}}{N + \alpha(N-j)\Pi_{j-1}}.$$

Each source executes a series of cycles: as the success probability of the activity attempt is $1 - \Pi$, their mean duration is:

$$E[c] = \frac{1}{\lambda} + \frac{1-\Pi}{\mu}.$$

The traffic handled by each source will be given by the activity rate of the source:

$$a_h = \frac{(1-\Pi)/\mu}{E[c]} = \frac{\alpha(1-\Pi)}{1 + \alpha(1-\Pi)}.$$

The total traffic handled (carried) will be N times this quantity. The same holds for the offered traffic. The traffic offered per source is $a_o = \alpha/[1 + \alpha(1 - \Pi)]$. The total offered traffic will be N times this quantity (this value is generally that given in tables).

6.4.9. *Models with limited capacity*

The M/M/1/K model corresponds to the configuration able to store at most K clients. Note that the customary use of K is to represent the total number of clients in the system, i.e. waiting or in service (we occasionally find the notation M/M/1/$K + 1$, indicating that K is on standby and 1 is in service).

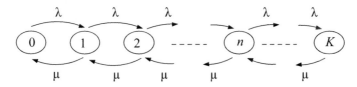

Figure 6.17. *State transition diagram for the limited-size queue*

The state diagram is obtained by truncating the M/M/1 diagram, and the equations easily give the result:

$$P_n = \frac{\rho^n (1 - \rho)}{1 - \rho^{K+1}}.$$

For a system with limited capacity, the performance criterion is of course the rejection probability. In this case, it is simply the stationary probability of observing K clients in the system, as an arriving client will then not be admitted:

$$\Pi = P_K = \frac{\rho^K (1 - \rho)}{1 - \rho^{K+1}}. \tag{6.54}$$

Of course, in this case it is possible to remove the usual stability condition $\rho < 1$, higher values of the load resulting in higher levels of rejection. It will be noted that the case $\rho = 1$ leads to a difficulty with the formula. This is only a mathematical problem, and it would be necessary to read for example:

$$\Pi = \frac{\rho^K}{1 + \rho + \rho^2 + \cdots + \rho^K},$$

which removes the difficulty.

6.5. More complex queues

6.5.1. *Multi-bitrate Erlang model*

The aim here is to evaluate the handling capacity of a system that concentrates traffic from sources with different levels of demands. This is typically the case of ISDN user concentrators, and synchronous network links, which have to handle calls with different bitrates (at $n \times 64$ kbit/s for example). It is in this context that the formula was derived, which explains the name, but above all, the analysis of this case forms the basis of statistical multiplex modeling for ADSL and IP traffic where bitrates differs per service type.

The aim is to evaluate the blocking probability B, for an offered traffic A issuing from x traffic classes, a class grouping all the demands requiring the same level of traffic. For instance, assume these are connections in a network and thus the demand is expressed in the form of bitrates.

Let c_1 be the bitrate (or capacity) required by the source demanding the lowest bitrate. We can take c_1 as bitrate unit (i.e. assume that $c_1 = 1$), and express bitrates of the other sources c_i as multiples of c_1. Let C be the total capacity to be shared among the flows.

The blocking probability is then given by the *generalized Erlang formula* applied to a system with $N = C$ servers. Let a_i be the activity level in Erlangs of bitrate class c_i. The probability $P(n_1, \ldots, n_x)$ of having $(n_1, \ldots, n_x)$ active sources in each class is then:

$$P(n_1, \ldots, n_x) = \frac{\prod_{i=1}^{x} \frac{a_i^n}{n_i!}}{\sum_{0 \le n_1 c_1 + \cdots + n_x c_x \le C} \left(\prod_{i=1}^{x} \frac{a_i^n}{n_i!} \right)}, \tag{6.55}$$

and the blocking probability of a demand with a bit rate c_i is:

$$B_i = \sum_{n_1 c_1 + \cdots + n_x c_x \ge C - c_i + 1} P(n_1, \ldots, n_x).$$

The average blocking, observed on the whole set of sources, is:

$$B = \frac{\sum_{i=1}^{x} B_i \times a_i}{\sum_{i=1}^{x} a_i}. \tag{6.56}$$

These fundamental formulae can give rise to relatively long calculations, although efficient algorithmic methods have been developed, see e.g. [ROS 95]. However, above all, they do not enable the rapid assessment of the impact made by the mix of services. It is for this reason that approximations have been developed, all of which are based on the adjustment of exact distribution moments with simpler distribution moments. We present later on the *peakedness factor method*, which is very simple to use and which is sufficiently precise for most practical purposes.

6.5.2. *The embedded Markov chain*

Up to now, the queues we have considered were such that their evolution was governed by a simple birth and death process. Here, we present a type of method which offers the possibility of dealing with arbitrary service time distributions. However, the arrival process will be such that the evolution of the system (clients and server) is what is known as a *semi-Markov process*.

The following stage, i.e. one capable of solving the case of arbitrary arrival and service distributions, will be presented later on, using the Pollaczek method.

For birth and death processes, the method consists of studying the state at an arbitrary instant, thanks to the memoryless properties of exponential distribution. This is no longer possible for general service laws. We overcome this difficulty by finding, in the system evolution, instants in which the past and future are independent. It is then possible to extract from this evolution a Markov chain (*embedded Markov chain*), which can be solved, possibly in numerical form.

End of service instants in particular enjoy this property, whereby knowing the instantaneous embedded state allows us to deduce the following one. The state of the system at these instants is characterized by the number of clients left by the departing one. We must be able to calculate the probability of having a certain number of arrivals during the next service duration, which depends only on the service duration and is independent of the system state. This imposes several conditions on the arrival process, such as the independence between arrivals occurring in the successive service durations.

We now follow Kendall's approach, and apply this method to a queue with general service distribution (i.e. the M/G/1 system), and we establish a quite interesting result concerning the number of clients in the system.

6.5.3. *The number of clients in a system*

Let us consider a queue, with service times distributed in accordance with a probability distribution, noted $B(t)$, and with an arrival process complying with the criterion given above (of the Poisson or Bernoulli kind, for example). The stationary analysis of birth and death processes is not applicable, because the probability of an end of service in the elementary interval $[t, t + \Delta t[$ will depend on the age of the service in progress (referring back to the result for the remaining service time, it will become obvious that the exponential law is the only law that demonstrates the memoryless property).

Now, let us denote as A_n the number of clients arriving during the service of the nth client, and (α) its probability distribution $(\alpha_k = P(A_n = k))$. The arrival process must be such that this probability may be calculated – e.g. Poisson or Bernoulli.

We observe the system at the successive ends of service. Let us denote as X_n the number of clients left behind after the departure of the nth customer. If X_n is greater than 0, another service starts immediately. If not, the server remains inactive, until the arrival of a client, who will be served without having to wait. In all cases, at the end of the next service, the system will have accommodated other clients, in the number of A_n. These clients are those who arrive during the time of the nth service. It is then possible to write a recurrence relation, whose resolution will give the probability distribution of X_n.

Let us assume first that $X_n > 0$. The departure of client n decreases the number of clients by one unit. Any arrivals during the next service will make the number of clients increase, and this will give:

$$X_{n+1} = X_n - 1 + A_{n+1}.$$

If on the other hand, $X_n = 0$, then the next client begins the service, and we then see that:

$$X_{n+1} = A_{n+1}.$$

These two cases are summed up by the abridged notation:

$$X_{n+1} = \left[X_n - 1\right]^+ + A_{n+1}, \tag{6.57}$$

where $[x]^+$ stands for $\max(x, 0)$ (we will see later, with the Pollaczek method, all the benefits we can draw from that kind of recurrence relation, applied to waiting times).

It is also possible to illustrate the system behavior (evolution of number of clients waiting or in service) with a diagram, similar to those preceding it, but which can no longer be termed "birth and death". Between the departure of clients n and $n + 1$, there may arrive 0, 1, 2, etc. clients, causing jumps corresponding to the recurrence relation. Note that it is possible to speak of a state: the number of clients *just after* the departure of the nth enables the accurate prediction of the probability distribution at the next departure. Indeed, the assumptions of the model allow us to calculate α_k, the probability that k clients arrive during a service.

If the departure of a client leaves the system in state $m > 0$, then a service begins immediately. If k clients now arrive during this service, the number remaining after the next departure will be $m - 1 + k$ (as the client served will leave the system): this happens with probability α_{m+1-j}. This is illustrated by the graph in Figure 6.18. In state 0, the server is inactive, and an arrival triggers a start of service. If m clients arrive during this service, the departure of the client starting up the period of activity will leave these m clients behind him, which explains the particularity of the transitions observed from state 0, compared with the transitions from the other states. The resolution of this system, i.e. the calculation of state probabilities, will follow the same general method as for birth and death processes. A system of

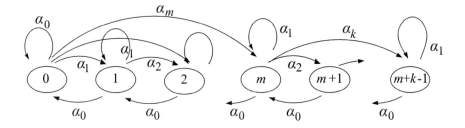

Figure 6.18. *State transition diagram of the embedded Markov chain*

Chapman-Kolmogorov equations will be written (flows entering and exiting from node k should equate):

$$P_0(1 - \alpha_0) = \alpha_0 P_1,$$
$$P_1(1 - \alpha_1) = \alpha_1 P_0 + \alpha_0 P_2,$$
$$P_2(1 - \alpha_1) = \alpha_2 P_0 + \alpha_2 P_1 + \alpha_0 P_3,$$

$$\vdots$$

$$P_m(1 - \alpha_1) = \alpha_m P_0 + \sum_{j=1}^{m-1} P_j \alpha_{m+1-j} + \alpha_0 P_{m+1}.$$

It is possible to solve this system of equations by truncating it and using the classical matrix resolution, or better by expressing it in the form of generating functions; we define:

$$P(z) = \sum P_k z^k, \quad A(z) = \sum \alpha_k z^k.$$

multiplying the equation of rank k by z^k, and summing the system, we obtain (the exercise is left to the reader):

$$P(z) = P_0 \frac{(1-z)A(z)}{A(z) - z}.$$

The normalization condition is written $P(1) = 1$, which here raises a problem as the above expression reduces to $0/0$. Making use of L'Hospital's rule removes the difficulty and yields the obvious relation $P_0 = 1 - \rho$.

Finally, we come to the important relation giving the transform of the number of clients in the system:

$$P(z) = A(z) \frac{(1-z)(1-\rho)}{A(z) - z}. \tag{6.58}$$

For Poissonnian arrivals, we have:

$$A(z) = \sum z^k \int \frac{(\lambda x)^k}{k!} e^{-\lambda x} dB(x) = \int e^{\lambda zx} e^{-\lambda x} dB(x) = B^*(\lambda - \lambda z)$$

(we have introduced $B^*(s)$, the Laplace transform of the service law). We finally arrive at this important result for the M/G/1 system:

$$P(z) = (1 - \rho) \frac{(1 - z)B^*(\lambda - \lambda z)}{B^*(\lambda - \lambda z) - z} \tag{6.59}$$

which is, as we will see later, one of the forms of the Pollaczek transform. As usual, we derive the moments of occupation probability from the transforms.

Actually, we can avoid direct calculation and indeterminate forms, using the following astute approach:

$$P(z)\big[B^*(\lambda - \lambda z) - z\big] = (1 - \rho)(1 - z)B^*(\lambda - \lambda z)$$

and to calculate the 2nd derivative (we omit the "*" and write B for $B(\lambda - \lambda z)$ to lighten notations; note that $B' = -\lambda B(\lambda - \lambda z)$):

$$P'(z)[B - z] - P(z)[\lambda B' - 1] = (1 - \rho)(1 - z)\lambda B' - (1 - \rho)B$$

$$P''(z)[B - z] - 2P'(z)[\lambda B' - 1] + \lambda^2 P(z)B'' = 2(1 - \rho)\lambda B' + \lambda^2(1 - z)(1 - \rho)B''$$

We make $z = 1$ in the last equation: $P(1) = 1$; $B(\lambda - \lambda z)|_{z=1} = 1$; $B'(\lambda - \lambda z)|_{z=1} = -E[s]$; and $B''(\lambda - \lambda z)|_{z=1} = E[s^2]$. Finally,

$$P'(1) = E[N] = \rho + \frac{\lambda E[s^2]}{2(1 - \rho)}.$$

Laplace transforms constitute an essential tool in the queueing analysis of complex systems. Here, we have illustrated the value of transforms for deriving the moments – e.g., allowing us to approximate the distribution by fitting a Gamma distribution. The characteristic function provides another expression for this, as developed in section 1.6. We will present other examples in section 6.6.3, this time relating to the powerful Pollaczek method.

6.5.4. Waiting times: Pollaczek formulae

6.5.4.1. Introduction: calculation of residual service time

Let us consider the server of the M/G/1 system at some arbitrary epoch. What is the time remaining until the end of the service in progress (zero if the server is inactive)? Note the difference with the calculation in section 6.2.2.2, where it was a matter of calculating the remaining time bearing in mind that y seconds have already elapsed.

Here the observation of the server occurs independently of the server state. We are therefore searching for the time average of the remaining service time – without knowing when it began.

We observe the system for a time θ. Note by $X(t)$ the remaining service time at some instant t. At each end of service, and if a client is present, a new service begins, triggering an instantaneous increase in $X(t)$, of a value equal to the requested service time (we will note by T_k the service time of client k). Finally, the evolution of the residual time evolves in accordance with the plot in Figure 6.19 below.

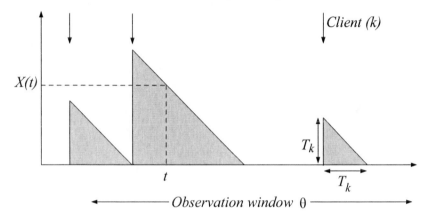

Figure 6.19. *Residual service time in the M/G/1 queue*

The pattern consists of initial jumps (at the start of each service, the remaining time is increased by the new service time), followed by segments with slope -1. The time average can be calculated:

$$\overline{X} = \frac{1}{\theta} \sum_1^{N(\theta)} \frac{T_k^2}{2},$$

where $N(\theta)$ represents the number of clients served in the interval, and T_k the sequence of service times. All the clients are statistically identical, and the passage to the limit gives:

$$\begin{aligned}
\overline{X} &= \lim_{\theta \to \infty} \frac{1}{\theta} \sum \frac{T_k^2}{2} \\
&= \frac{1}{2} \lim_{\theta \to \infty} \frac{N(\theta) E[T_1^2]}{\theta} \\
&= \frac{1}{2} \lambda E[T^2].
\end{aligned} \qquad (6.60)$$

This quantity is conventionally noted as W_0. It is worth pointing out that the calculation does not depend on the service discipline (i.e. on the choice that the server makes about the next client to be processed).

6.5.4.2. The Pollaczek-Khintchine formula

We remain in the context of the M/G/1 queue. A client who arrives in accordance with the Poisson process, and thus independently of the state of the queue, observes the queue's stationary state. He either finds a client in service or with its server inactive. He observes x, the corresponding residual service time. He also observes n other clients in the queue, who will be served before him (assuming here a first-come, first-served discipline). His wait will therefore be:

$$w = x + \sum_{1}^{n} T_i$$

(as above T_i stands for the service time of client i). We take the mean value of the expression. That of x has been calculated above, in equation (6.60). The mean of the sum will be $E[N]$ times the mean service time. However, $E[N]$, the mean number of clients waiting, is linked to $E[W]$, by the Little formula. Hence:

$$E[W] = W_0 + E\left[\sum_{1}^{n} T_i\right]$$
$$= W_0 + E[N]E[T]$$
$$= W_0 + \lambda E[W]E[T],$$

and finally the formula sought:

$$E[W] = \frac{W_0}{1-\rho} = \frac{\rho}{1-\rho} \times \frac{1+c^2}{2} \times E[T], \tag{6.61}$$

into which we have introduced the coefficient of variation of the service time: $c^2 = (\sigma(T)/E[T])^2$, which quantifies the "variability" of service times.

This is the Pollaczek-Khintchine formula, often designated as the PK-formula. We demonstrate this result again in what follows, this time, as a special result of the original Pollaczek method.

Its interpretation is extremely valuable. The first term quantifies the waiting phenomenon, which depends on the system utilization factor. The second illustrates the influence of the service variability, and the third is a "scale factor", the scale of the phenomenon being given by the mean service time.

6.5.4.3. *Example 1: the M/M/1 queue*

For the exponentially distributed service time, it has already been established that $E[T] = 1/\mu$, $E(T^2) = 2/\mu^2$, i.e. $c^2 = 1$. Hence:

$$E[W]_{M/M/1} = \frac{\rho E[T]}{1 - \rho}.$$

6.5.4.4. *Example 2: the M/D/1 queue*

Clearly, the variance of the service time is zero. Thus, $c^2 = 0$, and:

$$E[W]_{M/D/1} = \frac{\rho E[T]}{2(1 - \rho)} = \frac{1}{2} E[W]_{M/M/1}.$$

6.5.4.5. *Generalization: Takacs' formula*

The following result, attributed to Takacs, enables us to obtain successive moments of the waiting times for the M/G/1 queue. They involve the successive moments of the service time.

$$E[W^0] = 1$$

$$E[W^k] = \frac{\lambda}{1 - \rho} \sum_{i=1}^{k} \binom{k}{i} \frac{E[T^{i+1}]}{i + 1} E[W^{k-i}]. \tag{6.62}$$

We will leave it for the reader to verify by examples that, taking $k = 1$ in the preceding form, we again find the PK-formula. The following relations can be deduced for *sojourn times*:

$$E[S^k] = \sum_{i=0}^{k} \binom{k}{i} E[T^i] E[W^{k-i}]. \tag{6.63}$$

For example, for $k = 1$: $E[S] = E[T] + E[W]$.

6.5.5. **The Beneš method: application to the M/D/1 system**

The Beneš method focuses on unfinished work or virtual waiting time. It will be illustrated here by deriving the waiting time distribution in the M/D/1 queue.

The origin is any arbitrary instant and we denote as $A(t)$ the quantity of work arriving in the interval $[-t, 0[$. (We assume the server processes one unit of work per unit of time.) Let us call V_{-t} the working time, or virtual waiting time, remaining at the instant $-t$ (time to serve the waiting clients, plus the remaining time for any client in progress). We introduce $\xi(t) = A(t) - t$, the work in excess arriving in the interval. It can be seen that the unfinished work is given by:

$$V_{-t} = \sup_{u \geq t} \left(\xi(u) - \xi(t) \right).$$

In particular, $V_0 = \sup_{u \geq 0} \xi(u)$ (this is the strongest work surplus to have occurred in the past, the one whose effect remains at 0). The method is traditionally focused on the complementary distribution $Q(x)$:

$$Q(x) = P\left[V_0 > x\right].$$

The event $\{V_0 > x\}$ can also be written: "there exists a value of t, such that $\xi(t) > x$". We can thus condition on the last instant T_x (the largest interval) where we observed $\xi(t) = x$: this is $T_x = \sup\{t \geq 0; \xi(t) = x\}$. For more remote instants, we must have $\xi(t) < x$, such that $V_{-T_x} = 0$ (it is at this point that the difference is greatest). We can then write (this is the key point of the method):

$$Q(x) = \int_{u \geq 0} P\{V_{-u} = 0 \text{ and } \xi(u) \in (x, x + \mathrm{d}x)\}. \tag{6.64}$$

Application to the M/D/1 system. Let us call $n(t)$ the number of clients arriving in $[-t, 0[$. The service time is taken as the time unit, so that $\xi(t) = n(t) - t$. The integral is then rewritten as a sum:

$$Q(x) = \sum_{j > x} P\{n(j - x) = j \text{ and } V_{-(j-x)} = 0\}.$$

The arrival process is independent of the state of the queue: the probability is written as the product of the two terms. As the arrivals are Poissonian, this gives:

$$Q(x) = \sum_{j > x} \frac{[\rho(j - x)]^j}{j!} e^{-\rho(j-x)}(1 - \rho)$$

(λ and ρ are identical, as the service time is equal to 1). After manipulations involving combinatorics, the result is rewritten in the form of a finite (but alternate) sum:

$$Q(x) = 1 - (1 - \rho) \sum_{j > \lfloor x \rfloor} \frac{[\rho(j - x)]^j}{j!} e^{-\rho(j-x)}. \tag{6.65}$$

6.6. The G/G/1 queue

Many methods can be used to establish results relating to GI/G/1 queues. We will here make use of the *Pollaczek method*. Pollaczek was probably the very first to establish fundamental results relating to this type of queue, and above all introduced a technique capable of solving the most complex problems.

6.6.1. *Pollaczek method*

The value of this method, in addition to its elegance, is that it can be used for complex queueing problems, involving random variables governed by extremely general distributions. We present the main elements of this method below. For a full presentation, see [LEG 62, COH 82, SYS 86], and obviously the original papers by Pollaczek [POL 57, POL 61].

The principle is as follows:

– on the one hand, very often it is possible to establish simple relationships between independent random variables such as the waiting time of two consecutive clients, their service time and their inter-arrival time, whatever the arrival and service time distributions may be;

– on the other hand, in association with these relations we identify incompatible events, for example: depending on the arrival instants of two consecutive clients, either waiting takes place or it does not. These events, when introduced into the previous relations, define for the variable studied (waiting, holding time, etc.) one or more fundamental relations that may be called *stochastic relations associated with the stochastic variable studied*.

By associating this expression of the variable with its *indicator* (as defined previously in Chapter 1) we completely define its probability distribution. It is then sufficient to write characteristic functions and from this deduce the moments by derivation, and any other property such as the distribution function, by use of the inverse transform and residue calculation.

Clearly, a method of this type leads very rapidly to pure mathematical developments. In fact, from the second stage onwards it may almost be said that we have already left the pure domain of probability. This explains its attraction for those who love mathematics. The downside is that the approach quickly seems to become abstract, and very often the developments are relatively complex. This tends to put off the physicist. However, it will always be a good idea to refer to physical phenomenon to gain better control of the calculations, and particularly problems at the limits. In fact simply practicing the method more frequently opens up new perspectives, bearing in mind that the resolution of complex problems raised by the new world of telecommunications would prove difficult without such tools. It is in this spirit that we present, below, the method and its application to a system with a single server.

We will first introduce the method and show how the celebrated Pollaczek transform can be very simply obtained. Then we will give example applications.

Characteristic function of a random variable corresponding to two incompatible events. In the first stage, let us demonstrate a fundamental expression of the characteristic function of a random variable corresponding to two incompatible events.

Let Y be a random variable such that:

$$Y = X \quad \text{if } X > 0; \qquad Y = 0 \quad \text{if } X \leq 0.$$

This can also be noted as $Y = X^+ = \max(0, X)$, X being itself a random variable.

There are only two possible and incompatible events: E1 is the event $\{X > 0\}$ and E2 is the event $\{X \leq 0\}$. The corresponding indicators are respectively $H(X)$ and $H(-X)$ (the Heaviside functions). It should be recalled (see Chapter 1) that the event indicator $\{x - X > 0\}$ is $H(x - X)$

As events E1 and E2 are mutually incompatible and represent all the possible cases, we can write

$$e^{zY} = e^{zX} H(X) + H(-X).$$

By moving on to expectations, we have:

$$E\left[e^{zY}\right] = E\left[e^{zX} H(X)\right] + E\left[H(-X)\right]. \tag{6.66}$$

Recall this is the characteristic function of variable Y. Given the definition of the Heaviside function (as seen in Chapter 1) and taking for the integration two parallels to the imaginary axis C_ζ and C_u, such that $Re(\zeta) > 0$ and $Re(u) > 0$, we have:

$$H(-X) = \frac{1}{2\pi i} \int_{C\zeta} e^{-\zeta X} \frac{d\zeta}{\zeta}, \quad \text{where } Re(\zeta) > 0,$$

$$e^{zX} H(X) = \frac{1}{2\pi i} \int_{Cu} e^{(z+u)X} \frac{du}{u}, \quad \text{where } Re(u) > 0$$

and if we note $z + u = -\zeta$, therefore $z = -(u + \zeta)$ and $Re(z + \zeta) = -R(u) < 0$, thus $Re(\zeta) < Re(z)$. Let us take $0 < Re(\zeta) < Re(-z)$, then $Re(z) < 0$. We then obtain:

$$H(-X) = \frac{1}{2\pi i} \int_{C\zeta} e^{-\zeta X} \frac{d\zeta}{\zeta},$$

$$e^{zX} H(X) = \frac{-1}{2\pi i} \int_{C\zeta} e^{-\zeta X} \frac{d\zeta}{\zeta + z}, \quad \text{where } 0 < Re(\zeta) < Re(-z).$$

This finally gives us:

$$E\left[e^{zY}\right] = \frac{1}{2\pi i} \int_{C\zeta} E\left[e^{-\zeta X}\right] \left[\frac{1}{\zeta} - \frac{1}{\zeta + z}\right] d\zeta,$$

that is:

$$E\left[e^{zY}\right] = \phi(z) = \frac{1}{2\pi i} \int_{C\zeta} E\left[e^{-\zeta X}\right] \left[\frac{z}{\zeta(\zeta + z)}\right] d\zeta,$$

(6.67)

where $0 < Re(\zeta) < Re(-z)$.

This is the fundamental relation for the characteristic function of the variable $Y = X^+$ corresponding to two incompatible events of X.

6.6.2. Application to the stochastic relation of the queue to one server (GI/G/1 queue)

This result can be applied to the study of waiting in the simple case of an isolated queueing system (i.e. that can be considered in isolation, independently of any correlation with its environment).

The principle is to find an expression, relating to waiting, which translates two incompatible events of indicators with values 0 and 1.

The single server, with any service law, serves the clients, with any arrival law, in their order of arrival. The first client is noted as $n = 0$, the second $n = 1$, etc. Services and arrival instants are assumed to be independent.

Let the terms be as follows:
– X_n the random arrival instant of the nth client,
– T_n the random duration of its service.

Let: $Y_n = X_{n+1} - X_n$. The process Y_n is assumed to be regenerative (the Y_ns are therefore mutually independent).

The waiting time of the nth client W_n is the time interval separating its arrival instant from its start of service. As such, the nth client begins to be served at the random instant $X_n + W_n$ and has finished being served at $X_n + W_n + T_n$.

There are two possible events:
– either client $n + 1$ arrives before the departure of the nth, in which case:

$$\left(X_n + W_n + T_n\right) - X_{n+1} > 0,$$

and its random wait is:

$$W_{n+1} = \left(X_n + W_n + T_n\right) - X_{n+1} = W_n + T_n - Y_n;$$

– or it arrives after the departure of the nth, in which case:

$$\left(X_n + W_n + T_n\right) - X_{n+1} < 0,$$

and its wait is zero: $W_{n+1} = 0$.

This brings us finally to the following relation:

$$W_{n+1} = \max\left(W_n + T_n - Y_n, 0\right) = \left[W_n + T_n - Y_n\right]^+, \qquad (6.68)$$

which is the key stochastic relation of the GI/G/1.

By direct application to the relation giving the characteristic function of the wait established previously (equation (6.67)), we have:

$$E\left[e^{zW_{n+1}}\right] = \frac{-1}{2\pi i} \int_{C\zeta} E\left[e^{-\zeta(W_n+T_n-Y_n)}\right] \frac{z}{\zeta(\zeta + z)} \, d\zeta,$$

with $0 < Re(\zeta) < Re(-z)$.

Let us study this integral.

As the variables W_n, T_n, Y_n are assumed to be independent, and as W_0 is fixed at a constant arbitrary value, we have:

$$E\left[e^{-\zeta(W_n+T_n-Y_n)}\right] = E\left[e^{\zeta W_n}\right]E\left[e^{-\zeta T_n}\right]E\left[e^{+\zeta Y_n}\right] = E\left[e^{-\zeta W_n}\right]E\left[e^{-\zeta(T_n-Y_n)}\right].$$

Returning to the characteristic functions, we introduce the notations:

$$E\left[e^{zW_{n+1}}\right] = \phi_{n+1}(z), \quad Re(z) < 0,$$

$$E\left[e^{\zeta W_n}\right] = \phi_n(-\zeta), \quad Re(\zeta) > 0,$$

$$E\left[e^{-\zeta(T_n-Y_n)}\right] = \varphi(-\zeta) = E\left[e^{-\zeta T_n}\right]E\left[e^{+\zeta Y_n}\right] = \varphi_1(-\zeta)\varphi_2(\zeta),$$

where $\varphi_1(\zeta) = E[e^{\zeta T_n}]$ and $\varphi_2(\zeta) = E[e^{\zeta Y_n}]$. Thus, the integral studied is written:

$$\phi_{n+1}(z) = \frac{1}{2\pi i} \int_{C\zeta} \phi_n(-\zeta)\varphi(-\zeta)\frac{z}{(\zeta)(\zeta + z)} d\zeta, \qquad (6.69)$$

with $0 < Re(\zeta) < Re(-z)$.

This relation characterizes the GI/G/1 queue. Although very simple to establish, it is very important, and we will make use of it to demonstrate, in a very simple way, the celebrated Pollaczek transform, more particularly concerning the waiting time in an M/G/1 queue, following for this purpose the use of the Pollaczek method according to the approach set out in [LEG 62].

Pollaczek has demonstrated another more elaborate expression of the previous result, which however necessitates more complex developments to be established. We provide the main lines in section 6.9. The result, still for the GI/G/1 queue, is as follows[1]:

$$\phi(z) = \exp\left\{ -\frac{1}{2\pi i} \int_{-i\infty}^{i\infty} \ln\left[1 - \varphi(-\zeta)\right] \frac{z\,d\zeta}{(\zeta)(\zeta + z)} \right\}, \qquad (6.70)$$

where $\varphi(-\zeta) = \varphi_1(-\zeta)\varphi_2(\zeta)$, $Re(z) \leq 0$. Bearing in mind that in order to exist this stationary limit process requires compliance with the condition $|\varphi(-\zeta)| \leq \varphi[-Re(z)] < 1$.

In the following we will also use this formula to establish the result of the G/M/1 queue.

6.6.3. Resolution of the integral equation

6.6.3.1. Application to the M/G/1 queue

Let us reconsider the general expression (6.69):

$$\phi_{n+1}(z) = \frac{1}{2\pi i} \int_{C\zeta} \phi_n(-\zeta)\varphi(-\zeta)\frac{z}{\zeta(\zeta + z)}\,d\zeta,$$

where $\varphi(-\zeta) = E[e^{-\zeta T_n}]E[e^{\zeta Y_n}] = \varphi_1(-\zeta)\varphi_2(\zeta)$.

As the arrivals are Poissonian $F_2 = 1 - e^{-\lambda t}$ and $\varphi_2(\zeta) = \frac{\lambda}{\lambda - \zeta}$, where λ is the arrival rate.

The characteristic function becomes:

$$\phi_{n+1}(z) = \frac{1}{2\pi i} \int_{C\zeta} \phi_n(-\zeta)\varphi_1(-\zeta)\frac{\lambda}{\lambda - \zeta}\frac{z}{\zeta(\zeta + z)}\,d\zeta.$$

In the zone $Re(\zeta) > 0$, the function:

$$f(\zeta) = \phi_n(-\zeta)\varphi_1(-\zeta)\frac{\lambda}{\lambda - \zeta}\frac{z}{\zeta(\zeta + z)}$$

has two poles $\zeta = \lambda$ and $\zeta = -z$, which after applying the residue theorem gives:

$$\frac{1}{2\pi i} \int_{-i\infty - 0}^{+i\infty - 0} f(\zeta)d\zeta = -(R_1 + R_2)$$

(with a minus sign as we do not integrate in the positive direction, we close the contour on the right!).

At the pole $\zeta = -z$, we have:

$$R_1 = \left[(\zeta + z)f(\zeta)\right]_{\zeta=-z} = -\frac{\lambda\varphi_1(z)}{\lambda + z}\phi_n(z).$$

Similarly at the pole $\zeta = \lambda$ we have:

$$R_2 = \left[(\zeta - \lambda)f(\zeta)\right]_{\zeta=\lambda} = -\frac{z\varphi_1(-\lambda)}{\lambda + z}\phi_n(-\lambda),$$

and therefore:

$$\phi_{n+1}(z) = \frac{\lambda\varphi_1(z)}{\lambda + z}\phi_n(z) + \frac{z\varphi_1(-\lambda)}{\lambda + z}\phi_n(-\lambda).$$

In a stationary condition, the relation becomes independent of n and therefore:

$$\phi(z) = \frac{z\varphi_1(-\lambda)\phi(-\lambda)}{\lambda + z - \lambda\varphi_1(z)}.$$

Recalling that the series expansion of $\varphi_1(z)$ gives:

$$\varphi_1(z) = 1 + m_1 z + m_2\frac{z^2}{2!} + \cdots, \quad \text{where } m_1 = \varphi_1(0), \text{ and } \rho = \lambda m_1,$$

the condition $\phi(0) = 1$ finally gives, now noting $\phi(z) = \phi_w(z)$:

$$\phi_w(z) = \frac{(1 - \rho)z}{\lambda + z - \lambda\varphi_1(z)}. \tag{6.71}$$

This is the fundamental relation giving the characteristic function of the waiting time for the M/G/1 server. This is the Pollaczek transform, of which we will see example applications in the following sections.

The simplicity of the demonstration is remarkable. Returning to series expansion, it is now easy to derive the moments. Let us recall that:

$$\varphi_1(z) = 1 + z\varphi_1'(0) + \frac{z^2}{2!}\varphi_1''(z), \quad \text{that is:} \quad \varphi_1'(z) = \varphi_1'(0) + z\varphi_1''(0) + \cdots$$

In particular, the average waiting time is obtained:

$$W = \phi'(0) = \frac{\lambda}{2(1 - \rho)}\varphi''(0), \quad \text{which is written:}$$

$W = \frac{\rho(1+c_s^2)}{2(1-\rho)}\,\overline{T}$, where $\overline{T}$ is the mean service times and c_s^2 its coefficient of variation.

Again, by taking $\overline{T}$ as the time unit:

$$W = \frac{\rho(1 + \sigma^2)}{2(1 - \rho)}.\tag{6.72}$$

This is the celebrated Pollaczek-Khintchine formula, established for the first time by Pollaczek in 1930 and since then demonstrated many times by various methods (as we saw earlier, see section 6.5.4.2). We now need to calculate the sojourn time in the system. By definition, we have, by calling S_n the sojourn time of the nth client:

$$S_n = W_n + T_n,$$

and at equilibrium,

$$S = W + T,$$

Let us note: $E[e^{zS}] = \phi_S(z)$.

As the variables W and T are independent, we can write:

$$\phi_S(z) = \phi_W(z)\phi_1(z).$$

Hence:

$$\phi_S(z) = \varphi_1(z)\frac{(1 - \lambda)z}{\lambda + z - \lambda\varphi(z)}.\tag{6.73}$$

This is the characteristic function of the total time spent in the M/G/1 system.

By way of example, let us apply these results to a set of typical cases which allow us to determine practical bounds (upper and lower) for most of real cases.

M/M/1 queue. Let us first apply the previous results to the M/M/1 case. As the service law is exponential, we have $\varphi_1(z) = \mu/(\mu - z)$, and we immediately obtain:

$$\phi_W(z) = \frac{(\mu - z)(1 - \rho)}{\mu(1 - \rho) - z}.$$

The function has a single pole $z_1 = \mu(1 - \rho)$.

Let us now apply our solution of the inversion formula:

$$F(x) = 1 - \frac{R_1}{-z_1}e^{-z_1 x}, \quad \text{and} \quad P(> x) = \frac{R_1}{-z_1}e^{-z_1 x}.$$

The residue R_1 in z_1 is: $R_1 = -\mu\rho(1 - \rho)$. Hence:

$$P(> x) = \rho e^{-\mu(1 - \rho)x}.$$

Of course we obtain the result already established.

M/D/1 queue. Let us now apply this to the M/D/1 queue. We have already encountered the M/D/1 queue; as it gives rise to hardly manageable expressions, we will rather establish here an asymptotic expression of the waiting distribution. This is a very simple expression, which gives very precise results.

We start again from the Pollaczek transform. To simplify the expressions we take the service time as the unit. The Pollaczek transform is thus written:

$$\phi_W(z) = \frac{(1-\rho)z}{\rho + z - \rho\varphi_1(z)},$$

We now apply our asymptotic law as presented in Chapter 1:

$$P(> x) = \frac{R_1}{-z_1} e^{-z_1 x},$$

where $z_1 = \beta_0 > 0$ is a singular point for $\phi_W(z)$, and such that:

$$\rho + \beta_0 - \rho\varphi_1(\beta_0) = 0$$

(this is the point closest to the origin, and on the real axis, see Lévy's theorem), and R_1 residue at z_1.

Remember that (see section 1.6.1.5) we also have: $R_1 = P(z_1)/Q'(z_1)$. Hence:

$$P(> x) \simeq \frac{1-\rho}{\rho\varphi_1'(\beta_0) - 1} e^{-\beta_0 x}.$$

In the case of the M/D/1 system, we have $\varphi_1(z) = e^z$, and

$$\phi_W(z) = \frac{(1-\rho)z}{\rho + z - \rho e^z}.$$

We have β_0 such that $\rho + \beta_0 - \rho\varphi_1(\beta_0) = 0$, and $\rho\varphi_1'(\beta_0) - 1 = \rho e^{\beta_0} - 1$. Thus, we have:

$$P(> x) \simeq \frac{1-\rho}{\rho e^{\beta_0} - 1} e^{-\beta_0 x}. \tag{6.74}$$

This formula gives results that are sufficiently precise for most applications.

M/H2/1 queue. Now let us apply our results to the M/H2/1 system. This is to some extent the "opposite" of the M/D/1 case, from the viewpoint of the coefficient of variation, greater than 1, the M/M/1 case being "intermediate". We start again from the Pollaczek formula:

$$\phi_W(z) = \frac{(1-\rho)z}{\lambda + z - \lambda\varphi_1(z)},$$

$$P(> x) \simeq \frac{1-\rho}{\lambda\varphi_1'(\beta_0) - 1} e^{-\beta_0 x},$$

where $z_1 = \beta_0 > 0$, singular point for $\phi_W(z)$, and such that:

$$\lambda + \beta_0 - \lambda \varphi_1(\beta_0) = 0.$$

The service has a hyperexponential distribution H2, which gives

$$\varphi_1(z) = \frac{\alpha_1 \mu_1}{\mu_1 - z} + \frac{\alpha_2 \mu_2}{\mu_2 - z} \tag{6.75}$$

with μ, the service rate given by $\frac{1}{\mu} = \frac{\alpha_1}{\mu_1} + \frac{\alpha_2}{\mu_2}$. Hence:

$$\lambda + \beta_0 - \lambda \left(\frac{\alpha_1 \mu_1}{\mu_1 - \beta_0} + \frac{\alpha_2 \mu_2}{\mu_2 - \beta_0} \right) = 0$$

which gives, after a few developments, and introducing the load $\rho = \lambda/\mu = \frac{\alpha_1 \mu_1 + \alpha_2 \mu_2}{\mu_1 \mu_2}$:

$$\mu_1 \mu_2 (1 - \rho) + \beta_0 (\lambda - \mu_1 - \mu_2) + \beta_0^2 = 0,$$

the solution of which is:

$$\beta_0 = \frac{-(\lambda - \mu_1 - \mu_2) - \sqrt{(\lambda - \mu_1 - \mu_2)^2 - 4\mu_1 \mu_2 (1 - \rho)}}{2}. \tag{6.76}$$

We also have

$$\varphi_1'(\beta_0) = \frac{\alpha_1 \mu_1}{(\mu_1 - \beta_0)^2} + \frac{\alpha_2 \mu_2}{(\mu_2 - \beta_0)^2},$$

hence the distribution function of the waiting time:

$$P(> x) = \frac{1 - \rho}{\lambda \left(\frac{\alpha_1 \mu_1}{(\mu_1 - \beta_0)^2} + \frac{\alpha_2 \mu_2}{(\mu_2 - \beta_0)^2} \right) - 1} e^{-\beta_0 x}. \tag{6.77}$$

The reader may verify that, taking $\mu_1 = \mu_2 = \mu$, we find $\beta_0 = 1 - \rho$ as needed, and:

$$P(> x) = \rho e^{-\mu(1 - \rho)x}$$

which is the expression to be expected for the exponential service.

6.6.3.2. *Application to the G/M/1 queue*

Let us now study the symmetric case of the M/G/1 queue, beginning again with the Pollaczek method. This time let us start from the general expression (6.70) of Pollaczek. This gives:

$$\phi(z) = \exp \left\{ -\frac{1}{2\pi i} \int_{-i\infty-0}^{i\infty-0} \ln \left[1 - \varphi(-\zeta) \right] \frac{z \, d\zeta}{(\zeta)(\zeta + z)} \right\},$$

with $\varphi(-\zeta) = E(e^{-\zeta T_n})E(e^{\zeta Y_n}) = \varphi_1(-\zeta)\varphi_2(\zeta)$, or again:

$$\phi(z) = \exp\left\{ -\frac{1}{2\pi i}\int_{-i\infty-0}^{i\infty-0} \ln\left[1 - \varphi_1(-\zeta)\varphi_2(\zeta)\right]\frac{zd\zeta}{(\zeta)(\zeta+z)} \right\}.$$

As the service is governed by an exponential law with a rate μ, this gives:

$$F_1(t) = 1 - e^{-\mu t}, \quad \text{and} \quad \varphi_1(\zeta) = \frac{\mu}{\mu-\zeta},$$

and so:

$$\phi(z) = \exp\left\{ -\frac{1}{2\pi i}\int_{-i\infty-0}^{i\infty-0} \ln\left[1 - \frac{\mu\varphi_2(\zeta)}{\mu+\zeta}\right]\frac{zd\zeta}{(\zeta)(\zeta+z)} \right\}.$$

It will be noted that:

$$\frac{zd\zeta}{(\zeta)(\zeta+z)} = \left(\frac{1}{\zeta} - \frac{1}{z+\zeta}\right)d\zeta = d\ln\frac{\zeta}{z+\zeta}.$$

This gives:

$$\phi(z) = \exp\left\{ -\frac{1}{2\pi i}\int_{-i\infty-0}^{i\infty-0} \ln\left[1 - \frac{\mu\varphi_2(\zeta)}{\mu+\zeta}\right]d\ln\frac{\zeta}{z+\zeta} \right\}.$$

The integration is carried out by parts (the form is $u \cdot dv$), and we thus obtain:

$$\phi(z) = \exp\left\{ \frac{1}{2\pi i}\int_{-i\infty-0}^{i\infty-0} \ln\frac{\zeta}{z+\zeta}\frac{d}{d\zeta}\ln\left[1 - \frac{\mu\varphi_2(\zeta)}{\mu+\zeta}\right]d\zeta \right\},$$

or yet,

$$\phi(z) = \exp\left\{ \frac{1}{2\pi i}\int_{-i\infty-0}^{i\infty-0} \ln\frac{\zeta}{z+\zeta}\frac{d}{d\zeta}\ln\left[\frac{\mu+\zeta-\mu\varphi_2(\zeta)}{\mu+\zeta}\right]d\zeta \right\}.$$

Let us consider the last expression in the integral: $\mu + \zeta - \mu\varphi_2(\zeta)$, and let us apply Rouché's theorem to it (sum of two functions, see the Appendix). Inside the circle with the center $-\mu$ and of radius μ, such that $Re(\zeta) < 0$, we have $|\zeta + \mu| < \mu$.

According to Rouché's theorem applied to the expression on the circle considered, it has only a single root ζ_1 in the circle and thus also in the whole plane $Re(\zeta) < 0$. We may therefore write:

$$\phi(z) = \exp\left\{ \frac{1}{2\pi i}\int_{-i\infty-0}^{i\infty-0} \ln\frac{\zeta}{z+\zeta}\frac{d}{d\zeta}\ln\left[\frac{\zeta-\zeta_1}{\mu+\zeta}\right]d\zeta \right\}.$$

or,

$$\phi(z) = \exp\left\{ \frac{1}{2\pi i}\int_{-i\infty-0}^{i\infty-0} \ln\frac{\zeta}{z+\zeta}\frac{d}{d\zeta}\ln\left[\frac{1}{\zeta-\zeta_1} - \frac{1}{\zeta+\mu}\right]d\zeta \right\}.$$

Let us apply the residue theorem to both poles:

$$\zeta_1 \text{ such that } \mu + \zeta_1 - \mu\varphi_2(\zeta_1) = 0,$$

and: $\zeta_2 = -\mu$. We obtain:

$$R_1 = \ln \frac{\zeta_1}{z + \zeta_1}, \quad R_2 = -\ln \frac{\mu}{\mu - z}.$$

Finally, by now denoting $\phi_W(z)$ the characteristic function of the waiting time, we obtain:

$$\phi_W(z) = \frac{\zeta_1}{z + \zeta_1} \frac{\mu - z}{\mu}.$$

This gives the characteristic function of waiting time for the G/M/1 server. This expression is also written:

$$\phi_W(z) = \frac{(\mu - z)(1 - \varphi_2(\zeta_1))}{\mu - z - \mu\varphi_2(\zeta_1)}. \tag{6.78}$$

which, by introducing $\sigma = \varphi_2(\zeta_1) = \frac{\mu + \zeta_1}{\mu}$, becomes:

$$\phi_W(z) = \frac{(\mu - z)(1 - \sigma)}{\mu - z - \mu\sigma}. \tag{6.79}$$

This is a remarkable result as we find an expression similar to that of the M/M/1 queue, this time σ playing the role of ρ.

We immediately deduce from this the expression for the waiting time distribution:

$$P(> x) = \sigma\, e^{-\mu(1-\sigma)x}. \tag{6.80}$$

Just as for the M/G/1 system, we can apply these results to several practical cases approximating most realistic scenarios.

Application to M/M/1 queue. Before considering the more general cases, let us first apply the previous result to the M/M/1 case once more. As the arrival instants are governed by an exponential law, we have:

$$\varphi_2(-z) = \frac{\lambda}{\lambda + z},$$

the solution sought is such that $\mu - \beta_0 - \mu\sigma = \mu - \beta_0 - \mu\frac{\lambda}{\lambda + \beta_0} = 0$, hence $\beta_0 = \mu - \lambda$ and finally $\sigma = \lambda/\mu = \rho$, and:

$$P(> x) = \rho\, e^{-\mu(1-\rho)x}.$$

We again find the result already established.

Application to D/M/1 queue. This is symmetric to the M/D/1 case. In this case we have $\varphi_2(z) = e^{z/\lambda}$, where λ is the arrival rate (smaller than μ); the solution sought is such that:

$$\mu - \beta_0 - \mu\sigma = \mu - \beta_0 - \mu e^{-\beta_0/\lambda} = 0. \tag{6.81}$$

We thus have $\sigma = 1 - \beta_0/\mu$, and then:

$$P(> x) = \sigma\, e^{-\mu(1-\sigma)x},$$

or:

$$P(> x) = \frac{\mu - \beta_0}{\mu} e^{-\beta_0 x}.$$

Application to H2/M/1 queue. This is in a sense the opposite case to the D/M/1 case, in terms of the coefficient of variation (greater than 1), M/M/1 being an intermediate case.

In this case we have:

$$\varphi_2(z) = \frac{\alpha_1 \lambda_1}{\lambda_1 - z} + \frac{\alpha_2 \lambda_2}{\lambda_2 - z}.$$

λ is the arrival rate, $(\lambda < \mu)$: $\frac{1}{\lambda} = \frac{\alpha_1}{\lambda_1} + \frac{\alpha_2}{\lambda_2}$. The solution sought is such that:

$$\mu - \beta_0 - \mu\sigma = \mu - \beta_0 - \mu\left(\frac{\alpha_1 \lambda_1}{\lambda_1 - \beta_0} + \frac{\alpha_2 \lambda_2}{\lambda_2 - \beta_0} \right) = 0. \tag{6.82}$$

We have: $\sigma = 1 - \beta_0/\mu$ and $P(> x) = \sigma e^{-\mu(1-\sigma)x}$, or of course:

$$P(> x) = \frac{\mu - \beta_0}{\mu} e^{-\beta_0 x}.$$

6.6.4. *Other applications and extension of the Pollaczek method*

This time out interest is no longer in an isolated server, but rather in a group of servers belonging to a queueing network. Our intent here is not to develop the available results, which are complex and remain the domain of specialists. The reader should recall that the Pollaczek method, although seldom used as it is unfortunately considered as reserved to mathematicians, has nevertheless given rise to interesting developments; see especially [LEG 94].

The method by which to address such complex problems relies on the manipulation of stochastic relations. One the basic relations having been expressed, their manipulation (just as in classical algebra) allows us to derive expressions of

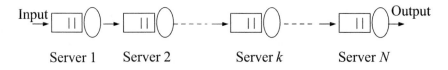

Figure 6.20. *Network of queues in series*

known characteristics, and thus to obtain their main properties. However, the exact calculation of the results remains complex. We mention here as an example the results which have been obtained for the M/M/.../1 system. This is a sequence of single servers with exponentially distributed service times and to which a Poisson process is offered: see Figure 6.20. This system gives rise to a specific phenomenon: the clients agglutinate as they progress towards the output node; the arrival processes in the successive servers are no longer Poissonian, and can hardly even be represented by an approximate law, due to the strong dependency between the successive stages. The analysis is fairly involved, but we can however prove the following simple result, which gives an asymptotic value for the waiting time at node k (see [FIC 04]):

$$\overline{W_k} \simeq_{k \to \infty} \ln\left[(k-2)\frac{\rho}{1-\rho}\right] + \gamma, \tag{6.83}$$

or, for very high k:

$$\overline{W_k} \simeq_{k \to \infty} \ln\left[k\frac{\rho}{1-\rho}\right] + \gamma, \tag{6.84}$$

where γ is the Euler constant ($\gamma \simeq 0.577$).

6.7. Queues with priorities

If a class of clients has a particular level of urgency, it is possible in most cases to set up priority mechanisms. For example, a processor must be able to process tasks relating to vital security functions very rapidly, even if this means delaying less critical tasks. Alternatively, a router will give preference to a packet whose quality of service requirements (in terms of delay) involve greater constraints. This service mechanism will be represented by a model with *priorities*.

The normal case, where clients are served in the order of their arrival, is the FIFO (*first-in, first-out*) discipline. Under the LIFO (*last-in, first-out*) discipline, the last to arrive is the first one to be served. In the case of the HoL discipline (*Head of Line*), each client belongs to a priority level, clients of a given level are served after those of a higher level have been served.

A further distinction is drawn between two variants in the analysis of priority queues, depending on whether they incorporate a pre-emption mechanism. In the case of pre-emptive priority, a client with a higher priority than the client in service will interrupt the latter's service, and immediately take the latter's place. On completion of the handling of the priority client, the client with a lower priority will resume his/her place in the service (and depending on the case, start from the beginning or continue his/her service, referred to as preemptive resume).

6.7.1. *Work conserving system*

Two viewpoints are considered in the analysis of systems with priorities: that of the client and that of the server. Understandably, in some cases the choice of client is indifferent to the server, in the sense that this choice does not change the total amount of work it must handle. The consequence is that at each instant, the server is capable of accounting for the quantity of work it is offered (*unfinished work*): the service time still to be provided to the current client, to which is added the sum of the services of clients waiting at the instant in question. This quantity can be evaluated at a fixed instant, but it is only meaningful if the remaining work does not depend on the next decision! So, let us denote as τ the unfinished work at instant t. Let us stop the arrival process at this instant, and observe the random behavior of the system: the server will work continuously until $t + \tau$, whatever the scheduling decisions taken after t.

A *work conserving* system is a system of this type in which the unfinished work does not depend on the choice discipline applied by the server. Although this is a common situation, counter-examples are a multi-queue system with switchover time; a system with impatience; a system in which the service time depends on waiting (ageing), etc. For most of these systems, it is not even possible to calculate this work at a given instant.

The M/G/1 conservation law [KLE 76]. It is clearly the case that, whereas the unfinished work does not depend on scheduling, the waiting time will depend on it. The conservation property operates from the server's viewpoint. For customers, we will see what is involved.

A queue receives several different flows. We note by λ_j the flow intensity of clients of type j (we speak of *classes of clients*) and by W_j the mean waiting time they experience. We note by λ the total flow submitted to the server. It is possible, experimentally for example, to measure waiting times while being unaware of the existence of the various classes. We note by $\overline{W}$ the corresponding quantity. This is a weighted sum, each of the flows contributing proportionally to its intensity:

$$\overline{W} = \sum_j \frac{\lambda_j}{\lambda} W_j.$$

The importance of this weighted mean time is that it may be impossible to measure any other quantity – as noted if the measurement process is unable to differentiate between classes.

CONSERVATION THEOREM. *Let us imagine a queue receiving clients belonging to different classes and served in accordance with any priority mechanism, which is conserving and non-pre-emptive. The conservation law is as follows:*

$$\sum_i \rho_i W_i = Constant = \frac{\rho W_0}{1 - \rho}, \quad with \quad W_0 = \sum_i \lambda_i \frac{E[T_i^2]}{2}. \tag{6.85}$$

Index i runs on all client classes; $\rho_i = \lambda_i E(T_i)$ represents the load in class i; $\rho = \sum \rho_i$ is the total load offered to the server.

The formula implies that the expression does not depend on the service discipline; note that at the difference of the average $\overline{W}$, here the weights in the formula are the ρ_is, instead of λ_is.

Special cases:

 – exponential law: $E[T^2] = 2(E[T])^2$, that is $W_0 = \sum \rho_i E[T_i]$,
 – constant time: $W_0 = \frac{1}{2} \sum \rho_i E[T_i]$.

Let us assume two flows, with different service times, but without priority. Their waiting times will therefore be identical, and the application of the formula gives:

$$W_1 = W_2 = \frac{1}{2(1 - \rho)} \sum \lambda_i E[T_i^2],$$

we return in this case to the PK formula.

Proof of the conservation law. We observe the system at an instant t, and we count $n(i)$ clients of class i (the classes are numbered: $1, 2, \ldots, P$); the client whose service is in progress requests additional service for a duration x_0. The unfinished work (the name explains the traditional notation U) is thus:

$$U(t) = x_0 + \sum_{i=1}^{P} \sum_{k=1}^{n(i)} T_{k,i}.$$

We have noted as $T_{k,i}$ the service time that will be requested by the kth client of class i. Taking the average,

$$E[U] = W_0 + \sum_{i=1}^{P} E\left[\sum_{k=1}^{n(i)} T_{k,i} \right].$$

Clients of the same class are assumed to be identical, i.e. to have the same service law, so that: $E[\sum_k T_{k,i}] = E[n_i]E[T_i]$. Bearing in mind that the use of the Little formula links the mean number of clients to their mean waiting time, this is re-written:

$$E[U] = W_0 + \sum_i \rho_i W_i.$$

Now, the unfinished work is independent of the scheduling mechanism – this is a direct consequence of the work conserving property. Thus its mean value will be the same as with a service in the order of arrivals, a case for which all W_i are equal, and in which $E(U) = W_0/(1 - \rho)$. Putting this expression into the previous one supplies the result sought. □

Priority between identical clients. In the case where all clients have identical characteristics (same service time distribution) and provided that the system is work conserving, the choice made by the server has no influence on the total occupation of the queue, and especially the mean number of clients is independent of the discipline. Therefore, the Little formula asserts that the mean waiting time does not depend on the discipline: for example, FIFO, LIFO, and random choice give the same mean waiting time.

6.7.2. *The HoL discipline*

We assume that there are P client classes, each class grouping clients with identical statistical characteristics. The server first processes clients of the highest priority class (by convention, this is noted as 1), and then, if there are no more priority clients in the queue, clients of lower priority (noted 2), etc., up to clients of class P, with the lowest priority. The service mechanism is work-conserving. This is the so-called *Head-of-Line* (HoL) discipline.

We introduce the notation:

$$\sigma_k = \sum_{n=1}^{k} \rho_n.$$

This is the sum of the partial loads contributed by classes with a priority greater than or equal to k. This is therefore the load seen by a client of class k, as it overtakes clients of lower classes. Note that a client of a given class will however be hindered by a client of a lower priority class in service on his/her arrival (as the discipline is not pre-emptive). Then we have:

$$W_1 = \frac{W_0}{1 - \sigma_1},$$

$$W_k = \frac{W_0}{(1 - \sigma_k)(1 - \sigma_{k+1})}, \quad k > 1. \tag{6.86}$$

In fact, for a non-pre-emptive discipline,

$$W_j = W_0 + \sum_{i \leq j} E[S_i] E[N_{ij}] + \sum_{i < j} E[M_{ij}].$$

W_j is the mean waiting time of clients in class j, and index i runs over classes $(i = 1, 2, \ldots, N)$; $E[N_{ij}]$ represents the mean number of clients in class i already present on the arrival of the client of type j and who will be served before him (in particular, the client does not overtake those of his own class). $E[M_{ij}]$ represents the mean number of clients in class i arriving during the wait of the client of type j and who will be served before him.

For our discipline, the Little formula gives

– $E[N_{ij}] = \lambda_i W_i, i = 1, \ldots, j$; and $E[N_{ij}] = 0, i > j$ (our test client overtakes clients in lower priority classes);

– and $E[M_{ij}] = \lambda_i W_j, i = 1, \ldots, j - 1$; $E[M_{ij}] = 0, i \geq j$ (only classes with strictly higher priority classes will overtake him).

Finally we have:

$$W_j = W_0 + \sum_{i \leq j} \rho_i W_i + \sum_{i < j} \rho_i W_j.$$

that is: $W_j(1 - \sigma_{j-1}) = W_0 + \sum_{i=1}^{j} \rho_i W_i$.

From this formula, we first calculate W_1, then W_2, etc.

6.8. Using approximate methods

The exact methods presented up to this point enable strict mathematical resolution of a limited number of problems. Real world systems rarely come into these models. Use must therefore be made of approximations. To this end, several approaches will be possible. The first attitude consists of looking for other mathematical models, enabling (at the price of numerical calculations which are often difficult to conduct) pseudo-exact models of very great complexity: for example, we have presented Coxian laws, which approximate general distributions by a superimposition of exponential stages, returning us to a Markovian analysis, which gives numerical results. This always leads to laborious calculations, and most often to useless complexity.

The second approach consists of forgetting some details of actual functioning that models cannot represent, and latching on to a known model (M/G/1 queue, HoL priority, etc.). The principle of this approach is to represent the behavioral essence through this model, while the results will be orders of magnitude, which are more or less exact. We can also approximate the actual probability distributions by simpler laws, for instance by fitting with the first moments.

We give hereafter several examples of approximate models, among the simplest and well-known ones. The goal is mainly to present an overview of the variety of possible techniques.

6.8.1. *Reattempts*

When congestion occurs, provoking rejection of the demands, or too lengthy response delays, user behavior has a strong impact on the operation of the whole system. In such circumstances, their impatient reactions, characterized by premature abandonments and retrials, induce an increase in the total effective load the system has to process, worsening the situation and potentially initiating chain reactions leading to complete collapse.

This phenomenon is extremely important in reality, particularly in the event of overloads, failures, traffic imbalance, etc. It has been shown that it leads, even in the event of initially slight overloads, to extremely severe overload situations. It is the role of regulation to protect systems and networks against these phenomena. It should also be noted that in these circumstances load measurement should be carried out with great care. This is because it is difficult to distinguish between fresh demands and reattempts, and the meaning to give to their respective blocking or rejection rate would be quite different.

Detailed modeling of these phenomena is both impossible and useless. We can only expect to describe the relation between the congestion and the demand increase that it induces. In that, the model renders the essence of the phenomenon, without taking account of the exact stochastic processes involved. We describe below a general model which links the final traffic offered to a server (handling system, transport system, network, etc.) to the traffic handled as a function of the probability of rejection by the server, and the source perseverance rate.

The phenomenon is characterized by the following features:

– offered traffic: we will note as λ_0 the flow of initial requests ("fresh" attempts) and as λ the total observed flow. Any client presenting himself in front of the service constitutes an attempt, which is a first attempt or a renewal;

– repetition factor: this is the ratio $\beta = \lambda/\lambda_0$, which measures the amplification caused by congestion; it enables us to relate the actual demand to observations;

– perseverance rate: in a very simple model, allowance is made for perseverance of demand using a probabilistic method: let H be the probability that a failed attempt will be presented again (one possible refinement would be to take H as a function of the rank of the attempt, of the nature of the failure, etc.);

– loss ratio: we note as p the probability of rejection of each attempt; this is assumed to be constant; reality is more complex (the failure rate differs depending on the rank of the attempt and the time interval between attempts);

– efficiency rate: we note as r the efficiency rate. This is an apparent efficiency rate, as it does not correspond to fresh traffic, with $r = 1 - p$. This is the only quantity that is generally observable as it is difficult and very expensive to separate fresh attempts from renewals in observations of systems and measurement campaigns.

Figure 6.21 shows the rejection and repetition mechanism in schematic form.

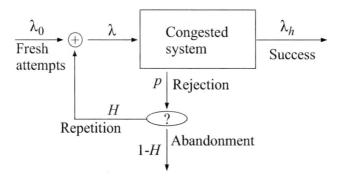

Figure 6.21. *Repeat attempts upon rejection*

We note as λ_h the intensity of the flow successfully handled. Finally, this schematic representation enables the estimation of the flows in each branch:

$$\lambda_h = (1 - p)\lambda, \quad \lambda = \lambda_0 + \lambda H p,$$

hence:

$$\lambda = \frac{\lambda_0}{1 - Hp}, \quad \lambda_h = \frac{\lambda_0(1 - p)}{1 - Hp}. \tag{6.87}$$

Thus, where $r = 1 - p$:

$$\beta = \frac{1}{1 - H(1 - r)}, \quad \lambda_0 = \frac{\lambda_h}{\beta r}. \tag{6.88}$$

This model must be understood for what it is: it explains the behavior observed, and in particular the difference between fresh, actual demand and observed traffic. Thus, by measuring apparent offered traffic and handled traffic, we can work out the fresh traffic for a given source perseverance rate hypothesis.

The model can help build an approximate analysis of the system, and an evaluation of the various flows, for instance by assuming that all flows resulting from the renewed attempts retain their Poissonian nature. This is an approximation, as the renewed attempts are clearly not independent of the system state, making the Poissonian assumption highly simplistic.

6.8.2. *Peakedness factor method*

We consider again the case of multiservices traffic (see section 6.5.1). The idea is to fit the generalized Erlang model to an equivalent simple Erlang loss system (a single equivalent offered traffic and a fictitious number of servers). The total occupancy is the sum of random variables $n_1, n_2, \ldots, n_x$ giving the number of communications per class, and we look for the set of probabilities $P(n_1, n_2, \ldots, n_x)$, assuming that each class generates independent Poisson traffic flows.

Here we make use of the classical result: the generating function of the sum of independent random variables is the product of their individual generating functions.

Consider a particular service, with offered traffic a. We note by (p_k) the distribution of the number of its simultaneous calls (assuming an infinite capacity). p_k takes only positive integer values. We can introduce their generating function, as already seen in section 6.4.4.2:

$$F(z) = \sum_k p_k z^k.$$

Assume the number of simultaneous connections for this service obeys a Poisson distribution. The problem is to estimate the total bitrate generated by all services. The Poisson law is, for this single service:

$$p_k = \frac{a^k}{k!} e^{-a},$$

and its generating function is:

$$F(z) = \sum_k \frac{a^k}{k!} e^{-a} z^k = \sum_k \frac{(az)^k}{k!} e^{-a}, \quad \text{i.e.} \quad F(z) = e^{a(z-1)}.$$

If this connection requires a bitrate equal to c, it amounts to saying that it consumes c units of transmission link resources, e.g. c megabits/s of the total capacity C (assumed to be infinitely large). When k sessions are simultaneously in progress the volume of resources they require is kc. Thus,

$$p(kc) = \frac{a^k}{k!} e^{-a},$$

and (this time, F stands for the generating function of the bitrates):

$$F(z) = \sum_k \frac{a^k}{k!} e^{-a} z^{kc} = e^{-a} \sum_k \frac{(az^c)^k}{k!}, \quad \text{i.e.} \quad F(z) = e^{a(z^c-1)}.$$

Now,

$$a(z^c - 1) = a[(1 + z - 1)^c - 1]$$

$$= a\left[1 + c(z - 1) + \frac{c(c-1)}{2!}(z-1)^2 + \cdots - 1\right]$$

and so:

$$F(z) = e^{a[(c(z-1)+\frac{c(c-1)}{2!}(z-1)^2+\cdots]}.\qquad(6.89)$$

This corresponds to a single service. Returning to our initial problem, assume that several services with bitrates $c_1, c_2, \ldots$ are offered, the sources being independent and Poissonnian. It immediately follows, for the total amount of bitrate, that:

$$F(z) = F(z_1)F(z_2)\cdots = \prod e^{a_i(z^{c_i}-1)},$$

and $F(z) = e^A$, with:

$$A = (a_1c_1 + a_2c_2 + \cdots)(z-1)$$
$$+ \frac{a_1c_1(c_1-1) + a_2c_2(c_2-1)\cdots}{2!}(z-1)^2 + \cdots.$$

This gives the characteristics of the distribution resulting from superposition. This is no longer a Poisson distribution, as we recognize by comparing it with the previous expressions. However, by introducing the parameter

$$\delta = \frac{a_1c_1^2 + a_2c_2^2 + \cdots}{a_1c_1 + a_2c_2 + \cdots},$$

we obtain:

$$A = \frac{(a_1c_1 + a_2c_2 + \cdots)}{\delta}\left[\delta(z-1) + \frac{\delta(\delta-1)}{2!}(z-1)^2 + \Psi(z-1)\right],$$

and thus:

$$F(z) = \exp\left[\frac{(a_1c_1 + a_2c_2 + \cdots)}{\delta}\left(\delta(z-1) + \frac{\delta(\delta-1)}{2!}(z-1)^2 + \Psi(z-1)\right)\right].$$

This expression can be compared with equation (6.89) for a single service, if the terms in $z-1$ of power higher than 2 (i.e. $\Psi(z-1)$) are neglected. The system for two services with different bitrates is thus approximately equivalent to a single Poisson source with parameter $a = (a_1c_1 + a_2c_2)/\delta$ and bitrate $\delta = \frac{a_1c_1^2 + a_2c_2^2}{a_1c_1 + a_2c_2}$. This is easily generalized to an arbitrary number of services.

The reader should note that, in the case where bitrates are the same $c = c_1 = c_2 \ldots$, we once more obtain a Poisson law with parameter $a = a_1 + a_2 + \cdots$.

An intuitive interpretation. In order to gain a deeper understanding of this result, the same problem can be addressed by means of the moments. For a single service, the definition directly gives the value of the first moments:

$$\overline{X} = c\sum kp_k = ac, \quad \overline{X^2} = c^2\sum kp_k = c^2(a^2 + a),$$

i.e. $m = ac$ and $\sigma^2 = \overline{X^2} - \overline{X}^2 = ac^2$.

As the variables are independent, the distribution of two superposition services has its first 2 moments given by:

$$m = a_1 c_1 + a_2 c_2 \quad \text{and} \quad \sigma^2 = a_1 c_1^2 + a_2 c_2^2.$$

In order to approximate this distribution by a unique Poisson law with parameters a and δ, we must have:

$$a\delta = a_1 c_1 + a_2 c_2 \quad \text{and} \quad a\delta^2 = a_1 c_1^2 + a_2 c_2^2,$$

giving

$$\delta = \frac{a_1 c_1^2 + a_2 c_2^2}{a_1 c_1 + a_2 c_2}, \quad a = \frac{a_1 c_1 + a_2 c_2}{\delta}.$$

This is the same expression once again. Approximating the exact result given by the generating function amounts to approximating a Poisson distribution by adjusting the first two moments. This allows us to represent the complex behavior of a multirate system by a much simpler Poisson process with a unique bitrate δ.

To summarize. In presence of several superpositional flows of different profiles, the classical results of probability theory make it possible to define an equivalent flow, replacing the x classes of individual bitrate c_i and activity a_i by a single flow offering activity A/z and bitrate z, such that:

$$A = \sum_{i=1}^{x} a_i c_i, \quad \text{and} \quad z = \frac{\sum_{i=1}^{x} a_i c_i^2}{\sum_{i=1}^{x} a_i c_i}. \tag{6.90}$$

z is called the *peakedness factor* and was initially introduced by Hayward to solve overflow traffic problems. It accounts for the *sporadicity* of the traffics. This is simply the ratio of the variance to the mean.

Therefore, a model equivalent to the initial one consists of a concentrator, with capacity C/z, to which a single traffic of intensity A/z is offered. The *average* blocking probability is thus obtained directly from the Erlang loss formula $E(A, N)$:

$$B \simeq E\left(\frac{A}{z}, \frac{C}{z}\right).$$

As for the different classes, we can obtain their respective blocking probability by interpolating the equivalent distribution between two consecutive values of z. We write, for values such that $n < z$:

$$E\left(\frac{A}{z}, \frac{C}{z} - 1\right) = E\left(\frac{A}{z}, \frac{C}{z}\right)\alpha_1^n;$$

$$E\left(\frac{A}{z}, \frac{C}{z} - 2\right) = E\left(\frac{A}{z}, \frac{C}{z} - 1\right)\alpha_2^n; \text{ etc.}$$

with

$$\alpha_1 = \left(\frac{E\left(\frac{A}{z}, \frac{C}{z} - 1\right)}{E\left(\frac{A}{z}, \frac{C}{z}\right)}\right)^{1/z} \approx \left(\frac{C}{A}\right)^{1/z};$$

$$\alpha_2 = \left(\frac{E\left(\frac{A}{z}, \frac{C}{z} - 2\right)}{E\left(\frac{A}{z}, \frac{C}{z} - 1\right)}\right)^{1/z} \approx \left(\frac{C - z}{A}\right)^{1/z}$$

(6.91)

and so on. We also have:

$$B_1 = \frac{1}{z} E\left(\frac{A}{z}, \frac{C}{z}\right),$$

(6.92)

and, for a service with for instance $c_2 = 2z + n, 0 < n < z$:

$$B_2 = \frac{1}{z} E\left(\frac{A}{z}, \frac{C}{z}\right) \alpha_1^z \alpha_2^z \alpha_3^n$$

As long as c_i is not too large (compared to C), we can simplify the expressions by keeping the α_i constant, $\alpha_i \approx \alpha_1 = \alpha = (C/A)^{1/z}$:

$$B_i \approx E\left(\frac{A}{z}, \frac{C}{z}\right) \cdot \left(\frac{\alpha^{c_i} - 1}{z(\alpha - 1)}\right)$$

(6.93)

$z = 2$						Generalized Erlang			Erlang loss (peakedness method)		
C	a_1	d_1	a_2	d_2	A	B_1	B_2	B	A/z	C/z	$E(A/z, C/z)$
200	105	1	7	5	140	9.71 10^{-5}	6.84 10^{-4}	1.34 10^{-4}	70	100	1.38 10^{-4}

$z = 10$						Generalized Erlang			Erlang loss (peakedness method)		
C	a_1	d_1	a_2	d_2	A	B_1	B_2	B	A/z	C/z	$E(A/z, C/z)$
200	38.5	1	1.5	21	70	9.18 10^{-6}	6.83 10^{-5}	3.45 10^{-5}	7	20	2.99 10^{-5}

Table 6.1. *Precision of the "peakedness factor" method*

Table 6.1 shows the precision of the approximation, for a mix of two traffic classes. We can note that in most situations a linear approximation provides sufficient precision:

$$B_i = \frac{1}{z} E\left(\frac{A}{z}, \frac{C}{z}\right) c_i \tag{6.94}$$

The peakedness method is naturally nothing more than an approximate approach; however, we can easily verify that it gives an excellent precision, even for large z, as long as the ratio C/c_x remains large – c_x being the highest bitrate requested. This ratio should remain larger than 10 to guarantee a good accuracy. Such a condition should hold in most situations where flows are multiplexed, thanks to the high capacity of modern networks.

6.8.3. *Approximate formulae for the G/G/R system*

At the present time, one of the best and most universal formulae is the Allen-Cunnen formula. It enables us to estimate the mean waiting time for a multiserver system with general arrival and service laws.

Let us denote by:

– c_T^2 the squared coefficient of variation of the service time, and $\overline{T}$ the average service time;

– c_a^2 the squared coefficient of variation of the inter-arrival time;

– $A = \lambda/\mu$ the offered traffic, and $\rho = A/R$ the utilization factor of each server;

– $C(A, R)$ the waiting probability of the M/M/R system (see section 6.4.6):

$$C(A, R) = \frac{A^R/R!}{\frac{A^R}{R!} + (1 - \rho) \sum_{n<R} \frac{A^n}{n!}}.$$

Then,

$$\frac{E[W]}{E[T]} \simeq \frac{C(A, R)}{R - A} \times \frac{c_T^2 + c_a^2}{2}. \tag{6.95}$$

This is in fact the formula for the M/M/R queue (an exact formula in this case), which is corrected by a factor that takes into account the coefficients of variation of the arrival and service laws. It is worth noting that:

– the formula is *exact* for the M/M/R queue;

– it is *exact* for the M/G/1 queue (it reduces to the Pollaczek-Khinchine formula).

Quantile calculation. Quantiles is the term given to an essential concept: the clients of a waiting system are not really sensitive to mean waits, but rather to inadmissible waits. In this respect, the reader must know that the QoS standards not only specify mean values to be complied with, but also values at $x\%$. Quantile estimation is a delicate process, as the distribution is rarely known explicitly, with the exception of M/M/c systems. Use is often made of an empirical formula, known as *Martin's formula*:

$$t_{90} = E[T] + 1.3\,\sigma_T,$$
$$t_{95} = E[T] + 2\,\sigma_T. \tag{6.96}$$

These formulae are in fact very general: they are based on the resemblance that inevitably exists between any good distribution and a Gamma law (see Chapter 2). This resemblance excludes non-unimodal or non-continuous distributions. It will be preferably applied to sojourn time, which has no discontinuity at the origin.

As an example, the table below shows the 90% quantile for the holding time of the M/D/1 queue (i.e. the time having 1 chance out of 10 of being reached or exceeded):

Load	Exact value	Approximation (Martin's formula)
0.3	1.85	1.73
0.5	2.5	2.35
0.7	4.1	3.6
0.8	6.0	5.1
0.9	11.8	9.6

Table 6.2. *Precision of Martin's formula*

The accuracy is satisfactory for a preliminary analysis. However, for more precise estimations, or for low probabilities, it is worth using an asymptotic formula when possible, e.g. equation (6.74) for the M/D/1 case.

6.9. Appendix: Pollaczek transform

We had:

$$\phi_{n+1}(z) = \frac{1}{2\pi i} \int_{C\zeta} \phi_n(-\zeta)\varphi(-\zeta)\frac{z\,\mathrm{d}\zeta}{\zeta(\zeta+z)}.$$

We can also write the characteristic function of the waiting time as follows:

$$\phi_n(-z) = \int_{0-}^{\infty} e^{-zt}\mathrm{d}W_n(t\mid w_0) = E\left[e^{-zW_n}\mid w_0\right],$$

and in particular for the first client:

$$\phi_0(-z) = E\left[e^{-zW_0}\right] = e^{-zW_0}.$$

Let us introduce the generating function:

$$\phi(z, v) = \sum_{n=0}^{\infty} \phi_n(-z) v^n,$$

which, applied to the integral studied (after development and summation), gives the relation:

$$\phi(z, v) - \frac{v}{2\pi i} \int_{C\zeta} \phi_n(\zeta, v) \varphi(-\zeta) \frac{z \mathrm{d}\zeta}{\zeta(z - \zeta)} = e^{-zW_0}.$$

In the case in which $W_0 = 0$, the solution of this equation is:

$$\phi_0(z, v) = \exp\left\{ -\frac{1}{2\pi i} \int_{C\zeta} \ln\left[1 - v\varphi(-\zeta)\right] \frac{z \mathrm{d}\zeta}{\zeta(z - \zeta)} \right\},$$

with $0 < Re(\zeta) < Re(z)$. The verification, which is relatively complex, is performed by inspection via expanding the logarithm in a Taylor expansion. Reference may be made to [LEG 62, SYS 86] for a detailed proof.

By application of the residue theorem at $\zeta = 0$, where $\frac{\ln[1-v\varphi(-\zeta)]}{\zeta} \approx \frac{1-v}{\zeta}$, this gives

$$\phi_0(z, v) = \frac{1}{1-v} \exp\left\{ -\frac{1}{2\pi i} \int_{-i\infty-0}^{i\infty-0} \ln\left[1 - v\varphi(-\zeta)\right] \frac{z \mathrm{d}\zeta}{\zeta(z + \zeta)} \right\},$$

The stationary limit process being independent of the initial condition W_0, we come to:

$$\phi(z) = \exp\left\{ -\frac{1}{2\pi i} \int_{-i\infty-0}^{i\infty-0} \ln\left[1 - \varphi(-\zeta)\right] \frac{z \mathrm{d}\zeta}{\zeta(z + \zeta)} \right\},$$

which is the characteristic waiting function that was sought, with $\varphi(-\zeta) = \varphi_1(-\zeta)\varphi_2(\zeta)$, $Re(z) \leq 0$. Bearing in mind that to exist the stationary limit process requires compliance with the condition $|\varphi(-\zeta)| \leq \varphi[-Re(z)] < 1$.

Recalling that the derivatives at $z = 0$ of the characteristic function give us the moments, or that the expansion in Taylor series of $\ln \phi(z)$ gives us the cumulants, we obtain in particular the mean wait, and more generally the cumulants:

$$W = -\frac{1}{2\pi i} \int_{-i\infty-0}^{i\infty-0} \ln\left[1 - \varphi(-\zeta)\right] \frac{\mathrm{d}\zeta}{\zeta^2},$$

$$C_n = \frac{(-1)^n n!}{2\pi i} \int_{-i\infty-0}^{i\infty-0} \ln\left[1 - \varphi(-\zeta)\right] \frac{\mathrm{d}\zeta}{\zeta^{n+1}}.$$

The probability of no waiting is also obtained directly from the characteristic function by growing $Re(z)$ to infinity by negative values. The waiting probability is its complement.

$$P(w = 0) = \exp\left\{ -\frac{1}{2\pi i} \int_{-i\infty-0}^{i\infty-0} \ln\left[1 - \varphi(-\zeta)\right] \frac{d\zeta}{\zeta} \right\}.$$

Chapter 7

Reliability Theory

This chapter presents the major elements of *reliability theory*, and more generally what is called *dependability*.

Dependability encompasses all these aspects of reliability, availability and maintainability, which play a major role in communication systems and networks. Indeed, ensuring the continuity of service is one of their first missions, especially in case of emergencies (e.g. calling fire brigade) and in any disaster situation. To reach such a goal, operators must deploy secured architectures. As this increases the cost of the system, it is worth evaluating efficiency. Reliability theory is the set of mathematical techniques to apply in order to perform this evaluation. This chapter presents these techniques, giving numerous examples.

7.1. Definition of reliability

According to the standardization and particularly to the IEC (International Electrotechnical Commission), reliability is "the probability that a system will perform its intended function for a specified time interval under stated conditions". This will correspond to the "success" of the mission. Conversely, the mission fails once the system breaks down. We will calculate the probability of success at time t, or probability of working for a given time interval t.

In the telecommunication domain, and particularly for terrestrial equipment that is generally repairable, another important feature is the long-term proportion of time the service is available; we then refer to this concept as *availability*. The availability function is defined as the probability that the system is working (into service) at any instant of time t, whatever could be the preceding states (failures and repairs may have occurred).

A system is thus characterized both by its reliability (probability of uninterrupted activity up to t) and by its availability (probability of being active at time t). As the availability is usually high, the probability being very close to 1, the *unavailability* is preferably used, generally expressed in the form 10^{-x}.

7.2. Failure rate and bathtub curve

The instantaneous failure rate $\lambda(t)$ is defined as follows: $\lambda(t)\mathrm{d}t$ is the probability that a system, working correctly at time t, fails within the time interval $[t, t + \mathrm{d}t]$.

During the lifetime of a repairable system, or of a population of identical equipment, the observation leads to distinguish three periods, according to the behavior of the failure rate.

The first period corresponds to the *early life period* (also called the *infant mortality period* or burn in period). It is characterized by the decrease of the failure rate as time increases. This corresponds to the period during which remaining (hardware or software) defaults, which have not been detected while debugging the system, are corrected after its deployment.

The second period, or *middle life period*, corresponds to what is also called the *useful life period* and is characterized by an approximately constant failure rate. During this phase, the longest of the lifetime, failures occur (either hardware or software) which are referred to as "catalectic" or "random", i.e. unpredictable. Actually, it is not possible, necessary and even profitable to identify and correct residual defaults as the failure rate becomes negligible.

The third period corresponds to the so-called *old age period*, also called the wear out period, during which the failure rate increases with time. This corresponds to irreversible degradation of the system, either due to a material degradation of its components, or to a lack of maintenance in the case of repairable systems. For terrestrial telecommunication systems this period is generally not considered because of the replacement of old equipment by new equipment, while it can be of importance for satellite systems.

The curve on Figure 7.1 illustrates these three successive modes. It is conventionally called the "bathtub curve" because of its shape. In the following, the focus is mainly on the useful life period. Moreover, since repairable systems are our main concern, the concept of MTBF (*Mean Time Between Failures*) will be of prime importance. This is the inverse of the constant failure rate of the system λ during the useful life period. Prior to beginning modeling the major reliability structures, it is worth defining the main functions used in reliability studies.

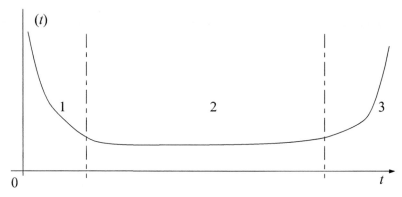

1 = early life period; 2 = useful life period; 3 = wear out period

Figure 7.1. *Bathtub curve (mortality curve)*

7.3. Reliability functions

$R(t)$ is the reliability function and represents the probability of survival at time t. We frequently characterize the reliability by

$$M = \theta = \int_0^{\infty} R(t)\mathrm{d}t. \tag{7.1}$$

M is the MTTF (*mean time to failure*) or MTBF for a repairable system where it represents the average time between failures. M is often denoted by θ.

$F(t)$ is the failure distribution function, $F(t) = 1 - R(t)$.

$\lambda(t)$ is the instantaneous failure rate (also called the hazard function). It corresponds to the probability that a system breakdown occurs between times t and $t + \mathrm{d}t$ provided that the system was on service at time t. Thus, we have:

$$\lambda(t) = \frac{\mathrm{d}F(t)}{\mathrm{d}t} \cdot \frac{1}{R(t)},$$

and thus:

$$\lambda(t)\mathrm{d}t = -\frac{\mathrm{d}R(t)}{R(t)}, \tag{7.2}$$

and also:

$$R(t) = e^{-\int_0^t \lambda(\tau)\mathrm{d}\tau}. \tag{7.3}$$

In the useful life period $\lambda(t) = \lambda$ is constant, hence:

$$R(t) = e^{-\lambda t}, \quad M = \frac{1}{\lambda}. \tag{7.4}$$

In what follows, our interest is mainly concentrated on that period. Note, however, that more complex functions can be used, in order to describe the reliability of the equipment during its whole lifetime. In particular, the Weibull distribution is often used (see Chapter 2 and [FIC 04]). Indeed, let us express the reliability distribution under the form of a Weibull law:

$$R(t) = e^{-(\frac{t-\gamma}{\eta})^{\beta}}. \tag{7.5}$$

Identifying this expression with general definition (7.3), we obtain:

$$R(t) = e^{-\int_0^t \lambda(\tau)d\tau} = e^{-(\frac{t-\gamma}{\eta})^{\beta}},$$

and thus:

$$\int_0^t \lambda(t)dt = \left(\frac{t-\gamma}{\eta}\right)^{\beta},$$

then:

$$\lambda(t) = \frac{\beta}{\eta}\left(\frac{t-\gamma}{\eta}\right)^{\beta-1}. \tag{7.6}$$

Denoting $\lambda_0 = \frac{1}{\eta^{\beta}}$, we obtain:

$$\lambda(t) = \lambda_0 \beta(t-\gamma)^{\beta-1}, \quad \text{i.e.} \quad R(t) = e^{-\lambda_0(t-\gamma)^{\beta}}. \tag{7.7}$$

Clearly, these expressions show that:

– the failure rate is decreasing with time for $\beta < 1$,

– the failure rate is constant for $\beta = 1$, and we again find the exponential distribution if $\gamma = 0$,

– the failure rate is increasing with time for $\beta > 1$.

7.4. System reliability

7.4.1. Reliability of non-repairable systems

In the following, any element of a system (component, card, rack, etc.) will be referred to as E_i. Any element will be itself decomposable in other elements.

We will assume that any element i may be in only two states: it is up, i.e. it works (E_i), or it is down ($\overline{E_i}$). We will also call these states good or bad respectively.

E and $\overline{E}$ are two mutually exclusive events:

$$P(E) + P(\overline{E}) = 1.$$

The reliability R is defined as the probability of being up, or probability of success (the time index is omitted, for short):

$$R = P(E) = 1 - P(\overline{E}).$$

Conforming to the usage, we will denote Q its complement, i.e. the probability of being down or probability of failure: $Q = 1 - R$.

7.4.1.1. *Reliability of the series configuration*

A system is said to be a series system if it fails as soon as any of its elements fails. It is symbolized by a *reliability diagram*, which is represented in Figure 7.2.

Figure 7.2. *Series configuration*

If $\overline{E}$ denotes the event "breakdown of the system" (or total failure) and $\overline{E_i}$ the event "failure of element i", we obtain:

$$\overline{E} = \overline{E_1} \cup \overline{E_2} \cup \ldots \overline{E_i} \cup \ldots.$$

Event algebra, and especially De Morgan's rule, allows us to write:

$$\overline{E} = \overline{E_1 \cap E_2 \cap \ldots E_i \cap \ldots},$$

hence: $E = E_1 \cap E_2 \ldots$. Going from the events to their probabilities, and considering the events as independent,

$$P(E) = \prod P(E_i),$$

and thus for reliability:

$$R = \prod R_i, \tag{7.8}$$

which may be merely formulated by the following rule: the reliability of a series configuration is the product of the reliabilities of its components. In the case where all the components have a failure rate exponentially distributed with parameter λ_i, we obtain:

$$R(t) = e^{-\sum \lambda_i t}. \tag{7.9}$$

The MTBF of the system is: $M = \int_0^t R(t)\mathrm{d}t$, and so:

$$M = \frac{1}{\sum \lambda_i}. \tag{7.10}$$

7.4.1.2. *Reliability of the parallel configuration*

A system is said to be parallel if the system fails only if all its elements fail. The reliability diagram is represented in Figure 7.3. Then we have:

$$\overline{E} = \overline{E_1} \cap \overline{E_2} \cap \ldots \overline{E_i} \cap \ldots.$$

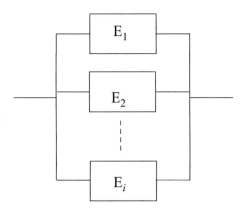

Figure 7.3. *Parallel configuration*

Hence:

$$P(\overline{E}) = \prod P(\overline{E_i}),$$

or, since Q denotes the probability of failure:

$$Q = \prod Q_i. \tag{7.11}$$

In other words, we have the following simple rule: the probability of failure of a parallel system is the product of the probabilities of failure of its components. Remember that we denote $Q = 1 - R$. Then we may write:

$$R = 1 - \prod \left(1 - R_i\right). \tag{7.12}$$

The system is working as long as *at least* one of its elements is working (note that this kind of manipulation, consisting of operating either on an event or on its complement is of great assistance in modeling such systems, and, more generally, each time the event of interest is a combination of elementary events: see the analysis of connecting networks, e.g. [FIC 04, PAT 97]). In the case where all elements have a failure law exponentially distributed with parameter λ_i:

$$R(t) = 1 - \prod \left(1 - e^{-\lambda_i t}\right). \tag{7.13}$$

In the simple case of two elements in parallel, we obtain the obvious result:

$$R(t) = R_1(t) + R_2(t) - R_1(t)R_2(t), \tag{7.14}$$
$$R(t) = e^{-\lambda_1 t} + e^{-\lambda_2 t} - e^{-\lambda_1 t}e^{-\lambda_1 t}.$$

The MTBF of the system is $M = \int_0^t R(t)dt$, and then:

$$M = \frac{1}{\lambda_1} + \frac{1}{\lambda_2} - \frac{1}{\lambda_1 + \lambda_2}. \tag{7.15}$$

7.4.1.3. *Reliability of the series-parallel configuration*

This configuration corresponds to a set of groups of elements in parallel, each one formed of elements in series: k branches of p elements for instance. The reliability diagram is represented in Figure 7.4.

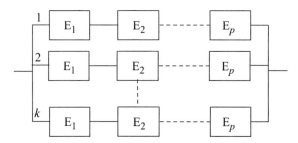

Figure 7.4. *Series-parallel configuration*

Proceeding as above immediately yields:

The reliability of one branch is $R_j = \prod_{i=1}^{p} R_i$.

The probability of failure of the whole system with k branches is: $Q = \prod_{j=1}^{k} Q_j$, and its reliability is $R = 1 - Q$, and thus:

$$R = 1 - \prod_{j=1}^{k} \left(1 - \prod_{i=1}^{p} R_i\right). \tag{7.16}$$

7.4.1.4. *Reliability of the parallel-series configuration*

The reliability diagram is represented in Figure 7.5.

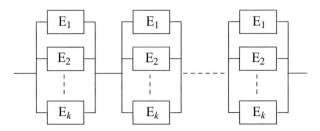

Figure 7.5. *Parallel-series configuration*

The reliability of one set of k elements in parallel is:

$$R = 1 - \prod_{j=1}^{k} \left(1 - R_j\right),$$

and the reliability of p sets in series is:

$$R = \prod_{i=1}^{p} \left[1 - \prod_{j=1}^{k} \left(1 - R_j\right)\right]. \qquad (7.17)$$

7.4.1.5. *Complex configurations*

The method is briefly developed using an example, illustrated in Figure 7.6. The generalization is straightforward.

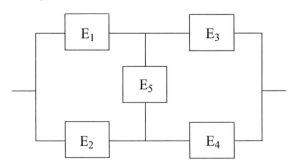

Figure 7.6. *"Meshed" configuration*

The direct approach distinguishes two cases, according to the state of E_5: E_5 is good, or E_5 is bad.

If E_5 has failed, the system is up, provided that at least one of the two branches (E_1, E_3) or (E_2, E_4) is working, i.e. the complement of the event "the two branches are down", the rule on elements in series giving the corresponding probability.

The probability of being up, corresponding to this case is:

$$(1 - R_5)[1 - (1 - R_1 R_3)(1 - R_2 R_4)].$$

If on the other hand E_5 is working, the system is up, provided that in each couple (E_1, E_2) and (E_3, E_4) at least one element is working, the probability of which is 1 minus the probability that both elements are down. That is:

$$R_5[1 - (1 - R_1)(1 - R_2)][1 - (1 - R_3)(1 - R_4)].$$

The reliability of the system is the sum of probability of these two mutually exclusive events:

$$
\begin{aligned}
R = {} & \left(1 - R_5\right)\left[1 - \left(1 - R_1 R_3\right)\left(1 - R_2 R_4\right)\right] \\
& + R_5\left[1 - \left(1 - R_1\right)\left(1 - R_2\right)\right]\left[1 - \left(1 - R_3\right)\left(1 - R_4\right)\right].
\end{aligned}
\tag{7.18}
$$

7.4.1.6. Non-repairable redundant configurations

The goal of such organizations is to ensure a higher reliability by inserting additional components in parallel. These structures are deployed especially in cases where it is impossible to replace failed components.

Simple redundancy. A breakdown of the system occurs if either all the elements in parallel are down (this is called *total simple redundancy*), or if a given proportion of them has failed (*partial simple redundancy*). For instance, a telecommunication system (switching or transmission equipment, a router, etc.) is built with many processing elements sharing the load. This leads us to consider different degraded states as a function of the number of failed elements. Notice however that terrestrial systems will generally be repairable, so that for them we are mainly concerned with availability, as will be seen below.

The total simple redundancy case corresponds directly to the parallel configuration: the system is down if all its components are down.

$$R = 1 - \prod_1^n \left(1 - R_j\right),$$

and thus with n identical elements:

$$R(t) = 1 - \left(1 - e^{-\lambda t}\right)^n \tag{7.19}$$

Hence the MTBF of the system is $M = \int_0^t R(t)\mathrm{d}t$,

$$M = \frac{1}{\lambda}\sum_{i=1}^{n}\frac{1}{i} \qquad (7.20)$$

For the simple case of two elements in parallel, we have:

$$M = \frac{3}{2\lambda}$$

The partial simple redundancy corresponds to the case where a part of the components is up. This is a special case of majority redundancy, which we examine here.

Partial redundancy and majority voting. In this case, the system is in service as long as at least r out of n elements are in service.

The system is called a *majority redundancy* system, or a *majority voting* system, if furthermore there exists a decision element in series (from the reliability standpoint), making it possible to detect whether or not at least r out of n elements are working. Rather than sharing the load, the system replicates the same vital function (e.g. power supplies or clocks). The decision element simply makes the comparison and issues a signal corresponding to the "majority opinion". Here too the mission will be said to be successful as long as, at least, r elements out of the n elements in parallel are good, provided however that the voter does not fail.

The corresponding reliability diagram is represented in Figure 7.7.

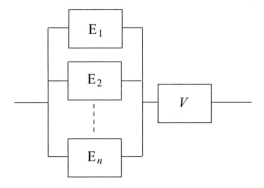

Figure 7.7. *Majority voting*

First let us consider the system without the majority voter (V). Its reliability function may be easily written using the binomial law:

$$R = \sum_{k=r}^{n}\binom{n}{k}R_j^k(1-R_j)^{n-k},$$

with $\binom{n}{k} = \frac{n!}{k!(n-k)!}$. Thus, with an exponential failure probability distribution:

$$R(t) = \sum_{k=r}^{n} \binom{n}{k} e^{-k\lambda t} \left(1 - e^{-\lambda t}\right)^{n-k}. \tag{7.21}$$

Now let us consider the system with its majority voter. From the reliability standpoint, the voter, with failure rate λ_V, is an element in series. Thus, the reliability of the whole system is:

$$R(t) = e^{-\lambda_V t} \sum_{k=r}^{n} \binom{n}{k} e^{-k\lambda t} \left(1 - e^{-\lambda t}\right)^{n-k}. \tag{7.22}$$

In the simple but common case of a three elements majority system with $r = 2$ (at least two elements must work), we have:

$$R(t) = e^{-\lambda_V t} e^{-2\lambda t} (3 - 2e^{-\lambda t}).$$

7.4.2. Reliability and availability of repairable systems

These systems are such that as soon as one of their components fails, the system itself or an external repair-person corrects the default after a certain amount of time. The equipment is then said to be returned to service. Here the notion of interest is the (mean) *availability*, i.e. the stationary probability of finding the system in service. The simplest example is a set of n components in total simple redundancy, on which a technician intervenes to re-establish the state with n components in service. The system alternates between *in service* and *degradated* states. The long-term proportion of time during which the system is operational, i.e. with n components active, is the availability. Availability is conventionally denoted A. Its complement, called the *unavailability* and denoted U, is also frequently used, as we will see below.

The period during which less than n elements are active is called the *degradated regime duration*. Clearly, this duration is shorter as failures are less frequent and repairs faster.

7.4.2.1. *State equations*

The process of going from state to state is nothing else than a *birth and death process*, as presented in Chapter 6. The present analysis introduces this notion in the context of reliability.

Let us denote by $i = 1, 2, \ldots, n$ the different system states, corresponding to i active elements, and let $P(i, t)$ be the probability that the system is in state i at time t. Whatever the specific structure of the system, a general basic set of equations describes the evolution of the state:

$$P(i, t + dt) = P(i + 1, t)d(i + 1, t)dt + P(i, t)\left[1 - d(i, t)dt\right]\left[1 - r(i, t)dt\right]$$
$$+ P(i - 1, t)r(i - 1, t)dt,$$

This equation translates the fact that $P(i, t + dt)$, the probability of finding the system in state i at time $(t + dt)$, is the sum of:

– the probability to be in state $(i + 1)$ at time t, and a failure has occurred, moving the system to state i in the interval dt, i.e. $d(i + 1, t)$;

– increased by the probability of being in state i at time t, i.e. $P(i, t)$, and no event has occurred during dt: no failure and no repair;

– and by the probability of being in state $(i - 1)$ at time t, $P(i - 1, t)$, and that a component has been repaired (rate $r(i - 1, t)dt$) moving to state i during the interval dt.

This holds, as the events are clearly mutually exclusive, neglecting simultaneous events (probability proportional to dt^2, see Chapter 6). The equation is transformed as follows:

$$\frac{P(i, t + dt) - P(i, t)}{dt} = P(i + 1, t)d(i + 1, t)$$
$$+ P(i - 1, t)r(i - 1, t) - P(i, t)\big[d(i, t) + r(i, t)\big].$$

Now, letting $dt \to 0$ and assuming the derivative exists, we obtain:

$$P'(i, t) = P(i + 1, t)d(i + 1, t) + P(i - 1, t)r(i - 1, t)$$
$$- P(i, t)\big[d(i, t) + r(i, t)\big]. \tag{7.23}$$

This result is quickly obtained, using Markov graphs, also called state transition diagrams, as already introduced in Chapter 6 (see Figure 7.8). As the states are mutually exclusive, we must have

$$\sum P(i, t) = 1 \quad \text{and thus} \quad \sum P'(i, t) = 0. \tag{7.24}$$

These equations must be completed by the initial conditions, i.e. the system state at $t = 0$. Generally, it is admitted that all elements are good at the origin, so that $P(n, 0) = 1$ if the system is composed with n elements and $P(i, 0) = 0$ for $i \neq 0$.

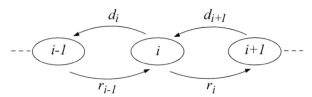

Figure 7.8. *Markov graph or state transition diagram*

Lastly, we consider generally that both the failure and repair processes are stationary: the probabilities $d(i, t)$ and $r(i, t)$ do not depend on t. The system should thus reach a state of statistical equilibrium as the time increases, characterized by the condition:

$$\lim_{t \to \infty} P'(i,t) = 0 \quad \text{for every state } i.$$

The set of these equations is a system of differential equations, which allows us to study reliability for various structures of the redundant repairable systems class.

7.4.2.2. Reliability of redundant repairable systems

We consider the same configurations as above, for non-repairable systems, and apply the method for exponentially distributed failure time and repair duration. This is in good accordance with actual observation, as explained in [FIC 04].

Simple redundancy with two elements

The system consists of two elements in parallel: if one fails, the second keeps working and the system survives.

First, let us calculate the system availability, i.e. the stationary probability of being in one of the states: one or two elements into service. For repairable systems, this is a major QoS criterion, as it reflects the availability degree from the user's viewpoint (examples concern the availability of telecommunication service for emergency calls).

As above, the state i is the one with i elements in service. Each element has a failure rate λ, so when i elements operate, the probability of any one failing is:

$$d(i,t) = i\lambda,$$

The repair process is such that failed elements are restored with a constant repair rate (one repair at one and the same time):

$$r(i,t) = \mu.$$

From the state transition diagram of Figure 7.9, we directly derive the set of differential equations:

$$P'(0,t) = \lambda P(1,t) - \mu P(0,t),$$
$$P'(1,t) = 2\lambda P(2,t) - (\lambda + \mu)P(1,t) + \mu P(0,t),$$
$$P'(2,t) = \mu P(1,t) - 2\lambda P(2,t).$$

At statistical equilibrium, probabilities $P(i,t)$ become independent of time, so that $P'(i,t) = 0$ and therefore:

$$\mu P_0 = \lambda P_1,$$
$$(\lambda + \mu)P_1 = \mu P_0 + 2\lambda P_2,$$
$$2\lambda P_2 = \mu P_1,$$

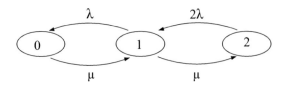

Figure 7.9. *Simple redundancy with two elements*

which yields:

$$P_1 = \frac{2\lambda}{\mu} P_2, \quad P_0 = \left(\frac{2\lambda}{\mu}\right)\left(\frac{\lambda}{\mu}\right) P_2.$$

Adding the condition: $P_0 + P_1 + P_2 = 1$, we obtain:

$$P_2 = \frac{1}{1 + \frac{2\lambda}{\mu} + \frac{2\lambda^2}{\mu^2}}, \quad P_1 = \frac{\frac{2\lambda}{\mu}}{1 + \frac{2\lambda}{\mu} + \frac{2\lambda^2}{\mu^2}}, \quad P_0 = \frac{\frac{2\lambda^2}{\mu^2}}{1 + \frac{2\lambda}{\mu} + \frac{2\lambda^2}{\mu^2}}. \qquad (7.25)$$

The state associated with P_0 corresponds to the breakdown of the system. Hence, the system availability A, from a service viewpoint, is given by:

$$A = 1 - P_0.$$

Therefore:

$$A = \frac{\mu^2 + 2\lambda\mu}{\mu^2 + 2\lambda\mu + 2\lambda^2}. \qquad (7.26)$$

In practice, the level of quality is such that the availability is close to unity (see below). The characterization is preferably performed by the system unavailability, denoted as U, expressed in the form 10^{-x}.

Obviously, $U = 1 - A = P_0$.

Given the relative magnitude of λ (between 10^{-4}/h and 10^{-6}/h, i.e. MTBF of several years), and of μ (0.1 or 0.2 per hour, i.e. repair times of a few hours), we can simplify the above expressions. It results that:

$$U = P_0 \approx \frac{2\lambda^2}{\mu^2}.$$

Often the repair procedures are such that the system, when down, will directly switch to the full availability state. The state transition diagram is then represented in Figure 7.10.

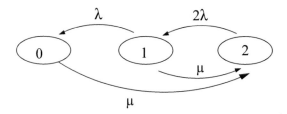

Figure 7.10. *Redundancy with return to total service*

From the diagram, we may directly write the following equations:

$$\mu P_0 = \lambda P_1,$$

$$(\lambda + \mu)P_1 = 2\lambda P_2,$$

$$2\lambda P_2 = \mu P_1 + \mu P_0.$$

which, combined with $P_0 + P_1 + P_2 = 1$, yields:

$$P_2 = \frac{1}{1 + \frac{2\lambda}{\lambda+\mu} + \frac{2\lambda^2}{\mu(\lambda+\mu)}},$$

$$P_1 = \frac{\frac{2\lambda}{\lambda+\mu}}{1 + \frac{2\lambda}{\lambda+\mu} + \frac{2\lambda^2}{\mu(\lambda+\mu)}},$$

$$P_0 = \frac{\frac{2\lambda^2}{\mu(\lambda+\mu)}}{1 + \frac{2\lambda}{\lambda+\mu} + \frac{2\lambda^2}{\mu(\lambda+\mu)}},$$

thus:

$$P_0 = \frac{2\lambda^2}{3\lambda\mu + \mu^2 + 2\lambda^2}, \qquad (7.27)$$

and finally:

$$A = \frac{3\lambda\mu + \mu^2}{3\lambda\mu + \mu^2 + 2\lambda^2}. \qquad (7.28)$$

Referring once again to the orders of magnitude, as here again $\mu \gg \lambda$, the unavailability is approximately:

$$U = P_0 \approx \frac{2\lambda^2}{\mu^2}.$$

From a practical viewpoint, the two models are equivalent.

k out of n elements redundancy. We consider here the system k out of n already discussed, assuming repairable elements. The system is considered as working correctly as long as k (at least) elements are operational.

We take account of the previous remarks about the practical equivalence between the repair procedures, and we only address the simply repairable case. The state transition diagram is represented in Figure 7.11.

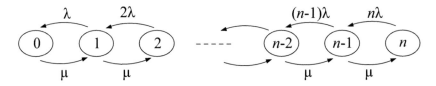

Figure 7.11. *k out of n elements redundancy*

From the diagram, we then easily derive the following relationships between the state probabilities:

$$P_{n-1} = \frac{n\lambda}{\mu} P_n,$$

$$P_{n-2} = \frac{n\lambda}{\mu} \frac{(n-1)\lambda}{\mu} P_n = \frac{n!\lambda^2}{(n-2)!\mu^2} P_n,$$

and more generally:

$$P_{n-i} = \frac{n!}{(n-i)!} \cdot \left(\frac{\lambda}{\mu}\right)^{n-i} P_n, \tag{7.29}$$

which may also be written:

$$P_j = \frac{n!}{j!} \cdot \left(\frac{\lambda}{\mu}\right)^{n-j} P_n,$$

and thus, for a k out of n redundant system,

$$A = \sum_{j=k}^{n} P_j, \quad U = \sum_{j=0}^{k-1} P_j.$$

Taking account of the current orders of magnitude once more, we obtain:

$$U \approx P_{k-1} \approx \frac{n!}{(k-1)!} \left(\frac{\lambda}{\mu}\right)^{n-k+1}. \tag{7.30}$$

Many real redundant systems consist of n elements, with only one of them as a spare. For instance, it will be a case of many processors sharing the load, or even performing different functions, with a standby processor, able to replace any other that fails.

For this type of system we then have $k = n - 1$. Thus:

$$U \approx P_{n-2} \approx n(n-1)\frac{\lambda^2}{\mu^2}.$$

NOTE. This kind of system is often called $n + 1$-redundant. The expression for U becomes:

$$U \approx (n+1)n\frac{\lambda^2}{\mu^2},$$

which is just a question of notation.

Sequential systems. Sequential systems are such that a single element is working while the other elements are all waiting in readiness to replace it in case of failure. This organization is called *standby redundancy*. The failure rate for all the states is:

$$d(i,t) = \lambda,$$

and the transition diagram is given in Figure 7.12, for the case of two elements.

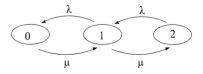

Figure 7.12. *Sequential redundancy*

We easily derive the following relationships:

$$\mu P_0 = \lambda P_1,$$
$$(\lambda + \mu)P_1 = \mu P_0 + \lambda P_2,$$
$$\lambda P_2 = \mu P_1,$$
$$P_0 + P_1 + P_2 = 1,$$

and thus:

$$A = \frac{\mu^2 + \lambda\mu}{\mu^2 + \lambda\mu + \lambda^2}. \tag{7.31}$$

Hence for the unavailability:

$$U = P_0 = \frac{\frac{\lambda^2}{\mu^2}}{1 + \frac{\lambda}{\mu} + \frac{\lambda^2}{\mu^2}}. \tag{7.32}$$

That is, given the orders of magnitude:

$$U \approx \frac{\lambda^2}{\mu^2}.$$

Such a redundant organization lowers unavailability, as can be expected since the standby unit is activated only if needed. However, its weakness is that all tasks in progress (call set-up, packet forwarding, etc.) are lost upon a failure of the active unit, as the spare unit does not process them in parallel. Furthermore, the general case of n elements with one spare element (type $n + 1$ redundancy) gives for the unavailability:

$$U \approx n^2 \frac{\lambda^2}{\mu^2},$$

which is not significantly different from the unavailability for simple redundancy, i.e. $U \approx n(n + 1)\frac{\lambda^2}{\mu^2}$, as soon as n is large enough.

That kind of organization generally does not apply for the hardware part of telecommunication equipment, as all elements, including standby elements, are permanently powered on and thus subject to failures. On the other hand, this model is quite well suited to software, as in the case of passive redundancy (see below), where the software modules are executed only when the element carrying them becomes active.

7.4.2.3. *Imperfect structures*

This term stands for systems with imperfections at the defence mechanism level. In most cases, defence mechanisms are very simple. Moreover, the usual orders of magnitude, as we have already noted, justify the application of simple and tractable models. However, we must always keep in mind certain critical aspects of real systems, and especially the imperfect nature of defence mechanisms. Therefore, we have to deal with structures, simple in their principles, but very much imperfect in reality. This leads to more complex models, as reliability modeling must take these imperfections into account.

This gives us the opportunity to summarize the major structures of redundant systems. Aside from the type of the structure: simple or partial redundancy, majority voting, etc., we have to distinguish between *passive* (or *standby*) redundancy and the *active* (or *static*) redundancy.

Passive redundancy. Elements in standby are activated only in case of failure. This type of redundancy is referred to as *dynamic*, as it implies a real time switching operation from standby to active state.

Active redundancy. All the components, those in use as well as those for redundancy, are simultaneously active. There is no explicit switching operation when a failure occurs, and we refer to this as static redundancy.

All these redundancy modes are widely in use in communication systems in order to ensure high service availability. The whole set of hardware and software resources implied constitute the defence mechanisms. They include all the decision processes associated with fault detection, isolation of the faulty element and traffic redirection to the working elements. Unfortunately, all these mechanisms are generally imperfect.

The following example, typical of a real system, serves to address these aspects of reliability.

Redundant structure with silent failure. In this system, the spare component is in passive redundancy and the detection mechanism is imperfect. Failure rates of both the active component and the spare component are identical (the common situation in telecommunication systems, although the analysis is easily generalized).

We assume that every fault in the active element is detected (a reasonable assumption, as the default appears rapidly at the application level). On the other hand, we will denote as c the coverage coefficient, which measures the efficiency of the detection mechanism in the passive element: this is the percentage of failures actually detected, for instance by periodic tests.

Lastly, we assume the probability of two successive failures in the passive element going undetected to be negligible. The state transition diagram is given in Figure 7.13.

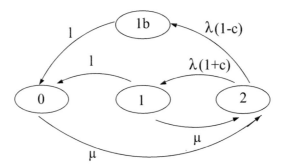

Figure 7.13. *Redundancy with silent failure*

State "1" corresponds to the failure of the active element, or a detected failure of the passive one. State "1b" follows an undetected failure of the passive element so that the system passes from state "1b" to state "0" upon the failure of the active element. We then derive the following system of equations:

$$\mu P_0 = \lambda P_1 + \lambda P_{1b},$$

$$(\lambda + \mu) P_1 = \lambda(1 + c) P_2,$$

$$\lambda P_{1b} = \lambda(1 - c) P_2,$$

$$\lambda P_2 = \mu P_0 + \mu P_1,$$

$$P_0 + P_1 + P_{1b} + P_2 = 1,$$

and thus with $A = 1 - P_0$,

$$A = \frac{3\lambda\mu + 2\mu^2 - c\mu^2}{4\lambda\mu - \lambda c\mu + 2\mu^2 - c\mu^2 + 2\lambda^2}. \tag{7.33}$$

For $c = 1$, we obtain the same results as for the system without any silent failure:

$$A = \frac{3\lambda\mu + \mu^2}{3\lambda\mu + \mu^2 + 2\lambda^2}.$$

It is worthwhile attempting to improve our understanding of the contribution of the coverage coefficient c. For this, let us take the expression of unavailability $U = 1 - A$:

$$U = \frac{\lambda\mu - \lambda c\mu + 2\lambda^2}{4\lambda\mu - \lambda c\mu + 2\mu^2 - c\mu^2 + 2\lambda^2}. \tag{7.34}$$

Then, observing that in practice (see [FIC 04]), we have $\mu \gg \lambda$,

$$U \approx \frac{\lambda\mu(1 - c) + 2\lambda^2}{\mu^2(2 - c)}.$$

So: when $c \to 1$, $U \approx \frac{2\lambda^2}{\mu^2}$ and for $c \to 0$, $U \approx \frac{\lambda}{2\mu}$.

Clearly, the effect of the coverage factor on unavailability is considerable (it goes from a linear dependency to a quadratic dependency).

7.4.3. *Using Laplace transform*

Up to now, our concern has been the availability of repairable systems. Let us now estimate the reliability of these systems. Here we look for the time-dependent probability to be in the different states, given that the system stops operating as soon as it reaches the state of total failure – state 0, where there is no possible repair. As previously, the system behavior is modeled by a system of differential equations.

However, instead of statistical equilibrium state probabilities, we are now interested in the time-dependent state probabilities.

An example demonstrates how the Laplace transform can help in solving the problem. Again we take the configuration with two elements in simple redundancy. Figure 7.14 gives the state transition diagram.

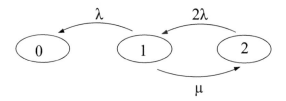

Figure 7.14. *Simple redundancy (reliability)*

The corresponding equations are:

$$P'(0,t) = \lambda P(1,t),$$
$$P'(1,t) = 2\lambda P(2,t) - (\lambda + \mu)P(1,t),$$
$$P'(2,t) = \mu P(1,t) - 2\lambda P(2,t).$$

Let us denote as $F^*(s)$ the Laplace transform of $f(t)$. Remember that:

$$F^*(s) = \int_{0-}^{\infty} f(t)e^{-st}\mathrm{d}t.$$

This relationship is symbolized by:

$$f(t) \Longleftrightarrow F^*(s).$$

We also have:

$$\frac{\mathrm{d}f(t)}{\mathrm{d}t} \Longleftrightarrow sF^*(s) - f(0),$$

$$\int_{0-}^{\infty} f(t)\mathrm{d}t \Longleftrightarrow \frac{F^*(s)}{s},$$

and in particular for the exponential function:

$$Ae^{-at} \Longleftrightarrow \frac{A}{s+a},$$

and for the unit step function:

$$\mu(t) \Longleftrightarrow \frac{1}{s}.$$

Now, let us apply the Laplace transform to the above set of differential equations and, for the sake of simplicity, let P_i^* denote the transform of $P(i, t)$.

We first determine the initial conditions. Assuming (logically) that all the elements are good at time $t = 0$, we have for the initial states: $P_2(0) = 1$, $P_1(0) = P_0(0) = 0$.

Then the application of the Laplace transform combined with the above result yields the following set of linear equations:

$$sP_0^* = \lambda P_1^*,$$
$$sP_1^* = 2\lambda P_2^* - (\lambda + \mu)P_1^*,$$
$$sP_2^* - 1 = \mu P_1^* - 2\lambda P_2^*.$$

This gives:

$$P_0^* = \frac{2\lambda^2}{s(s^2 + s(3\lambda + \mu) + 2\lambda^2)}, \tag{7.35}$$

or, if a_1 and a_2 are the denominator roots:

$$P_0^* = \frac{2\lambda^2}{s(s - a_1)(s - a_2)},$$

with

$$a_1 = \frac{-(3\lambda + \mu) + \sqrt{\lambda^2 + \mu^2 + 6\lambda\mu}}{2}, \quad a_2 = \frac{-(3\lambda + \mu) - \sqrt{\lambda^2 + \mu^2 + 6\lambda\mu}}{2}.$$

Then, observing that:

$$\frac{1}{(s - a_1)(s - a_2)} = \frac{1}{a_1 - a_2}\left(\frac{1}{s - a_1} - \frac{1}{s - a_2}\right),$$

and that we can decompose $\frac{1}{s(s-a)} = \frac{1}{a}\left(\frac{1}{s-a} - \frac{1}{s}\right)$, we obtain:

$$\frac{1}{s(s - a_1)(s - a_2)} = \frac{1}{a_1 - a_2}\left[\frac{1}{a_1}\left(\frac{1}{s - a_1} - \frac{1}{s}\right) - \frac{1}{a_2}\left(\frac{1}{s - a_2} - \frac{1}{s}\right)\right],$$

This result returns us to the original (untransformed) function:

$$P(0, t) = \frac{2\lambda^2}{a_1 - a_2}\left(\frac{e^{a_1 t}}{a_1} - \frac{1}{a_1} - \frac{e^{a_2 t}}{a_2} + \frac{1}{a_2}\right).$$

This result is combined with: $a_1 a_2 = 2\lambda^2$, yielding:

$$P(0,t) = 1 - \frac{a_1 e^{a_2 t} - a_2 e^{a_1 t}}{a_1 - a_2}. \tag{7.36}$$

So finally the reliability function is:

$$R(t) = \frac{a_1 e^{a_2 t} - a_2 e^{a_1 t}}{a_1 - a_2}, \tag{7.37}$$

and the MTBF:

$$\theta = \int_0^\infty R(t) \mathrm{d}t = -\frac{a_1 + a_2}{a_1 a_2},$$

or,

$$\theta = \frac{3\lambda + \mu}{2\lambda^2}. \tag{7.38}$$

This last result could of course be easily obtained directly from the diagram as seen in section 7.4.2, but not the expression of $R(t)$ as a function of t.

This example clearly shows the power of the method, but also that its application to complex systems rapidly becomes tedious. We explain in the next section how to numerically analyze certain aspects of complex systems by means of matrix methods. However, whatever the approach, approximations are most often mandatory in order to derive explicit results, especially when retrieving the original function. This emphasizes the importance of being able to detect states with negligible probability, even for availability at statistical equilibrium.

7.4.4. *Use of matrices*

In order to estimate the reliability – or the unavailability – we have proceeded, up to now, by directly solving the system of differential equations derived from the state transition diagram. Another approach is to represent the system in its matrix form and then to solve, either analytically or numerically, the matrix equation through appropriate software tools.

For instance, let us reconsider the case of two elements in simple redundancy, as already studied in section 7.4.2.2. Starting from the graph shown in Figure 7.14 we obtain the equations:

$$P'(0,t) = \lambda P(1,t)$$
$$P'(1,t) = 2\lambda P(2,t) - (\lambda + \mu)P(1,t)$$
$$P'(2,t) = \mu P(1,t) - 2\lambda P(2,t)$$

Writing these equations in matrix form, the system reduces to a single matrix equation, as follows:

$$\begin{bmatrix} P'(0,t) \\ P'(1,t) \\ P'(2,t) \end{bmatrix} = \begin{bmatrix} 0 & \lambda & 0 \\ 0 & -(\lambda+\mu) & 2\lambda \\ 0 & \mu & -2\lambda \end{bmatrix} \begin{bmatrix} P(0,t) \\ P(1,t) \\ P(2,t) \end{bmatrix}$$

The equation which may also be directly derived from the graph, since the matrix coefficients a_{ij} (index i stands for rows and j for columns) are merely the transition rates from state i to state j.

Let us now consider the duration T of the first time period (cycle) leading to the system down state. The integration of the matrix equation from 0 to T yields:

$$\int_0^T P'(i,t)\mathrm{d}t = P(i,T) - P(i,0),$$

and also: $\int_0^T P(i,t)\mathrm{d}t = T_i$, average time spent in state i.

Then, integrating the equation yields the following very general matrix relationship:

$$\begin{bmatrix} P(0,T) - P(0,0) \\ P(1,T) - P(1,0) \\ P(2,T) - P(2,0) \end{bmatrix} = [\Lambda] \begin{bmatrix} T_0 \\ T_1 \\ T_2 \end{bmatrix}, \tag{7.39}$$

where $[\Lambda]$ denotes the transition rates matrix.

Now, taking account of the initial conditions, we obtain for our example:

$$\begin{bmatrix} 1-0 \\ 0-0 \\ 0-1 \end{bmatrix} = \begin{bmatrix} 1 \\ 0 \\ -1 \end{bmatrix} = [\Lambda] \begin{bmatrix} T_0 \\ T_1 \\ T_2 \end{bmatrix},$$

whose resolution, through the corresponding system of equations, gives:

$$T_2 = \frac{\lambda+\mu}{2\lambda^2}, \quad \text{and} \quad T_1 = \frac{1}{\lambda}.$$

The average time up to the down state, i.e. the MTBF, is merely the sum of T_2 and T_1, thus:

$$\theta = \frac{3\lambda+\mu}{2\lambda^2}. \tag{7.40}$$

This is the same result as already obtained in equation (7.38). The main advantage of this approach is that it offers the possibility of numerically solving the matrix system (exact solution by matrix inversion, or approximate methods, such as Euler or Runge-Kutta methods). This is especially attractive for complex systems with a large number of states and equations. We now present this kind of resolution.

7.4.4.1. *Exact resolution by inversion*

Before exploring an illustrative example, we briefly recall the method of inverse matrices.

Let us call I the set of initial states, and T the unknown average durations in the different states. From the previous general matrix equation (7.39) we have:

$$[I] = [\Lambda][T],$$

and then:

$$[T] = [\Lambda]^{-1}[I],$$

provided that the inverse matrix exists, which fortunately is the case for most practical applications. Furthermore, in our problems, matrices are also generally square matrices and thus regular (every matrix that may be inverted is regular).

There are essentially two methods for matrix inversion: the direct *determinant method* and the *triangulation*, or *Gaussian elimination*. Although it requires more calculations, let us recall the simple determinant method, as it allows us to refresh all the basic notions concerning matrices:

– permute rows and columns,

– replace each element by its cofactor,

– divide by the determinant.

Of course, the method applies equally well to availability as to reliability calculation, and we now describe an example of application in the case of statistical equilibrium.

First, let us recall how to obtain the determinant of a matrix. The determinant associated with a matrix A of elements ($i = $ row, $j = $ column) is defined by (expanding for instance with respect to the first row):,

$$\det(A) = |A| = \sum_j (-1)^{j+1} \det\left(A_{1,j}\right) \tag{7.41}$$

where $A_{1,j}$ is the submatrix of A, and $\det(A_{1,j})$ the cofactor of $a_{1,j}$, obtained when the first row and the jth column are deleted. For instance, for the basic case of a four term matrix, we have:

$$|A| = \begin{vmatrix} a_{1,1} & a_{1,2} \\ a_{2,1} & a_{2,2} \end{vmatrix} = a_{1,1}a_{2,2} - a_{2,1}a_{1,2}.$$

Then for a nine term matrix we have:

$$|A| = \begin{vmatrix} a_{1,1} & a_{1,2} & a_{1,3} \\ a_{2,1} & a_{2,2} & a_{2,3} \\ a_{3,1} & a_{3,2} & a_{3,3} \end{vmatrix} = a_{1,1} \begin{vmatrix} a_{2,2} & a_{2,3} \\ a_{3,2} & a_{3,3} \end{vmatrix} - a_{1,2} \begin{vmatrix} a_{2,1} & a_{2,3} \\ a_{3,1} & a_{3,3} \end{vmatrix} + a_{1,3} \begin{vmatrix} a_{2,1} & a_{2,2} \\ a_{3,1} & a_{3,2} \end{vmatrix}$$

Now, let us reconsider the case of a redundant repairable system composed of two elements, as in section 7.4.2.2. We have (see Figure 7.9):

$$P'(0,t) = \lambda P(1,t) - \mu P(0,t),$$
$$P'(1,t) = 2\lambda P(2,t) - (\lambda + \mu)P(1,t) + \mu P(0,t),$$
$$P'(2,t) = \mu P(1,t) - 2\lambda P(2,t),$$

and of course the conservation condition:

$$\sum_i P(i,t) = 1.$$

This set of equations may be written:

$$\begin{bmatrix} 1 \\ P'(0,t) \\ P'(1,t) \\ P'(2,t) \end{bmatrix} = \begin{bmatrix} 1 & 1 & 1 \\ -\mu & \lambda & 0 \\ \mu & -(\lambda + \mu) & 2\lambda \\ 0 & \mu & -2\lambda \end{bmatrix} \begin{bmatrix} P(0,t) \\ P(1,t) \\ P(2,t) \end{bmatrix}.$$

In steady state, or statistical equilibrium, the state probabilities are independent of time and derivatives are equal to zero, then we have:

$$\begin{bmatrix} 1 \\ 0 \\ 0 \\ 0 \end{bmatrix} = [\Lambda] \begin{bmatrix} P_0 \\ P_1 \\ P_2 \end{bmatrix}, \quad \text{with} \quad [\Lambda] = \begin{bmatrix} 1 & 1 & 1 \\ -\mu & \lambda & 0 \\ \mu & -(\lambda + \mu) & 2\lambda \\ 0 & \mu & -2\lambda \end{bmatrix}.$$

Furthermore, we can easily verify that only two out of the three initial equations are independent. Thus, deleting for instance the last row (note that this is the sum of the two preceding rows), the system reduces to:

$$\begin{bmatrix} 1 \\ 0 \\ 0 \end{bmatrix} = [\Lambda] \begin{bmatrix} P_0 \\ P_1 \\ P_2 \end{bmatrix}, \quad \text{with} \quad [\Lambda] = \begin{bmatrix} 1 & 1 & 1 \\ -\mu & \lambda & 0 \\ \mu & -(\lambda + \mu) & 2\lambda \end{bmatrix},$$

the determinant of which is:

$$|\Lambda| = 1 \times \begin{vmatrix} \lambda & 0 \\ -(\lambda + \mu) & 2\lambda \end{vmatrix} - 1 \times \begin{vmatrix} -\mu & 0 \\ \mu & 2\lambda \end{vmatrix} + 1 \times \begin{vmatrix} -\mu & \lambda \\ \mu & -(\lambda + \mu) \end{vmatrix},$$

that is: $|\Lambda| = 2\lambda^2 + 2\lambda\mu + \mu^2$.

Now we transpose the matrix:

$$[\Lambda]^T = \begin{bmatrix} 1 & -\mu & \mu \\ 1 & \lambda & -(\lambda + \mu) \\ 1 & 0 & 2\lambda \end{bmatrix}.$$

Then, replacing each term by its cofactor, we obtain the cofactor matrix $[\Lambda]^C$:

$$[\Lambda]^C = \begin{bmatrix} \begin{vmatrix} \lambda & -(\lambda + \mu) \\ 0 & 2\lambda \end{vmatrix} & -\begin{vmatrix} 1 & -(\lambda + \mu) \\ 1 & 2\lambda \end{vmatrix} & \begin{vmatrix} 1 & \lambda \\ 1 & 0 \end{vmatrix} \\ -\begin{vmatrix} -\mu & \mu \\ 0 & 2\lambda \end{vmatrix} & \begin{vmatrix} 1 & \mu \\ 1 & 2\lambda \end{vmatrix} & -\begin{vmatrix} 1 & -\mu \\ 1 & \lambda \end{vmatrix} \\ \begin{vmatrix} -\mu & \mu \\ \lambda & -(\lambda + \mu) \end{vmatrix} & -\begin{vmatrix} 1 & \mu \\ 1 & -(\lambda + \mu) \end{vmatrix} & \begin{vmatrix} 1 & -\mu \\ 1 & \lambda \end{vmatrix} \end{bmatrix},$$

or:

$$[\Lambda]^C = \begin{bmatrix} 2\lambda^2 & -(3\lambda + \mu) & -\lambda \\ 2\lambda\mu & 2\lambda - \mu & -\mu \\ \mu^2 & \lambda + 2\mu & \lambda + \mu \end{bmatrix}.$$

Finally, dividing by the determinant:

$$\begin{bmatrix} P_0 \\ P_1 \\ P_2 \end{bmatrix} = \frac{1}{|\Lambda|} [\Lambda]^C \begin{bmatrix} 1 \\ 0 \\ 0 \end{bmatrix}.$$

We obtain:

$$P_0 = \frac{2\lambda^2}{\mu^2 + 2\lambda\mu + 2\lambda^2}, \quad P_1 = \frac{2\lambda\mu}{\mu^2 + 2\lambda\mu + 2\lambda^2}, \quad P_2 = \frac{\mu^2}{\mu^2 + 2\lambda\mu + 2\lambda^2}.$$

These are obviously the results already obtained. As mentioned before, these calculations are attractive only because they can be automated, allowing numerical resolutions of complex systems.

We can find numerous mathematical packages that perform such calculations. They make use of methods demanding less run time, such as Gaussian elimination.

7.4.4.2. *Approximate solutions*

These methods are especially suited to evaluate such quantities as reliability at a given time t (as we have seen with Laplace transforms). Indeed, they operate directly on the differential system and seek the solution iteratively. The two major methods are the Euler and Runge-Kutta methods, both being based upon the same principle. The Runge-Kutta method is clearly the most precise, at the price of more extensive calculations. Here too, numerous software packages implement these methods.

We recall here the basic principle through the presentation of the Euler method. We are given the equation $y' = f(x, y)$, with the initial conditions x_0, y_0. We seek a solution in the interval $[x_0, x]$. The interval is decomposed into elementary sub-intervals $[x_{n-1}, x_n]$, and for each interval boundary, we write $y_n = y_{n-1} + f(x_{n-1}, y_{n-1}) \times (x_n - x_{n-1})$, beginning from the initial point $y_1 = y_0 + f(x_0, y_0)(x_1 - x_0)$, and going step by step up to the target point x.

This amounts to approximating the curve f by its tangent at x_i (actually we write $y_1' = (y_1 - y_0)/(x_1 - x_0)$). This is the Euler method. The precision depends on the increment, and the error accumulates on each step from 0 to the target x. The Runge-Kutta method proceeds the same way, stepwise, except that at each point it uses a Taylor development, generally of the fourth order (note that the Euler method requires no more than the use of a Taylor series of order 1, see the Appendix). This increases the precision, at the expense of processing time. For a Runge-Kutta of order 4, we have the following formulae:

$$y_n = y_{n-1} + \frac{1}{6}\left(k_0 + 2k_1 + 2k_2 + k_3\right),$$

with

$$k_0 = hf\left(x_{n-1}, y_{n-1}\right),$$

$$k_1 = hf\left(x_{n-1} + \frac{h}{2}, y_{n-1} + \frac{k_0}{2}\right),$$

$$k_2 = hf\left(x_{n-1} + \frac{h}{2}, y_{n-1} + \frac{k_1}{2}\right),$$

$$k_3 = hf\left(x_{n-1} + h, y_{n-1} + k_2\right), \quad h = x_n - x_{n-1}.$$

7.5. Software reliability

Software reliability raises several specific issues, and we detail some of them in this section. We must first stress the importance of this point, as software complexity keeps increasing with the development of the services and becomes a major factor in system dependability.

The analysis of software reliability proceeds in a similar way to that presented for hardware, and several notable behaviors may be distinguished: reliability growth and constant failure rate. The phenomenon is complex but two main periods may nonetheless be identified. During the developing and debugging period, the reliability grows as errors are detected and corrected. Then, during the operational (or useful life period), an almost constant failure rate is observed. More exactly, successive periods are observed, with the failure rate increasing, then decreasing and remaining constant.

For telecommunication products, this corresponds to the introduction of new releases, which introduce corrections and new services, but also bring with them new early-life defaults. Furthermore, despite the continuous correction effort during the test and operational phases, a certain number of defaults are likely to remain, associated with quite specific operating conditions, and this will be tolerated. That is the reason why our focus will be on redundancy which, as we will see, tolerates most of these defaults, and our effort will be concentrated in eliminating those faults which provoke the total breakdown of the system.

Finally, we do not observe any wear out period, at least for terrestrial equipments, as these products are generally replaced before reaching this phase.

7.5.1. *Reliability growth model, early-life period*

We are concerned here with the reliability increase related to the progressive correction of the residual defaults in the system. Note that we address this issue in the context of software reliability, but this is a global characteristic for both hardware and software components of communication systems, where new releases are permanently issued, and similar considerations may apply to hardware as well as to software.

Numerous reliability increase models have been proposed: Jelinski-Moranda, Shooman, Musa, Littlewood-Verral, etc. Musa's model seems the best suited to the cases we have in mind.

Let N_0 be the number of errors (defaults) remaining at $t = 0$, and $n(\tau)$ the number of errors corrected at date $t = \tau$, then we have:

$$\lambda(\tau) = K\left[N_0 - n(\tau)\right] \tag{7.42}$$

where K is a proportionality constant which relates error exposure frequency to code linear execution frequency (no error can occur as long as no code is executed, as already explained).

Assuming that no new errors are spawned in the error correction process, the error correction rate will be equal to the error exposure rate. Then we have:

$$\frac{dn}{d\tau} = \lambda(\tau), \tag{7.43}$$

which, combined with the relationship above, yields:

$$n(\tau) = N_0\left(1 - e^{-K\tau}\right) \tag{7.44}$$

and the MTTF, average up to the next fault occurrence (following the default exposure), is:

$$T = \frac{1}{\lambda(\tau)} = \frac{1}{K N_0} \exp(K\tau),$$

or, introducing $T_0 = \frac{1}{K N_0}$:

$$T = T_0 \exp\left(\frac{\tau}{N_0 T_0}\right). \tag{7.45}$$

Obviously, the MTTF increases with time, up to the useful lifetime period where it is approximately constant, although a certain amount of variability remains (related, as explained, to the introduction of new releases).

This expression allows us to estimate the duration of the early-life period and the failure risks during this period. For instance, the MTTF is multiplied by 3 after a time τ in the order of $N_0 T_0$ (i.e. N_0 times the initial MTTF when the equipment is brought into service) and by 10 for a period 2.3 times longer, in accordance with the exponential distribution. Practice shows that often a new system reaches its operational (useful life) period when its initial MTTF has been multiplied by 3. If we denote as θ the MTBF (now equal to the MTTF) of the equipment during its useful-life period, the early-life duration is then $\tau = (N_0/3)\theta$. This emphasizes the impact of residual errors on system reliability.

7.5.2. *Useful-life period model*

Here the goal is to measure the impact of failures due to residual software errors on the system availability. During the useful-life period, the software failure rate is assumed as being constant: the system is assumed stable, the last version has been delivered and the early-life defaults have been corrected.

The effect of the failures related with software assumes an increasing importance. However, most of the residual defaults lead to failures which are quite easy to recover, thanks to the defence mechanisms such as *hot restarts*. To illustrate this, let us analyze a simple example of the relative influence of the three failure categories: software defaults said to be *recoverable* simply by restarting the failed machine, *severe* defaults, giving rise to a full system reset using remote elements, and lastly hardware failures calling for human intervention.

Consider a system composed of two elements in passive redundancy. The master component can break down, due to hardware or software failure. The passive element cannot breakdown, except due to hardware cause, as it executes no code (or hardly any code: for instance, a test routine).

For software failures, we distinguish those recoverable through an automatic system restart, from those, called "severe", asking for human intervention.

The two components being in operation, upon a recoverable software fault in the active element, the system switches the control to the standby component, which becomes active. Then, quasi-instantaneously, the system returns to normal operation (two elements in order of service), the faulty one being rapidly and automatically reloaded (by replication from the other, for instance). This transition is absolutely negligible from the perspective of unavailability.

If after a switching on the standby element due to a non-recoverable or hardware fault (ie. with only one element in service) a recoverable software default is detected, the system (out of service) is reset by automatically reloading from a remote site. The duration of this operation is non-negligible but still moderate compared to human intervention in the case of equipment replacement.

Let us denote by:

$- \lambda_h$ the hardware failure rate,

$- \lambda_{ss}$ the severe software failure rate, i.e. which cannot be repaired by an automatic restart of the station (this is equivalent to an hardware failure),

$- \lambda_{sr}$ the recoverable software failure rate: failures recoverable through automatic restarts of the station. This operation is almost instantaneous if replication from the other element is possible; otherwise, the re-initialization lasts a few minutes,

$- \mu_h$ the hardware repair rate, corresponding to an intervention duration of a few hours,

$- \mu_r$ the reset rate, corresponding to a reset duration of a few minutes.

Let us take:

• $\lambda_1 = \lambda_h + \lambda_{ss}$,
• $\lambda_2 = 2\lambda_h + \lambda_{ss}$,
• $\lambda_3 = \lambda_{sr}$.

The state diagram is represented in Figure 7.15.

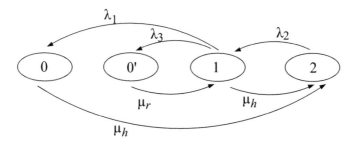

Figure 7.15. *Redundancy with software failures*

The set of equations is:

$$\lambda_2 P_2 = \mu_h (P_1 + P_0),$$

$$(\lambda_1 + \lambda_3 + \mu_h) P_1 = \lambda_2 P_2 + \mu_r P_0,$$

$$\mu_h P_0 = \lambda_1 P_1,$$

$$\mu_r P_{0'} = \lambda_3 P_1,$$

$$P_0 + P_{0'} + P_1 + P_2 = 1.$$

The system of equations being redundant, we discard one of them, for example, the second, and we derive:

$$P_0 = \frac{\frac{\lambda_1}{\mu_h}}{1 + \frac{\lambda_1}{\mu_h} + \frac{\lambda_3}{\mu_r} + \frac{\lambda_1 + \mu_h}{\lambda_2}}, \tag{7.46}$$

$$P_{0'} = \frac{\frac{\lambda_3}{\mu_r}}{1 + \frac{\lambda_1}{\mu_h} + \frac{\lambda_3}{\mu_r} + \frac{\lambda_1 + \mu_h}{\lambda_2}}. \tag{7.47}$$

Such expressions clearly show the importance of recoverable software failures (terms in the order of λ_3 / μ_r).

Indeed, the availability of the system is $A = 1 - (P_0 + P_{0'})$:

$$A = \frac{1 + \frac{\lambda_1 + \mu_h}{\lambda_2}}{1 + \frac{\lambda_1}{\mu_h} + \frac{\lambda_3}{\mu_r} + \frac{\lambda_1 + \mu_h}{\lambda_2}},$$

which may also be written as:

$$A = \frac{(\lambda_2 + \lambda_1) \mu_h \mu_r + \mu_h^2 \mu_r}{(\lambda_2 + \lambda_1) \mu_h \mu_r + \mu_h^2 \mu_r + \lambda_2 \lambda_1 \mu_r + \lambda_2 \lambda_3 \mu_h}. \tag{7.48}$$

We can first verify that, suppressing the possibility of software faults ($\lambda_3 = 0$ and $\lambda_2 = 2\lambda_1$ in the first expression of A above), we again find the basic system.

Using unavailability makes visualizing the impact of the software failure rate more straightforward:

$$U = \frac{\lambda_2 \lambda_1 \mu_r + \lambda_2 \lambda_3 \mu_h}{(\lambda_2 + \lambda_1) \mu_h \mu_r + \mu_h^2 \mu_r + \lambda_2 \lambda_1 \mu_r + \lambda_2 \lambda_3 \mu_h}. \tag{7.49}$$

When severe software failures are in the majority and recoverable software failures are negligible ($\lambda_3 = 0$), we have:

$$U \approx \frac{\lambda_1 \lambda_2}{\mu_h^2},$$

with the system behaving just as if the hardware failure rate had worsened.

When severe software failures are negligible, which is the case if the defence mechanisms operate correctly: $\lambda_2 = 2\lambda_1 = 2\lambda_h$, and so:

$$U \approx \frac{2\lambda_h^2}{\mu_h^2} + \frac{2\lambda_h \lambda_{sr}}{\mu_h \mu_r}.$$

The impact of re-initializations is relatively moderate, as μ_r is much lower than μ_h. For instance, with a reset duration 10 times shorter than the human intervention, and software failure rates twice as large as hardware failure rates, unavailability is increased by only 20%. This clearly shows the importance of implementing efficient defence mechanisms.

7.6. Spare parts calculation

This section is devoted to evaluating the quantity of spare parts to be provided for maintenance, in order to guarantee a given *stock-out probability* (*shortage*). This is another important component of QoS, as it helps to quantify maintenance costs for the operator. Note also that stock shortage can severely impact service availability, especially if *restocking delays* turn out to be non-negligible (a point which absolutely must be checked).

7.6.1. *Definitions*

Call N the total amount of equipment in the district to be secured by the spare parts store. Only the case of identical components is considered. Let P_s denote the stock-out probability (probability of stock shortage), λ the component failure rate and μ the restocking rate (this rate corresponds to the time needed by the repair center, local or central, to replace the missing equipment in the spare parts store, also called *turnaround time*).

Two major strategies can be deployed. The first consists of periodically restocking the store with a period T (generally large, e.g. one year). This corresponds to machines far from production or repair centers (for instance, in a foreign country). The second strategy works by continuously restocking each item in the stock. In that case we introduce the restocking rate μ. This fits situations where the district has a repair center in its vicinity, or it can be a first-level store, making use itself of a centralized stock of second level.

7.6.2. Periodical restocking

The stock being of size S, the stock-out probability (or shortage) is the probability of having more than S failures during the period T. We assume the on-site replacement delay to be much shorter than the restocking delay. In this case, as long as no shortage is observed, the failure rate in the district is equal to $N\lambda$, and it gives the decrease rate of the stock size.

Thus, the Poisson law with parameter $N\lambda T$ gives the answer:

$$P_s = 1 - \sum_{k=0}^{S} \frac{(N\lambda T)^k}{k!} e^{-N\lambda T}. \tag{7.50}$$

We then evaluate the (integer) value for S which allows us to reach the targeted value for P_s.

7.6.3. Continuous restocking

The system is composed of equipment, both on-site and in stock. Its behavior is described by the transition diagram in Figure 7.16. It is a birth-death process with a constant failure rate as long as a spare part exists in the stock, and a decreasing failure rate as soon as the S spare parts of the stock have been used.

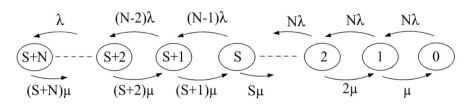

Figure 7.16. *Continuous restocking*

From the diagram we obtain:

$$P_k = \frac{\left(\frac{N\lambda}{\mu}\right)^k}{k!} P_0, \quad k \le S,$$

$$P_k = \frac{N!}{(N+S-k)!} \cdot \frac{S!}{k!} \left(\frac{\lambda}{\mu}\right)^{k-s} P_s, \quad \text{for } S \le k \le N+S.$$

Then taking: $\alpha = N$, for $k \le S$, and $\alpha = N+S-k$ for $k > S$, we have the general expression:

$$P_k = \frac{N!}{\alpha!} N^{\alpha-N+k} \frac{\left(\frac{\lambda}{\mu}\right)^k}{k!}, \quad \text{where} \begin{cases} \alpha = N, & k \le S \\ \alpha = N+S-k, & k > S \end{cases} \tag{7.51}$$

with of course:

$$\sum_{k=0}^{N+S} P_k = 1 \quad \text{and} \quad P_0 = 1 - \sum_{k=1}^{N+S} P_k.$$

The stock-out probability is then defined as the long-term proportion of requests for replacements that are not immediately satisfied due to a shortage of spare parts in the stock:

$$P_s = \frac{\sum_{k=S}^{N+S} \alpha_k P_k}{\sum_{k=0}^{N+S} \alpha_k P_k}, \tag{7.52}$$

with α_k and P_k as defined above. The stock size S will be defined as the lower value of S that yields a stock-out probability P_s less than the specified value.

If N is large enough compared to S the failure rate is approximately constant $N\lambda$, and the system may be modeled by a Poisson law with parameter $N\lambda/\mu$:

$$P_s \approx \sum_{k=S}^{N+S} P_k \approx \sum_{k=S}^{\infty} P_k, \tag{7.53}$$

and then:

$$P_k = \frac{\left(\frac{N\lambda}{\mu}\right)^k}{k!} e^{-N\lambda/\mu}. \tag{7.54}$$

Chapter 8

Simulation

The previous chapters have given prominence to the power and efficiency of the analytical approach to communication systems modeling and analysis. However, many realizations make use of such specific mechanisms that their analysis is beyond the scope of mathematical tools. In that case, simulation provides an efficient way to overcome the difficulty.

A simulation experiment aims at reproducing dynamic system behavior (customers, servers, message errors, component failures, filtering or coding algorithms, etc.) using a computer program, most often run on specific software tools. On this software model, observations are performed, which give the figures of interest, such as spectral density, error rate, detection rate, loss and delay probabilities, mean or variance, etc. Clearly, the goal is not to reproduce the microscopic level of detail in the original system exactly, but to take account of those peculiarities in the mechanisms responsible for the overall behavior. It takes a careful analysis of the system, and a good understanding of transmission, coding, filtering, routing, queueing, defense mechanisms, etc., to extract the strict set of details compatible with the degree of precision required and the budget set for the study, expressed both in terms of the time needed to elaborate and validate the model as well as the duration of each simulation run.

Actually, simulation happens to offer quite a powerful approach for the engineer: not only does it allow a quantitative analysis of complex systems to be made, but it provides a *software prototype* of the system under development, whose role is the same as the experiment for the researcher. Indeed thanks to simulation we can observe and understand complex system behaviors, hypotheses can be formulated and verified, alternative technological solutions may be experimented with, eventually giving rise to an improved solution and its model.

However, simulation is generally not a definitive answer to performance problems. The large variety of external conditions (especially assumptions about traffic) and the evolution of the services offered are such that synthetic and tractable analytical tools, even if they are approximate, are mandatory for the equipment provider or the operator. Actually, it would be quite expensive to run the simulation program for each new set of parameters or for each new customer demand. The real goal of a simulation experiment is the derivation of a set of rules or models, as simple and robust as possible.

Two main approaches have been developed, referred to as *roulette simulation* and *discrete-event simulation*. Both make use of random number generators as the basic tool to emulate the environment (customer's behavior, random signal, occurrence of failures, etc.). Another simulation method is sometimes described as *continuous simulation*. In the latter, the system state is revaluated at short time intervals, just as in solving a differential equation by numerical integration.

8.1. Roulette simulation

Although use of this technique is somewhat restricted, it is a powerful method, especially in terms of execution speed.

The principle is quite simple. Assume the system can be represented through a set of denumerable states enjoying the memoryless property. For instance, the system could be a multistage subscriber concentrator, where the occupancy varies at each beginning and end of communication with exponentially distributed communication duration; or it could be a cluster of redundant processors, where failures occur according to a Poisson process, etc. The point is that we are able to calculate the transition probabilities from each state to the next one. Simulating such a system amounts to reproducing the sequence of transitions, by drawing the next state to be reached at each step. Simultaneously, all necessary counting is performed, allowing us to estimate state probabilities. Evidence suggests that this technique is fairly well suited to Markovian systems, such as those studied in Chapters 6 and 7. Especially, if service durations or time intervals between breakdowns, etc., are exponentially distributed, the probabilities are the transition matrix coefficients already introduced (in fact, roulette simulation is just a kind of empirical resolution of the state equations summarized in the matrix).

EXAMPLE. We consider the simulation of a subscriber concentrator (or a traffic sources multiplexer) offering R servers to N Poissonian sources, generating calls at a rate λ, with exponentially distributed duration with average $1/\mu$. This system has already been considered in Chapter 6: it is the Engset problem. The state transition diagram is recalled in Figure 8.1: "state" stands for the number of calls in progress in the concentrator. Elementary events are:

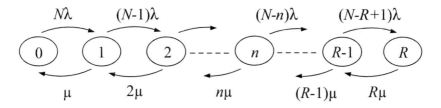

Figure 8.1. *State transition diagram of the concentrator*

– the arrival of a new request, which changes the state from n to $n + 1$ if $n < R$. In state n, $N - n$ sources are only idle and able to issue a request: the birth rate is $(N - n)\lambda$;

– the end of a call, with a rate $n\mu$, which changes the state from n to $n - 1$.

Given the state n the transition probabilities to adjacent states are respectively:

$$P(n \rightarrow n - 1) = \frac{n\mu}{n\mu + (N - n)\lambda},$$

$$P(n \rightarrow n + 1) = \frac{(N - n)\lambda}{n\mu + (N - n)\lambda}.$$

(8.1)

Clearly the events are complementary, the probabilities summing up to 1. The simulation experiment runs as follows:

a) Draw a random number r, uniformly distributed in the interval $(0, 1)$.

b) Test if $r < \frac{n\mu}{n\mu+(N-n)\lambda}$. If yes (a departure occurs), move the system to the state $n - 1$. If no (an arrival occurs), move to $n + 1$.

c) Repeat operations a) and b) until the number of events reaches the limit assigned to the experiment.

As will become clear, the present method enjoys simplicity and efficiency, especially at run time, as compared with the classical discrete-event approach presented in the next section, as the code to be processed reduces to execute simple calculations and to update a few counters. In the case of simulating a large network, for instance, it reduces to choosing the destination, looking for an available path, according to the routing algorithm and the architecture, and marking the corresponding resources as busy. Also, the occurrence of an end of service depends on the total number of ongoing connections. Powerful computers currently available make it possible to investigate fairly large structures this way.

However, this real simplicity raises several issues. The first two are common to all simulation techniques: the accuracy of the result, function of the simulation duration, and the measurement technique. The reader is directed to Chapter 3, and specialized books on statistics for an in-depth treatment of these issues, the main aspects of which are summarized below.

The major drawback with roulette simulation is that it does not incorporate any notion of time. As already mentioned, the memoryless property of all the processes is central to the method, so that non-exponential service or inter-arrival durations cannot be accounted for. However, it is always possible to approximate arbitrary processes, replacing them with a combination of exponential distributions (e.g. Erlang-k distribution, see Chapters 2 and 6).

More important, the principle of the method makes it incapable of measuring any delay, such as waiting times, busy periods, etc. Here again various tricks may be used, e.g. counting the number of events between significant state changes (possibly adding that null events occur according to an exponential distribution), and deducing from it the corresponding duration. In fact, as soon as time is the parameter of central concern, discrete-event simulation will be the preferred approach.

8.2. Discrete-event simulation

This technique is commonly used in all specialized software packages, e.g. Simula, Simscript, SES-Workbench, QNAP, OPNET. As previously, the system being studied can be described in terms of the states among which it progresses. Formally, a state is a set of state variables (number of busy servers, number of clients in a queue, date of the next arrival or departure, etc.) giving all the information necessary to predict the future evolution (on a probabilistic basis). Especially, the epoch of the next event is included in the state variables. Each transition is caused by an event (arrival, failure, etc.). The events occur at *discrete epochs*, and are described in the simulation program. So, the evolution of the system is fully reproduced, but only by jumping from one event of date to the next, as nothing occurs between events from the simulation standpoint.

As opposed to roulette simulation, this method provides a full mastery of time and allows its precise measurement. Also, the gain as compared with continuous simulation is obvious, since in this last method much time is devoted to increasing the clock without effective action (since nothing occurs between events).

However, this method requires us to estimate the date of a future event, which is obtained by generating random intervals according to a given probability distribution. For instance, when an exponentially distributed service duration begins, its duration is drawn using the properties of the exponential distribution, determining the event date of the end of service occurrence. This operation is even simpler when the service is of constant duration. These techniques are further discussed in section 8.4.

As events occur on a discrete-time basis (no simultaneous events) they are processed chronologically, in the following way: the *event notices* describing them (date of occurrence, actions to be executed) are stored in a timetable (event list, sequencing set) in order of increasing dates. The simulation logic scans the event at the head of the list, jumps immediately to the date of the first event and executes the corresponding actions (new request, end of session, failure of an element, etc.). Most often, the processing ends by generating new future events (a beginning of service generates an end of service) which are inserted at the appropriate location in the event list. Then the logic scans the head of the list again, etc.

The efficiency of such a process depends first on the complexity of the actions to be executed, but also on the number of simultaneous events to be handled in the event list. Dedicated software tools incorporate sophisticated and powerful algorithms for managing the event list: inserting or extracting events (the so-called *synchronization kernel*).

The event list. Let us briefly describe a possible structure for the event list. It can be built using a circular two-way list, where each entry (event notice) is linked by forward and backward pointers to the next and previous event notice.

Each event notice is a data structure storing the event reference, its date of occurrence, a pointer to the code simulating it, pointers to the previous event and to the next one (see Figure 8.2). Adding an event at a given date is accomplished by inserting a new notice and updating the pointers (sophisticated techniques are used to optimize the process).

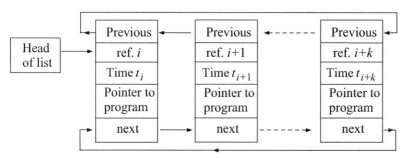

Figure 8.2. *An event list organized as a circular buffer*

Compared with continuous simulations, where the system keeps increasing time and testing possible actions, here the computer executes only the code pieces corresponding to the events. The gain in terms of run-time is important, and such a method allows us to build powerful simulators, suited to traffic analysis of machines with ever greater capacity (e.g., switches and call servers handling several millions of calls per hour, or routers handling packets). The techniques to manage event lists are not restricted to traditional simulations, and the performance engineer may be required to create such a structure for his own machines, and especially for *load tests* (in labs or field trials for instance). Actually, consider the realization of a call generator, creating traffic for testing a system with a real size load. At a given date a call is initialized by an *open* message sent to the system (e.g. request for call set-up). The generator then stands waiting for an answer from the system (connection set up) initializing the communication, communication which will be interrupted by the sending of a *close* message to the system, generated after a random duration. Another open message will then be generated at a date depending on the load level, etc.

As can be seen, an event list storing the scheduled dates for the beginning and end of calls is perfectly suited to the design of this call generator.

Managing event lists is one of the examples emphasizing the interest, for the specialist, of having a sound understanding of language simulation techniques, as they may be re-used for the design and optimization of all real-time systems.

8.3. Measurements and accuracy

Two difficult issues are related to simulation, whatever the technique in use (roulette or discrete-event approach): the precision of the measurement and confidence to put in the results, and the observation technique allowing measurement (of sojourn time in various states, of number of events, etc.). The reader is referred to statistical methods; for further developments, see Chapter 3. Here are a few basic principles.

8.3.1. *Measurements*

The ideal measure should supply a random sampling of the states the system goes through during the simulation. We must always keep in mind this fundamental rule, as numerous traps may distort the observation process. For instance, consider how we may measure queue lengths in the case of deterministic or bulk arrivals, or how to measure the load of a cyclic server, etc.

Fortunately, in the most common cases it is possible to describe the phenomenon to be observed precisely in terms of queueing theory. The simulation experiment then simply implements the measurement corresponding to the definition. Remember however that the observation cannot tell more than what has been defined, including all the *a priori* implicit in most of our reasoning. Experiments, using random observations are always fruitful in this respect (they may make some unsuspected property appear).

These issues are less crucial in the case of roulette simulation, as the memoryless property allows us to simply increase the number of visits in a given state and the total number of transitions, the state probability being simply the ratio of these quantities.

8.3.2. *Accuracy*

Regarding measurement accuracy, it is simply reduced to a question of *estimation*, as we now explain.

Assume we want to estimate some state probability (for instance, the probability of having n busy servers, or the probability of more than n customers in a buffer). If the estimation is made in a series of k time units (event driven simulation), or of k transitions (roulette simulation), the results can be displayed in the form of curves, similar to those in Figure 8.3. The value observed is the ratio: number of outcomes over k. The parameter k must be large enough that two successive series may be seen as approximately independent.

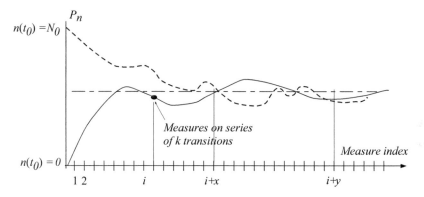

Figure 8.3. *Trajectories of the observed state*

These curves are called *trajectories* of the measurement process. Two different curves are represented, corresponding to two different initial states of the simulation. After a transient period, the process goes to a stable limit as the number of measurements increase. This is because the system reaches a stationary regime so that the state probabilities have constant values and the measurement process converges toward these values. This represents the situation of almost all systems to be considered. Based on the evidence, if the initial state is closer to the stationary regime, the results are more rapidly significant.

On this subject, sophisticated techniques have been developed that lead to a reduction in the simulation duration, for a given accuracy, especially in the case where rare events are to be observed. The idea is to restart the simulation when the trajectory of the system state reaches a zone of interest (i.e. where critical states are likely to be found). See [VIL 91] for further developments.

Let us now consider the trajectory once the stationary regime has been reached (after rank i, for example). Then traditional methods for estimating means and variances apply. The set of values observed from the measures of rank $(i + x)$ to $(i + y)$ is our *sample*. However, we clearly have no knowledge about the probability distribution of the measures, and this implies several assumptions. Most of the time, the process is considered as being stationary, and the traditional estimation approach gives the answer (point estimators as well as confidence intervals). In most cases the normal assumption holds (as soon as $n > 30$): this is the consequence of the *central limit theorem*; see Chapter 3.

Notably, traditional results for the mean value give:

$$P\left(\hat{m} - \frac{\sigma}{\sqrt{n}} u_{1-\alpha_2} < m < \hat{m} + \frac{\sigma}{\sqrt{n}} u_{\alpha_1}\right) = 1 - \alpha, \tag{8.2}$$

n being the sample size, $\hat{m}$ the observed value, $1 - \alpha$ the confidence level and σ the standard deviation of the population. An unbiased estimator for this quantity, usually unknown, is

$$s = \sqrt{\frac{n}{n-1}} \hat{\sigma}, \quad \hat{\sigma} \text{ being the values observed on the sample.}$$

So finally, $\hat{m} - u_{1-\alpha_2}\frac{s}{\sqrt{n}} < m < \hat{m} + u_{\alpha_1}\frac{s}{\sqrt{n}}$, or yet:

$$\hat{m} - u_{1-\alpha/2}\frac{s}{\sqrt{n}} < m < \hat{m} + u_{1-\alpha/2}\frac{s}{\sqrt{n}}, \tag{8.3}$$

for a risk symmetrically distributed. For instance, the 95% and 90% centered confidence intervals (values in common use) are:

$$\begin{aligned}
&\left[\hat{m} - 1.96\frac{s}{\sqrt{n}} < m < \hat{m} + 1.96\frac{s}{\sqrt{n}}\right], \\
&\left[\hat{m} - 1.65\frac{s}{\sqrt{n}} < m < \hat{m} + 1.65\frac{s}{\sqrt{n}}\right]
\end{aligned} \tag{8.4}$$

Remember that the above results also hold for small size samples n, provided the coefficients t are taken from the Student-Fischer table, in the column corresponding to the risk level (see e.g. [FIC 04]).

This method (sometimes referred to as *batch means*) is of great importance, as it visualizes both the transient period and the optimal measurement interval – when the stationary regime is reached. Taking only the cumulative result may lead to erroneous predictions, related for instance to a biased measurement during the transient period or also to the use of random number generators with too short periods, provoking non-stationary behaviors. This last remark applies especially to home-made generators, as modern simulation languages provide correct enough generators.

We can also point out the value of the several states measure, in helping to obtain the whole probability distribution, and for different conditions, e.g. different load levels. This allows us to draw curves and thus to extrapolate the results for low probabilities. This can also reinforce the confidence towards the measures as the curve obtained should present a plausible shape.

However, it will always be preferable to consider lengthening the simulation duration, or improving the simulation process (e.g. using the restart methods [VIL 91]), before trying any extrapolation.

Regardless, we must retain the usefulness of diagrammatic representation, which greatly helps to clarify the validity of the simulation process and to improve our confidence towards results.

8.4. Random numbers

Although random number generators are a facility offered by most computers, it is worth understanding their basic principles, as their usage goes far beyond the needs of simulation experiments. Here again the specialist, in addition to his own knowledge of simulation languages, must make use of or even design random number generators for specific needs (noisy sound generation, real traffic simulators, failure generation for system testing, measurements, etc.).

Generally speaking, the problem is to generate a sequence of numbers obeying a given probability distribution as accurately as possible, this distribution being given by measurements, by the assumption in the model, etc.

8.4.1. *Generation according to a distribution*

The principle is as follows: we want to generate a series of numbers X (say, service durations) obeying a known distribution probability:

$$F(x) = P[X \leq x].$$

The method consists of drawing a random number u uniformly distributed between 0 and 1, and estimating $X = F^{-1}(u)$ (as the probability is between 0 and 1). Figure 8.4 illustrates the principle. We can verify that the number is such that $P[X \leq x] = F(x)$. In fact, $P[X \leq x] = P[F^{-1}(u) \leq x] = P[u \leq F(x)]$, and $P[u \leq F(x)] = F(x)$, as u is uniformly distributed in the interval $(0,1)$.

The important example of exponential distribution serves to illustrate the method. The distribution is $F(t) = 1 - \exp(-\mu t)$.

The successive drawings yield a sequence of numbers u. As we want an exponential distribution we have $u = 1 - \exp(-\mu t)$, from which the values of the variable t are given by:

$$t = -\frac{\ln(1 - u)}{\mu}. \tag{8.5}$$

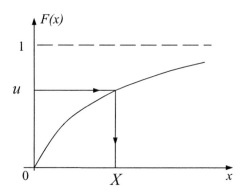

Figure 8.4. *Principle of the generation of a random number distributed according to a given probability law*

It is immediately clear that the method can be generalized to the generation of complex laws, by combining several drawings. Of special importance is the case of distributions combining several exponential laws, such as the Erlang-k or hyperexponential distributions; see Chapter 6. For instance, the Erlang-k distribution is simply obtained by adding k successively drawn exponentially distributed variables.

Moreover, the method can be extended to the case of empirical distributions. This is of particular importance for performance tests where it may be necessary to reproduce a specific behavior (experimental processing time distribution, complex packet arrival process observed at the output of a multiplexer, etc.). Assume the empirical distribution is given (actually a cumulated histogram). The target value X_k is obtained by looking for the interval (X_k, X_{k+1}) containing the random variable u, i.e.:

$$F(X_k) < u \le F(X_{k+1}).$$

Other methods have been developed (especially for the case where no closed form is available for F^{-1}); see for instance [FIS 78, FIS 96].

All these developments assume the availability of a uniformly distributed random variable. Let us now indicate how we may solve this problem.

8.4.2. *Generating pseudo-random variables*

We introduce here the concept of *pseudo-randomness*. Actually, the methods in common use for generating "random" numbers rely on algorithms, which are rather sophisticated but perfectly deterministic and periodic. The method will be such that the series *looks like* a random sequence, presenting an autocorrelation as low as possible and a period of maximum length.

Numerous methods have been successively experimented with for generating such sequences. The first used quite empirical approaches (e.g. the *mid-square* method introduced by Von Neumann), but they were quickly discarded, in favor of more formal algorithms generating series which were open to theoretical analyses (based upon the results of algebraic number theory) guaranteeing optimal properties, with respect to periodicity and correlation.

We can mention the congruential method (multiplicative or additive), the use of shift registers, the use of specific series such as the successive decimals of π, and lastly the shuffling of several generators. The presentation here is restricted to congruential methods and shuffling, which are the most commonly used methods in our applications.

Congruential methods. The method is based upon the following property: if I is an irrational number, then the sequence of the numbers $u_n = nI$, $(\bmod\,1)$, is uniformly distributed (Weyl-Jacobi theorem). The congruential method consists of taking $u_n = ku_{n-1}$, $(\bmod\,m)$, that is $u_n = k^n u_0$, $(\bmod\,m)$. The value u_0 is the *seed*. The generator period is at best $m - 1$. The recommended values for m are $2^p - 1$, with $p = 2, 3, 5, 7, 13, 17, 19, 31, 61$, etc. (Fermat numbers). If $m = 2^q$, $q \geq 4$, which simplifies the modulo calculation, the maximum period is at best equal to $m/4$. Table 8.1 provides example parameters for good generators (see also [FIS 78, FIS 96]).

k	m	period
16807 (= 7^5)		
62089911		
4177924 (*)	$2^{31} - 1$	$2^{31} - 2$
1226874159 (*)		
1099087573		
69069		
1099087573	2^{32}	2^{30}
2824527309		
3125	$2^{35} - 31$	$2^{35} - 32$
133955583 ($2^{27} - 2^{18} - 1$)		
68909602460261	2^{48}	2^{46}

(*) These values are presented as "best choices" in [FIS 96]

Table 8.1. *Parameters for random generators using the multiplicative congruence method*

The additive congruence makes use of the Fibonacci series $u_n = u_{n-1} + u_{n-2}$ (mod m). An example is given by $u_0 = u_1$ (mod 2^p), p being the machine data width in bits (e.g. 32). The following algorithm shows the practical use of the method:

```
Initialize      Choose the seed u₀ (between 0 and 30),
|               m (arbitrary, large),
|               u₁ (number < module m);
|               Take α = u₀ and β = u₁
|   1) Take k = α + β;
|      Test if k > m; If yes take k = k - m;
|      Take α = β and β = k;
|      Take u = k/(m+1); "u is the random number drawn, 0 < u < 1"
    Repeat 1).
```

This method, although fast and simple to implement, usually provides worse generators than those based on multiplicative congruence. However, combining generators of poor quality may overcome this weakness.

Shuffling generators. Shuffling two generators of low period is a means to generate another generator of improved quality. This procedure is appealing as it offers a way to use basic and fast generators, easy to be implemented. This is of special importance in field trials, where an artificial load is generated, where failures are simulated, etc. The principle is to use a first generator to fill a *shuffling table* which is accessed randomly using the second generator (the successive outcomes of this are used as entry addresses in the table). Each number read in the table is then replaced by a new drawing of the first generator. A table with around 100 entries happens to give satisfactory results.

A single generator can even be shuffled with itself: the algorithm is as follows.

```
1) Initialize the table with the first 100 drawings of
the generator: tᵢ = uᵢ, i = 1,...,100.
```

```
2) Draw the following random number u_k and normalize it
so as to obtain a value between 1 and 100. This yields i.
      Entry i of the table gives the random number tᵢ;
      Draw the following random number u_{k+1} and update
tᵢ = u_{k+1}.
    Repeat 2).
```

The design of a random number generator is not a common task in the life of engineers. It relies on sophisticated results of number theory, and is mainly a matter for specialists. Various tests for estimating the randomness of generators have been devised, see [FIS 96]: they aim at testing autocorrelation, uniformity, etc. (see Chapter 3). More complex methods – of increased computing complexity – have been proposed, for situations calling for high-quality randomness or large period (see the *Mersenne twister* for an example [MAT 98]). Combining simple congruential generators results in sequences with increased periods. We present here the case of a combination of two generators, see [L'E 97] for more details.

Two generators are built, with $k_1 = 40014$, $m_1 = 2^{31} - 85$, and $k_2 = 40692$, $m_2 = 2^{31} - 249$:

At step j we draw $X_{1,j}$ and $X_{2,j}$;
– Let $Y_j = X_{1,j} - X_{2,j} \bmod 2^{31} - 85$.
– The result is $r_j = Y_j / 2147483563$ if $Y_j > 0$, and $1 - 1/2147483563$ if not.

This algorithm generates a sequence with period $(m_1 - 1)(m_2 - 1)$, around 2×10^{18}.

Appendix

Mathematical Refresher

In this appendix we recall several basic definitions and theorems concerning the different fields addressed by this book: functions of the complex variable, series expansions, algebraic structures, polynomials in the binary field, matrices. These reminders – the choice of which remains arbitrary to a large extent – are not required for the reading of this book. However, they may be of some help for various specific concepts, or preparation for the study of specialized textbooks.

A.1. The function of the complex variable: definition and theorems

Definition of the function of the complex variable. Let Ω be an open set of the complex number field C. A function of the complex variable on Ω is an application from Ω to C, which for every z in Ω yields a complex number denoted as:

$$Z = f(z).$$

This can always be written as:

$$Z = X(x, y) + iY(x, y).$$

The set Ω is the function *domain*.

Uniform function. The function $f(z)$ is said to be uniform (or single-valued) if every z in Ω has a single image $Z = f(z)$.

Continuity. Definitions about the limits of complex functions are identical to those concerning scalar functions.

Specifically, z being a continuous function in the complex plane, every polynomial in z is a continuous function on the whole plane. Similarly, every rational fraction of

z is continuous on the plane, except in these points, where its denominator vanishes (these points are the fraction *poles*).

Analytical function. A function of the complex variable is derivable (sometimes termed *complex derivable*) at a point z_0 of the complex plan if a number a exists (denoted as $f'(z_0)$), such that:

$$\lim_{z \to z_0} \frac{f(z) - f(z_0)}{z - z_0} = a$$

(the limit being independent of the way z goes to z_0). It is said to be analytic in a domain if it is derivable at every point of this domain.

A necessary and sufficient condition for the derivability of the function $f(z)$ at point $z = x + iy$ is that its real and imaginary parts $X(x, y)$ and $Y(x, y)$ are differentiable in $m(x, y)$, image of z, and that their partial derivatives verify the Cauchy-Riemann equations:

$$\frac{\partial X}{\partial x} = \frac{\partial Y}{\partial y}, \quad \text{and} \quad \frac{\partial X}{\partial y} = -\frac{\partial Y}{\partial x}.$$

Holomorphic function. A function $f(z)$ is said to be holomorphic at a point z_0 if $f(z)$ is derivable in z_0 and if a circle of center z_0 exists in which $f(z)$ is continuous and uniform.

A function $f(z)$ is said to be holomorphic within a domain $\mathcal{D}$ if it is uniform in every point of $\mathcal{D}$, and if it has a derivative at each point of $\mathcal{D}$.

Singular points and poles. Every point z_0 where the function $f(z)$ is not holomorphic is said to be a singular point (or *singularity*) of the function. The critical points of a multiple-valued function, and the poles of a fraction, are singularities. More generally,

$$z = z_0 \text{ is a pole of } f(z) \text{ if } 1/f(z) \text{ is holomorphic in } z_0.$$

Integral of a continuous function. Let AB be a smooth arc in the complex plane:

$$\int_{AB} f(z) dz = \int_{AB} (X + iY)(dx + idy)$$

$$= \int_{AB} X dx - Y dy + i \int_{AB} Y dx + X dy.$$

The integral of a complex function is a linear combination of line integrals. It possesses all properties of the ordinary integral.

A basic important integral: $\int_C \frac{dz}{z-a}$ where C is the circle of center $z = a$ and radius ρ.

Let us denote $\rho = |z - a|$ and $z - a = \rho e^{i\theta}$. We obtain:

$$\int_C \frac{dz}{z-a} = \int_0^{2\pi} \frac{i\rho e^{i\theta}}{\rho e^{i\theta}} d\theta = \int_0^{2\pi} i d\theta = 2\pi i.$$

Cauchy integral theorem. Given a smooth closed curve C, and a function $f(z)$, holomorphic in the domain D inside C, and continuous on $D \cup C$, then:

$$\int_C f(z)dz = 0.$$

Cauchy integral:

$$f(a) = \frac{1}{2i\pi} \int_{C+} \frac{f(z)}{z-a} dz,$$

$C+$ meaning that the integral is evaluated along the positive direction (trigonometric, or counterclockwise sense).

Paul Lévy theorem. If $\phi(z)$ is an indefinitely derivable function, and if the series $\sum_{n=0}^{\infty} \frac{\phi^{(n)}(0)}{n!}(iu)^n$ is convergent, u being a real number, in a circle of radius a, then $\phi(z)$ is an analytic function in the band $-a < R(z) < a$, $R(z)$ being the real part of z.

Corollaries:

   – if $\phi(x)$ exists for x real, $\alpha < x < \beta$, $\phi(z)$ is analytic in the band $\alpha < R(z) < \beta$;

   – the singular point of $\phi(z)$ the closest to the origin, being necessarily on the convergence circle and outside the band of analyticity, is necessarily real.

Rouché theorem. If $f(z)$ and $g(z)$ are analytical inside and on a closed contour C, and if $|g(z)| < |f(z)|$ on C, then $f(z)$ and $f(z) + g(z)$ have the same number of zeros inside C.

A.2. Usual z-transforms

In these formulae (Table A.1), $\delta(n)$ represents the Dirac delta function and $u(n)$ the unit step (also denoted as $\mu(n)$).

A.3. Series expansions (real functions)

Taylor formula. Let f be a continuous function in the interval $[a, b]$, with derivatives up to order n, continuous in the interval, and a $n + 1$ order derivative in the interval $]a, b[$, then there exists c on $]a, b[$ such that:

$$f(b) - f(a) = \frac{(b-a)}{1!} f'(a) + \frac{(b-a)^2}{2!} f''(a) + \cdots$$

$$+ \frac{(b-a^n}{n!} f^{(n)}(a) + \frac{(b-a)^{n+1}}{(n+1)!} f^{n+1}(c)$$

Signal $x(n)$	Transform $X(z)$	Convergence domain
$\delta(n)$	1	C
$u(n)$	$\dfrac{1}{1-z^{-1}}$	$|z|>1$
$a^n u(n)$	$\dfrac{1}{1-az^{-1}}$	$|z|>|a|$
$na^n u(n)$	$\dfrac{az^{-1}}{(1-az^{-1})^2}$	$|z|>|a|$
$-a^n u(-n-1)$	$\dfrac{1}{1-az^{-1}}$	$|z|<|a|$
$-na^n u(-n-1)$	$\dfrac{az^{-1}}{(1-az^{-1})^2}$	$|z|<|a|$
$\cos(n\omega_0)u(n)$	$\dfrac{1-z^{-1}\cos(\omega_0)}{1-2z^{-1}\cos(\omega_0)+z^{-2}}$	$|z|>1$
$\sin(n\omega_0)u(n)$	$\dfrac{z^{-1}\sin(\omega_0)}{1-2z^{-1}\cos(\omega_0)+z^{-2}}$	$|z|>1$
$a^n\cos(n\omega_0)u(n)$	$\dfrac{1-az^{-1}\cos(\omega_0)}{1-2az^{-1}\cos(\omega_0)+a^2z^{-2}}$	$|z|>|a|$
$a^n\sin(n\omega_0)u(n)$	$\dfrac{az^{-1}\sin(\omega_0)}{1-2az^{-1}\cos(\omega_0)+a^2z^{-2}}$	$|z|>|a|$

Table A.1. *Table of usual z-transforms*

A practical form for this result is:

$$f(x) = f(a) + \frac{(x-a)}{1!}f'(a) + \frac{(x-a)^2}{2!}f''(a) + \cdots$$

We obtain the Maclaurin expansion if $a = 0$:

$$f(x) = f(0) + \frac{x}{1!}f'(0) + \frac{x^2}{2!}f''(0) + \cdots$$

Here are the expansions of several functions which are of constant use.

Binomial theorem. Let us apply the Taylor formula to the function, with n integer. We have:

$$(a + b)^n = a^n + \frac{b}{1!}na^{n-1} + \cdots + \frac{b^p}{p!}n(n - 1) \cdots (n - p + 1)a^{n-p}$$

$$+ \cdots + \frac{b^{n-1}}{1!}na + b^n.$$

The binomial coefficient is:

$$\binom{n}{p} = \frac{n(n - 1) \cdots (n - p + 1)}{p!} = \frac{n!}{p!(n - p)!} \quad \text{for } p > 0, \text{ and } \binom{n}{0} = 1.$$

$\binom{n}{p}$ is also denoted as C_n^p (European notation), from which the binomial theorem is written:

$$(a + b)^n = \binom{n}{0}a^n + \binom{n}{1}a^{n-1}b + \cdots + \binom{n}{p}a^{n-p}b^p + \cdots + \binom{n}{n}b^n.$$

Note that

$$\binom{n}{p} = \binom{n}{n - p}.$$

We easily verify that:

$$\binom{n}{p} = \binom{n - 1}{p - 1} + \binom{n - 1}{p}$$

(a relation which allows us to build a Pascal triangle).

Using the binomial theorem, the expansion of the function $(1 + x)^n$ is:

$$(1 + x)^n = 1 + \binom{n}{1}x + \cdots + \binom{n}{p}x^p + \cdots + \binom{n}{n}x^n.$$

Exponential function:

$$e^x = 1 + \frac{x}{1!} + \frac{x^2}{2!} + \cdots + \frac{x^n}{n!} + x^n\epsilon(x),$$

with $\epsilon(x)$ such that $\epsilon(x) \to 0$ as $x \to 0$, for every value of x.

Power function:

$$a^x = 1 + \frac{x \log a}{1} + \frac{(x \log a)^2}{2!} + \cdots, \quad \text{for every value of } x$$

Polynomial:

$$(1+x)^m = 1 + mx + \cdots + \frac{m(m-1)}{2!}x^2 + \cdots$$

$$+ \frac{m(m-1)\cdots(m-p+1)}{p!}x^p + \cdots + x^m,$$

for arbitrary m positive or negative, integer or fractional. If m is integer, we again find the binomial development:

$$(1+x)^m = 1 + \binom{m}{1}x + \cdots + \binom{m}{2}x^2 + \cdots + \binom{m}{p}x^p + \cdots$$

The following is an important special case:

$$\frac{1}{1+x} = 1 - x + x^2 - x^3 + \cdots + (-1)^n x^n + x^n \epsilon(x), \quad \text{if } |x| < 1,$$

and also:

$$\frac{1}{1-x} = 1 + x + x^2 + x^3 + \cdots + x^n + \cdots$$

Taking the derivative, we obtain:

$$\frac{1}{(1-x)^2} = 1 + 2x + 3x^2 + \cdots$$

Logarithm:

$$\ln(1+x) = x - \frac{x^2}{2} + \frac{x^3}{3} - \frac{x^4}{4} + \cdots, \quad \text{for } -1 < x \le 1,$$

$$\ln(x) = 2\left[\frac{x-1}{x+1} + \frac{1}{3}\left(\frac{x-1}{x+1}\right)^3 + \frac{1}{5}\left(\frac{x-1}{x+1}\right)^5 + \cdots\right], \quad \text{for } x > 0.$$

A.4. Series expansion of a function of the complex variable

Taylor series. A function $f(z)$, holomorphic inside a circle C of center a and on the circle itself, is expandable in the powers of $(z-a)$ and the series is convergent as long as z remains inside the circle C. The expansion is unique; this is the Taylor expansion of $f(z)$ about $z = a$:

$$f(z) = f(a) + \frac{(z-a)}{1!}f'(a) + \frac{(z-a)^2}{2!}f''(a) + \cdots + \frac{(z-a)^n}{n!}f^{(n)}(a) + \cdots$$

which is of the same form as in the real domain.

The expansions of the usual functions are identical to those obtained for the real variable, inside their *radius of convergence R*. For instance,

$$e^z = 1 + \frac{z}{1!} + \frac{z^2}{2!} + \cdots + \frac{z^n}{n!} + \cdots$$

the radius of convergence R being infinite.

$$\frac{1}{1+z} = 1 - z + z^2 - z^3 + \cdots + (-1)^n z^n + \cdots,$$

with $R = 1$.

Laurent series expansion. A function $f(z)$ holomorphic inside an annulus of center a and on its limits formed by the circles C and γ (γ inside C) is the sum of two convergent series, the first in the positive powers of $(z - a)$, the other in the powers of $\frac{1}{z-a}$. We obtain:

$$f(z) = \cdots + \frac{A_{-n}}{(z-a)^n} + \cdots + \frac{A_{-1}}{(z-a)} + A_0$$
$$+ A_1(z-a) + \cdots + A_n(z-a)^n + \cdots$$

which is the Laurent series of $f(z)$ about $z = a$, with:

$$A_n = \frac{1}{2\pi i} \int_{C+} \frac{f(u)}{(u-a)^{n+1}} du,$$

$$A_{-n} = \frac{1}{2\pi i} \int_{\gamma+} (u-a)^{n-1} f(u) du.$$

If a is the only singular point inside γ, then the Laurent series provides the expansion of $f(z)$ around the singularity $z = a$ (the result holds for z as close at possible of a but not for $z = a$). A_{-1} is the residue of $f(z)$ in a. This is also the coefficient of $(z-a)^{n-1}$ in the Taylor expansion of $(z-a)^n f(z)$.

A.5. Algebraic structures

We consider a set M on which a binary operation is defined, that is, a function f defined on the Cartesian product $M \otimes M \rightarrow M$, and which associates with each pair (x, y) of $M \otimes M$ an element of M, $f(x, y)$ usually denoted as $x + y$ or $x * y$. If the application operates on $\Omega \otimes M \rightarrow M$, Ω and M being two different sets, we are dealing with an external binary operation.

An algebraic structure is a set M on which one or several (possibly external) binary operations has been defined.

Groups. A group is a set E (of finite or infinite size) where a binary operation denoted as "+" here (or any other symbol "$*$", "$\circ$", etc.) is defined, satisfying the following axioms:

- E is closed for +: if $x, y \in E$, then $x + y \in E$;
- associativity: for all $x, y, z \in E$, $x + (y + z) = (x + y) + z$;
- there exists an identity element e: $x + e = e + x = x$;
- each element x possesses an inverse x' (or x^{-1}) such that $x + x' = x' + x = e$.

The group is denoted $(E, +)$.

There are numerous examples of groups: $\mathbb{Z}$ (the set of integers) under the usual addition; a set under intersection; etc. A commutative group (i.e. such that $x + y = y + x$) is called Abelian.

Rings. A ring is a set $(A, +, *)$, equipped with two binary operations, here denoted arbitrarily "+" "$*$", and such that:

- $(A, +)$ is a commutative group;
- the operation "$*$" is associative: $x * (y * z) = (x * y) * z$;
- the operation "$*$" is distributive with respect to "+": $x * (y + z) = x * y + x * z$.

If the operation "$*$" possesses an identity element, i.e. $x * e = e * x = x$, the ring is called a unit ring (or unitary ring).

Moreover, if the operation "$*$" is commutative ($x * y = y * x$) and such that the equation $x * y = 0$ has only $x = 0$ or $y = 0$ as solution (0 being the identity element of +), the ring is referred to as an *integral domain*. The integer set $\mathbb{Z}$, under the usual addition and product, is an integral domain.

Ideal. An ideal I is a subset of a ring, such that $(I, +)$ is an Abelian group, and closed for "$*$" – i.e. $x \in A, y \in I \rightarrow x * y \in I$. The element $y \in I$ is said to divide $x \in I$ (or to be a divisor of x) if there exists a $z \in I$ such that $x = y * z$. Elements x, y are said to be relative prime if they have no common divisor. A necessary and sufficient condition in which $x, y \in I$ are relative prime is that there exists $a, b \in I$ such that $ax + by = 1$ (Bezout's identity).

K being a field (see below), polynomials in x are a ring, the *polynomial ring* denoted traditionally as $K[x]$.

Congruence classes (or residue classes) modulo p. As mentioned, integer set $\mathbb{Z}$, equipped with the classical operations of arithmetics (addition, multiplication) is an integral domain. Let us take an arbitrary integer p, we can define the modulo: two numbers, a and b, are said to be congruent modulo p (or sometimes equal modulo p), which is denoted as $a \equiv b \pmod{p}$ if they have the same remainder, when divided by p:

$$a = xp + r, \quad b = yp + r \quad \text{(in other terms, } a - b \text{ is a multiple of } p\text{)}.$$

This is an equivalence relation:
– it is reflexive: $a \equiv a \pmod{p}$;
– it is symmetric: if $a \equiv b \pmod{p}$ then $b \equiv a \pmod{p}$;
– it is transitive: if $a \equiv b \pmod{p}$ and $b \equiv c \pmod{p}$ then $a \equiv c \pmod{p}$.

This relation allows us to define *equivalence classes*: given an arbitrary a, its equivalence class contains all integers having the same remainder when divided by p.

The equivalence classes defined this way on $\mathbb{Z}$ are termed congruence classes (or residue classes) modulo p. They are denoted as $\mathbb{Z}_p$ and form a ring.

Field. A field is a unit ring $K(+, *)$, where each element has an inverse for $*$. Rational numbers (numbers p/q, $p, q \in \mathbb{Z}$, $q \neq 0$) as well as real and complex numbers are commutative fields.

The characteristic $\mathrm{char}(K)$ of the field K is the smallest natural number p such that $p.1 = 0$. If $\mathrm{char}(K) = p$ then p is prime.

The residue class ring $\mathbb{Z}_p$ with p prime is a field. If p is not a prime number, this ring *is not* a field: for instance, in $\mathbb{Z}_6$, we have $2 * 3 = 0$ (hence the ring is not an integral domain), and similarly there is no x such that $2 \times x = 1$ (this would mean that, for integer numbers, we could write $2 \times x = 6k + 1$).

Galois fields. The fields $\mathbb{Z}_p$ of the residue classes modulo p, with p prime, are the Galois fields (with p elements) denoted as $\mathrm{GF}(p)$.

The algebraic field extension of degree n of the basic field $\mathrm{GF}(p)$ is the field denoted as $\mathrm{GF}(p^n)$, p being a prime number, and made with the elements $0, 1, \ldots, p^n - 1$. In this book the case of $\mathrm{GF}(2^n)$ where $p = 2$ is abundantly used, and especially $\mathrm{GF}(2)$ which makes use of the classical binary operations: $0 + 0 = 0$; $0 + 1 = 1 + 0 = 1$; $1 + 1 = 0$; $0 * 1 = 1 * 0 = 0$; $1 * 1 = 1$.

Vector space. We consider a set E, on which a binary operation "$+$" is defined such that $(E, +)$ is an Abelian group (commutative). Also, we consider a commutative field K (the operations on it are also denoted as "$+$" and "$*$" without any ambiguity). We define on E an external binary operation, denoted as "$\cdot$":

For every pair $x \in E$, $u \in K$ then $u \cdot x \in E$.

E is said to be a vector space on K if the operation "·" has the properties of being associative and distributive:

$u \cdot (x + y) = u \cdot x + u \cdot y$; $(u + v) \cdot x = u \cdot x + v \cdot x$, for every $u, v \in K$ and $x, y \in E$; $(uv) \cdot x = u \cdot (v \cdot x)$

The elements of the vector space are the vectors, while the elements of K are referred to as scalars.

Taking a subset $(x_1, x_2, \ldots, x_n)$ of elements of E, then the elements of the form $\sum u_i \cdot x_i$ define a *subspace*, which is a vector space by itself. The $(x_1, x_2, \ldots, x_n)$ constitute a basis of the subspace.

If the equation $\sum u_i.x_i = 0$ has no solution but $u_i = 0$, the x_is are said to be linearly independent, and form an *orthogonal basis* of the subspace (which has dimension n).

Algebra. Let I be a commutative unit ring. The set A is an algebra over I if:

   o A is a ring;

   o A is a module over I;

   o $1 * x = x$ and $u \cdot (x \cdot y) = (u \cdot x) \cdot y = x \cdot (u \cdot y)$, for every $u \in I$, and every $x, y \in A$.

If the ring I is a (commutative) field K, then A is an algebra over the field K.

A.6. Polynomials over the binary finite field

Irreducible binary polynomials. Let F be a field, a polynomial of degree n in the variable x on F is the expression $f(x) = a_n x^n + a_{n-1} x^{n-1} + \cdots + a_1 x + a_0$, with $a_i \in F$. The set of polynomials with coefficients in F has a ring structure denoted $F[x]$. In the ring $F[x]$ the multiples of a polynomial $p(x) \in F[x]$ form an *ideal*.

A binary polynomial of degree n, $f(x) = a_n x^n + a_{n-1} x^{n-1} + \cdots + a_1 x + a_0$ is a polynomial having its coefficients a_i in the Galois field $GF(2)$ with 2 elements 0 and 1.

A polynomial $f(x)$ in $F[x]$ is said *irreducible* if no polynomial $g(x)$ with $0 < \text{degree}(g) < \text{degree}(f)$ divides it.

If the only common divisor of $f(x)$ and $g(x)$ is of degree zero, the polynomials are said to be *relative prime*. As for integers, the elements of $F[x]$ can be organized in congruence classes modulo $p(x)$ about the ideal $P[x]$ made of all the multiples of a polynomial $p(x)$ with degree n. The congruence classes modulo $p(x)$ form an algebra, denoted as $f(X)$.

An element α of $GF(2^m)$ is called a *primitive root* if all the (non-zero) elements $n = 2^m - 1$ of $GF(2^m)$ can be written as powers of α. α verifies the relation $\alpha^n = 1$. If one of the roots of the irreducible polynomial $g(x)$ of degree m with coefficients in $GF(2)$ is a primitive root of the field $GF(2^m)$, $g(x)$ is called a *primitive polynomial*.

As an example, here are the binary irreducible polynomials up to degree 5, indicating the ones who *are not* primitive ones:

○ $x + 1$ (not a primitive polynomial),

○ $x^2 + 1, x^2 + x + 1,$

○ $x^3 + x + 1, x^3 + x^2 + 1,$

○ $x^4 + x^3 + x^2 + 1$ (not a primitive polynomial), $x^4 + x + 1, = x^4 + x^3 + 1,$

○ $x^5 + x^2 + 1, x^5 + x^3 + 1, x^5 + x^4 + x^3 + x + 1, x^5 + x^4 + x^3 + x^2 + 1,$ $x^5 + x^3 + x^2 + x + 1$, etc.

Factorization of polynomials in the binary field. Here is the list of all binary polynomials, up to the fourth degree, with their factorization (when it exists):

○ 1;

○ $x, x + 1$;

○ $x^2 + 1 = (x + 1)^2, x^2 + x + 1$;

○ $x^3 + 1 = (x + 1)(x^2 + x + 1), x^3 + x + 1, x^3 + x^2 + 1, x^3 + x^2 + x + 1 = (x + 1)^3$;

○ $x^4 + x^2 + x + 1 = (x + 1)(x^3 + x^2 + 1), x^4 + x^3 + 1$;

○ $x^4 + x^3 + x + 1 = (x + 1)^2(x^2 + x + 1), x^4 + x^3 + x^2 + 1 = (x + 1)(x^3 + x + 1),$

○ $x^4 + x^3 + x^2 + x + 1$, etc.

For polynomials of the form $x^n + 1$ the decompositions (up to degree 9):

○ 1;

○ $x + 1$;

○ $x^2 + 1 = (x + 1)^2$;

○ $x^3 + 1 = (x + 1)(x^2 + x + 1)$;

○ $x^4 + 1 = (x + 1)^4$;

○ $x^5 + 1 = (x + 1)(x^4 + x^3 + x^2 + x + 1)$;

○ $x^7 + 1 = (x + 1)(x^3 + x + 1)(x^3 + x^2 + x + 1)$;

○ $x^8 + 1 = (x + 1)^8$;

○ $x^9 + 1 = (x + 1)(x^2 + x + 1)(x^6 + x^3 + x + 1)$, etc.

A.7. Matrices

Sum of matrices

$$A = \begin{bmatrix} a_{11} & a_{12} \\ a_{21} & a_{22} \end{bmatrix}; \quad B = \begin{bmatrix} b_{11} & b_{12} \\ b_{21} & b_{22} \end{bmatrix}; \quad A + B = \begin{bmatrix} a_{11} + b_{11} & a_{12} + b_{12} \\ a_{21} + b_{21} & a_{22} + b_{22} \end{bmatrix};$$

Scalar multiplication

$$\lambda A = \begin{bmatrix} \lambda a_{11} & \lambda a_{12} \\ \lambda a_{21} & \lambda a_{22} \end{bmatrix}$$

Product of two matrices

$$A \cdot B = \begin{bmatrix} a_{11} & a_{12} \\ a_{21} & a_{22} \end{bmatrix} \cdot \begin{bmatrix} b_{11} & b_{12} \\ b_{21} & b_{22} \end{bmatrix} = \begin{bmatrix} a_{11}b_{11} + a_{12}b_{21} & a_{11}b_{12} + a_{12}b_{22} \\ a_{21}b_{11} + a_{22}b_{21} & a_{21}b_{12} + a_{22}b_{22} \end{bmatrix}$$

Transpose of a matrix

$$A^T = \begin{bmatrix} a_{11} & a_{21} \\ a_{12} & a_{22} \end{bmatrix}$$

$$(A^T)^T = A; \quad (A + B)^T = A^T + B^T; \quad (A \cdot B)^T = B^T \cdot A^T.$$

Inverse of a square matrix. Given a square matrix A, its inverse, denoted as A^{-1}, is such that:

$$A \cdot A^{-1} = I.$$

Recall here the basic inversion method using determinants (see Chapter 7 for an example application):

○ take the transpose of the matrix,

○ replace each element by its cofactor (or minor),

○ divide each element by the determinant of the initial matrix.

The determinant of a matrix A with elements a_{ij} (i indicates the row and j the column) is obtained, for instance by developing according to the first row:

$$\det(A) = |A| = \sum_j (-1)^{j+1} \det\left(A_{1,j}\right),$$

where $A_{1,j}$ is a sub-matrix of A associated with element a_{1j}, obtained by removing the first row and the jth column. Its determinant is the *cofactor*, or minor. For instance, for a $2 \otimes 2$ matrix:

$$A = \begin{bmatrix} a_{11} & a_{12} \\ a_{21} & a_{22} \end{bmatrix} \longrightarrow |A| = a_{11}a_{22} - a_{12}a_{21}$$

$$\longrightarrow A^T = \begin{bmatrix} a_{11} & a_{21} \\ a_{12} & a_{22} \end{bmatrix}$$

$$\longrightarrow A^{-1} = \frac{1}{|A|} \begin{bmatrix} a_{22} & -a_{12} \\ -a_{21} & a_{11} \end{bmatrix}.$$

Bibliography

[ALB 03] ALBRIGHT S., WINSTON W. and ZAPPE C., *Data Analysis and Decision Making with Microsoft Excel*, Brooks Cole, Pacific Grove, CA, 4th edition, 2003.

[BEL 00] BELLANGER M., *Digital Processing of Signals: Theory and Practice*, John Wiley & Sons, Chichester, 3rd edition, 2000.

[BER 93] BERROU C., GLAVIEUX A. and THITIMAJSHIMA P., "Near Shannon limit error correcting coding and decoding : turbo-codes", *IEEE Int. Conf. on Commun.*, Geneva, May 1993, p. 1064–1070, 1993.

[CIN 75] CINLAR E., *Introduction to Stochastic Processes*, Prentice Hall, Inc., Englewood Cliffs, NJ, 1975.

[COH 82] COHEN J., *The Single Server Queue*, vol. 8 of *North-Holland Applied Mathematics and Mechanics Series*, North Holland Pub. Co., Amsterdam, 2nd edition, 1982.

[COO 65] COOLEY J.W. and TUKEY J.W., "An algorithm for the machine calculation of complex Fourier series", *Math. Comput.*, vol. 19, p. 297–301, 1965.

[CRO 97] CROVELLA M. and BESTAVROS A., "Self-similarity in World Wide Web traffic: evidence and possible causes", *IEEE/ACM Transactions on Networking*, vol. 5, num. 6, p. 835–846, December 1997.

[DUH 90] DUHAMEL P. and VETTERLI M., "Fast Fourier transforms: a tutorial review and a state of the art", *Signal Processing*, vol. 19, p. 259–299, 1990.

[FEL 71] FELLER W., *An Introduction to Probability Theory and its Applications*, John Wiley & Sons, New York, 3rd edition, 1971.

[FIC 04] FICHE G. and HÉBUTERNE G., *Systems and Communicating Networks; Traffic and Performance*, Innovative technology series, Kogan Page Science, London, 2004.

[FIS 78] FISHMAN G., *Principles of Discrete-Event Simulation*, John Wiley & Sons, New York, 1978.

[FIS 96] FISHMAN G., *Monte Carlo, Concepts, Algorithms and Applications*, Springer series in operations research, Springer Verlag, New York, 1996.

[GAU 66] GAUSS C.F., "Nachlass: Theoria interpolationis methodo nova tractata", *Werke band 3 (Königliche Gesellschaft der Wissenschaften, Göttingen)*, p. 265–327, 1866.

[HAM 50] HAMMING R., "Error detecting and error correcting codes", *The Bell Technical Journal*, vol. 29, p. 147–160, 1950.

[HAN 03] HANKERSON D., HARRIS G. and JOHNSON P. J., *Introduction to Information Theory and Data Compression*, Chapman & Hall/CRC, Boca Raton, FL, 2nd edition, 2003.

[HAY 86] HAYKIN S., *Adaptive Filter Theory*, Prentice Hall, Englewood Cliffs, NJ, 1986.

[KLE 74] KLEINROCK L., *Queueing Systems vol. 1: Theory*, John Wiley & Sons, New York, 1974.

[KLE 76] KLEINROCK L., *Queueing Systems vol. 2: Computer applications*, John Wiley & Sons, New York, 1976.

[KNU 85] KNUTH D. E., "Dynamic Huffman coding", *Journal of Algorithms*, vol. 6, num. 2, p. 163–180, June 1985.

[KUN 93] KUNT M., GRANLUND G. and KOCHER M., *Traitement numérique des images*, Collection technique et scientifique des télécommunications, Presses Polytechniques et Universitaires Romandes, Lausanne, 1993.

[L'E 97] L'ECUYER P. and ANDRES T., "A random number generator based on the combination of four LCGs", *Mathematics and Computers in Simulation*, vol. 44, 1997.

[LEG 62] LEGALL P., *Les systèmes avec ou sans attente et les processus stochastiques*, Dunod, Paris, 1962.

[LEG 94] LE GALL P., "The overall sojourn time in tandem queues with identical successive service times and renewal input", *Stochastic Processes and their Applications*, vol. 52, p. 165–178, 1994.

[LÉV 25] LÉVY P., *Calcul des probabilitiés*, Gauthier-Villard, Paris, 1925.

[MAT 98] MATSUMOTO M. and NISHIMURA T., "Mersenne twister: a 623-dimensionally equidistributed uniform pseudorandom number generator", *ACM Trans. Model. Comput. Simul.*, vol. 8, num. 3, 1998.

[MOO 86] MOOD A., GRAYBILL F. and BOES D., *Introduction to the Theory of Statistics*, McGraw-Hill series on probability and statistics, McGraw-Hill, 3rd edition, 1986.

[MOR 97] MOREAU N., *Techniques de compression des signaux*, Collection Technique et Scientifique des Télécommunications, Masson, Pariss, 1997.

[OSW 91] OSWALD J., *Diacritical Analysis of Systems: A Treatise on Information Theory*, Ellis Horwood series in electrical and electronic engineering, E. Horwood Ltd, New York, 1991.

[PAT 97] PATTAVINA A., *Switching Theory: Architectures and Performance in Broadband ATM Networks*, John Wiley & Sons, New York, 1997.

[PET 72] PETERSON W. and WELDON E., *Error Correcting Codes*, The MIT Press, Cambridge, 2nd edition, 1972.

[POL 57] POLLACZEK F., *Problèmes stochastiques posés par le phénomène de formation d'une queue d'attente à un guichet et par des phénomènes apparentés*, vol. 136 of *Mémorial des sciences mathématiques*, Gauthier Villars, Paris, 1957.

[POL 61] POLLACZEK F., *Théorie analytique des problèmes stochastiques relatifs à un groupe de lignes téléphoniques avec attente*, vol. 150 of *Mémorial des sciences mathématiques*, Gauthier Villars, Paris, 1961.

[RIV 78] RIVEST R., SHAMIR A. and ADELMAN L., "A method for obtaining digital signatures and public-key cryptosystems", *Communications of the ACM*, vol. 21, num. 2, p. 120–126, 1978.

[ROS 95] ROSS W., "Multiservice loss models for broadband telecommunication networks", in *Telecommunication Networks and Computer Systems*, Springer Verlag, Berlin, 1995.

[RUD 91] RUDIN W., *Functional Analysis*, McGraw-Hill Science, 2nd edition, 1991.

[SCH 96] SCHNEIER B., *Applied Cryptography Protocols, Algorithms, and Source Code in C*, John Wiley & Sons, New York, 1996.

[SCH 01] SCHECHTER M., *Principles of Functional Analysis*, Graduate studies in mathematics, American Mathematical Society, 2nd edition, 2001.

[SHA 48] SHANNON C., "The mathematical theory of communication", *The Bell System Technical Journal*, vol. 27, p. 379–423, October 1948, Available at cm.bell-labs.com/cm/ms/what/shannonday/paper.html.

[SHA 49] SHANNON C., "Communication theory of secrecy systems", *The Bell System Technical Journal*, vol. 28, num. 4, p. 656–715, 1949.

[SHE 95] SHENOI K., *Digital Signal Processing in Telecommunications*, Prentice Hall PTR, Upper Saddle River, NJ, 1995.

[SPA 87] SPATARU A., *Fondements de la théorie de la transmission de l'information*, Presses Polytechniques Universitaires Romandes, 1987.

[STI 06] STINSON D.R., *Cryptography: Theory and Practice*, CRC Press series on discrete mathematics and its applications, Chapman & Hall/CRC, Boca Raton, 3rd edition, 2006.

[SYS 86] SYSKI R., *Introduction to Congestion Theory in Telephone Systems*, vol. 4 of Studies in telecommunication, North-Holland, Amsterdam, 2nd edition, 1986.

[VIL 91] VILLÉN M. and VILLÉN J., "RESTART: A method for accelerating rare event simulation", *Proceedings of the 13th ITC*, Copenhaguen, June 1991, International Teletraffic Congress, 1991.

[WEH 03] WEHENKEL L., Théorie de l'information et du codage (notes de cours), Université de Liège Faculté des sciences appliquées, 2003, available at http://www.montefiore.ulg.ac.be/ lwh/Info/.

[WID 85] WIDROW B. and STEARNS S., *Adaptive Digital Processing*, Prentice Hall, Englewood Cliffs, NJ, 1985.

Index